Book Two

READING FASTER AND UNDERSTANDING MORE

Third Edition

Book Two

READING FASTER AND UNDERSTANDING MORE

Third Edition

Wanda Maureen Miller
El Camino College

Sharon Steeber de Orozco
Santa Monica College

Scott, Foresman/Little, Brown Higher Education
A Division of Scott, Foresman and Company
Glenview, Illinois   London, England

An Instructor's Edition of *Reading Faster and Understanding More, Book 2* is available through your local Scott, Foresman representative or by writing the English Editor, Higher Education and Professional Division, Scott, Foresman and Company, 1900 East Lake Avenue, Glenview, Illinois 60025.

ISBN 0-673-39939-7 Student Edition
ISBN 0-673-49652-X Instructor's Edition

123456 VIK 949392919089

A NOTE TO THE INSTRUCTOR

Organization

The *Reading Faster and Understanding More* series of two graded workbooks is designed for the young adult or mature adult reader whose vocabulary and comprehension are at the developmental level. The readings in Book 1 progress through levels E, F, G, H and in Book 2 through levels H, I, J, K.*

Each lesson in both books includes:

1. *Lesson Objectives,* a list at the start of each lesson that enumerates the skills for the students to learn.
2. *Perception and Comprehension Exercises,* a set of six timed drills using words, phrases, and sentences.
3. *Reading Instruction,* a two-page presentation of one or more basic principles of good comprehension.
4. *Theme for the Reading Selections,* a brief introduction to the subject matter of each lesson's reading selections.
5. *Practice Paragraphs,* three paragraphs that allow the student to apply immediately the reading principle(s) presented in the preceding Reading Instruction.
6. A *Words in Context* exercise, taken from the upcoming longer readings, to familiarize the students with difficult vocabulary words or expressions.
7. A *Previewing Exercise* that precedes each reading selection.
8. In most lessons, two timed *Short Readings,* with comprehension questions.
9. A timed *Long Reading,* with comprehension questions.
10. Optional *Writing and Discussion Activities.*

We recommend that students work through each of the twelve lessons in chronological order, particularly in the first seven lessons, because each lesson has been carefully designed to build on and reinforce the principles presented in the earlier lessons. In the Table of Contents, each lesson indicates the principles of good reading comprehension that the text covers. (Also see the Instructor's Manual, p. 1, following the Appendix.)

Homework Lessons

At the end of the workbook are twelve Homework Lessons. These lessons cover dictionary use and vocabulary or word-attack skills, including uses of Latin and Greek roots, prefixes and suffixes. (Book 1 also includes a phonics review.) The pages are designed so that the exercises may be torn out and handed in.

Answer Keys

At the end of the book are answer keys for the comprehension and perception exercises; two of each lesson's three Practice Paragraphs; Words in Context; and the Short and Long Readings. Most of the answer keys for the Practice Paragraphs are instructive; that is, they explain why a particular answer is correct and better than the other choices.

---

*Based on Edward Fry's Readability Formula.

Instructor's Manual

The Instructor's Manual has answers to the Pretests, Posttests; Homework Lessons; and one Practice Paragraph for each Lesson. The outlines for the reading selections in Lesson 7 (study-reading) are also in the manual.

In addition, the manual provides a guide to graded reading materials; a selected list of reading lab materials; a checklist of observable clues to vision problems; and suggestions for teaching each of the twelve lessons. The Instructor's Manual also contains copyable vocabulary quizzes, skills tests, and other instructional aids.

The Third Edition

This revised edition of *Reading Faster and Understanding More, Book 2* reflects the comments of students and instructors who are currently using the series. The third edition:

1. Shifts the readability levels, for the most part, from HIJ to IJK, retaining some of the H-level readings at the beginning.
2. Introduces a new Lesson, *"Reading Critically,"* in which students learn to determine an author's purpose, distinguish fact from opinion, and evaluate the reliability of facts and opinions.
3. Provides a brief *Previewing* Exercise before all Short and Long Readings to help students "tune in" and read with a purpose.
4. Introduces a diagram and instruction to help students progress from finding the main idea of a paragraph to *finding the thesis* of a Short or Long Reading.
5. Adds an *additional comprehension question* to each Short Reading and two additional questions to each Long Reading. Usually these additional questions require some basic critical thinking, or attention to graphic aids or punctuation.
6. Presents *skimming* after PRO, the study-reading technique, because the students' experience with the preceding skills is a natural lead-in to looking actively for main ideas and overall structure. *Scanning* is now in the appendix because we believe it is a reading skill most students already practice regularly.
7. Places *Practice Paragraphs* after the *Theme for the Reading Selections* since they now share the same general subject matter and help the students build a larger base of information for the writing and discussion topics.
8. Updates reading selections, adding more articles on current issues, while maintaining a balance of readings by and about women and minorities.
9. Streamlines the reading instruction for skimming, determining inference, and interpreting literature.
10. Consolidates *Answer Keys* at the end of the book. Instructors will have the option of collecting all Answer Keys at the beginning of the term.

A Word of Appreciation

We wish to thank a number of instructors across the country who made suggestions for this third edition of *Reading Faster and Understanding More, Book 2:* the reading instructors at El Camino College and Santa Monica College, in particular Julie Uslan; Mary Carmichael, College of the Sequoias; Cathlene S. Denny, St. Johns River Community College; Helen M. Gladson, West Hills College; Deanna J. Prillaman, Delaware Technical and Community College; Gerald Schug, Chippewa Valley Technical College; Barry Selinger, Northern Virginia Community College; Rose Lyons Smith, Wayne Community College.

We also thank Doris Flood Ladd and Anne Dye Phillips, who helped co-author the original 1976 text of *Reading Faster and Understanding More* from which the series evolved.

CONTENTS

PRETESTS   1

Comprehension and Rate Pretest
   "How Fast Should a Person Read?"
      George Guomo   2
Vocabulary Pretest   5

LESSON 1

PREPARING FOR A NEW COURSE   9

Perception and Comprehension Exercises   10
Reading Instruction   22
   Practice Paragraphs   24
Reading Selections—Theme: Looking Back
   Words in Context   26
   Short Reading 1G   28
      from *The Diary of Anne Frank, Anne Frank*
   Short Reading 1H   30
      from *The Autobiography of Mark Twain,
      Samuel Langhorne Clemens*
   Long Reading 1I   32
      from *The Story of My Life, Helen Keller*
Writing and Discussion Activities   35

LESSON 2

FINDING THE MAIN IDEA   37

Perception and Comprehension Exercises   38
Reading Instruction   44
Reading Selections—Theme: Feeling Good
   Practice Paragraphs   46
   Words in Context   48
   Short Reading 2G   51
      "Research Debunks Old Myths About
      Mind's Decline"
   Short Reading 2H   53
      "Pain in the Neck is All in Your Head,"
      George Alexander
   Long Reading 2I   55
      "Is Your Sex Life Going Up in Smoke?"
      Genell J. Subak-Sharpe
Writing and Discussion Activities   59

LESSON 3

MORE ABOUT MAIN IDEA   61

Perception and Comprehension Exercises   62
Reading Instruction   70
Reading Selections—Theme: Contemporary Living
   Practice Paragraphs   73
   Words in Context   75
   Short Reading 3G   76
      from "A World Without Honor," Anthony Brandt
   Short Reading 3H   78
      from "Reading Between the Subliminals,"
      Lorraine Bennett
   Long Reading 3I   80
      "Can't Anybody Fix Anything Any More?"
      Jean Kerr
Writing and Discussion Activities   84

LESSON 4

RETAINING DETAILS   85

Perception and Comprehension Exercises   86
Reading Instruction   92
*Reading Selections—Theme: Creatures, Strange
   and Common*
   Practice Paragraphs   96
   Words in Context   99
   Short Reading 4G   100
      "Pet Pigs," Wanda Maureen Miller
   Short Reading 4H   102
      "The Unicorn in the Garden," James Thurber
   Long Reading 4I   104
      "The Yahoos and the Houyhnhnms,"
      Jonathan Swift
Writing and Discussion Activities   107

LESSON 5

RECOGNIZING TRANSITIONS   109

Perception and Comprehension Exercises   110
Reading Instruction   116

Reading Selections—Theme: Tracing Our Roots
  Practice Paragraphs 118
  Words in Context 120
  Short Reading 5G 122
    from *"Jesse Jackson: The Power or the Glory?"*
    Gail Sheehy
  Short Reading 5H 124
    from *One Flew Over the Cuckoo's Nest,*
    Ken Kesey
  Long Reading 5I 126
    "Carnival Queen," Jeanne Wakatsuki Houston
    and James Houston

Writing and Discussion Activities 129

LESSON 6

ORGANIZING THOUGHTS 131

Perception and Comprehension Exercises 132
Reading Instruction 138
Reading Selections—Theme: Study Skills
  Practice Paragraphs 141
  Words in Context 144
  Long Reading 6G 145
    "Preparing for Tests," William H. Armstrong
  Long Reading 6H 150
    "Taking Tests," William H. Armstrong

Writing and Discussion Activities 155

LESSON 7

USING P R O — HOW THE PROS
STUDY–READ 157

Perception and Comprehension Exercises 158
Reading Instruction 164
Selections for Study-Reading—Theme:
  The Sciences
  Words in Context 167
  Long Reading 7G 168
    "Interpersonal Conflict," Ronald B. Adler
    and Neil Towne
  Long Reading 7H 174
    "Resolving Interpersonal Conflict,"
    Ronald B. Adler and Neil Towne

Writing and Discussion Activities 179

LESSON 8

SKIMMING FOR OVERVIEW 181

Perception and Comprehension Exercises 182
Reading Instruction 188

Reading Selections—Theme: Stories of
  Famous People
  Words in Context 189
  Short Reading 8G 191
    "A Friend of the Environment," John Hartley
  Short Reading 8H 194
    from *Golda: The Life of Israel's Prime Minister,*
    Peggy Mann
  Long Reading 8I 197
    from *Lyndon Johnson and the American Dream,*
    Doris Kearns

Writing and Discussion Activities 201

LESSON 9

READING CRITICALLY 203

Perception and Comprehension Exercises 204
Reading Instruction 210
Reading Selections—Theme: Current Problems
  Practice Paragraphs 212
  Words in Context 214
  Long Reading 9G 215
    "The Right to Arms," Edward Abbey
  Long Reading 9H 218
    "Why Do People Own Handguns?" Pete Shields

Writing and Discussion Activities 222

LESSON 10

DETERMINING INFERENCE 223

Perception and Comprehension Exercises 224
Reading Instruction 230
Reading Selections—Theme: Beyond Sex Roles
  Practice Paragraphs 233
  Words in Context 235
  Short Reading 10G 236
    from *Men are Just Desserts, Sonya Friedman*
  Short Reading 10H 238
    "Men's Liberation from Etiquette," Jack Smith
  Long Reading 10I 240
    "Click!" Jane O'Reilly

Writing and Discussion Activities 243

LESSON 11

READING DEEPER FOR INFERENCES 245

Perception and Comprehension Exercises 246
Reading Instruction 252
Reading Selections—Theme: Imaginative Prose
  Practice Paragraphs 254

Words in Context   256
Long Reading 11G   257
   "A Modest Proposal," Jonathan Swift
Writing and Discussion Activities   261

LESSON 12

INTERPRETING LITERATURE   263

Perception and Comprehension Exercises   264
Reading Instruction   270
Reading Selections—Theme: Conflicts in Literature
   Practice Passages   272
   Words in Context   274
   Short Reading 12G   275
      "Amelia" from Vanity Fair,
         William Makepeace Thackeray
   Short Reading 12H   277
      "Rebecca" from Vanity Fair,
         William Makepeace Thackeray
   Long Reading 12I   279
      "The Sacrifice" from Vanity Fair,
         William Makepeace Thackeray

Writing and Discussion Activities   281

HOMEWORK   283

Homework Lesson 1   285
   How to Use the Dictionary

Homework Lesson 2   291
   Twenty Ways to Compliment Your Friends

Homework Lesson 3   293
   Twenty Ways to Insult Your Enemies

Homework Lesson 4   295
   Word Analysis:
   Twenty Common Greek and Latin Roots

Homework Lesson 5   301
   Twenty More Greek and Latin Roots

Homework Lesson 6   305
   Even More Greek and Latin Roots

Homework Lesson 7   309
   Still More Greek and Latin Roots

Homework Lesson 8   313
   Twenty Common Prefixes

Homework Lesson 9   317
   Twenty More Prefixes

Homework Lesson 10   321
   Twenty-five Noun Suffixes

Homework Lesson 11   325
   Seven Verb Suffixes

Homework Lesson 12   327
   Nineteen Adjective Suffixes and One
      Adverb Suffix

POSTTESTS   331

*Comprehension and Rate Posttest: "I was a
   Speed-Reading Dropout," J. M. Flagler*   332
Vocabulary Posttest   337

APPENDIX   341

Additional Perceptual Drills   342
Scanning Instruction and Exercises   348
Personal Vocabulary List   358
*Alphabetical List of Prefixes, Roots, and
   Suffixes*   359
Rate (WPM) Chart for Long Readings   364
Progress Chart for Short and Long Readings   367
Progress Chart for Pretest and Posttest   368
*Answer Keys for Lessons 1–12 and Scanning
   Exercises*   369

PRETESTS

1. Comprehension and Rate Pretest
2. Vocabulary Pretest

Read the following selection as rapidly as you can but with good comprehension. Wait for a signal from your instructor before you begin reading. (This reading should be timed.)

How Fast Should a Person Read?

George Guomo

It's probably useless to hope to talk sensibly any more about so-called speed reading. The extremists have overrun the field and, as usual, ridiculous statements and foolish misconceptions make good copy. Amidst the din, quieter voices go unheard.

The extremists of the left—using such effective platforms as television talk shows—tell us that we should be reading at ten thousand words a minute, fifteen thousand, twenty thousand. . . .

Their right-wing counterparts thunder back with equal irrelevance. George Stevens's piece in the August 26, 1961, issue of this magazine, entitled *Faster, Faster!* is typical. Why not, he suggests, keep reading faster and faster until we can read all of Gibbon's *Decline and Fall* over a cup of instant coffee?

Why not, one could suggest in turn, carefully train ourselves to read slower and slower until it takes us a minute to read a single word? We could then blissfully spend something like 21,000 solid hours—or 2,625 eight-hour days—reading *Decline and Fall.*

To some, not knowing their reading rate is a source of pride. They don't want to know. One's reading rate is God-given, and to measure or question it or, heaven forbid, to try to improve it, is blasphemy. The assumption, of course, is that everybody's reading rate is just dandy as it is. Perhaps. But the facts scarcely encourage such a carefree attitude.

At the other end of the scale, we have those whose pride springs from rates measured in rapidly multiplying tens of thousands. Bosh and foolishness, I say. Up in the rare heights of 20,000 or 30,000 words a minute, a person is skimming, or surveying, or "getting the gist of the thing." But he isn't reading with anything resembling full or specific comprehension. With few exceptions most people cannot read effectively at much better than 2000 words per minute. Perhaps it would pay us to leave the extremes where they belong and look at the whole question realistically. The average adult, for instance, reads about 250 words a minute. This is also the average I've found among college freshmen. But the variations in my classes run from 125 to 900. This means that some students were reading over *seven* times as fast as others. There's probably an even greater spread among the general public.

All right, one is tempted to reply, some people are simply faster readers than others, as they may also be taller, fatter, or better looking. But speed itself does not tell the whole story. And no one except the figure-worshippers of the left and the figure-haters of the right is concerned with speed alone. What counts is a person's overall reading ability. But in this, speed plays an important and usually misunderstood part. Every reputable study has shown that reasonably fast readers perform not only as well as slower readers, but often better.

Probably the most common and groundless misconception about reading is the one that equates even moderate speed with sloppiness. Actually, the slow readers are the sloppy ones. They read aimlessly and passively and have more trouble concentrating than do faster readers. In addition, they do not understand as much, do not evaluate as well, and do not remember as effectively. The person who says he always reads slowly because he is being careful is just fooling himself. He is neither as careful nor as diligent as he likes to think. He is simply inefficient. He's driving along a smooth, clear highway in the same low gear he uses to get his car out of the mud.

The fast reader is fast because he is alert and skillful. He has been trained—or has trained himself—to use his ability and his intelligence effectively. Thousands of persons, including [former] President Kennedy, have proved that such training is both possible and practical.

The methods used cannot be fully explained in a brief article, but they are based on sound principles and have been approved by many respected and conservative educators. More important, they have consistently worked. A person is taught, for instance, to read several words, or a phrase, or perhaps a whole line, at a single eyestop, instead of making such a stop for every word.

A person with a rate of less than 250 words per minute almost always reads word by word. This method is so slow and inefficient that it actually hinders comprehension. In learning to read by meaningful word groups, a person enables his brain to function much closer to its capacity and almost invariably improves his comprehension.

No matter how hard some people try to ignore the fact, reading is a learned process, in which certain techniques operate more successfully than others. No one is born knowing how to read; he must be taught. He can be taught well or poorly. What most often happens, however—and this seems to be what the "slower, slower" people are fighting for—is that he is not taught at all. Left to his own devices, he typically develops a surprising number of bad reading habits, among which is the habit of reading too slowly for maximum comprehension or enjoyment.

The real issue here is not whether a person should or shouldn't read 20,000 words a minute, or even whether he can or can't. The real issue is much more mundane than that, and much more important. It is whether the average person—now reading 250 words a minute— would not be a better reader in every way if he learned to read effectively at 600, 800, or 1000 words a minute. The evidence is quite convincing that he would.

A person whose rate is 250 words a minute is not only kept from reading well, but is often kept from reading at all. Let's take another look at *Decline and Fall*. At 250 words a minute, a person will take eighty-three hours to read it. How often does he, faced with such a task, simply decide he hasn't got time for it? Rightly or wrongly, this is often his decision, for he has only two alternatives: to spend eighty-three hours on it or no hours.

And this brings us to an important and generally neglected point. In actual fact, a person does not have a single reading rate. He has— or should have—many rates. He should be able to read as fast or as slow as he wants, or as the situation warrants.

But all people have what can be considered a "base" rate—the rate at which they normally read more or less average material. It is from this base that they should speed up or slow down in accordance with the demands of the material.

However, the reader with a low base rate—around 250—rarely does this. He reads Shakespeare and Spillane at essentially the same pace. And even when he does try to shift gears, he isn't very successful. He can't get much faster because he's too unskilled, and he can't get much slower without coming to a dead halt.

The reader with a better base rate—say 800 words a minute—has a far broader range of differing speeds. He can easily move up to 1000 words or better for casual reading. And he can always slow down as much as he wants for studying or for the reading of difficult or specialized material. The rapid reader is not a slave to speed. The slow reader *is* a slave to slowness.

Thus it's absurd to argue about "speed reading." The term is meaningless because critics insist on interpreting it to mean that a person must read everything as fast as he possibly can. He must race headlong through Yeats and Milton and Donne and dash madly through *Moby Dick*. Quite the contrary. If a person learns his lesson well, he will not be limited in reading a good-sized novel to a choice of either no hours or ten hours. He can spend on it any number of hours in between. He can spend on it as much time and effort as he feels it deserves. More than that no writer, not Gibbon, nor Shakespeare, nor Spillane, can fairly ask of any reader.

Now, for the life of me I can't see why encouraging sensible reading techniques, and pointing out that most people read too slowly for satisfactory comprehension or appreciation, should be considered evil or anti-intellectual. Perhaps the explanation lies in the startling emotional investment most people have in their reading habits. Almost everyone who has worked in the field has noticed this. You can criticize a person's ignorance of arithmetic or spelling or sex or politics, but mention his reading techniques and immediately he's insulted. Good, bad, or indifferent, they're his and he loves them.

The whole question can really be put quite simply. If someone can prove to me that a reasonable increase in a person's reading rate causes disadvantages—such as loss of comprehension or a lessening of that person's appreciation or enjoyment—I'll happily throw the whole business over and learn all the chants of the "slower, slower" crowd.

By the same token, I'd like to see these people agree that if a person *could* read faster—without any such losses and usually with appreciable gains—then the increase in speed would be a desirable goal and worth working for.

This doesn't seem too much to ask. But the radicals will probably howl anyway.*

TOTAL READING TIME _____

Immediately answer the following questions without referring to the selection.

---

*"How Fast Should a Person Read?" by George Guomo. Adapted from *The Saturday Review*, April 21, 1962. Copyright © 1962 by the Saturday Review/World, Inc. Reprinted by permission.

1. Choose the statement that best expresses the main idea (or thesis).

    (a) People cannot read effectively when reading over 2000 words per minute.

    (b) The average reading speed is 250 words per minute.

    (c) Readers can be trained to read faster and more effectively.

    (d) An increase in reading speed means a decrease in comprehension for most readers.

2. We can assume that the author disagrees both with the extremists who encourage speed reading and those who encourage slow reading.   **T**   **F**

3. One's reading rate, like a big nose, is God-given and should not be changed.   **T**   **F**

4. The author found that the college freshmen in his classes read at about the same speed—slow.   **T**   **F**

5. The fast reader usually comprehends more because he is alert and skillful.   **T**   **F**

6. The author recommends a base reading rate of _____.

7. The author suggests that most people are defensive about their reading habit.   **T**   **F**

8. Readers can read Shakespeare as fast and as effectively as they can read Spillane if they have trained properly.   **T**   **F**

9. What is the most common misconception about even moderate speed readers? _____

10. The author's main purpose is to **(a)** inform **(b)** persuade **(c)** entertain **(d)** a combination of (a) and (b).

Check your answers with your instructor. Then turn to the Rate Chart on page 364 to get your words per minute for this selection. Finally, record your scores below and on the progress chart on page 368.

WORDS PER MINUTE _____

% COMPREHENSION _____

Note: Question 1, marked with a circle O, deals with the thesis (main idea) of the selection. Any question marked with a triangle △ deals with inference (or drawing a conclusion). Questions unmarked by symbols are detail questions.

VOCABULARY PRETEST

This test is made up mostly of words taken from the Homework sections, Word Comprehension exercises, and Words in Context. Since you have not yet begun to study these vocabulary words, you probably will not know as many as when you take the Posttest at the end of the book. You should then be able to score much higher. (Your instructor may want you to take this test in class using a separate answer sheet.)

A. Matching 1–5

In the blank before each word, write the letter of the best definition.

_____	**1.** synonymous	**(a)**	commotion
_____	**2.** pilfer	**(b)**	opponent
_____	**3.** adversary	**(c)**	prank
_____	**4.** turmoil	**(d)**	similar
_____	**5.** caper	**(e)**	steal

B. Short Definitions, 6–15

In the blank at the left, write the letter of the word that is being defined.

_____ **6.** save

(a) finesse (b) pseudonym (c) seclude (d) salvage

_____ **7.** cat

(a) wench (b) feline (c) amateur (d) oculist

_____ **8.** rude

(a) surly (b) prominent (c) sufficient (d) oblivious

_____ **9.** follower

(a) physician (b) politician (c) disciple (d) sultry

_____ **10.** watch

(a) casualty (b) horde (c) delinquent (d) vigil

_____ **11.** assess

(a) nominate (b) evaluate (c) smudge (d) accumulate

_____ **12.** ruler

(a) sovereign (b) pedestrian (c) replica (d) scoundrel

_____ **13.** clever

(a) mammoth (b) remedial (c) ingenious (d) swarthy

_____ **14.** sarcastic

(a) devious (b) formidable (c) snide (d) ornate

_____ **15.** secret

(a) grotesque (b) boisterous (c) listless (d) cryptic

C. Context—Phrases, 16–30

In the blank at the left, write the letter of the best definition for the *italicized word.*

_____ **16.** was *inexpressibly* glad

(a) can't be talked about (b) can't be described (c) inexcusably (d) obnoxiously

_____ **17.** persisted in *confounding* the two

(a) forgetting (b) remembering (c) writing (d) confusing

_____ 18. due to old age or *senility*

(a) a serious disease (b) occasional forgetfulness (c) physical and mental weakness because of old age (d) giving up on life

_____ 19. grass and dirt that *evoke* the countryside

(a) are similar to (b) are different from (c) call to mind (d) are near to

_____ 20. *comparable* to the earliest combinations of children

(a) different from (b) similar to (c) bigger than (d) leading up to

_____ 21. a *proportionate* degree of reason

(a) balanced (b) sufficient (c) tremendous (d) small portion

_____ 22. to my everlasting *mortification*

(a) delight (b) amusement (c) embarrassment (d) anger

_____ 23. inside in that *squalor*

(a) miserable filth (b) small dwelling (c) dense forest (d) abandoned nursery

_____ 24. trying to *mediate*

(a) listen (b) make a fresh start (c) act quickly (d) help people reach an agreement

_____ 25. a *furtive* gesture

(a) frightening (b) insignificant (c) sneaky (d) colorful

_____ 26. can *divine* the meaning of all things

(a) foretell (b) soothe (c) hasten (d) forget

_____ 27. with an *impassive* stare

(a) showing no emotions (b) hostile (c) angry (d) deceptively sweet

_____ 28. using vivid *imagery*

(a) lies (b) characters (c) word pictures (d) funny stories

_____ 29. in a *solicitous* tone

(a) expressing concern (b) hypocritical (c) sarcastic (d) harshly critical

_____ 30. so *guileless* and good natured

(a) smiling (b) simple (c) foolish (d) passionate

D. Context—Sentences, 31–40

In the blank at the left, write a *T* if the statement is true; write an *F* if the statement is false. (Emphasis is on the correct use of the *italicized word* rather than on facts.)

_____ 31. If you get *tangible* results from your efforts, you won't be able to see or feel those results.

_____ 32. *Repentance* means never having to say you are sorry.

_____ 33. To *dispel* a rumor is to confirm it.

_____ 34. Strong friendships are based on mutual *antipathy.*

35. A graceless dancer *lumbers* across the floor.

36. An inept *neurologist* could do a lot of damage to your garden.

37. Mules are known for their *obstinance*.

38. Because of our *infinite* nature, we must all one day die.

39. Their marriage is so *complacent* that they fight all the time.

40. He certainly is a *precocious* child; at eleven years old he still cannot tie his shoelaces.

E. Roots, Prefixes, and Suffixes—Matching, 41–50

In the blank at the left, write the letter of the best definition for the root (main word part), prefix (beginning word part), or suffix (ending word part).

Roots

_____	41. ocul	(a)	to lead
_____	42. vers, vert	(b)	eye
_____	43. duc, duct	(c)	earth
_____	44. terra	(d)	wishing, willing
_____	45. volens	(e)	to turn

Prefixes and Suffixes

_____	46. arch-	(a)	one who (noun)
_____	47. -esque	(b)	chief, principal
_____	48. bi-	(c)	two
_____	49. -cide	(d)	having the quality of (adj.)
_____	50. -ster	(e)	killing (noun)

Check your answers with your instructor. Record your score below and on the progress chart on page 368 in the Appendix.

% CORRECT _____

1

Preparing for a New Course

IN THIS LESSON, YOU WILL

1. learn perception and comprehension exercises;
2. check your good and bad reading habits;
3. apply *previewing* skills;
4. read in logical phrases of meaning;
5. read three articles applying the skills you have learned.

Directions for Word Perception

These drills consist of a key word on the left, followed by five words on the right. The key word is repeated once in the words at the right. Find the same word as quickly as you can and cross it out, as in the following example:

Key Word

student   dents   study   student   stewed   sputter

Continue until you finish all twenty items. Look up and your instructor will indicate your time in seconds.

Check your work for errors. Then write your time and number of errors at the bottom of the drill.

► Exercise 1A—Word Perception

Key Word

1.	bedroll	bedrest	rollick	bedroll	bedrail	bedside
2.	observe	obsess	observe	servant	obstruct	obscure
3.	permit	permeate	permute	remit	permit	permissive
4.	scream	screech	scratch	cream	screen	scream
5.	unison	uniform	unison	union	universal	nestle
6.	switch	switch	swatch	witch	swathe	watch
7.	learned	leaven	earned	learned	leather	lectern
8.	pupil	papal	puppet	pilfer	pupil	pulpit
9.	turnspit	turnplate	turret	spittle	turnstile	turnspit
10.	spindle	spinal	spindle	spindly	poodle	spinet
11.	virtuoso	virtuoso	virtuous	virulent	riotous	virtual
12.	rotation	rotary	nation	rotation	rotate	notation
13.	whisker	whistle	skirt	whisper	whisker	whist
14.	hustle	bustle	hustle	hurtle	hurried	nestle
15.	aversion	avenue	aviation	version	average	aversion
16.	cartilage	cartilage	cartridge	carriage	partition	cartwheel
17.	devout	devour	devote	devout	evoke	devoid
18.	foundry	founder	foundling	foundry	laundry	fountain
19.	ulterior	interior	ulterior	ultimate	ulcerate	exterior
20.	engrave	engrain	gravity	engrave	engross	enhance

TIME _____

ERRORS _____

These word perception drills help train you to react to size and shape rather than to meaning or sound. You are not expected to know the meanings of the words, nor should you sound them out to yourself. This will only slow you down unnecessarily.

Of course, slight changes in a word can affect the meaning. A *trail* is very different from a *trial.* And a *fiancé* is different from *finance.* But in actual reading, you see the word in context, and your brain usually makes the necessary corrections as you follow the thought of the sentence.

So do not be afraid of making errors. Do not go back to correct any errors. Do not linger over any word. Form a picture in your mind of the whole key word. Then find the identical words as fast as possible.

► *Exercise 1B—Word Perception*

Key Word

1.	blanket	blank	blanket	bland	strand	blankly
2.	conviction	convection	victory	conviction	convention	convince
3.	foliage	foliage	folio	folder	tollgate	folk
4.	natal	natural	nation	fatal	natal	nasal
5.	merely	mercy	surely	mercury	merrily	merely
6.	jackal	jabbed	jacket	jackal	tackle	jackpot
7.	party	partial	partly	party	poorly	rapidly
8.	honor	honey	honor	honest	honed	boner
9.	passion	fashion	passive	passerby	passion	passenger
10.	shame	shame	sham	tame	shank	share
11.	transcribe	transform	transcend	ascribe	transcript	transcribe
12.	warlock	warhorse	warrant	warlock	locket	warpath
13.	yokel	yodel	yoke	yogurt	token	yokel
14.	gymnast	gypsum	gymnast	gypsy	nasty	gyrostat
15.	hatchet	hatchway	hateful	patch	hatchet	hatter
16.	jigger	jigger	jigsaw	trigger	jiggle	jiffy
17.	manage	mangle	manacle	manage	marriage	mandate
18.	obtuse	obtain	obtuse	obstruct	truck	obtrusive
19.	quarrel	quarter	quarry	quartz	laurel	quarrel
20.	slither	slipper	slinky	lithe	slither	sliding

TIME _____

ERRORS _____

Directions for Word Comprehension

Unlike the preceding perceptual drills, you must know the meaning of these words. Look at the key word in boldface print in the phrase on the left and think of its meaning. Next, quickly locate the *synonym,* or the word with the closest meaning, among the three words on the right. Then cross it out, as in the following example:

Key Word

the tall **man**   boy   m̷ale   woman

Continue until you finish all twenty items. Look up and your instructor will indicate your time in seconds.

Check your work with the answer key at the back of the book. Write your time and number of errors at the bottom of the exercise.

► *Exercise 1C—Word Comprehension*

Choose the word closest in meaning to the key word in **boldface** print.

Key Word

1.	**ornate** furniture	beautiful	plain	elaborate
2.	to **meditate** on problems	ponder	sleep	worry
3.	in a **surly** mood	pleasant	tender	bad-tempered
4.	pain in an **extremity**	middle	neck	outermost part
5.	to **spurn** a lover	accept	reject	help
6.	a subtle **aroma**	odor	sight	perfume
7.	**malicious** gossip	interesting	boring	spiteful
8.	a **superfluous** amount	necessary	small	extra
9.	**compelled** to act	paid	forced	asked
10.	**lust** for life	desire	broken	ill
11.	to **idolize** a parent	degrade	introduce	worship
12.	the rain to **abate**	increase	subside	pour
13.	an **aptitude** for sports	inability	ability	hatred
14.	to **stifle** a cough	let out	hear	smother
15.	to **delete** curse words	omit	replace	add
16.	the **nimble** dancer	stiff	agile	slow-moving
17.	a **formidable** opponent	dishonest	impressive	cowardly
18.	to **lament** sadly	celebrate	sing	mourn
19.	a brief **siesta**	nap	picnic	party
20.	to pull off a **caper**	jacket	prank	table

TIME _____

ERRORS _____

NOTE: Remember, all answers are in the key on page 369.

These exercises are more complex than the perceptual drills. You are working to develop not only rapid eye movement and reaction, but also a quick grasp of meaning.

The exercise requires some familiarity with the key words, their meaning in the phrase, and corresponding *synonyms* (words similar in meaning). But do not agonize over a word you do not know; go on to the next item. Also, do not look for fine distinctions between synonyms. Look only for the one word that is closest in meaning.

Notice that the synonym can usually replace the key word in the phrase and the phrase will still make sense. Both the key word and the synonym will be the same part of speech (noun, verb, adjective, or adverb). However, sometimes the synonym will require a different structure word (article or preposition) to fit smoothly into the phrase. For example, in Exercise 1C, item 17, the article *a* before *formidable* would have to be changed to *an* before *impressive*. (Rule: Use *an* before a word beginning with a vowel, and use *a* before a word beginning with a consonant.)

As soon as you find the correct answer, go on to the next item. Trust your judgment. Don't waste time double checking with the other possible answers. Concentrate! Do not be fooled by *antonyms* (words opposite in meaning); use them as clues. Use an active approach—know what meaning you are looking for. Do not wait passively for the meaning to occur to you.

Remember too that in English a single word may have several different meanings.

EXAMPLE:

The *bear* went into hibernation. (noun)

He will *bear* a large part of the cost. (verb)

No attempt has been made to confuse you. But keep your mind open to a definition other than the one you are most familiar with. Choose the definition that fits the context of the phrase.

Note: The words in these exercises have been taken from a basic list of words appropriate to your reading level. It is important for you to know them. Check your answers with the key at the back of the book. If you miss any item, circle both the key word and the correct answer for that item and enter both words in your "must learn" Personal Vocabulary List in the Appendix on page 358.

► *Exercise 1D—Word Comprehension*

Choose the word closest in meaning to the key word.

Key Word

1. to **exterminate** the bugs	help	protect	destroy
2. to **pilfer** the money	borrow	steal	give
3. to **deplore** the war	disapprove	witness	approve
4. to **reprimand** the child	compliment	scold	lecture
5. another **vanquished** hero	honored	renewed	conquered
6. to **redeem** his reputation	recover	ruin	forget
7. a **tedious** task	well-paid	boring	interesting
8. a charming **anecdote**	hymn	novel	story
9. to **comply** with the law	defy	agree	argue
10. a **renowned** scientist	famous	foreign	unknown
11. to **agitate** the water	pollute	disturb	serve
12. to suffer from **insomnia**	insults	dreams	sleeplessness
13. **illegible** writing	unreadable	neat	readable
14. an exact **replica**	statement	time	copy
15. to **dismantle** the car	repair	take apart	take back
16. the **ebb** of the tide	receding	power	wetness
17. the **gist** of the story	end	point	middle
18. to **sever** a tie	treasure	bind	cut off
19. **indelible** ink	erasable	permanent	dark
20. to leap in **ecstasy**	joy	pain	fear

TIME _____

ERRORS _____

NOTE: Don't forget to add the words you missed to your Personal Vocabulary List in the Appendix on page 358.

Directions for Phrase Perception

These drills consist of a key phrase on the left, followed by three phrases on the right. The key phrase is repeated once among the three phrases on the right. Find the same phrase as quickly as you can and cross it out, as in the following example:

Key Phrase

bed rest   red vest   best vest   ~~bed rest~~

Continue until you finish all twenty items. Look up and your instructor will indicate your time in seconds.

Check your work for errors. Then write your time and number of errors at the bottom of the page.

► *Exercise 1E—Phrase Perception*

Key Phrase

1.	prepared for	program for	four pastels	prepared for
2.	those flowers	rose bowers	those flowers	these fingers
3.	does need	does need	those weeds	did bleed
4.	to be as	to see us	to be as	have been to
5.	our own	our own	four gowns	on loan
6.	first year	third gear	first year	yellow bird
7.	also ran	also ran	false run	ran also
8.	my turn	his churn	my turn	too stern
9.	has enjoyed	joyful noise	have rejoiced	has enjoyed
10.	practical joke	practical joke	heavy yoke	praying jockey
11.	as you are	are you as	as you are	your orange
12.	for rent	for rent	poor recital	recent file
13.	last week	very meek	last week	lost wine
14.	is new	as new	as few	is new
15.	their car	they're here	their car	this tar
16.	about noon	about nine	nice abbot	about noon
17.	onto the floor	out the door	into the flour	onto the floor
18.	near home	rear tire	home free	near home
19.	empty mug	empty mug	dug into	entry rug
20.	demand more	reprimand him	demon rum	demand more

TIME _____

ERRORS _____

Like the Word Perception drills, these exercises require you to react to the size and shape of the phrase *as a whole*, not as separate letters or words. The exercises are designed to widen your eye span and get you used to longer units of print.

If you find yourself reading each word in a phrase separately, try focusing on the dot above each phrase. You should be able to see the entire phrase through your peripheral vision, without moving your eyes. (If you cannot, turn to the Perceptual Drills in the Appendix for additional help in increasing your eye span. Especially see Perceptual Drill 4 to see how raising your point of focus can help you.)

Soon you will be able to see, perceive, and think in phrases, and eventually to read faster and more intelligently. These drills can help you cross the gap between reading word by word and reading phrases and ideas.

► *Exercise 1F—Phrase Perception*

NOTE: All key phrases are adjective-noun combinations.

Key Phrase

1. rock singer	rock salt	rock singer	jazz singer
2. up a creek	sip a coke	sup on cake	up a creek
3. over the hill	over the hill	into the hat	took the pill
4. the bird nest	the brown nest	the red vest	the bird nest
5. good reader	good reading	book reader	good reader
6. having a shot	have a shot	having a shot	having pots
7. dirty glass	dirty grass	dirty glass	dusty glass
8. loud noise	crowd noise	loud noise	long nose
9. fast foods	fast foods	first foods	fresh food
10. bad news	sad news	bad news	bad and new
11. hungry dog	hungry dog	hunting dog	hungry god
12. bright shirt	bright shorts	bright shirt	bright shift
13. high heels	high peals	high heels	higher heels
14. lift weights	lift weights	lose weight	lifting weights
15. for a price	for a price	for the rice	found a price
16. a hard course	a heavy course	a hard cause	a hard course
17. a dream house	a dream house	a dream horse	a dreary house
18. foreign leader	friendly leader	foreign leader	foreign reader
19. traffic jam	traffic cop	traffic jam	trifling jam
20. go to court	gone to court	go to count	go to court

TIME _____

ERRORS _____

Are you satisfied with how well you read? No matter how successful, intelligent, or highly educated a person is, almost everyone would like to become a better reader. That's because reading is a skill that one way or another touches almost every activity in our lives, from our jobs to our schoolwork to our free time.

The best way to improve your reading ability is, of course, to read. But sheer plodding through pages and pages of printed words is not the quickest or easiest way to read better or faster. In fact, it may turn you off reading altogether. *The single most important influence on how much and how fast you will become a better reader is your attitude.*

The importance of attitude

You must cultivate a creative, positive attitude. That means you must be willing to break some old habits and try new approaches. You must be willing to be uncomfortable at times as you get used to reading more actively. You must believe that you indeed have the ability to read faster and understand more, and that you will.

The importance of commitment

Believing that you can and will read faster and understand more requires a commitment from you to this course of study. This decision will carry you over any hard or uncomfortable moments you might find as you strive to practice the techniques that will make you a more effective reader. It will also help you meet demands in your personal life that can sometimes distract or discourage you if you let them. Most of all, your attitude should include patience, especially toward yourself. You are learning, and learning occurs step by step, not instantly.

Tips to help you start

Here are seven suggestions to help you prepare for this new course of study:

1. **Relax.** Reading, like everything else in life, is best done when you're relaxed, not tense. First, check your breathing. Make sure you're not holding your breath and that your breathing is even and regular. Then use your imagination to make reading a pleasure. Surrender yourself to the characters in the story, the ideas in the article, the colorfulness of the details.

2. **Concentrate.** If just the word "concentration" makes you feel tired, you have the wrong idea of its meaning. Another word for concentration could be "awareness." The reading process requires physical and mental awareness. You may have heard already of the five Ws that newspaper reporters use: *Who, What, When, Where,* and *Why.* Add to this list *How.* Look for these elements in what you read. Try to create a picture of what you're reading, and your concentration (and memory) will automatically improve.

3. **Form good physical habits.** Do you:

   a. Hold the book about 16 inches from your face?

   b. Choose a quiet spot to read?

   c. Read during the time of the day when you're at your mental best? (Are you a day person or a night person?)

   d. Have a 100-watt bulb illuminating your reading area?

   e. Know your eyesight is adequate and doesn't need correcting?

4. **Use a preview-skimming technique.***

   a. Prepare to read by surveying the author's clues, such as titles, subtitles, marginal aids (like the ones in this book), italics, and boldface print to help you focus on what is most important.

---

*Lesson 7 presents a study-method called PRO which builds on this preview-skimming technique.

b. Read introductions and summaries carefully before reading the main text.

c. Be curious as you preview-skim. Form questions that you will want to find the answers to when you start the actual reading.

5. **Correct poor physical habits.**

    a. Lip movements. Do your lips move, even slightly, when you read? Are you sounding out every word with your lips?

    b. Subvocalizing. Do you say the words "aloud" in your mind as you read? Do you form the words in your throat? Does your breathing change even when you are not reading something exciting?

    c. Squinting. Are your eyes straining to see the lines? If so, what can you do to correct the problem?

6. **Correct poor mental habits.**

    a. Do you sometimes read in the same way you take a shower, letting the words wash over you, retaining whatever meaning from them that just happens to strike you?

    b. Do you read without a purpose? In other words, do you dawdle and poke along? Do you sometimes forget what the beginning of a sentence was about by the time you get to its end?

    c. Do you often regress (have to reread phrases, sentences, or even whole paragraphs, sometimes whole pages)? Do you find you have passed your eyes over a page, recognizing the words but remembering nothing?

    d. Do you tend to zoom right over commas and periods or not notice when a new paragraph starts?

7. **Read in phrases.** One comprehension technique that will immediately help you is reading in phrases (or wholes). Consider this example:

> To train yourself to read in phrases, use the natural rhythm
> of the language to guide you.

The reader who pauses on every word in that sentence will be stopping (fixating) seventeen times. The person who reads in phrases, though, will group chunks of words that belong together and pause once for each chunk. Here is how a more effective reader might see the sentence.

> To train yourself / to read in phrases, / use the natural rhythm /
> of the language / to guide you.

The slashes mark logical "bites" of meaning to take at one time. Did you notice how punctuation such as commas and periods also marks natural places to stop and read? This second reader would pause only five times, once on each chunk. This reader would, therefore, be reading three times as fast, just because of reading in phrases instead of word by word! Also, this reader would understand more of what he or she is reading. To "bite off" chunks of meaning, a reader has to be paying attention to what the words are saying as a whole, not just to how they look or sound.

As you get more practice, you'll be able to digest longer and longer phrases at a time. The drills at the beginning of this Lesson introduce you to phrase perception and in Lesson 3 to phrase comprehension. These skills are then reinforced in the rest of the Lessons.*

---

*For more practice, see the Perceptual Drills starting on page 342 in the Appendix.

Most of the Lessons in this book have three practice paragraphs, each for the purpose of applying the reading principle just learned. Read the following paragraphs and try to use some of the suggestions you just learned. Then answer the questions for each paragraph and check the Answer Key at the back of the book.

A. When a person uses his peripheral vision, he uses his ability to see to the left and right and above and below the point where his eyes fixate (or focus). A driver, for example, uses his peripheral vision when he drives. He sees not only directly ahead of his car, but he is aware of cars behind him and on both sides. He sees "out of the corners of his eyes." Similarly, a reader who uses his peripheral vision can read faster by seeing

   1. (Finish the author's last sentence:)
- **(a)** cars on each side.
- **(b)** more than one word at a glance.
- **(c)** one whole word at a time.
- **(d)** spots in front of his eyes.

   2. What is a good title for this paragraph? _____

   3. Mark slashes between each natural phrase unit.

B. One way to use peripheral vision and read faster right away is to stop *margin-reading*. You margin-read if you automatically focus on the first word on every line, because the left side of your peripheral vision is on the blank space in the margin. The margin communicates nothing. What a waste of focus! You similarly waste the right side of your peripheral vision if you always automatically focus on the last word when you come to the end of a line. Why not get in the habit of beginning your focus on the second word on every line and ending your focus on the next to the last word. Then you are using your peripheral vision to the maximum. You are using the edges of your peripheral on

   1. (Finish the author's last sentence:)
- **(a)** words in the margins.
- **(b)** words and the margins.
- **(c)** words instead of blank space.
- **(d)** all words except the first and last on each line.

   2. What is a good title for this paragraph? _____

   3. Mark slashes between each natural phrase unit.

C. A person reads more efficiently by getting a "mental set"—preparing to read the material or zeroing in on the subject. One effective method is to *preview* the article first. That is, read the title, author's name, subtitles, and first and last paragraphs. Having done this, the reader will then

   1. (Finish the author's last sentence:)
- **(a)** have no need actually to read the material.
- **(b)** have set his mind to reading everything in the article except the first and last paragraphs.

(c) be able to take a rest.

(d) be able to understand more when he reads the material because he has a general idea of the content.

2. What is a good title for this paragraph? _____

3. Mark slashes between each natural phrase unit.

Theme: Looking Back

The two Short and one Long Readings that follow are taken from autobiographies. The three famous authors are writing about their early lives. Although they led completely different lives, each had the same kind of "growing pains" we all have had.

Words in Context

The following sentences are from the reading selections in this Lesson. They contain words that may be new to you. This exercise introduces them now so they will not slow you down while you read the selections.

Words in context means that you will learn these words, not as isolated words, but, as part of an idea in a sentence. Many times the *context* (the rest of the sentence) gives you a clue to the meaning of the new word. But other times you will need to use the Word Attack Skills you'll be learning in the Homework section at the back of this book. This means you'll *analyze the parts* that make up the word. Occasionally, the meaning of a word isn't clear from either of those two approaches. Then you may have to check your *dictionary.* But where possible, we provide an extra clue in brackets [ ] after the sentence to help guide you to the correct choice below each sentence. Even though the clue may seem obvious, it may teach you a word attack skill.

For each *italicized* word, choose the meaning that best fits its context or that best relates to the extra clue.

► *Short Reading 1G*

1. I am simply a young girl, badly in need of some *rollicking* good fun.

    (a) happy and carefree **(b)** innocent **(c)** physically active **(d)** inexpensive

► *Short Reading 1H*

2. It was the first time I had ever had a chance to tell anything on him, and I was *inexpressibly* glad. [Extra Clue: The prefix *in* means *not.*]

    (a) can't be talked about **(b)** can't be described **(c)** inexcusably
    (d) obnoxiously

► *Long Reading 1I*

3. Have you ever been at sea in a dense fog, when it seemed as if a *tangible* white darkness shut you in? [Extra Clue: A chair is tangible; a thought is not.]

    (a) invisible **(b)** brilliant **(c)** able to be touched **(d)** imaginary

4. When I finally succeeded in making the letters correctly, I was *flushed* with childish pleasure and pride. [Extra Clue: **(a)** can be the *cause* of flushing.]

    (a) embarrassed **(b)** turning pink with excitement **(c)** tired **(d)** on the verge of tears

5. Earlier in the day we had had a *tussle* over the words "m-u-g" and "w-a-t-e-r." [Extra Clue: The correct answer is the opposite of **(d)**.]

    (a) struggle **(b)** joke **(c)** exercise **(d)** agreement

6. Miss Sullivan had tried to impress it upon me that "m-u-g" is mug and that "w-a-t-e-r" is water, but I persisted in *confounding* the two.

   (a) forgetting   **(b)** remembering   **(c)** writing   **(d)** confusing

7. In the still, dark world in which I lived there was no strong *sentiment* or tenderness. [Extra Clue: Examine the root *sent* or *sens*.]

   (a) wrongdoing   **(b)** feeling   **(c)** power   **(d)** gloom

8. Then my eyes filled with tears; for I realized what I had done, and for the first time I felt *repentance* and sorrow.

   (a) sadness   **(b)** happiness   **(c)** repetition   **(d)** regret

Check your answers with the key in the back of the book.

Directions for Short Readings

To help you improve your concentration and speed, these next readings are timed. When your instructor gives you the signal, you will read each article from the beginning. After one minute, circle the number at the end of the line you are reading. That is your words per minute (WPM). Immediately finish reading the article and answer the questions without looking back at the selection.

Question 1, marked with a circle, is about the main idea (or thesis) of a selection. Questions marked with a triangle △ are inference (reasoning or judgment) questions. Unmarked questions ask details related to the main idea.

Remember to practice reading whole phrases at a single glance.

This selection is an entry from Anne Frank's diary, written during the two years she and her family hid from the Nazis in the attic of an office building in Amsterdam. She started the diary when she was thirteen and died when she was fifteen in a concentration camp at Bergen-Belsen, two months before the liberation of Holland.

Preview: *Take 20 seconds (or less) to survey the first and last sentences of the article. Write here what you think this reading might be about:* _____

_____

Now wait for a signal from your instructor before you begin reading. Circle your WPM (words per minute) after one minute.

from Anne Frank: The Diary of a Young Girl

WPM

Today . . . Mrs. Koophuis comes and tells us about her daughter Cor- 11
ry's hockey club, canoe trips, theatrical performances, and friends. I 20
don't think I'm jealous of Corry, but I couldn't help feeling a great 33
longing to have lots of fun myself for once, and to laugh until my 47
tummy ached. Especially at this time of the year with all the holidays 60
for Christmas and the New Year, and we are stuck here like outcasts. 73
Still, I really ought not to write this, because it seems ungrateful and 86
I've certainly been exaggerating. But, still, whatever you think of me, 97
I can't keep everything to myself, so I'll remind you of my opening 110
words—"Paper is patient." 114
When someone comes in from outside, with the wind in their 125
clothes and the cold on their faces, then I could bury my head in the 140
blankets to stop myself thinking: "When will we be granted the privi- 152
lege of smelling fresh air?" And because I must not bury my head in 165
the blankets, but the reverse—I must keep my head high and be 178
brave, the thoughts will come, not once, but, oh, countless times. Be- 189
lieve me, if you have been shut up for a year and a half, it can get too 207
much for you some days. In spite of all justice and thankfulness, you 220
can't crush your feelings. Cycling, dancing, whistling, looking out 229
into the world, feeling young, to know that I'm free—that's what I 242
long for; still, I mustn't show it, because I sometimes think if all eight 256
of us began to pity ourselves, or went about with discontented faces, 268
where would it lead us? I sometimes ask myself, "Would anyone, ei- 279
ther Jew or non-Jew, understand this about me, that I am simply a 292
young girl badly in need of some rollicking fun?" I don't know, and I 306
couldn't talk about it to anyone, because then I know I should cry. 319
Crying can bring such relief. . . .* 324

Immediately answer the following questions without referring to the selection.

1. Choose the sentence expressing the main idea (or thesis) of this article.

   (a) The author is jealous of Corry Koophuis.

*From *Anne Frank: The Diary of a Young Girl.* Copyright 1952 by Otto H. Frank. Reprinted by permission of Doubleday, a division of Bantam Doubleday Dell Publishing Group, Inc.

(b) She is filled with self pity after being isolated so long.

(c) She is trying to be brave, but wants to be free and have fun like other girls.

(d) She is beginning to predict her coming death.

2. Her isolation is relieved occasionally by being able to go outside and breathe fresh air. **T**   **F**

3. To whom is the author speaking in this article? _____

4. Her isolation is more difficult because it is holiday time. **T**   **F**

5. When she writes this diary entry, she has been shut up for

(a) a few months. **(b)** a year. **(c)** a year and a half. **(d)** two years.

Check your answers with the key at the end of the book. Each comprehension question in a Short Reading is worth 20%. Record your scores below and on the progress chart on page 367.

WORDS PER MINUTE _____

% COMPREHENSION _____

Samuel Langhorne Clemens is the real name of Mark Twain, the famous, nineteenth-century, American writer and humorist. You probably are most familiar with his novels, Tom Sawyer *and* Huckleberry Finn. *In the selection below, you will see similarities between him as a boy and the characters in those books.*

Preview: *Take 20 seconds or less to preread a few sentences at the beginning and the end of the article. Then write in the blanks below what you expect the article to be about:* _____

_____

Wait for a signal from your instructor before you begin reading. (Reread the sentences you just previewed.) Remember to read in phrases. After one minute, circle the number at the end of the line you are reading. Then finish the article and answer the questions.

from The Autobiography of Mark Twain

Samuel Langhorne Clemens

WPM

My mother had a good deal of trouble with me, but I think she	14
enjoyed it. She had none at all with my brother Henry, who was two	28
years younger than I. I think that the unbroken monotony of his	40
goodness and truthfulness and obedience would have been a bur-	50
den to her but for the relief and variety which I furnished in the	63
other direction. I was a tonic. I was valuable to her. I never thought of	78
it before but now I see it. I never knew Henry to do a vicious thing	94
toward me or toward anyone else—but he frequently did righteous	105
ones that cost me as heavily. It was his duty to report me, when I	120
needed reporting and neglected to do it myself. He was very faithful	132
in discharging that duty.	136
[Once I had an opportunity to report Henry.] Henry never	146
stole sugar. He took it openly from the bowl. Mother knew he	158
wouldn't take sugar when she wasn't looking, but she had her doubts	170
about me. Not exactly doubts, either. She knew very well I *would*. One	183
day when she was not present Henry took sugar from her prized and	196
precious old-English sugar bowl, which was an heirloom in the fam-	206
ily. And he managed to break the bowl. It was the first time I have ever	221
had a chance to tell anything on him, and I was inexpressibly glad. I	235
told him I was going to tell on him but he was not disturbed.	249
When my mother came in and saw the bowl lying on the floor	262
in fragments, she was speechless for a minute. I allowed that silence	274
to work; I judged it would increase the effect. I was waiting for her to	289
ask, "Who did that?"—so that I could fetch out my news. But it was an	305
error of calculation. When she got through with her silence she	316
didn't ask anything about it. She merely gave me a crack on the skull	330
with her thimble that I felt all the way down to my heels. Then I	345
broke out with my injured innocence, expecting to make her very	356
sorry that she had punished the wrong one. I expected her to do	369
something remorseful and pathetic. I told her that I was not the	381
one—it was Henry. But there was no upheaval. She said, without	393

emotion, "It's all right. It isn't any matter. You deserve it for something that you are going to do that I shan't hear about."*

Answer these questions without referring to the selection.

(1.) State the main idea (or thesis) of the selection in a complete sentence. _

_____

_____

2. The two brothers loved each other too much to report on each other's misdeeds.   **T**   **F**

3. What object was broken? _____

4. The mother apologized to her son for punishing him unjustly.   **T**   **F**

5. Why was the author's moment of silence an "error of calculation?"
   (a) Henry used it to tell on him [the author].
   (b) His mother automatically assumed he, not Henry, was guilty.
   (c) He wished he had used the time to run away.
   (d) He knew he should have spent the time repenting his sins.

Check your answers with the key at the end of the book, and record your scores below and on the progress chart on page 367.

WORDS PER MINUTE _____

% COMPREHENSION _____

Directions for Long Readings

The Long Reading exercises are different lengths, but all are over 800 words. Wait for a signal before you begin reading. Then, after finishing, look up and your instructor will indicate your reading time.** Record the time in the space provided, and immediately go on to answer the ten questions below the selection.

Check your answers with the key at the end of the Lesson. If you made a mistake, review the reading to find the correct answer.

Use the rate chart on page 364 to find your words per minute for each exercise. Record your words per minute and percent of correct answers at the bottom of the exercise and on the progress chart on page 367.

---

*Clemens, Samuel. From *The Mark Twain Autobiography,* edited by Charles Neider. Published by Harper & Row, Publishers, Inc.

**If you are timing yourself, write down both your starting and your finishing time and subtract for total reading time, as follows:

	hr.	min.	sec.
finishing time	10	21	0
starting time	–10	15	30
total reading time		5	30

LESSON 1   31

Helen Keller, the author of the next selection, was a celebrated author and lecturer, who, like Mark Twain, grew up in the nineteenth century. She relates a key episode from her early life that helped her learn to communicate in spite of being blind and deaf.

Preview: *Read the title, first paragraph, and last paragraph in less than 30 seconds. Then write in the blanks below your guess about why this day was important:*

_____

_____

Wait for a signal from your instructor before you begin. Read the entire article, including the parts you just previewed.

from The Story of My Life

Helen Keller

The most important day I remember in all my life is the one on which my teacher, Anne Mansfield Sullivan, came to me. . . . It was the third of March, 1887, three months before I was seven years old.

On the afternoon of that eventful day, I stood on the porch, dumb, expectant. I guessed vaguely from my mother's signs and from the hurrying to and fro in the house that something unusual was about to happen, so I went to the door and waited on the steps. The afternoon sun penetrated the mass of honeysuckle that covered the porch, and fell on my upturned face. My fingers lingered almost unconsciously on the familiar leaves and blossoms which had just come forth to greet the sweet southern spring. I did not know what the future held of marvel or surprise for me. . . .

Have you ever been at sea in a dense fog, when it seemed as if a tangible white darkness shut you in, and the great ship, tense and anxious, groped her way toward the shore . . . and you waited with beating heart for something to happen? I was like that ship before my education began, only I was without compass . . . and had no way of knowing how near the harbour was. "Light! give me light!" was the wordless cry of my soul, and the light of love shone on me in that very hour.

I felt approaching footsteps. I stretched out my hand as I supposed to my mother. Someone took it, and I was caught up and held close in the arms of her who had come to reveal all things to me, and, more than all things else, to love me.

The morning after my teacher came she led me into her room and gave me a doll. . . . When I had played with it a little while, Miss Sullivan slowly spelled into my hand the word "d-o-l-l." I was at once interested in this finger play and tried to imitate it. When I finally succeeded in making the letters correctly, I was flushed with childish pleasure and pride. Running downstairs to my mother I held up my hand and made the letters for doll. I did not know that I was spelling a word or even that words existed; I was simply making my fingers go in monkey-like imitation. In the days that followed I learned to spell in this uncomprehending way a great many words, among them *pin, hat, cup* and a few verbs like *sit, stand,* and *walk.* But my teacher had been with me several weeks before I understood that everything has a name.

One day, while I was playing with my new doll, Miss Sullivan put my big rag doll into my lap also, spelled "d-o-l-l" and tried to make me understand that "d-o-l-l" applied to both. Earlier in the day we had had a tussle over the words "m-u-g" and "w-a-t-e-r." Miss Sullivan had tried to impress it upon me that "m-u-g" is *mug* and that "w-a-t-e-r" is *water,* but I persisted in confounding the two. In despair she had dropped the subject for the time, only to renew it at the first opportunity. I became impatient with her repeated attempts and, seizing the new doll, I dashed it upon the floor. I was keenly delighted when I felt the fragments of the broken doll at my feet. Neither sorrow nor regret followed my passionate outburst. I had not loved the doll. In the still, dark world in which I lived there was no strong sentiment or tenderness. I felt my teacher sweep the fragments to one side of the hearth, and I had a sense of satisfaction that the cause of my discomfort was removed. She brought me my hat, and I knew I was going out into the warm sunshine. This thought, if a wordless sensation may be called a thought, made me hop and skip with pleasure.

We walked down the path to the well-house, attracted by the fragrance of the honeysuckle with which it was covered. Someone was drawing water and my teacher placed my hand under the spout. As the cool stream gushed over one hand she spelled into the other the word *water,* first slowly, then rapidly. I stood still, my whole attention fixed upon the motions of her fingers. Suddenly I felt a misty consciousness as of something forgotten—a thrill of returning thought; and somehow the mystery of language was revealed to me. I knew then that "w-a-t-e-r" meant the wonderful cool something that was flowing over my hand. That living word awakened my soul, gave it light, hope, joy, set it free! There were barriers still, it is true, but barriers that could in time be swept away.

I left the well-house eager to learn. Everything had a name, and each name gave birth to a new thought. As we returned to the house, every object which I touched seemed to quiver with life. That was because I saw everything with the strange, new sight that had come to me. On entering the door I remembered the doll I had broken. I felt my way to the hearth and picked up the pieces. I tried vainly to put them together. Then my eyes filled with tears, for I realized what I had done, and for the first time I felt repentance and sorrow.

I learned a great many new words that day. I do not remember what they all were; but I do know that *mother, father, sister, teacher* were among them—words that were to make the world blossom for me. . . . It would have been difficult to find a happier child than I was as I lay in my crib at the close of that eventful day and lived over the joys it had brought me, and for the first time longed for a new day to come.*

TOTAL READING TIME _____

Immediately answer the following questions without referring to the selection.

_____
*Helen Keller, *The Story of My Life.* Doubleday, Page, & Company: 1903.

(1) Choose the statement that best expresses the main idea (or thesis).

   (a) Helen Keller was filled with despair over her blindness and deafness.

   (b) Helen resisted Anne Mansfield Sullivan's efforts to teach her words for a long time.

   (c) Helen's realization that everything had a name was her key to learning and a turning point in her life.

   (d) Helen was a quick and eager student.

2. Before her teacher came to her, Helen felt ready for something significant to happen in her life.   **T**   **F**

3. How old was Helen when she first met her teacher? _____

4. Miss Sullivan first tried to teach Helen the signs for *mother.*   **T**   **F**

5. Helen learned to "finger-spell" several words without realizing they were words.   **T**   **F**

6. Miss Sullivan taught Helen Keller the word for *water* by making her drink it out of a mug.   **T**   **F**

7. Many details in the story suggest that Helen was especially aware of smells and textures.   **T**   **F**

8. Once she learned the signs *w-a-t-e-r* meant *water,* Helen was immediately eager to learn the name of everything around her.   **T**   **F**

9. What was Helen's reaction to breaking the doll?

   (a) first satisfaction, then repentance

   (b) first repentance, then satisfaction

   (c) anger at the doll

10. What was the significance of the new words Helen remembered learning that day?

   (a) The number of words she learned proved how smart she was.

   (b) The words represented the people important to her.

   (c) She realized she could learn to read then.

Check your answers with the key at the back of the book. Each comprehension question in a Long Reading is worth 10%. Then turn to page 364 to get your words per minute for this selection. Finally, record your scores below and on the progress chart on page 367.

WORDS PER MINUTE _____

% COMPREHENSION _____

How to Improve—Short and Long Readings

1. Always preview or survey for the title and topic. This habit helps you "tune in" and concentrate.

2. Continue to practice reading in phrases. Read for ideas, not single words. This technique will also help you concentrate.

3. Don't regress or reread.

4. Don't move your lips. This bad habit (and reading word-by-word) will make it hard for you to read more than 150 to 200 WPM.

1. Certain key events or people in our lives have influenced who or what we've become. Many of these influences were positive, others negative or painful. Think back over your childhood and teenage years. Then make a list of some people and events that helped to shape the kind of person you are today. After you make the list, choose one of these influences to explain or describe in a detailed paragraph.

2. Start a reading journal. Choose one or more of the articles you just read. Write your feelings about the author's story. Have you had a similar experience?

2

Finding the Main Idea

IN THIS LESSON, YOU WILL

1. continue perception and comprehension exercises;
2. learn to identify the *topic* of a reading selection;
3. learn to distinguish between *topic* and *main idea;*
4. learn to state the author's *main idea* in paragraphs;
5. learn to find the author's *thesis* in articles.

► *Exercise 2A—Word Perception*

Pick out the word identical to the key word.

Key Word

1.	geology	geography	geometry	geology	radiology	genuflect
2.	pickle	picked	pickup	nickle	pickle	picket
3.	repellent	repealer	repellent	excellent	repentant	replicate
4.	extrovert	extrovert	extricate	extravagant	convert	expletive
5.	glide	gilt	slide	glade	gild	glide
6.	notation	nation	ovation	notation	vacation	notional
7.	scurry	scurvy	scurry	curry	scruffy	scuffle
8.	financial	fineness	pension	finagle	financial	finality
9.	hayrick	hayrick	hayrack	rickets	haywire	hayseed
10.	metaphor	metaphase	euphoric	metamorphic	meteor	metaphor
11.	kidney	kindle	kinder	hinder	kidnap	kidney
12.	generic	genesis	generic	genetic	regenerate	general
13.	hamster	sterile	hamper	hamster	hammer	handler
14.	cricket	cricket	ricket	crinkle	critic	crinkly
15.	breadth	breach	bread	break	breadth	reach
16.	appeal	appear	pealed	appall	appeal	appease
17.	flotation	rotation	flotation	flotsam	notation	fluoridated
18.	grumble	humble	crumble	grunter	grunion	grumble
19.	wastrel	waster	wasteful	wastrel	minstrel	wassail
20.	sprig	sprig	spring	string	prig	sprite

TIME _____

ERRORS _____

► *Exercise 2B—Word Perception*

Pick out the word identical to the key word.

Key Word

1. graduate	gradient	graduate	radiator	gradual	radical
2. equality	equalize	quality	equality	equal	qualify
3. mean	middle	men	main	mean	level
4. sensation	soaring	sore	sensitive	sensible	sensation
5. tactile	tactile	traction	attractive	track	contact
6. politic	pompous	pills	politic	politician	radical
7. whip	which	whip	whit	hipster	wick
8. penalty	penalize	purify	legality	penalty	petrify
9. approve	prove	applaud	poverty	approval	approve
10. leopard	lioness	partner	leopard	jeopardy	lizard
11. revenue	revenue	reveal	avenue	renew	revel
12. exalt	exit	exalt	solid	excite	salt
13. dreariness	dearness	nearness	harness	dreariness	dreadful
14. anyone	someone	known	anybody	annoy	anyone
15. origin	original	rigorous	origin	orifice	artificial
16. titillate	titular	titillate	titled	scintillate	stifle
17. quaint	quantity	saint	quality	quandary	quaint
18. borough	borough	borrow	thorough	brought	through
19. paragon	paragraph	antagonize	parallel	paragon	paraffin
20. shipboard	overboard	shiftless	shipboard	shipment	shipbuilder

TIME _____

ERRORS _____

► *Exercise 2C—Word Comprehension*

Choose the word closest in meaning to the key word in **boldface** print.

Key Word

1. an **articulate** speaker	talkative	fluent	artistic
2. an **obstinate** child	shy	agreeable	stubborn
3. the **arid** land	dry	wet	fertile
4. to **abhor** rudeness	approve	witness	detest
5. **wary** around strangers	friendly	cautious	careless
6. an **extravagant** cost	cheap	moderate	excessive
7. **abolition** of slavery	termination	beginning	amendment
8. to **secrete** the truth	uncover	hide	tell
9. revealed as a **sham**	fake	reality	nude
10. a **valiant** soldier	pretentious	brave	cowardly
11. an **astounding** development	new	suspicious	surprising
12. burying the **deceased**	alive	unclean	corpse
13. to **imply** an insult	suggest	infer	refer
14. to become **destitute**	humble	rich	poor
15. to **wane** in power	increase	decline	glory
16. to render **mute**	talkative	loud	silent
17. **famished** for food	starved	looking	satisfied
18. a **trivial** pursuit	important	petty	dangerous
19. an **obscure** point	clear	interesting	vague
20. a **sublime** experience	noble	subtle	ordinary

TIME _____

ERRORS _____

NOTE: Remember, all answers are in the key at the back of the book.

► *Exercise 2D—Word Comprehension*

Choose the word closest in meaning to the key word in **boldface** print.

Key Word

1. asking for an **encore**	song	repeat	play
2. sewing on an **insignia**	signature	button	emblem
3. throwing a **tantrum**	ball	fit	game
4. to **rove** the countryside	wander	photograph	raise
5. a **fabulous** dress	expensive	common	wonderful
6. to **apprehend** the thief	capture	chase	convict
7. to **forgo** the benefit	give in	give up	take
8. to **concede** the point	give in	give up	win
9. to **cleave** in two	march	split	count
10. to **avert** danger	expect	attract	turn aside
11. the **expired** patient	dead	breathing	live
12. a worthy **adversary**	partner	opponent	friend
13. to **captivate** an audience	charm	beg	gather
14. to **smite** the enemy	fight	caress	strike
15. to **amputate** the leg	cut off	sew on	break
16. an eager **apprentice**	veteran	carpenter	learner
17. a clever **strategy**	trap	plan	tournament
18. a **commanding** voice	soft	masterful	loud
19. for **tangible** results	doubtful	touching	concrete
10. to pay **homage** to the flag	raise	penalty	honor

TIME _____

ERRORS _____

Circle the key words in each of these sentences. Look for the topic (the noun or pronoun that tells what the sentence is about) and the action (verb) that tells what happens or happened.

EXAMPLE:

The(boat)full of English professors(was sinking)slowly.

When you finish the exercise, check your time and record it on the line at the end of the exercise. Then check your answers with the key at the back of the book and record the number of your errors.

▶ *Exercise 2E—Sentence Comprehension*

1. An ape can be a clumsy, gross person.
2. The fatigued executive went to an ashram, a secluded place, for meditation.
3. The bobwhite, a small, North American quail, has white and brown markings on its gray body.
4. They constructed a breezeway, or a covered passageway, between the house and the garage.
5. Some people flavor their coffee with cinnamon.
6. The ambassador received diplomatic immunity from taxes while abroad.
7. Larry McMurtry's book, *Lonesome Dove,* has been made into a television mini-series.
8. In a direct primary election, candidates are chosen by the people in a direct vote, instead of by convention delegates.
9. The Gulf Stream flows from the Gulf of Mexico along the Eastern coast of the United States.
10. Holly leaves and berries frequently are used as Christmas decorations.

TIME _____

ERRORS _____

Every sentence has two key parts—what it is about (the topic) and what is going on. Often the topic is the first or second word. But sometimes descriptive words come before the topic. Notice where the topic is in each of these sentences:

Pink and hairless, newborn (mice) look transparent.

In the meadow near the lake, the (bears) are eating someone's picnic.

► *Exercise 2F—Sentence Comprehension*

Circle the key words in each of these sentences.

1. On November 22, 1963, Lyndon Johnson took the oath of office as President in the Presidential jet plane in Dallas.
2. A **simile** is a figure of speech in which one thing is compared to another without the use of **like** or **as**.
3. The articulate politician gave a spirited defense of his fund-raising methods.
4. Terra cotta, a hard brown-red earthenware, is used for sculpture and pottery.
5. Terrorists have made Americans afraid to travel.
6. The embarrassed woman wore a turban to cover her bald head.
7. "God dwells where we let God in." Menachem Mendel.
8. Martin Van Buren was the eighth president of the United States.
9. Many people suffer from vertigo, a feeling of dizziness.
10. In spite of the fierce competition, he won a gold medal at the 1988 Olympics in Korea.

TIME _____

ERRORS _____

NOTE: Before you read this unit, practice the survey technique you learned in Lesson 1. Read the title. Before reading the entire unit, quickly read the first and last paragraphs and marginal notes.

The first and most essential skill that will improve your reading comprehension is finding the main idea, whether of a paragraph, an essay, a chapter, or a book. It is another aid that will help you see the whole instead of getting lost in the parts. To begin, we will examine the main idea in the simplest unit, the paragraph. If you can find the main idea in a paragraph, you can find it in an article. Of course, you must be able to recognize a paragraph.

Remember that a paragraph is a group of sentences on the same topic. These sentences explain, define, or develop a dominant idea. The first sentence in this group is indented several spaces from the left margin to show where the paragraph begins. Each paragraph has (1) a topic, (2) a main idea about that topic, and (3) details that explain or "prove" the main idea.

First, finding the topic—like a title

Because the main idea tells you something about the author's topic, you must first decide what the topic is. The topic is what a paragraph (or longer piece of writing) is about in general. You can almost always state the topic in a word or short phrase. For example, the topic might be "Vitamin A" *or* "Talking to Your Plants" *or* "Television in the 90s." When you state the topic of a paragraph, you may find it helpful to think of it as similar to a title that gives the subject the author is discussing.

Next, looking for the main idea about the topic

After you have found the topic, you must discover what main point the writer is making about that topic. In other words, see how the writer expands the topic. For example, "Vitamin A is essential for normal bone growth, vision, and skin" *or* "Plants are sensitive to sound" *or* "The 1990s have seen a rise in high-quality movies made for television" are examples of the main idea statement that gives more information about the topic.

The main idea statement presents the author's opinion, point of view, or concept that will be explained in the paragraph. It is the central point of the paragraph (or of an article, chapter, or book). The author usually states the main idea in one of the sentences in the paragraph. This sentence is called a topic sentence. Other times the main idea is not stated directly but is implied (suggested).

Telling main ideas from topics

To help you practice telling statements from topics, a list of topics and main ideas follows. Place a check in front of those groups of words that are not just topics but actually make statements. You are looking for an opinion, a judgment, or a fact that could be explained. (A clue is that a statement is a complete sentence and that a topic is usually a fragment.)

_____ 1. Warm currents in the Pacific Ocean.

_____ 2. Warm currents in the Pacific Ocean are destroying the fish off the coast of Peru.

_____ 3. A diet high in fiber can help prevent cancer of the colon.

_____ 4. A shortage of teachers in math and science.

_____ 5. How to make money in real estate.

_____ 6. The only way to learn how to write is to write.

_____ 7. Watching the horse that won the Kentucky Derby.

_____ 8. War is hell.

If you marked 2, 3, 6, and 8 as statements, you understand the difference between a topic and a statement. Remember: a statement is a complete sentence.

Where to find the
main idea

Writers usually state their topics at the beginning, often in the title. Writers of a textbook—informative prose—usually state the main idea about the topic at the beginning of the unit. For example, the topic of this section is announced in the title "Finding the Main Idea." And the main point is stated in the third sentence of the second paragraph. Whether you are reading a paragraph or a whole chapter, 70 to 90 percent of the time you will find the main idea(s) at the beginning. The rest of the time you will find it in the middle or end of the unit. Sometimes it is stated at the beginning, then repeated in a conclusion or summary at the end.

Topic sentence

In a short unit like a paragraph, the main idea may be clearly stated in a *topic sentence.* Sometimes, of course, the writer does not conveniently provide you with a topic sentence. Then you must infer, or judge, from the details or organization just what the main point is. (You will learn more about how to infer the main idea in Lesson 3.)

Whether stated for you or implied, the main idea statement is like an umbrella. It covers all the details, but does not introduce any new ones. Notice the function of the supporting details. They hold up the main idea statement.

Said another way, the main idea statement makes the author's point. It is a general statement. The rest of the paragraph will be the details that explain or prove—in other words, support—the main point.

The most important
and difficult reading
skill

Finding the main idea is the most important reading skill. Yet most readers have more trouble with this skill than they do with others, such as understanding and remembering colorful details. This skill is the key to increasing understanding and speed, because once you have that main idea in mind, everything that follows seems to click into place. You see the parts (details, minor points, inferences) in relationship to the whole (main idea). In every reading selection in this book, you will be asked to locate the topic and the main idea before anything else. Main idea questions are marked with a circle: ○.

To make sure you understand terms that will be used throughout this book, define and discuss the following:

1. topic _____

2. main idea _____

3. main idea statement _____

4. topic sentence _____

Theme: Feeling Good

These readings discuss different aspects of your health. They especially stress the connection between your body and your mind.

Practice Paragraphs

Read the following paragraphs to find the topic or subject being discussed. Then, find the writer's main idea about that topic. Remember that the main idea is not always stated clearly in one sentence. After answering the questions for each paragraph, check with the key at the back of the book.

A. (1) One effective treatment for the sharp, crippling pain of migraine headaches has been biofeedback training. (2) This kind of headache is often set off by too much flow of blood to the brain. (3) Doctors teach patients to divert the extra blood flow to the hands. (4) An instrument that is very sensitive to temperature changes is attached to the patient's hand. (5) As more blood flows to the hand, the temperature rises. (6) The instrument emits higher and higher sounds. (7) Patients have learned to increase blood flow to the hands enough to raise the temperature ten degrees in two minutes. (8) As this happens, the migraine is headed off. (9) At the Menninger Foundation in Kansas, researchers have helped 75 percent of the migraine patients they first treated with this method.*

1. What is the general topic of the paragraph? (Consider the topic like a title. Remember to capitalize the first letter of the first word and all important words in a title.) _____

2. In your own words, what is the main idea about this topic? (State the idea in a complete sentence.) _____
_____

3. Is the main idea stated in a topic sentence? _____

If so, what is the number of the sentence? _____

B. (1) Pay attention to your breathing. (2) How you breathe can tell you how relaxed you are. (3) For example, when you are calm, your breathing is deep and steady. (4) Your breath comes from the stomach, not the chest. (5) But when you are nervous, excited, or under stress, your breathing changes. (6) It becomes shallow and ragged, almost like panting. (7) It comes from the chest or throat. (8) Sometimes, when upset, you may even catch yourself holding your breath without knowing it. (9) Or you may exhale more quickly than you inhale. (10) So whenever you want to calm down, try to breathe to a rhythm. (11) Inhale to the count of three, exhale to the count of four. (12) Then get in the habit of checking

---

*Adapted from John J. Fried, "Biofeedback: Teaching Your Body to Heal Itself," *Family Health*, February 1974.

your breathing from time to time to make sure you stay relaxed and at your best.

1. What is the general topic of the paragraph? (Consider the topic like a title. Remember to capitalize the first letter of the first word and all important words in a title.) _____

2. In your own words, what is the main idea about this topic? (State the idea in a complete sentence.) _____

   _____

3. Is the main idea stated in a topic sentence? _____

   If so, what is the number of the sentence? _____

C. (1) Self-hypnosis can lessen social fears such as excessive shyness, nervousness, awkwardness, and even fear of flying. (2) It not only helps people shed fat, but can improve their eating habits, and help them sleep more soundly. (3) It can also help cure more serious habits such as smoking, alcoholism, and drug abuse. (4) Further, doctors have successfully used it as an anaesthesia for patients during dental work, childbirth, and certain operations where the patient must remain conscious. (5) Self-hypnosis is indeed a powerful tool that has varied benefits and reminds us that mind and body are one.

1. What is the general topic of the paragraph? (Consider the topic like a title. Remember to capitalize the first letter of the first word and all important words in a title.) _____

2. In your own words, what is the main idea about this topic? (State the idea in a complete sentence.) _____

   _____

3. Is the main idea stated in a topic sentence? _____

   If so, what is the number of the sentence? _____

For each *italicized* word, choose the best meaning below.

▶ Short Reading 2G

1. In the cases where the older person's mind really seems to decay, it is not necessarily a sign of decay due to old age or *senility*. [Extra Clue: Another form of *senile*.]

   (a) excellent health **(b)** occasional forgetfulness **(c)** weakness in body and mind because of old age **(d)** giving up on life

▶ Short Reading 2H

2. Many techniques, including *biofeedback*, hypnosis, and yoga, could be used to control tension. [Extra Clue: The root *bio* means *life*.]

   (a) a machine hooked up to the body and feeding back information about physiological responses **(b)** a well-paying job **(c)** a method of transcending earthly concerns **(d)** a mild drug

▶ Long Reading 2I

3. The carbon-monoxide intake reduces the blood oxygen level and impairs *hormone* production. [Extra Clue: Both men and women have them.]

   (a) a sexual attitude **(b)** related to the female reproductive system **(c)** a drug causing male characteristics in females **(d)** a chemical substance formed by one organ and carried to another that it affects.

4. "If you're short of breath, tired, perhaps suffering from *vascular* disease complicated by smoking, then you're not going to feel much like engaging in sex." [Extra Clue: From Latin meaning small vessel.]

   (a) spots on the skin **(b)** excessive coughing **(c)** system of vessels for carrying blood **(d)** a condition caused by the white blood cells destroying the red

5. What sperm he did produce were sluggish—displaying low *motility*. [Extra Clue: Look at the root *mot* or *mov*.]

   (a) intelligence **(b)** ability to reproduce **(c)** motion, movement **(d)** color quality

6. "There is some strong evidence that smoking mothers have a significantly greater number of unsuccessful pregnancies due to stillbirth and *neonatal* death." [Extra Clue: The prefix *neo* means *new*.]

   (a) before birth **(b)** a newborn infant **(c)** after birth **(d)** false labor

Moving Beyond the Paragraph: The Main Idea in a Longer Reading

Longer readings, such as articles in magazines and newspapers, also have a main idea. This main idea is the major point for the entire piece of writing. It is the controlling idea that, like an umbrella *for the whole article,* helps the author write about only the ideas that fit under that topic.

In your writing classes, you may have heard the main idea for an article or essay called a thesis or thesis statement. In this book, we use the term *thesis* to refer to the main idea for a whole article.

An author usually states the thesis of an essay or article in the first or second paragraph, just as the main idea for a paragraph is often in the first or second sentence. Study the following diagram to see other ways a paragraph and an essay are similar.

Study These Two Diagrams to See How the Key Elements of a Paragraph and an Essay Are Alike.

The Structure of An Essay or Article

The Structure of A Paragraph

The structure of a paragraph usually follows the same order as the structure of an essay. Most of the time the TOPIC and the MAIN IDEA are in a topic sentence in the first part of the paragraph. . . . .
. . . .
. . . .
. . . . The rest of the paragraph has DETAILS that explain or support the main idea. . . . .
. . . .
. . . .
. . . .

Sometimes a paragraph has a CONCLUSION. It might restate the main idea.

The Title *May* Give the Topic or the Main Idea

The INTRODUCTION presents general information about the topic to catch your interest. . . .
. . . .
The main idea *for the whole essay* often comes at the end of the introduction. The main idea of an essay is called the THESIS.

The BODY of an essay has one or more paragraphs. These paragraphs give DETAILS that explain or prove the THESIS. . . . .
. . . .
. . . .
. . . .
. . . .

Usually a writer needs more than one paragraph to explain the thesis. Look for the main idea of each paragraph in a topic sentence. See how it supports the thesis. . . . .
. . . .
. . . .
. . . .
. . . .

The CONCLUSION can state the thesis again in different words in a final paragraph. Or it might point out what we can learn from the thesis or why it's important.

This first reading contradicts the popular belief that senility has to accompany old age.

Preview: *In 15 seconds or less, read the title and the first paragraph. The first paragraph is often the introduction of an article. As you read, guess at what the thesis (main idea for the whole article) might be, and write it in these blanks:*

_____

_____

Now wait for a signal from your instructor before you start to read the article from the beginning. (You will be rereading the introduction.) After one minute, circle the number at the end of the line you are reading. Then finish the article and answer the questions.

Research Debunks Old Myths About Mind's Decline

	WPM
Many of us believe that a person's mind becomes less active as	12
he grows older. But this is not true, according to Dr. Lissy F. Jarvik,	26
professor of psychiatry at the University of California, Los Angeles,	36
and a board member of the New Center for Aging at the Veterans	49
Hospital. She has studied the mental functioning of aging persons	59
for several years. For example, one of her studies concerns 136 pairs	71
of identical twins, who were first examined when they were already	82
60 years old. As Dr. Jarvik continued the study of the twins into their	96
70s and 80s, their minds did not generally decline as was expected.	108
However, there was some decline in their psycho-motor	117
speed. This means that it took them longer to accomplish mental	128
tasks than it used to. But when speed was not a factor, they lost very	143
little intellectual ability over the years. In general, Dr. Jarvik's studies	154
have shown that there is no decline in knowledge or reasoning abil-	166
ity. This is true not only into the 30s and 40s, but into the 60s and 70s	178
as well.	180
As for learning new things, and ability to remember, studies	190
by Dr. Jarvik and others show that the old are equal to the young. It is	206
true that older people themselves often complain that their memory	216
is not as good as it once was. However, much of what we call "loss of	232
memory" is not that at all. There usually was incomplete learning in	244
the first place. For example, the older person perhaps had trouble	255
hearing, or poor vision, or inattention, or was trying to learn the new	268
thing at too fast a pace.	274
In the cases where the older person's mind really seems to	285
decay, it is not necessarily a sign of a decay due to old age or	300
"senility." Often it is simply a sign of a depressed emotional state.	312
This depression usually can be counteracted by counseling, therapy	321
with a psychologist, or medications which fight depression.	328
In American society, when an older person loses something,	337
we tend to call him or her "senile." But notice that when a younger	351

person loses something, he does not blame it on senility or loss of memory. He finds some other excuse!*

Answer the following questions without referring to the article.

1. According to Dr. Jarvik's studies, middle-aged and older persons should expect to

(a) remember less. **(b)** reason better. **(c)** learn fewer new things. **(d)** lose little ability to remember, reason, or learn.

2. Both younger and older persons should realize that senility, or mental decay due to aging, is much less common than most of us believe.　　　**T**　　**F**

3. A long-term study of 136 pairs of twins showed that the only factor that declined over the years was psycho-motor speed.　　　**T**　　**F**

4. Usually, what appears to be senility is really _____.

5. Loss of memory is usually *not* caused by

(a) poor hearing or vision. **(b)** inattention. **(c)** senility. **(d)** trying to learn too fast.

Record your scores below and on the progress chart in the Appendix.

WORDS PER MINUTE _____

% COMPREHENSION _____

Bonus Question

The title expresses the thesis for the reading selection.　　　**T**　　**F**

NOTE: The key to this extra question (and to those following in the Short and Long Readings) follows the other answers in the Answer Key at the back of the book. These extra questions need not be included in the comprehension score.

---

*"Research Debunks Old Myths About Mind's Decline," *UCLA Monthly,* October, 1974. Reprinted by permission.

The next reading comments on the power of the mind to control tension.

Preview: *In 25 seconds or less, read the title, first paragraph, and last paragraph of the article. Then guess at what the thesis (main idea of the whole article) might be:*

———————————————————————————————————

———————————————————————————————————

Wait for a signal from your instructor before you read the entire article. Be sure to reread the parts just previewed. After a minute, circle the number of words on the line you are reading. Finish the article and answer the questions.

Pain in the Neck Is All in Your Head

George Alexander

WPM

The busy executive who makes a phone call with his fists | 11
clenched unconsciously and the secretary who types with her knees | 21
pressed together tightly are suffering from the same problem. They | 31
both have tension caused by too much use of muscles not really | 43
involved with their tasks. | 47

Speakers this weekend at the first meeting of the American | 57
Association for the Advancement of Tension Control kept making | 66
the same point. The damaging effects of tension are caused by the | 77
tensing of extra muscles for a long time. They stressed the belief that | 90
tension starts with the brain's giving commands to tense muscle | 100
bundles throughout the body. In short, that pain in your neck is all in | 114
your head. | 116

The speakers pointed out that people can create their own | 126
headaches, backaches, high blood pressure, as well as other ailments | 136
linked to tension. By the same token, they could also be the agents of | 150
their own recovery. Many techniques—including biofeedback, hyp- | 158
nosis and yoga—could be used to control tension. Most tension | 168
control techniques are based on the belief that all behavior is | 179
learned and can be unlearned. | 184

Dr. Edmund Jacobson, an eighty-six-year-old Chicago physi- | 191
cian, has an approach that involves simple exercises. At first the | 201
patient uses only the big muscles in the arms and legs. He learns to | 215
recognize the presence and the absence of tension in those muscles. | 226
He then learns to concentrate on relaxing the muscles until all the | 238
signs of tension are gone. Those who use this method say they can | 251
get rid of tension even in the small muscles around their eyes. They | 264
simply close their eyes for a few minutes and relax the muscles at | 277
will. | 278

One speaker, Charles Beach, a doctoral candidate at Michi- | 287
gan State University, described tension control techniques for ath- | 295
letes. He has worked for the past few years with Los Angeles Dodger | 307
pitching star, Mike Marshall. Beach said that an athlete needs some | 318
tension to compete well. Yet he went on to make the point that the | 332
tensing of muscles not directly needed to hit or throw a baseball can | 345

keep an athlete from playing well. Choking the bat can be one result 358
of too much muscular tension. 363

Beach discussed a tension control program that he and Marshall ran. The high school athletes who completed the program reported that while they might not perform any better, they could block out crowd noises and get rid of butterflies in their stomachs at crucial times. "So they didn't make herky-jerky motions taking a foul shot in the last few seconds of a basketball game," Beach points out. He further states that herky-jerky motions are nearly always the result of too much muscular tension.* 373 382 393 406 417 430 442 447

Immediately answer the following questions without referring to the selection.

(1.) State the thesis of the selection in a complete sentence. _____

_____

2. The speakers at the meeting suggest that tension can cause headaches, backaches, and high blood pressure. T   F

3. Tense behavior is learned and can be unlearned. T   F

4. Which of the following was not recommended in the article for tension control?

(a) biofeedback **(b)** hypnosis **(c)** mild tranquilizers **(d)** yoga

5. After the high school athletes completed the tension control program, they had

(a) better performance. **(b)** fewer butterflies in their stomachs. **(c)** more meaningful relationships. **(d)** less desire to compete.

Record your scores below and on the progress chart in the Appendix.

WORDS PER MINUTE _____

% COMPREHENSION _____

Bonus Question

Is the second sentence or the last sentence the topic sentence for the second paragraph? _____

*From "Pain in the Neck Is All In Your Head" by George Alexander, *Los Angeles Times,* October 14, 1974. Copyright © 1974 Los Angeles Times. Reprinted by permission.

This reading points out the damaging effects of smoking on one's sexual health.
Preview: *In 45 seconds or less, read the title and the first and last paragraphs.*
Write below what the author's thesis (main idea for the article) might be: _____

_____

Wait for a signal from your instructor before you start to read. Look for the thesis of the article and for topic sentences expressing the main idea of each paragraph.

Is Your Sex Life Going Up in Smoke?

Genell J. Subak-Sharpe

A large number of doctors are convinced that there is a link between smoking and sex. One of them is Alton Ochsner, a seventy-six-year-old senior consultant to the Ochsner Foundation Hospital in New Orleans. His views were twenty-four years ahead of the Surgeon General's report on the dangers of smoking. Dr. Ochsner described, on the basis of observing patients, a cause-and-effect relationship between heavy cigarette smoking and lung cancer. The same kind of clinical proof has convinced him that cigarette smoking can be dangerous to one's sexual health.

Ironically, he says, he is much more successful in convincing patients to stop smoking because of dangers to sexual health than because of more serious threats. "It has been estimated," Dr. Ochsner says, "that tobacco use kills about 360,000 people a year in this country alone. Yet people go right on smoking. But when I tell them that tobacco may have an adverse effect on their sexual activities, they suddenly take notice."

Dr. Ochsner likes to tell about a seventy-three-year-old man, a heavy smoker for forty-five years, who had a lung abcess removed. "I told him he had to stop smoking, so he did. Two months later, the lung had healed completely. Before he stopped smoking, he told me, he'd had sexual relations once every four to six months. Now it's three or four times a week."

More support comes from Joel Fort, M.D., director of San Francisco's Center for Solving Special Social and Health Problems. This center helps people both to overcome the cigarette habit and to deal with sexual problems. Dr. Fort automatically counsels smokers who complain of impotence to enroll in the center's stop-smoking clinic. The overwhelming majority of men who do so, says Dr. Fort, report their sex lives markedly improved. He gives the same advice to women who complain of lack of interest in sex.

Dr. Fort thinks that smoking impairs sexual performance in two primary ways. (1) The carbon-monoxide intake reduces the blood oxygen level and impairs hormone production. (2) The nicotine intake shrinks the blood vessels. It is the swelling of the blood vessels that is the central mechanism of sexual excitement and erection.

Dr. Fort also cites secondary effects of heavy smoking. Lung capacity is reduced, cutting back on the ability to "last" during intercourse. Also, nicotine discolors the teeth and taints the breath, reducing the smoker's sexual attractiveness.

Only a few scientific studies of the relationship between smoking and sexual capabilities have been undertaken, however. Two Paris researchers, Dr. H. Cendron and J. Vallery-Masson, published a study of the effects of age, tobacco, and other factors on male sexual activity. They took 70 men, 45 to 90 years old. The men were divided into two groups: 31 who smoked one or more packs a day, and 39 who either were nonsmokers or consumed fewer than five cigarettes a day. Slightly more than half the men had reported a decline in sexual activity between the ages of 25 and 40. "On this sample," the research team reported, "there is a significant difference between the smokers and nonsmokers. Sexual activity between ages 25 and 40 decreased more often in the first group than in the second group."

Notes one physician: "If you're short of breath, tired, perhaps suffering from vascular disease complicated by smoking, then you're not going to feel much like engaging in sex. But if a patient stops smoking, increases his exercise, and starts feeling more fit, his sexual interest and ability may improve too."

Such was the case with Ken Farrell. He was worried about a marked decline in his sexual capabilities. "I kept reading about guys in their 70s who are still going strong," he confided to his doctor. "And here I'm having trouble at 31!" He was smoking four packs a day when he finally consulted a doctor. The doctor found him underweight, but with nothing seriously wrong. "He advised me, though, to quit smoking, or at least to cut down," Farrell says. "About the same time I enrolled in an exercise program." In three months, Farrell reduced his smoking—to about ten cigarettes a day—and gained 15 pounds. He found himself much happier with both his health and his sex life.

Dr. Ochsner hopes that today's emphasis on sex will spur more scientific interest in studying the effects of smoking on sexual response. "The ironic thing," says Dr. Ochsner, "is that many men don't recognize they have a libido problem until after they quit smoking, and then they realize what they've been missing. It just seems sad to wait until you're 73 to make this discovery."

Also under consideration is the effects of smoking on fertility. One of the pioneer researchers in the field is Carl Schirren, M.D., a professor at Hamburg University, Germany. He studied fertility patterns in nearly 5000 men and reports that "no firm conclusions" can be drawn about smoking and male infertility. But he did observe "severe disturbances of sperm motility" in a group of men who smoked.

"A possible connection between their childlessness and the sperm damage by nicotine was made clear to these patients," Dr. Schirren reports. "And if they stopped smoking entirely, within six to ten weeks a considerable improvement in sperm motility resulted." He contends that "in every case of reduced male fertility, smoking should cease completely if children are desired."

Other studies tend to confirm this. For example, noted Australian biochemist Michael Briggs has found that heavy smoking does indeed lower testosterone (male sex hormone) production. Even more important, he found that hormone levels increase if smoking is stopped.

This happened in the case of Paul Conrad. He and his wife, Linda, had been married six years. Ever since their third anniversary Linda had gone from doctor to doctor in a vain attempt to discover why "we can't seem to have a baby." Finally, Paul agreed to be tested too. His examination turned up a normal level of the male hormone but a low sperm count. What sperm he did produce were sluggish—displaying "low motility." Then his doctor learned that Paul smoked three packs of cigarettes a day and had been a heavy smoker for 15 years. He advised the would-be father to stop smoking and return in three months for more tests.

Paul was doubtful, but he did kick the habit. When he was retested, there was marked improvement in sperm count and motility. Four months later, Linda was pregnant.

The evidence that women's smoking may affect ability to bear healthier children is more conclusive—and damning. Take Patricia Lansing, a chain smoker since high school. Her first pregnancy seemed normal, although her doctor did urge her to cut down from her four packs a day. Her baby was born dead, full-term yet more than two pounds lighter than normal nine-month babies. Patricia was understandably shattered.

Then she read a summary of a 1973 Surgeon General's report, *The Health Consequences of Smoking.* One sentence jumped out at her: "There is some strong evidence that smoking mothers have a significantly greater number of unsuccessful pregnancies due to still-birth and neonatal death." "That statement was like a knife stabbing me," she remembers.

It would be almost impossible to prove that Patricia's smoking was responsible for her baby's death. But statistically, women who smoke run a far greater risk of a tragedy like Patricia's than do nonsmokers. Says the 1973 Surgeon General's report: "On the average, the smoker has nearly twice the risk of delivering a low-birthweight infant as that of a nonsmoker." Such undersized infants run a higher risk of sickness and death than do larger babies.

On the brighter side is evidence gathered from a study of nearly 17,000 pregnancies in Britain. It suggests that women who give up smoking by the fourth month of pregnancy may avoid the risks to their babies. "The most damage from smoking comes in the second half of pregnancy," explains Joseph Warshaw, M.D., Director of the Yale University division of prenatal medicine. "I would advise any pregnant woman to stop smoking," he adds.

The potential harmful effects of smoking on fertility, childbirth, and sex life are worrisome. Again, data are skimpy, but many sex counselors and drug researchers are convinced, from personal observations, that a relationship exists.*

TOTAL READING TIME _____

Immediately answer the following questions without referring to the selection.

1. Choose the answer that best completes the thesis. Although it has not been proven beyond any doubt,

    (a) smoking reduces the smoker's sexual attractiveness because it discolors the teeth and taints the breath.

---

*"Is Your Sex Life Going Up in Smoke?" by Genell Subak-Sharpe. Adapted from an article first published in *Today's Health,* August, 1974 and condensed in *Reader's Digest,* January 1975. Reprinted by permission.

(b) some doctors believe that smoking can be damaging to one's sexual capacity, fertility, and ability to bear healthy children.

(c) men are not sexually attracted to women who smoke.

(d) smoking is the major factor in the decline of sexual performance.

2. According to Dr. Ochsner, people are more likely to quit smoking because of danger to their

   (a) sexual health. **(b)** lungs. **(c)** throats.

3. The 73-year-old man who stopped smoking because of lung surgery had what side benefit? _____

4. The swelling of the blood vessels plays an important part in sexual performance. **T   F**

5. There is little evidence to support the claim that a woman who smokes has less chance of bearing a healthy baby. **T   F**

6. One solution for a man with the problem of sperm with "low motility" is to drink plenty of liquids. **T   F**

7. Dr. Carl Schirren, M.D., is thoroughly convinced that smoking affects male fertility. **T   F**

8. According to Dr. Warshaw, the most damage to babies from smoking mothers comes in the second half of pregnancy. **T   F**

9. According to the 1973 Surgeon General's report, there is very little risk to the infant of a smoker. **T   F**

10. The British study suggests that a woman may avoid risks to her baby if she gives up smoking by which month?

    (a) fourth. **(b)** sixth. **(c)** seventh. **(d)** ninth.

Turn to the Rate Chart in the Appendix to get your words per minute for this selection. Then record your scores below and on the progress chart in the Appendix.

WORDS PER MINUTE _____

% COMPREHENSION _____

Bonus Question

Which sentence in the first paragraph is the topic sentence for that paragraph and also is the thesis for the entire selection? _____

How to Improve Getting the Thesis/Main Idea

As you apply the reading principles you are learning in this book to your outside reading, you may notice certain things:

1. The thesis is not usually the first sentence in an article or essay. The author often starts with a little story (called an anecdote) to get your interest and introduce the topic. Or the author may start with some surprising facts or statistics. *The thesis may not be stated until the end of the first paragraph or even until the second paragraph.*

2. The thesis in writing for newspapers and magazines is often more general than the type of thesis you are learning to write for school assignments. It doesn't always list *all* the main ideas that the article will develop. Instead, it may just give the main point the author will expand on in the rest of the article.

3. Looking for the article's thesis and main ideas is a thinking skill. You cannot always spot the thesis of an article nor the main idea of a paragraph the first time you see it. Only when you *compare what a sentence is saying to what the other sentences are saying* can you tell which statement is the most general, the umbrella for the others.

WRITING AND DISCUSSION ACTIVITIES

1. Write a letter to your boss. In the letter give your ideas about what your company or business could do to improve the general well-being of the employees. You may wish to use some of the ideas from the articles you just read. But feel free to add other ideas that come to you. When you finish, your instructor may want you to break into small groups of three or four and discuss the ideas in each other's letters. (If you have no job, imagine the conditions you'd like to have once you start to work.)

2. Continue your reading journal. Give your feelings about one or more of the articles you just read. Start by summing up your feelings in a single sentence. This will be your topic sentence. In the rest of the paragraph, explain why you feel this way.

3

More About
Main Idea

IN THIS LESSON, YOU WILL

1. continue perception and comprehension exercises;

2. learn to form a generalization about a list of specifics;

3. learn to tell the *general idea* in a paragraph from the supporting details;

4. learn to generalize the main idea in paragraphs and the thesis in articles that have both implied and stated main ideas.

► *Exercise 3A—Phrase Perception*

Pick out the phrase identical to the key phrase.

Key Phrase

1. to save gas	to have gas	two saved gas	to save gas
2. control pollution	central pollution	control pollution	controlled pullout
3. owning a car	owning cars	owning a car	the owner's car
4. slow driving	slow driver	slow driving	slow drive
5. a seat belt	a neat belt	a seat belt	a near belt
6. car pool	car pooling	car pool	careful pal
7. pedal travel	pedal travel	pedal traveled	pedal drag
8. careful driver	careful driver	careful diver	scared of driving
9. radial tires	radial tires	radial tire	radical tire
10. make and model	make a model	make and model	maker's model
11. a popular item	a populous item	a popular item	a popular mite
12. having overdrive	having overhang	having overdrive	having overdone
13. lower rpm	lower rim	lower rpm	slower rpm
14. air filter	air filter	fair filter	air flight
15. natural resource	national resource	nature's resource	natural resource
16. harmful emissions	harmful omissions	harmless emissions	harmful emissions
17. wasting energy	wasteful energy	wasting energy	wasting energies
18. use the brakes	abuse the brakes	fuse the brakes	use the brakes
19. road tested	toad rested	rod tested	road tested
20. camping trip	camping trip	camping tent	camper rip-off

TIME _____

ERRORS _____

► **Exercise 3B—Phrase Perception**

Pick out the phrase identical to the key phrase.

Key Phrase

1.	six swimming swans	swat six swans	six sweet sins	six swimming swans
2.	this covered wagon	the costly wigs	this covered wagon	that wagging dog
3.	the dripping faucet	the file cabinet	the worst fault	the dripping faucet
4.	downfall of man	downfall of man	fall of women	many funny clowns
5.	a clean ashtray	a clean ashtray	clear an aisle	a betrayed clod
6.	gangster movie	big motorcycle gang	picture of mother	gangster movie
7.	smokefilled lungs	smokefilled lungs	dreadful smog	broken filling
8.	polka-dot bikini	yellow dotted bikini	polka-dot bikini	dance the polka
9.	down narrow streets	down narrow streets	marrow of bones	deft right turns
10.	dance a jig	dance a jig	a rigged dance	a fancy jig
11.	in slow motion	in slow motion	inside the track	an insolent action
12.	a crossword puzzle	a crossword puzzle	a jigsaw puzzle	a puzzling word
13.	handle with care	careful handling	handle with care	a hot handle
14.	put to sleep	a sleazy slut	but not there	put to sleep
15.	cook your goose	cook your goose	goose your crook	cupful of gin
16.	pray for peace	pray for peace	pans of pears	prey on people
17.	win the war	war to win	win the war	the won war
18.	the lost letter	a lost letter	the better lot	the lost letter
19.	tread on me	tread on me	read this too	one dread night
20.	rip it across	cross the rip	trip it across	rip it across

TIME _____

ERRORS _____

► Exercise 3C—Word Comprehension

Choose the word closest in meaning to the key word in **boldface** print.

Key Word

1.	an **abominable** meal	expensive	disgusting	delightful
2.	a **wayward** child	willful	obedient	sickly
3.	to fall into the **abyss**	bankruptcy	pool	deep hole
4.	to **verify** his story	confirm	dispute	doubt
5.	the thief's **accomplice**	victim	helper	tools
6.	a social **upheaval**	disturbance	improvement	standard
7.	to **adapt** to the heat	dislike	adjust	give in
8.	an honored **tradition**	accomplishment	medal	custom
9.	to **adhere** to policy	stick	ignore	approve
10.	the **titanic** rock	tiny	huge	hard
11.	to **administer** a business	manage	buy	build up
12.	to **thwart** justice	seek	aid	stop
13.	suffering from **afflictions**	hives	weather	misfortunes
14.	the **tempo** of music	rhythm	volumn	timelessness
15.	an **aggressive** move	smart	forceful	shy
16.	his **swarthy** skin	light	thick	dark
17.	to **amass** a fortune	waste	accumulate	desire
18.	to **surpass** her dreams	exceed	forget	fulfill
19.	an **analysis** of the play	financing	banning	examination
20.	to **suppress** a yawn	hold back	let out	hide

TIME _____

ERRORS _____

► *Exercise 3D—Word Comprehension*

Choose the word closest in meaning to the key word in **boldface** print.

Key Word

1. to **commend** her behavior	command	praise	study
2. a **complex** idea	complicated	simple	unpopular
3. an **ingenious** plan	clumsy	unworkable	clever
4. **elegantly** dressed	expensively	tastefully	sloppily
5. to **compute** the cost	estimate	ignore	calculate
6. remarkable **insight**	vision	understanding	glasses
7. his **dwindling** confidence	shrinking	growing	shattered
8. an **indispensable** item	useless	necessary	cheap
9. some **remedial** techniques	advanced	prescribed	helping
10. a life of **drudgery**	hard work	good deeds	nice smells
11. a **quest** for peace	payment	search	request
12. a **random** choice	careful	planned	unplanned
13. a room in **turmoil**	commotion	peace	change
14. **preface** to a book	cover	summary	introduction
15. a sense of **foreboding**	anger	warning	forbidden
16. the **ravaged** village	destroyed	rebuilt	thriving
17. a **disciple** of God	follower	law	prayer
18. a **flaw** in the gem	shine	defect	price
19. to **subdue** the enemy	fear	bribe	overcome
20. a **staunch** friend	strong	selfish	false

TIME _____

ERRORS _____

Directions for Phrase Comprehension

These drills allow you to practice reading in meaningful chunks. They consist of a key phrase on the left, followed by three phrases on the right. Look at the key phrase and think of its meaning. Next, quickly locate the phrase with similar meaning among the three on the right. Then cross it out, as in the following example:

Key Phrase

unusual story   strange ~~tale~~   weird book   bad lie

Continue until you finish all twenty items. Look up and your instructor will indicate your time in seconds. Check your work with the Answer Key at the back of the book. Finally, write your time and number of errors at the bottom of the exercise.

Reread your errors to see if you have a pattern of poor perception or poor comprehension. For instance, do you consistently omit one important word in a phrase? Do you substitute look-alike words? Do you pay attention to only the first or the last word in a phrase? Try to correct your bad habit in the next exercise.

Choose the phrase identical to the key phrase.

Key Phrase

1. going places	stationary life	traveling about	packed suitcase
2. large painting	big picture	cold lard	soft pillow
3. sour fruit	celery stick	ripe fig	bitter lemon
4. engraved name	grave man	carved letters	entire story
5. common mistake	ordinary error	misty weather	unusual blunder
6. torn pages	painful torment	soiled book	ripped paper
7. quick snooze	long sleep	awful nightmare	short doze
8. quiet place	silent spot	quick reply	evil person
9. thick book	short poems	fat volume	thin blood
10. earnest endeavor	earned wages	hard task	serious attempt
11. to tumble	to fall	to jump	to halt
12. reverse order	revealing picture	backward position	forward march
13. thorough review	careful reexamination	through rivers	three views
14. nice compliment	simple complaint	pleasant praise	sharp insult
15. extra money	additional income	exact examination	copper coins
16. to differ strongly	two different opinions	too strange	to disagree forcefully
17. having a frolic	a sad occasion	engaging in merriment	foaming water
18. solve a problem	find a solution	make a statement	inquire inside
19. total cost	more money	complete price	cheap clothes
20. very appropriate	out in the cold	doesn't fit situation	fits in most cases

TIME _____

ERRORS _____

These phrase-reading exercises add another building block to your reading skills. Perceptually, they give you more practice in widening your eye span. Intellectually, they require you to quickly understand an idea formed by several words. English is a phrasal language; reading by phrases is the last step before reading entire sentence units.

Search only for the phrase closest in meaning to the key phrase. Stop when you find it, and go on to the next item. As in the Phrase Perception exercises, focus only once per phrase, preferably on the dot above the phrase. Continue the sweeping eye movement and active search for meaning.

Notice that the phrases tend to get longer in later Lessons. Continue to perceive (see with understanding) each phrase at one glance, just as you perceived the single words and shorter phrases in earlier drills.

► *Exercise 3F—Phrase Comprehension*

Choose the phrase identical to the key phrase.

Key Phrase

1. entire story	devious lie	complete tale	inside story
2. unusual error	common mistake	strange manner	weird blunder
3. being troubled	very worried	horror movies	frightened look
4. obvious contrast	plainly opposite	constant pressure	clear similarity
5. according to plans	as arranged	cordless instrument	haphazard action
6. horrible dream	dreamless sleep	awakened early	bad nightmare
7. brief encounter	countless millions	short meeting	new breed
8. vacuumed rug	vast holdings	clean carpet	firm cushion
9. shorn head	shearing sheep	close haircut	headless rider
10. desolate field	dissolved pill	lonely area	late friend
11. funny comedian	silent movie	runny nose	comic actor
12. having courage	being brave	feeling cowardly	listening carefully
13. captured criminal	capsule summary	caught crook	law officer
14. seeming calm	easily excited	appearing serene	callow youth
15. sorrowful expression	sad look	mournful tale	full house
16. smelling trouble	smart trucker	sniffing brandy	expecting problems
17. feeling satisfied	being content	fried pies	uneasy peace
18. vast wasteland	wasted moment	endless emptiness	distant mirage
19. finished project	famished person	left undone	completed job
20. smooth sailing	easy to handle	romantic swoon	overturned boat

TIME _____

ERRORS _____

In Lesson 2, you learned that before you could find the main idea in a piece of writing, you first have to identify the topic (what the paragraph or article is about). The main idea is the author's opinion, judgment, or idea about the topic. It is the overall idea that the author wishes to prove or explain. The details are the proof or explanation that support this general concept. Generally, then, a paragraph has three elements: a topic, a main idea, and supporting details. You also learned in Lesson 2 not to confuse the topic with the main idea. *In this Lesson we will concentrate on telling the difference between the main idea and the details.*

General versus specific

Remember that the main idea is a generalization, whereas the supporting details are more specific. Consider this list of four items: raccoon, fox, animal, rabbit. Which item is the most general and thus covers or includes the others? The answer is "animal" because it sums up all three of the remaining items. The other items (raccoon, fox, rabbit) are specific kinds of animals.

Practice identifying the general and specific in the three lists that follow. Circle one word in each column that is the most general, or, in other words, covers or includes the others.

Mars	vehicle	carrots
Jupiter	bicycle	peas
planet	car	onions
Venus	truck	vegetables
Saturn	wagon	radish

Forming generalizations

Did you recognize the general words to be "planet," "vehicle," and "vegetables"? The next list presents specifics only. On the line write a general heading that would be appropriate for each column of details.

_____	_____	_____
carburetor	behind the stove	sneezing
steering wheel	on the counter	runny nose
radiator	in the cupboard	coughing
tires	near the fridge	low energy
dashboard	under the sink	tight lungs

You generalized accurately if you made headings like "parts of an automobile," "locations in a kitchen," and "symptoms of a cold or flu." Now it's just a small step to telling the difference between the general and the specific in a paragraph. Read the following paragraph, looking for the idea that is the most general. This main idea is like the top of an umbrella because it covers the details.

> The ancient Egyptians may have known what they were doing when they applied honey over a wound. A recent five-year study shows that sugar can be a great healer of burns, ulcers, and open wounds. The combination of sugar and sponges worked even better than antibiotics, claimed one of the scientists. In addition, sugar absorbs moisture and may help cut the swelling caused by fluids rushing to the damaged tissue. It may also nourish the new surface cells.*

---

*Adapted from Robert Wallach, *Total Health*.

Now see if you can fill in the umbrella sketch below. First, write the topic on the line at the top. Then put the main idea across the top of the umbrella. (Be sure to write a statement, in other words, a complete thought.) On the spokes of the umbrella, write the details that support the main idea. (*Hint*: The main idea statement is not always the first sentence.)

TOPIC: _____

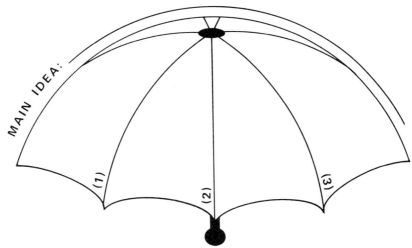

Now check your work. *Topic*: Sugar's effects. *Main idea*: Sugar can help heal burns, wounds, and ulcers. *Supporting details*: (1) is better than antibiotics; (2) absorbs moisture to cut down swelling; (3) may feed the new cells.

Implied main idea

Remember that, just as the main idea statement is not always at the beginning of the paragraph, sometimes it's not stated at all. In those cases, you must infer, or judge, from the details what the main idea is. What main idea do the details in the paragraph below suggest? To answer, first identify the topic. Then decide what all the details tell you about that topic. Fill in the topic and then the details on the following umbrella sketch before you state the main idea.

Aunt Stella never forgets to send a card on the birthdays of her friends. She remembers anniversaries and graduations better than anyone else in the community. If she says she'll lend you a book or send you an article she saw in the newspaper, she always comes through. And somehow she manages to keep straight not just the names of her fifteen nieces and nephews, seven brothers and sisters, and their thirty-five children, but she also remembers such things as who loves the color blue and who hates chartreuse and who loves roller-skating and who despises trips to the beach.

TOPIC: _____

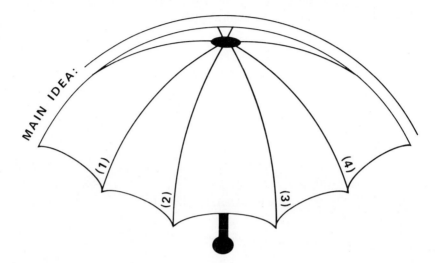

Let's check your comprehension again. All the sentences have something to do with Aunt Stella's memory, so that is the topic. What specifics do you learn about her memory? She remembers (1) birthdays of friends, (2) anniversaries and graduations, (3) promises, (4) names and interests of family members. Each of these details should be written on the spokes of the umbrella. Now what general statement can you make about Aunt Stella's memory, judging from the details you just listed? *Main idea*: Aunt Stella has a very good memory regarding her friends and family. If you wrote a main idea similar to this one, you have inferred (or drawn a conclusion) accurately.

Think once more of the paragraph as an expanding whole. The details are an expansion of the main idea, that is, in turn, an expansion of the topic.

Theme: Contemporary Living

"Progress is a comfortable disease," wrote the poet e. e. cummings. Nobody would argue that the new technology of this century has brought us much progress. The following paragraphs are about some changes in people as a result of our advances. But the longer readings may make you wonder if we're really better off than when our lives were simpler.

Practice Paragraphs

As you read the paragraphs below, first find the topic. Then look for the writer's main idea about that topic. Remember: (1) the main idea may be implied instead of stated in a topic sentence; and (2) the topic sentence is not always the first sentence in a paragraph.

A. (1) What's your girlfriend doing right now? (2) Or your sister? (3) Or your mother, for that matter? (4) Chances are good that she's got her nose deep in a type of book that tops the list of best-selling books week after week. (5) These women are reading the historical romance, a kind of novel that's really more romance than it is history. (6) It is full of danger and adventure. (7) Strong men and pretty women, with lots of nerve and verve, prance across every page. (8) And the things they put themselves through—all in the name of love. (9) Pirates! (10) Kidnapping! (11) Close calls! (12) The Wild West! (13) Lover's fights! (14) Passion! (15) Could it be that these books—so popular with women—tell us something important about what we've lost? (16) Are we tired of being such tame city dwellers? (17) Do we long for the brave deed and bold kisses of a more romantic time gone by?

1. What is the general topic of the paragraph? (Consider the topic like a title. Remember to capitalize the first letter of the first word and all important words in a title.) _____

2. In your own words, what is the main idea about this topic? (State your idea in a complete sentence.) _____

_____

3. Is the main idea stated in a topic sentence? _____

If so, what is the number of the sentence? _____

B. (1) "There are estimates that 20% to 25% of the blue-collar work force in the auto and steel industries is illiterate," says Anthony St. John, vice president of human resources for Chrysler. . . . (2) Five years ago, a national commission called America "a nation at risk." (3) Yet the economy has recovered from recession and created millions of jobs. (4) Could the case for education be overstated? (5) How much, after all, do assembly workers have to know? (6) The case is anything but overstated. (7) Workers today must know more all the time because modern industry piles responsibility on their shoulders. (8) Working with robots and computers isn't pushing buttons but knowing how to make the hourly chartings demanded by zero-rejects, quality-first production. (9) It takes high levels of literacy and numeracy.*

1. What is the general topic of the paragraph? (Consider the topic like a title.) _____

2. In your own words, what is the main idea about this topic? (State your idea in a complete sentence.) _____
   _____

3. Is the main idea stated in a topic sentence? _____

   If so, what is the number of the sentence? _____

C. (1) Amid current discussions of rising college costs, a recent U.S. Census Bureau survey reveals that the price of a sheepskin pays off, no matter what its price. (2) According to the Census report, a college graduate in 1984 earned $1,910 on average each month, while the average monthly income of a high school graduate was $1,045. (3) Among individuals with degrees beyond high school, those earning professional diplomas had the highest mean monthly income—$3,871. (4) Graduates with a bachelor's degree earned $1,841 on average each month.**

1. What is the general topic of the paragraph? (Consider the topic like a title.) _____

2. In your own words, what is the main idea about this topic? (State your idea in a complete sentence.) _____
   _____

3. Is the main idea stated in a topic sentence? _____

   If so, what is the number of the sentence? _____

---

*From "Helping Johnny Learn to Read is Top Priority," by Jim Flanigan. Copyright © 1988, *Los Angeles Times*. Reprinted by permission of Los Angeles Times Syndicate.
**From "A College Degree Pays," *On Campus*, December 1987/January 1988. Reprinted by permission of the American Federation of Teachers.

Words in Context

For each *italicized* word, choose the best meaning below.

► *Short Reading 3G*

1. During exams no one *monitored* you; instructors came in, handed out the blue books, handed out the exams, and left.

   (a) questioned **(b)** stared at **(c)** watched or checked on **(d)** bothered or interfered

2. Now we have become *cynical* about such things. The nation lies, fights unjustifiable wars; the nation robs the poor to give to the rich.

   (a) doubting the sincerity **(b)** angry and violent **(c)** depressed and sad **(d)** cheerful

3. At my college the students used to agree to inform on their friends rather than suffer a *breach* in the honor code. [Extra Clue: A breach of promise could lead to a lawsuit.]

   (a) a breaking of trust **(b)** strong support **(c)** new trousers **(d)** change shirt

4. Morality thereby becomes a matter of *expediency*. [Extra Clue: Skimming an assigned textbook chapter instead of studying it is a matter of *expediency*.]

   (a) convenient at the moment **(b)** being nonexistent **(c)** something to strive for **(d)** imitating your friends

► *Short Reading 3H*

5. It's done in ways you don't perceive because the manipulation is *subliminal*. [Extra Clue: The prefix *sub* means *under*.]

   (a) illegal **(b)** below the level of awareness **(c)** by instinct **(d)** expensive submarine

6. To prove his point about the *prevalence* of skulls in liquor ads, Key holds up an ad for a popular rum. [Extra Clue: Another form of *prevail*.]

   (a) black and white pictures **(b)** absence **(c)** frequent occurrence **(d)** infrequence

7. While it is commonly recognized and accepted that sex—sometimes *blatant* sex—sells products, it is not so established that death images sell them, too.

   (a) tasteful **(b)** obvious **(c)** perverted **(d)** attractive

► *Long Reading 3I*

8. All of these *traumatic* experiences fill me with nostalgia for a summer I spent in the Pocono Mountains when I was eight years old.

   (a) pleasant **(b)** realistic **(c)** emotionally painful **(d)** dangerous illness

9. Alas, we can't return to this *halcyon* past.

   (a) tranquil and happy **(b)** primitive and inconvenient **(c)** distant **(d)** unforgotten

10. That would be breaking the *inexorable* laws of the universe: fish gotta swim and birds gotta fly.

    (a) unbelievable **(b)** moral **(c)** unrelenting **(d)** cruel

This first Short Reading raises the question of honor in our modern world. Is this a concept that has become outdated?

Preview: *In 25 seconds or less, read the title and the first paragraph of the article; then write what the thesis of the article might be.*

_____

_____

Wait for a signal from your instructor before you start reading. (You will be rereading the introduction.) Circle your WPM after one minute. Read for the thesis of the article and the main idea of each paragraph.

from "A World Without Honor"

Anthony Brandt

WPM

	WPM
The sense of honor appears to be dying. Who fights duels to	12
defend his reputation anymore? The idea merely strikes us as odd.	23
How often does someone resign public office as a form of protest	35
against his government's policies about this or that? Most of us sub-	47
merge our consciences in the policies of our company or organiza-	58
tion (and in our own self-interest) and regard loyalty as more	68
important than dishonor.	71
We had an honor code where I went to college; that was in the	85
late 1950s. During exams no one monitored you; instructors came	95
in, handed out the blue books, handed out the exams, and left.	107
During the four years I was there, I can recall only one case of cheat-	122
ing. Students simply did not break the code.	129
In World War II men died more or less willingly for the nation	142
and the nation's honor, and they were honored for it in return. Now	155
we have become cynical about such things; the nation lies, fights	166
unjustifiable wars; the nation robs the poor to give to the rich.	178
At my college the students used to agree to inform on their	190
friends rather than suffer a breach in the honor code. A sense of	203
honor is a sense that there are standards of behavior one *must* live up	217
to, even at the cost of one's personal happiness, even at the cost of	231
one's life. Without such a sense one has to make up one's rights and	245
wrongs as one goes along—usually, as it happens, to one's own ad-	257
vantage. Morality thereby becomes a matter of expediency: nothing	266
seems worth dying for, and life loses its beauty and some of its value.	280
Our recent history has deprived us of models. I cherish the	291
story of John Stubbs, a Puritan divine of Queen Elizabeth's time who	303
strongly opposed her projected marriage to the Duke of Alencon.	313
Stubbs knew the penalty for doing so, which was the loss of a hand;	326
nevertheless, he published a pamphlet against the marriage. He was	336
accordingly tried, convicted, and led out for public execution of the	347
sentence. Stubbs laid his right hand on the block, the ax fell, and he	361
rose to his feet, lifted the bloody stump high in the air, and cried out	376
to the crowd, "Long live the queen!"	383

In spite of the blood and the horror, it is the beauty of such an act that stands out. A man lives up to his beliefs; he acts with courage and great style and literally gives of himself in the service of something he feels is greater than himself. We cannot help but honor him, whether we agree with his beliefs or not.*

398
413
426
428
446

Immediately answer the following questions without referring to the selection.

1. The article's thesis is that
  (a) More students cheat on exams now than in the past.
  (b) Each era has a different concept of honor.
  (c) There are still many individuals today who have a sense of honor.
  (d) Our society no longer highly values a sense of honor.

2. Earlier in this century, giving one's life for one's country was not considered an honorable thing to do. **T** **F**

3. In the author's college days, students valued the honor code more than loyalty to one another. **T** **F**

4. What did John Stubbs lose as a result of opposing the Queen's marriage?

_____

5. The author admires John Stubbs because **(a)** he agrees with Stubbs' beliefs. **(b)** Stubbs made a great sacrifice for his beliefs. **(c)** Stubbs died for his Queen. **(d)** Stubbs could suffer without crying.

Record your scores below and on the progress chart in the Appendix.

WORDS PER MINUTE _____

% COMPREHENSION _____

Bonus Question. Which sentence in the first paragraph expresses the thesis for the whole selection? _____

---

*From "A World Without Honor" by Anthony Brandt, *Esquire,* August, 1983. Reprinted by permission of the author.

LESSON 3   77

The next reading explores a questionable new method used in advertising to influence us.

Preview: *In 20 seconds or less, read the title and the first paragraph. Then write what you think the thesis will be:*

_____

_____

Wait for a signal from your instructor before you read the entire article. (Reread the first paragraph.) Circle your WPM after one minute. Look for the main idea of each paragraph as you read.

from "Reading Between the Subliminals"

Lorraine Bennett

WPM

He sees skulls in liquor ads, severed hands and the word *cancer*	12
in cigarette ads, and the letters S E X when a popular sink cleanser	24
floats the grease down the drain. Is Dr. Wilson Bryan Key crazy?	37
Some people think so. Is it an overactive imagination that makes	49
him find such things? Maybe. But Key, who is absolutely serious	61
about all this, can be very convincing. Key says that almost every time	74
you pick up a magazine, turn on the TV, or look at a billboard you	88
are being manipulated. It's done in ways you don't perceive because	98
the manipulation is subliminal.	101
To prove his point about the prevalence of skulls in liquor	112
ads, Key holds up an ad for a popular rum. In the foreground is a	127
glass filled with ice cubes and liquid, and among the stacked ice	139
cubes Key finds the outline of a toothy, grinning skull. The image is	152
unapparent to the uninitiated eye, but when Key outlines it, tracing	163
his pen along the ice cubes, the viewer can see nothing but a skull. Is it	179
real or imagined?	182
From a thick folder he pulls a two-page color ad selling ciga-	194
rettes and depicting two hockey players who are grappling on the	204
ice. The ad is filled with motion, but more is going on here than the	219
uninitiated eye will detect, says Key. Amid the scramble of arms and	231
legs is a third hand. It cannot possibly belong to either player or to a	246
referee partly hidden behind them. People rarely notice the hand	256
until it is pointed out, says Key. Beside the hand is an empty glove,	270
and on the glove is written the manufacturer of the hockey equip-	282
ment. People hardly notice that word, either, until he shows them.	292
Nonsmokers almost immediately perceive the word, which is dis-	300
torted in the ad, as "cancer," Key says. Smokers generally don't see it	313
that way at first, and about 20 percent of those who smoke never see	327
"cancer" at all.	330
It's not your imagination, Key says emphatically. The lines	339
were put there by people who knew what they were doing. They	351
attracted you because they appealed to your unconscious self. While	361
it is commonly recognized and accepted that sex—sometimes bla-	371

tant sex—sells products, it is not so established that death images **382**
sell them, too. But Key believes they do, especially when the products **394**
can be addictive. **397**

If subliminal suggestion is going on, couldn't it be harmless? **407**
Well, maybe, he concedes, but what he resents is the feeling you're **419**
being had when you don't know it. "I believe nothing can hurt you as **433**
long as you can decide whether to look or not look at it. But this **448**
material goes into your brain at the speed of light. We've put people **461**
under hypnosis, and we think some of it stays in your brain for life."* **475**

Immediately answer the following questions without referring to
the selection.

(1.) Write a sentence expressing the thesis of this article:

_____

_____

2. What does Key see in certain liquor ads? _____
3. Key thinks that ads containing images of death won't help sell the prod-
   uct. **T   F**
4. Regarding advertising, Key would agree with the old adage that what you
   don't know can't harm you. **T   F**
5. What Key resents about subliminal suggestion in advertising is
   (a) it makes people buy more than they need.
   (b) it reminds people of death.
   (c) it manipulates people without their knowledge.
   (d) it frightens people.

Record your scores below and on the progress chart in the Appendix.

WORDS PER MINUTE _____

% COMPREHENSION _____

Bonus Question. Which two sentences in the opening paragraph
present the thesis for this article? _____

---

*From "Reading Between the Subliminals" by Lorraine Bennett, *Los Angeles Times,* April 28, 1977.
Copyright © 1977 Los Angeles Times. Reprinted by permission.

This reading takes a humorous look at the joys of trying to get all our modern conveniences repaired and running right. Have modern conveniences really improved the quality of our lives?

Preview: *In 30 seconds or less, read the title and the first and last paragraphs. Guess at what you think the thesis might be:*

_____

_____

Wait for a signal from your instructor before you read the entire article. Look for the main idea of each paragraph as you read.

Can't Anybody Fix Anything Any More?

Jean Kerr

If I sounded all out of breath, it's because I had three repairmen here this afternoon. Actually, it wasn't the mess that bothered me, or the fact that there were *several* cables snaking through the kitchen—which, quite naturally, caused all the fuses to blow twice. That was really all right. I *have* extra fuses. The argument started about something else.

You've probably noticed that the first thing every repairman does, right after he spreads his tools all over the floor, is to ask if he can use your telephone. (Who is it, do you suppose, that he is so desperate to make contact with? His dispatcher? A loved one? Some support group? One doesn't ask, and, in any case, I've always obliged.) It became a problem today only because all three of them wanted to use the phone at the same time. When I suggested that they take turns, they became not only morose but downright testy. Look, life isn't easy for any of us. As it happened, each of them had to make several calls, so the phone was completely tied up for an hour and a half. Or so my husband discovered when he tried to call me from the airport.

Since I mentioned *three* repairmen, you will suppose I had the misfortune of having three appliances break down on a single day. Not at all. The electric oven broke down last Easter. The ice maker died quietly during the night of the Fourth of July, which only reinforces my suspicion that holidays are indeed a strain on us all. What is really puzzling is that the washer should have gone on the blink today. Why today? It wasn't a holiday; it wasn't even Monday. I'd say that it was just my good luck that the washer should break down on a day when I had to sit there anyway, waiting for other repairmen to come back: the one who has been trying to stabilize the new ice maker since July 18th, plus the man who is coming to replace the men who have failed to replace the switch on the electric oven.

Years of experience may have taught you that *no* repairman ever comes on the day he *says* he will come. Nevertheless, you do have to stay right there, glued to the spot, faithful as a sentry. Once I heedlessly went into the garden for three minutes to pick zinnias and totally missed the plumber who (I deduce from his answering service) subsequently left the country.

Anyway, during the weeks—now months—that I have been here keeping vigil, I've had plenty of time to think. (There really isn't much else to do after the dishes are done. It doesn't seem like wisdom to mop the linoleum *before* it gets messed up. And, ovenless, I can't whip up a batch of brownies.) So I think. I ask myself questions. What went wrong? How does it happen that I, who once had dreams, ambitions, hopes, spend all my time in an empty kitchen waiting for strangers?

So far as the electric oven is concerned, I see now that my mistake was in taking out a service contract. It was explained to me that, if I paid 180 dollars in advance, I would get free service all year. Well, the "service" may be questionable but the "all year" part is beginning to seem like prophecy. They *said* that they would send a man any time I needed one. What they did not make clear is that they would never, ever send the same man twice. I don't think they *have* the same man twice. I think they fire them every day—for good and sufficient reasons.

Perhaps I exaggerate the incompetence of these gentlemen. (They're called "technicians," though not by me.) Perhaps they're just unfortunate. Maybe (yes, this could be it) they each have only one bad day a year, and I get that day. The only thing they have had in common is that every one of them dismantled the entire stove, then slammed it back together while muttering, "Definitely gotta order a new switch," and left. In other ways they differ.

The first one put the dialing wheels that control the top burners on backward, so that when the burners (which did continue bravely to work) were turned to the "Off" position they were actually on "High." This was easy to figure out once the copper bottom of the kettle melted.

The next technician got the dialing wheels back on correctly, but, while replacing the large drawer just under the oven, he jammed the drawer off its tracks so that it could not be opened by an unskilled person like myself. Which meant, of course, that all of our frying pans were locked away, unavailable. You do understand that we *needed* frying pans because of our inability to roast anything. But that problem was easily solved. After we got tired of sending the kids out for Chinese food, we sent one out to buy a frying pan.

The fourth man, a spirited fellow who hummed "Swanee" while he worked, was able to free the drawer in a jiffy, or two jiffys. However, this liberator managed (somehow or other) to break off one of the legs of the stove. Though, as he pointed out, three legs are usually enough to keep an appliance stable.

As for the man who came to replace the leg, I really liked him. He had integrity. When I brought up the always touchy subject of the oven switch, he said, "Lady, I'm a maintenance man. Those damn things are a mystery to me." This honesty was not only refreshing; it did a lot to restore my faith in human nature. It did nothing, however, to restore the oven.

But we all know there are two sides to everything. So let me say that I have nothing but sympathy for the technicians who are supposed to be fixing the new ice maker. In one sense, since the ice maker never really worked, it cannot fairly be said to have broken down. And, as one ice-maker man pointed out, brushing cubes off his shoulder, "It *does* make ice." True enough. The problem is that it does not drop the ice cubes down into the box directly underneath. It shoots the ice sideways so that the cubes plop all over the ice cream and the packages of frozen food.

They even plop directly on top of the two spare ice-cube trays that we keep on a shelf in the freezer. This would seem almost a solution to the problem except, of course, that the cubes made by the ice-maker aren't really cubes at all, they're sort of oval and consequently they do not fit into the ice-cube trays. However, my immediate concern is with the cubes that fall on the linoleum. If I am not careful to search out and destroy every vagrant cube, *I* fall on the linoleum. It does help that we now have a large bath mat in front of the refrigerator.

All of these traumatic experiences fill me with nostalgia for a summer I spent in the Pocono Mountains when I was eight years old. My parents rented a charming cottage with a private deck directly on a pretty, pine-circled lake. There were huge, comfortable sofas covered in brightly flowered chintz, four-poster beds, a long swing on the front porch, and window seats everywhere to curl up in. There was, however, no electricity, no indoor plumbing. We had a pot-bellied stove, a pump, and an actual outhouse with cement seats. The pump was near the back door, and every morning my little sister and I filled up all the buckets with water and brought them into the kitchen, which we considered great fun. My baby brother made his contribution by filling his little sand pail with lumps of coal from the bin and pouring them into the coal scuttle. Dad replaced the kerosene in all the lamps at night.

What I remember most vividly, most fondly, and with some envy, is that my mother (pregnant at the time) spent all afternoon, every afternoon, sitting on the dock sunning herself and reading novels while she kept an eye on her chicks splashing in the lake. As I see it now, the reason that she had all this lovely, lazy time is that nothing *ever* broke down. She had no appliances to make her life easier.

Alas, we can't return to this halcyon past. Nor can we look to a future in which a machine (any machine) is going to be designed in such a way as to make it fail-safe. That would be breaking the inexorable laws of the universe: fish gotta swim and birds gotta fly and some rockets gotta fizzle on their launching pads. And, yes, sooner or later your refrigerator *will* break down. I have no trouble accepting that. Look, I break down myself every so often. That's the way it is.

All I ask, all I'm looking for, is for somebody else to sit here and wait for all these repairmen. That must be possible. Listen, we hire people to baby-sit and to walk dogs. I know a young woman who makes a good living going to people's houses and watering their plants. Why can't we pay people to meet repairmen? They might be called Meeter Men and Meeter Maids. The work is certainly easier than baby-sitting since an appliance, when broken down, does nothing at all. All that these Meeter Persons would be required to do would be to sit there, answer the doorbell, greet the repairman, and point to the afflicted appliance.

It occurs to me that unemployed actors would be excellent for the purpose. You might find a George C. Scott type who could terrorize a technician into doing his best work. Or you might want to play it the other way and find a young woman who had some of Liv Ullmann's melting charm and for whom even the thinnest-blooded man would strive to succeed.

Wait, I just had an inspiration. Last month I saw a college production of *The Caine Mutiny Court Martial*. And the young man who played Captain Queeg was chilling, really bloodcurdling. I believe that he is available at the moment. He'd be perfect, absolutely perfect.

As soon as the telephone is free, I'll call him.*

TOTAL READING TIME _____

Immediately answer the following questions without referring to the selection.

1. Choose the statement that best expresses the thesis.
  (a) Repairmen tend to use the telephone excessively.
  (b) Repair service is inefficient and inconvenient.
  (c) People who do repairs should be trained to be more competent.
  (d) Waiting for repairmen to show up gives the homeowner a chance to read.

2. The author suffered the misfortune of having three appliances break down on the same day.   T   F

3. "It was explained to me that, if I paid 180 dollars in advance, I would get free service all year. . . . the all year part is beginning to seem like prophecy." The word "prophecy" implies the repairs are being completed each visit.   T   F

4. The author considers the people who repair modern appliances to be true technicians.   T   F

5. For Jean Kerr, life would be harder without modern labor-saving devices.   T   F

6. The four repairmen who came to Jean Kerr's home to fix the stove had something in common.   T   F

7. The author implies that even extreme terror or extreme charm wouldn't get a repair person to do the job right.   T   F

8. She accepts the fact that modern conveniences will sometimes break down.   T   F

She proposes two solutions to the problem:

9. Hire Meeter Men and Meeter Maids who will _____

10. Hire an unemployed actor or actress to _____

Turn to the Rate Chart in the Appendix to get your words per minute for this selection. Then, record your scores below and on the progress chart in the Appendix.

WORDS PER MINUTE _____

% COMPREHENSION _____

Bonus Question. Which topic sentence in the last three paragraphs best states the author's thesis about waiting for repairmen to show up? ____

_____

_____

*From "Can't Anybody Fix Anything Any More?" by Jean Kerr, *McCall's,* November, 1983. Reprinted by permission of the author.

1. After reading the articles, which century would you choose to live in? Make a list of the reasons for your choice. Then use this list to compose a paragraph about your choice. (Use what you know about main idea to form a topic sentence. The supporting details in your paragraph will be the reasons drawn from your list and put in sentence form.) When you are finished, exchange paragraphs with the person sitting next to you. On what do you agree? Disagree?

2. Have you had a bad experience with a "labor-saving" machine or a modern "time-saving" plan? Tell about your experience in a paragraph or two. Make a topic sentence (main idea statement) for each paragraph. Then give enough details so that a reader can understand why your experience was so frustrating. (If you are keeping a journal, your instructor may wish you to write your experience there.)

LESSON

Retaining Details

IN THIS LESSON, YOU WILL

1. continue perception and comprehension exercises;

2. learn four ways to help you *remember details* in your reading:

   a. find the topic and the main idea;

   b. connect the details with the main idea;

   c. remember only the important details;

   d. recognize the eight patterns authors most often use to organize their ideas;

3. apply the skills you have learned to practice paragraphs and articles.

► Exercise 4A—Phrase Perception

Pick out the phrase identical to the key phrase.

Key Phrase

1.	with sticks	white strips	while sick	with sticks
2.	passing parks	parking cars	passing parks	tossing pills
3.	since morning	since morning	adorning fences	marvelous sense
4.	green shirt	green shirt	clean skirt	great shift
5.	below surface	scarred face	below surface	low surf
6.	less rapid	least rancid	last race	less rapid
7.	against walls	against walls	whole skin	huge gains
8.	through streams	though straight	through streams	small throat
9.	some money	some money	soft moans	bear market
10.	abstract idea	abstract idea	trace house	arbitrary solution
11.	grocery cart	grammar school	gross error	grocery cart
12.	startling features	staring faces	startling features	starting friction
13.	by the fence	buy the fedora	by the fence	bright felon
14.	burned house	brown mouse	high brow	burned house
15.	calm mother	motheaten collar	calm mother	cold monkey
16.	past the door	past the door	pass the flour	passed test
17.	extreme stealth	extremely wealthy	extra shirts	extreme stealth
18.	broken nose	broken nose	broker's loan	bronchial tube
19.	annual return	anemic regent	annual return	real angle
20.	over a hill	after the bill	over a hill	owe the bill

TIME _____

ERRORS _____

► *Exercise 4B—Phrase Perception*

Pick out the phrase identical to the key phrase.

Key Phrase

1. idealized girl	real whirl	whiter pearl	idealized girl
2. sailing the ship	nailing the strip	sailing the ship	sifting the pail
3. executive's daughter	excellent draught	executive's daughter	edible doughnut
4. across the street	the six acres	across the street	acting the role
5. favorable report	favorable report	flavorful roll	favorite review
6. magnetic attraction	mechanical accuracy	magnetic attraction	active magnet
7. lofty thought	tight logic	tawdry location	lofty thought
8. at the top	in a pot	at the top	after the hop
9. chipped polish	chipped polish	charity ball	picked chicken
10. stolen passage	seamy paragraph	stolen passage	second path
11. grocery cart	grocery cart	graduate school	groaning craft
12. jumped hurdle	bumped horse	honest judge	jumped hurdle
13. regarding him	retarding progress	reverting back	regarding him
14. collection plate	late recollection	collection plate	careful plot
15. running the race	ruining the rice	raising the roof	running the race
16. serious drama	serious drama	dramatic series	frantic search
17. silver pen set	salt shaker	pinned corsage	silver pen set
18. eclipsed moon	eclipsed moon	escaped man	ecstatic moan
19. to think of	to sink to	a thought of	to think of
20. science fiction	scant favor	secret friction	science fiction

TIME _____

ERRORS _____

► *Exercise 4C—Word Comprehension*

Choose the word closest in meaning to the key word in **boldface** print.

Key Word

1.	**oblivious** to danger	conscious	unaware	obvious
2.	a bloody **skirmish**	fight	operation	shot
3.	**tolerable** conditions	unbearable	welcome	acceptable
4.	to **segregate** races	unite	separate	integrate
5.	an **eccentric** hermit	odd	common	wealthy
6.	an **appalling** error	costly	minor	horrifying
7.	the **ultimate** threat	meanest	final	harmless
8.	arousing his **ire**	grief	anger	irritation
9.	to **compile** the data	scatter	add	gather
10.	to lie **dormant**	awake	sleeping	frequently
11.	a wide **panorama**	view	highway	window
12.	**silhouette** on the wall	painting	sunlight	outline
13.	upper **strata** of society	houses	levels	income
14.	**ensemble** actors	stage	trained	group
15.	an **inquisitive** reporter	arrogant	curious	passive
16.	to **designate** positions	elect	find	appoint
17.	to **flail** helplessly	beat	plead	cry
18.	to **evaluate** options	overlook	assess	create
19.	**deficient** in funds	plentiful	complete	lacking
20.	a deep **incision**	cut	hole	thought

TIME _____

ERRORS _____

► *Exercise 4D—Word Comprehension*

Choose the word closest in meaning to the key word in **boldface** print.

Key Word

1. two **diverse** options	similar	different	stubborn
2. to **annihilate** the enemy	destroy	fool	satisfy
3. a **furtive** move	quick	forthright	sneaky
4. to **allay** your fears	aggravate	relieve	ignore
5. to **enhance** the moment	improve	worsen	treasure
6. a **mediocre** job	terrible	ordinary	wonderful
7. at a **crucial** point	special	sharp	important
8. a **naive** young girl	innocent	dumb	sophisticated
9. a **genteel** family	coarse	large	well-bred
10. an **accessible** route	closed	available	sensible
11. stuck in the **mire**	mud	water	glue
12. a **chronic** cold	timely	constant	brief
13. the **diligent** worker	lazy	difficult	hard-working
14. the **immature** bride	undeveloped	old	frightened
15. the **despondent** widow	happy	depressed	silent
16. **bedlam** in the classroom	order	learning	confusion
17. a **demure** maiden	shy	immoral	bold
18. a **droll** story	mournful	amusing	dramatic
19. a need for **discretion**	belief	judgment	gossip
20. to **convalesce** after illness	shake	relapse	recuperate

TIME _____

ERRORS _____

These exercises have a key sentence that expresses a specific idea. Read this sentence carefully and think about its meaning. Ten sentences follow the key sentence. Read each one quickly and determine if the central thought is the same as (or similar to) the idea expressed in the key sentence. If it is basically the same, put a check in the right-hand column, as in the following example:

Key Sentence: It is not always wise to buy tires at "sale" prices.

1. Buying tires at special sales can be risky.   ✔
2. Tires "on sale" are not guaranteed to be good buys.   ✔
3. You should wait until a special sale before buying your tires.   _____
4. Some people get good tire buys at sales, and some people get stuck with lemons.   ✔

As soon as you finish all ten items, look up and your instructor will indicate your time in seconds.

Check your work against the answer key at the end of the book. Then write your time and number of errors at the bottom of the exercise.

► *Exercise 4E—Sentence Comprehension*

Key Sentence: If anything can go wrong, it will. ("Murphy's Law")

1. You might as well prepare for the worst.   _____
2. If there's a remote chance that something will go wrong, you can expect it to do so.   _____
3. Things will go better if you "think positive."   _____
4. God watches over saints and fools.   _____
5. It is realistic to expect things to go wrong.   _____
6. Unless something is absolutely fool-proof, trouble will occur.   _____
7. If you plan very carefully, you will avoid failure.   _____
8. With most things, there's a 50–50 chance that all will be well.   _____
9. Difficulties will occur, whether we expect them to or not.   _____
10. We have every reason to be optimistic about the future.   _____

TIME _____

ERRORS _____

The Sentence Comprehension exercises deal with even larger chunks of meaning than the other drills. Therefore, you must read the key sentence carefully and think about it *before* deciding whether the sentences that follow are alike or different.

Read every word of the key sentence. Look for the topic and the action words. Understand the whole sentence, not just a part of it.

Notice whether the statement is broad and loose ("usually," "sometimes") or limited ("always," "only"). Notice whether it is positive or negative.

Remember that the addition of one word can change the entire meaning. It is useful to *paraphrase* the key sentence—to put it mentally into your own words. Then you can recognize the same idea even when the sentence structure is different.

► *Exercise 4F—Sentence Comprehension*

Place a check after the sentences that express the same idea as the key sentence.

Key Sentence: Your story of the incident would be incredible if I had not witnessed it myself.

1. I cannot believe your story of what happened. _____
2. You are not telling the truth. _____
3. I would not believe you if I didn't know you well. _____
4. I would not believe you if I hadn't seen it myself. _____
5. You tend to have a low regard for the truth. _____
6. You and I really made up a good story. _____
7. In this case, seeing was believing. _____
8. I believe you because you have a good reputation. _____
9. If I had not been a witness myself, I would not have believed your story. _____
10. It's odd how the same incident can seem totally different to two different witnesses. _____

TIME _____

ERRORS _____

If you're starting this section expecting to learn "How to Remember Everything You Read, In Two Easy Steps, With Our Magic Memory Formula"—sorry! There is no such formula. However, you should keep in mind some helpful hints. Some are based on research by psychologists and other learning experts on how we forget and remember. Other hints are based on plain logic and common sense.

Finding the main idea

The most important hint is **understand and remember the main idea before you look for the details.** See the whole before you examine the parts. Otherwise, the parts are meaningless. When we locate a friend's apartment, we find the area and street, and then the building, before we look for the apartment number. To use another analogy (comparison), we need to see the forest before we examine each tree. In Lessons 2 and 3, you learned the importance of locating the **main idea** in any reading. If you understand the overall point, the minor points will not slip away from you.

Relating details to the main idea

The second hint is **fit the details to the main idea.** Details don't add up to anything by themselves, even if they are understood and remembered perfectly. The human brain wants things to "add up." For example, try to retain the following details as they stand:

"Group 4, walk 4 minutes, jog 6 minutes, walk 3 minutes, jog 6 minutes. Group 5, walk 4 minutes, jog 15 minutes. Group 6, walk 2 minutes, jog 17 minutes. Group 7, jog 19 minutes."

Look away from those sentences and try to "recite" the details. It's hard, unless you're a whiz at rote memory.

But suppose you had been reading a pamphlet about the physical fitness class at your local gym. One of the main ideas in the pamphlet is that the class is divided up on the basis of "fitness" into ten groups, from group 1 (beginners) to group 10 (the physically fit). The lower-numbered groups walk more and jog less; the higher-numbered groups walk less and jog more. Now read the details again. "Recite" again. The exact numbers (4, 6, and so on) are not important. But you should retain more of the details, more meaningfully, because you now have a main idea or framework to unify them. The little trees are now grouped into a forest. The supporting details are now under the main idea umbrella.

Remembering the most important details

A third hint is **notice and try to retain only those details that are necessary.** Don't overload the circuits unnecessarily. Many readers seem to retain easily minor facts and figures, or unimportant details, and nothing else. Why remember "$4000–$6000 a year" from a paragraph unless you also remember what it refers to? Why remember a photograph of a mouse terrifying a large cat unless you also remember the purpose of that experiment? Think in terms of remembering the approximate dates the Civil War began and ended rather than the exact date of a minor battle.

Recognizing the pattern of details

The fourth hint is **recognize the pattern of the details.** What shape can a framework of details or writings take? They may take as many shapes as there are thoughts. But we do tend to communicate ideas through the use of certain recognizable patterns. If you, the listener or reader, can identify the pattern, you can remember the details more easily. You can also anticipate what details you will read next.

A list of the most common patterns for organizing detailed material usually includes the following: **description, process, time sequence (chronology), example or illustration, classification, cause and effect, comparison and contrast,** and **addition.**

As you read the following patterns, be aware that you should also use them in your writing:

Description. Details that fit this pattern tell who, what, or how about the main idea. These details often describe the surface, or appearance, of someone or something. Note that descriptive details often appeal not only to the sense of sight, but also to the senses of smell, taste, sound, and touch:

> My brother is a handsome fellow. His crisp, curly, dark hair and clear green eyes give him the good looks of a movie star. Plus, he has the firm, trim body of an athlete. When he goes out on a date, he wears silk or velvet shirts and a spicy cologne. His dates admire him almost as much as he admires himself.

Process. Patterns may often overlap. Sometimes descriptive details tell the steps in a *process*. Often this pattern will use words like *first, second, then, next* to introduce each new step:

> Changing a tire is a matter of four simple steps. First, jack up the side of the car where you want to change the tire. Second, twist off the lug nuts in the middle of the wheel. Next. . . .

Time Sequence. Details are sometimes presented in the order in which they took place. This pattern is called *time sequence* and is used to tell a story or narrative:

> The early years of Lisa's life were marked by wealth. She was born in 1955 to a family with vast landholdings in Montana. When Lisa was just one year old, her grandmother died suddenly, willing her three city blocks in Manhattan. In 1958, still more riches graced her life when . . .

Example or Illustration. This pattern uses specific, representative cases to move from the general (often in the topic sentence) to the particular. In the following paragraph, look for the three examples that support or explain the main idea stated in the first sentence:

> Tom avoids doing his homework by "inventing" other work for himself. For example, he may suddenly decide his car just can't go without a washing another day. Or he might convince himself he has to sit down and pay all his bills before he cracks his history book. Or maybe all at once he feels he's getting too flabby and so hurries off to shoot some basketball. Meanwhile, he hasn't started on that ten-page term paper due tomorrow.

Classification. Paragraphs that separate details into categories or *classes* and then discuss each class fit this pattern. You might find classification when you read about a broad topic that needs to be manageable. The students at your college, for instance, might be grouped—or *classified*—according to their religions; that is, Catholic, Protestant, Jew, Moslem, Buddhist. Or they might be classified by marital status, personality type, or study habits. But just *one* basis of classification is used to determine the grouping, and there are usually at least three groups. A paragraph that classified students according to study habits might be organized like this:

> Most of the students at our college fall into one of the following categories when it comes to study habits: the grind, the balancing artist, and the "what, me worry?" The grind is at the books day and night, or so it seems. This student is the type who's likely to spend even spring break boning up in the library. The balancing artist, though, believes in the golden mean. This type of student may not get

top grades but does get some pleasure. The balancing artist will work hard when necessary but knows when to forget it and go fishing. And then there's the "what, me worry?" kid who seldom passes up a party and just as seldom passes a test. This student's average life span in college is about one semester.

Cause and Effect. This pattern starts with a cause (topic sentence) and gives its effects (supporting details). Or vice versa, it may give an effect or result (topic sentence) and then tell what caused it (supporting details). Which method does the following paragraph use?

> When I was a young girl, I longed to be a doctor. Partly this was because I wanted to be like my favorite aunt, who was a doctor. But this wish was also the result of all the many TV shows I watched about doctors and hospital drama. Partly too it was because I loved the image of myself as a heroine who could save people when all else had failed.

(Note that related patterns are "problem-solution" and "question-answer.")

Comparison and Contrast. The details point out what two or more subjects do or do not have in common. Comparison points out similarities; contrast points out differences. These paragraphs are often organized in one of two ways. The paragraph may present, in turn, each point of similarity or difference between subject A and subject B. Or it may discuss all aspects of subject A, then all aspects of subject B. These paragraphs will often have transition (or signal) words like *but, however, on the other hand*. Notice whether the following paragraph uses mostly comparison or contrast:

> Many high school graduates go straight on to college. Others go to work full-time, then decide later to start college. The graduate who goes off to a job always runs the risk of being unable to let go of that paycheck. It just may be too hard to live the lean life of a student again. However, once that person does return to college, she usually brings a maturity that's a big asset in the classroom. True, that student will be older than the others when she finally gets that college degree. On the other hand, this older student more often knows from experience what kind of job best suits her. This student is less likely to end up in a make-do job after college.

Addition. This pattern (sometimes called enumeration) is one of the simplest and most common. Supporting details are organized into a list of points: first one point, then another, then another. Addition can overlap other patterns. For example, you might have a list of causes, effects, similarities, or steps in a process. The points are usually made to prove or support the main idea:

> After weighing the pros and cons, Sharon decided to move from her isolated beach house to the city. She felt that the most important advantage was job opportunities. A second important advantage was that she would be closer to her friends. Of lesser importance, she would have easier access to the theatre, good restaurants, and better shops.

Again, the patterns often combine or overlap. You can discover this for yourself if you try to think in any organized way about even a one-word topic such as "dogs." You will recognize this problem in looking for patterns in the reading exercises that follow this discussion.

Look for these common patterns in your other verbal activities—listening, talking, writing. You'll see them too in advertising, political speeches, course lectures, conversation with friends, even in your own thinking. They are simply logic patterns used by logical thinkers.

Finally, to retain important details, you should:

1. Find the topic and the main idea.

2. Associate details with the main idea.

3. Remember only the important details.

4. Recognize the pattern by which the main idea is developed.

Theme: Creatures, Strange and Common

The paragraphs and longer readings in this Lesson are about creatures, both common and uncommon—or almost human. As you read these selections, you will see that these creatures have much in common with us humans.

Practice Paragraphs

As you read these paragraphs, remember to look for the topic and main idea first, just as you did in Lessons 2 and 3. Then notice how the supporting details are organized.

A. (1) That cockroach you just stepped on with disgust is not just any old bug. (2) It is above all else a Survivor. (3) It has survived almost unchanged for millions of years and may just outlive the human race. (4) How does the cockroach manage? (5) For one thing, it adapts easily to changing conditions. (6) For another, it eats almost anything. (7) Also, it has few natural enemies; birds and mammals soon find out that eating a cockroach makes them sick. (8) In fact, eating a cockroach would probably make *me* sick.*

1. In your own words, what is the main idea of the paragraph? (Write a complete sentence.) _____

_____

2. Is the main idea stated in a topic sentence? _____

If so, what is the number of the topic sentence? _____

3. The supporting details are organized in what type of pattern(s)? Check one or more:

cause and effect _____   classification _____

time sequence _____   contrast _____

4. List four reasons why the cockroach has survived:

_____   _____

_____   _____

B. (1) On my fifth birthday, I was given a dog. (2) It was the most shattering thing that ever happened to me; so shattering, such unbelievable joy, that I was unable to say a word. (3) When I read that well-known cliché "so and so was struck dumb," I realize that it can be a simple statement of fact. (4) *I* was struck dumb—I couldn't even say thank you. (5) I could hardly look at my beautiful dog. (6) Instead I turned away from him. (7) I needed, urgently, to be alone and come to terms with this incredible happiness. (I have done the same thing frequently during my later life. Why is

*by Anne Dye Phillips

one so idiotic?) (8) I think it was the lavatory to which I retired—a perfect place for quiet meditation, where no one could possibly pursue you. (9) Lavatories were comfortable, almost residential apartments in those days. (10) I closed the heavy mahogony shelf-like seat, sat on it, gazed unseeingly at the map that hung on the wall, and gave myself up to realization. (11) "I have a dog . . . a dog . . . (12) It's a dog of my own . . . my very own dog. . . . (13) It's a Yorkshire terrier . . . my dog . . . my very own dog. . . ."*

1. In your own words, what is the main idea of this paragraph? (Write a

   complete sentence.) _____

   _____

2. Is the main idea stated in a topic sentence? _____

   If so, what is the number of the topic sentence? _____

3. The supporting details are organized in what type of pattern(s)? Choose one or more:

   contrast   _____   addition   _____

   description   _____   time sequence   _____

4. Describe three things the author did that were unusual reactions to

   receiving a nice gift. _____

   _____

   _____

C. (1). . . Mickey Mouse turned a respectable fifty last year. (2) To mark the occasion, many theaters replayed his debut performance in *Steamboat Willie* (1928). (3) The original Mickey was a rambunctious, even slightly sadistic fellow. (4) In a remarkable sequence, exploiting the exciting new development of sound, Mickey and Minnie pummel, squeeze, and twist the animals on board to produce a rousing chorus of "Turkey in the Straw." (5) They honk a duck with a tight embrace, crank a goat's tail, tweak a pig's nipples, bang a cow's teeth as a stand-in xylophone, and play bagpipe on her udder. (6) Christopher Finch, in his semi-official pictorial history of Disney's work, comments: "The Mickey Mouse who hit the movie houses in the late twenties was not quite the well-behaved character most of us are familiar with today. (7) He was mischievous, to say the least, and even displayed a streak of cruelty."**

---

1. In your own words, what is the main idea of the paragraph? (Write a complete sentence.) _____

_____

2. Is the main idea stated in a topic sentence? _____

If so, what is the number of the topic sentence? _____

3. The supporting details are organized in what type of pattern(s)? Check one or more.

addition _____   contrast _____

example _____   time sequence _____

4. List six details that support the picture of an earlier, more mischievous Mickey Mouse.

_____   _____

_____   _____

_____   _____

Words in Context

For each *italicized* word, choose the best meaning below.

► Short Reading 4G

1. I gradually became *callous* to all animals, including my pets.

   (a) unfeeling **(b)** loving **(c)** unkind **(d)** murderous

2. They became *indistinguishible* from the other pigs.

   (a) less well known than **(b)** not showing a difference **(c)** more famous than **(d)** better liked

► Short Reading 4H

3. A white unicorn with a gold horn was quietly *cropping* the roses in the garden. [Extra Clue: This would not help the roses' growth.]

   (a) smelling **(b)** planting **(c)** cutting off **(d)** trampling

4. The unicorn is a *mythical* beast.

   (a) has two tongues **(b)** appears in tales and legends **(c)** enjoys music **(d)** likes to play pranks

5. She was very excited and there was a *gloat* in her eye. [Extra Clue: Usually a verb.]

   (a) disease **(b)** speck of dust **(c)** look of great satisfaction **(d)** sadness

► *Long Reading 4I*

6. Several of this cursed brood leaped into the tree I stood under and began to discharge their *excrements* on my head. [Extra Clue: One would prefer to duck.]

   (a) baskets of fruit **(b)** weapons **(c)** angry words **(d)** bodily wastes

7. I never beheld in all my travels so disagreeable an animal, or one against which I naturally had so strong an *antipathy*. [Extra Clue: *Anti* means *against; path* means *feeling*.]

   (a) hatred **(b)** curiosity **(c)** affection **(d)** irritation

8. They gently struck each other's right hoof before neighing several times by turns, and varying the sound, which seemed to be almost *articulate*. [Extra Clue: Usually used as a compliment.]

   (a) able to be heard **(b)** artistic **(c)** having the power of speech **(d)** too talkative

9. I concluded that, if the inhabitants of this country possessed a *proportionate* degree of reason, they must be the wisest people upon earth.

   (a) balanced relationship **(b)** sufficient **(c)** tremendous **(d)** small portion

10. I was soon to learn the meaning of that word to my everlasting *mortification*.

   (a) grief **(b)** amusement **(c)** embarrassment **(d)** anger

Preview: *Think about any facts you may already know about pigs, and imagine having one as a pet. Then in 30 seconds or less, preview the title and first and last paragraphs of this reading. Write below what you think the thesis might be and any two supporting details you noticed:*

Thesis: _____

Details: (1) _____

(2) _____

Wait for a signal from your instructor before you begin to read the whole article. (You should reread the first and last paragraphs.) Circle your WPM after one minute. Find the topic and main idea. Then notice how the details explain or support the main idea.

Pet Pigs

Wanda Maureen Miller

WPM

For the first eighteen years of my life I lived among animals, in and 14
out-of-doors, on a small farm in Arkansas. Some of these animals I 26
played with, slept with, fed, and cared for. Others I killed and ate. 39
They were always a part of my life, underfoot like a carpet of feath- 53
ered or hairy flesh. I stumbled over them or kicked them aside every 65
day in the yard. I fed them my leftover food and stepped in their 79
excrement with my bare feet. My nose became accustomed to their 90
smell, and my ears learned to close out their squawks, squeals, and 102
bleats when they were killed. We ate their meat at least twice a day, 116
sometimes three. As a result, I gradually became callous to all ani- 128
mals, including my pets. 131

When my brother, sister, and I were younger, my daddy often gave 143
us a pet pig to play with. He could sometimes be gentle and protective 157
with small helpless things. These pigs were the runts that were re- 168
jected by their mothers, who wouldn't let them suck. The sow instinc- 180
tively knew the runts wouldn't survive and let them die. We kept 191
each little pink pig in the house, fed it with a bottle, and fought over 206
who could play with it. I have a picture of the whole family posed in 221
our Sunday clothes standing in front of the red Studebaker truck. We 233
are all smiling. At our feet is one of our pet pigs sucking a bottle set 249
on a small block of wood. Mama complained about the mess these 261
pets made, but nobody paid any attention to her. 270

When the pigs got too big to be cute and made too much noise 284
clumping through the house, we kept them in the yard for a while, 297
and they slept under the house where it was cool in the summer and 311
warmer in the winter. 315

One day an uncle and aunt from town visited us. Their little boy, 328
only about three, stuck his head under the edge of the house, expect- 341
ing to see a cat or a dog. One of these half-grown pigs thrust his head 356
out with a loud "Unnngh!" Our little cousin screamed in terror. We 368
all laughed that he would be frightened by a pig. 378

When the pet pigs got so big that the house shook as they tried to   393
reach their cool spot underneath, they were returned to the pigpen   404
and forced to take their chances at the trough. They had to "root, hog,   418
or die." They became indistinguishable from the other pigs. In the   429
winter, they were all butchered and eaten.   436

When my brother, sister, and I lost our interest in pets, the runt   449
pigs were left to their fate. I know I must have loved some of these   464
pigs, but I can't remember any of their names. I try to eat less pork   479
now because of its fat content, but it is still my favorite meat.   492

Immediately answer the following questions without looking back
at the article.

1. The thesis of this article is that the author becomes callous about pets
because
   (a) she is spoiled by having so many pets given to her.
   (b) she is surrounded every day by animals that are routinely killed.
   (c) her cousin has an unpleasant experience with her pet pig.
   (d) she was given the wrong kind of pet—pigs instead of cats or dogs.

2. The children were given the runt pigs as pets, mostly so these pigs could
survive.   T   F

3. When the pigs got too big to pet, they were not immediately returned to
the pigpen.   T   F

4. What was the ultimate fate of the pet pigs?

_____

5. The author eats less pork because of
   (a) her memories of the pet pigs.
   (b) its fat content.
   (c) it no longer being her favorite food.
   (d) it no longer being easily available.

Record your scores below and on the progress chart in the Appendix.

WORDS PER MINUTE _____

% COMPREHENSION _____

Bonus Question: Check the pattern that best indicates how the details
are organized around the main idea:

addition   _____   time sequence   _____

cause and effect   _____   classification   _____

The next reading is a classic fable about an uncommon animal in a common place. It is written by James Thurber, a famous American humorist, so don't take him literally. See if you can form an opinion about his attitude, or "tone."

Preview: *In 15 seconds or less, read the title and the first sentence of each paragraph. Then write what you think is the main event in the story:* _____

_____

Wait for a signal from your instructor before you start to read. (Reread the sentences you previewed.) Circle your WPM after one minute. As you read the article, look first for the thesis. Then notice how the details are organized.

The Unicorn in the Garden

James Thurber

WPM

Once upon a sunny morning a man who sat in a breakfast | 12
nook looked up from his scrambled eggs to see a white unicorn with | 25
a gold horn quietly cropping the roses in the garden. The man went | 38
up to the bedroom where his wife was still asleep and woke her. | 51
"There's a unicorn in the garden," he said. "Eating roses." She | 62
opened one unfriendly eye and looked at him. "The unicorn is a | 74
mythical beast," she said, and turned her back on him. The man | 86
walked slowly downstairs and out into the garden. The unicorn was | 97
still there; he was now browsing among the tulips. "Here, unicorn," | 108
said the man, and he pulled up a lily and gave it to him. The unicorn | 124
ate it gravely. With a high heart, because there was a unicorn in his | 138
garden, the man went upstairs and roused his wife again. "The uni- | 150
corn," he said, "ate a lily." His wife sat up in bed and looked at him | 165
coldly. "You are a booby," she said, "and I am going to have you put in | 181
the booby-hatch." The man, who had never liked the words "booby" | 192
and "booby-hatch," and who liked them even less on a shining morn- | 204
ing when there was a unicorn in the garden, thought for a moment. | 216
"We'll see about that," he said. He walked over to the door. "He has a | 231
golden horn in the middle of his forehead," he told her. Then he | 244
went back to the garden to watch the unicorn; but the unicorn had | 257
gone away. The man sat down among the roses and went to sleep. | 270

As soon as the husband had gone out of the house, the wife | 283
got up and dressed as fast as she could. She was very excited and | 297
there was a gloat in her eye. She telephoned the police and she tele- | 311
phoned a psychiatrist; she told them to hurry to her house and bring | 323
a strait-jacket. When the police and the psychiatrist arrived, they sat | 334
down in chairs and looked at her, with great interest. "My husband," | 346
she said, "saw a unicorn this morning." The police looked at the | 358
psychiatrist and the psychiatrist looked at the police. "He told me it | 370
ate a lily," she said. The psychiatrist looked at the police and the | 383
police looked at the psychiatrist. "He told me it had a golden horn in | 397
the middle of its forehead," she said. At a solemn signal from the | 410
psychiatrist, the police leaped from their chairs and seized the wife. | 421

They had a hard time subduing her, for she put up a terrific struggle, **435**
but they finally subdued her. Just as they got her into the strait-jacket, **448**
the husband came back into the house. **455**

    "Did you tell your wife you saw a unicorn?" asked the police. **467**
"Of course not," said the husband. "The unicorn is a mythical beast." **479**
"That's all I wanted to know," said the psychiatrist. "Take her away. **491**
I'm sorry, sir, but your wife is as crazy as a jay bird." So they took her **508**
away, cursing and screaming, and shut her up in an institution. The **520**
husband lived happily ever after. **525**

    Moral: Don't count your boobies until they are hatched. * **534**

    Immediately answer the following questions without referring to
the selection.

1. State the thesis of the selection in a complete sentence.

_____

_____

2. What did the unicorn have on its head? _____

3. The husband tried to stop the police from taking his wife to the booby-
hatch.   **T**   **F**

4. Revenge is sweet.   **T**   **F**

5. The author's attitude (or *tone*) is least sarcastic towards which of the
following characters? **(a)** wife **(b)** police **(c)** psychiatrist **(d)** husband

    Record your scores below and on the progress chart in the Appendix.

WORDS PER MINUTE _____

% COMPREHENSION _____

Bonus Question. Check the pattern(s) that best describe the way in
which the details are organized around the main idea:

description	_____	time sequence	_____
cause and effect	_____	comparison and contrast	_____

The last reading is an excerpt from Gulliver's Travels *by Jonathan Swift. This writer of satire from the eighteenth century presents animals as a reflection of mankind. Notice, as you read, which animals seem more human—physically or mentally.*

Preview: *In one minute or less, read the title and the first and last paragraphs of the selection. Then write what you think the thesis of the article might be:* _____

_____

Wait for a signal from your instructor before you begin. (Read the entire article.) As you read, see if your guess at the thesis is correct. Look for details that help prove your guess.

The Yahoos and the Houyhnhnms

Jonathan Swift

I was set ashore in a strange country and walked about to discover its inhabitants. I resolved to deliver myself to the first savages I should meet. I would purchase my life from them by some bracelets, glass rings, and other toys, which I had about me.

The land was divided by long rows of trees, not regularly planted, but naturally growing. There was plenty of grass and several fields of oats. I walked very carefully for fear of being surprised, or suddenly shot with an arrow from behind or on either side. I fell into a beaten road. There I saw many tracks of human feet, and some of cows, but most of horses.

At last I saw several animals in a field, and one or two of the same kind sitting in trees. Their shape was unusual and deformed, which a little upset me. So I lay down behind a thicket to observe them better.

Some of them, coming forward near the place where I lay, gave me an opportunity of examining them more carefully. Their heads and breasts were covered with a thick hair, some frizzled and others lank. They had beards like goats, and a long ridge of hair down their backs and the fore-parts of their legs and feet. The rest of their bodies were bare, so that I might see their brown buff-colored skins. They had no tails, nor any hair at all on their buttocks, except about the anus. This hair, I presume, helped them as they sat on the ground. This posture they used, as well as lying down, and often stood on their hind feet. They climbed high trees as nimbly as a squirrel, for they had strong extended claws before and behind, ending in sharp, hooked points. Several of this cursed brood leaped into the tree I stood under and began to discharge their excrements on my head. I escaped but was almost stifled with the filth, which fell about me on every side.

Upon the whole, I never beheld in all my travels so disagreeable an animal, or one against which I naturally had so strong an antipathy.

In the midst of this distress, I observed them all to run away all of a sudden as fast as they could. I ventured to leave the tree and go to the road, wondering what it was that could put them into this fright.

Looking to my left, I saw a horse walking softly in the field. This was the cause of my persecutors' flight. The horse started a little when he came near me, but soon recovering himself, looked full in my face with obvious wonder. He looked at my hands and feet, walking round me several times. I would have walked away, but he placed himself directly in the way. Yet he looked at me mildly, never offering the least violence.

We stood gazing at each other for some time. At last I took the boldness to reach my hand towards his neck, with the intention of stroking it. I used the common style and whistle of jockeys when they are going to handle a strange horse. But this animal seemed to receive my friendliness with contempt. He shook his head and bent his brows, softly raising up his right forefoot to remove my hand. Then he neighed three or four times, but so strangely that I almost began to think he was speaking to himself in some language of his own.

Then another horse came up, who applied himself to the first in a very formal manner. They gently struck each other's right hoof before neighing several times by turns, and varying the sound, which seemed to be almost articulate. They went some paces off, as if it were to confer together, walking side by side, backward and forward, like persons deliberating upon some important affair. But they often turned their eyes towards me, as if to watch that I might not escape. I was amazed to see such actions and behavior in brute beasts. I concluded that, if the inhabitants of this country possessed a proportionate degree of reason, they must be the wisest people upon earth.

The two horses neighed frequently towards each other, as if they were engaged in serious conversation. I could frequently distinguish the word *Yahoo,* which was repeated by each of them several times. I do not know what the word meant, yet while the two horses were busy in conversation, I tried to practice this word upon my tongue. And as soon as they were silent, I boldly pronounced *Yahoo* in a bold voice. I imitated, at the same time, as near as I could, the neighing of a horse. They were both visibly surprised at this. The gray horse repeated the same word twice, as if he meant to teach me the right accent. I spoke after him as well as I could, and found myself to improve every time.

Then the bay horse tried me with a second word, much harder to be pronounced. But I reduced it to English letters and spelled it *Houyhnhnm.* I did not succeed in this so well as the first word. But after two or three farther trials, I had better fortune, and they both appeared amazed at my ability.

The gray horse then took me to a long kind of building, made of timber stuck in the ground. I now began to be a little comforted. I took out some toys, which travellers usually carry for presents to the savage Indians of America and other parts, in hopes the people of the house would be thereby encouraged to receive me kindly.

As I waited, the horse neighed three or four times, and I waited to hear some answers in a human voice. But I heard no other response than the same dialect of horses, only one or two a little shriller than his. I began to think that this house must belong to some person of great note among them, because there appeared so much ceremony before I could gain admittance.

Finally, the gray horse led me into a room where I saw a very comely mare. She sat with a colt and foal, sitting on their haunches upon mats of straw, not unartfully made, and perfectly neat and clean. The mare rose from her mat, and coming up close, observed my hands and face. She then gave me a most contemptuous look. As she turned to the gray horse, I heard the word *Yahoo* often repeated between then. I was soon to learn the meaning of that word to my everlasting mortification.

The mare led me out into a kind of court, where there was another building at some distance from the house. Here I saw three of those detestable creatures whom I first met after my landing. They were all tied by the neck and fastened to a beam. The horse ordered the largest of these animals to be untied. The beast and I were brought close together and compared. The horse thereupon repeated several times the word *Yahoo*.

My horror and astonishment are not to be described, when I observed in this abominable animal a perfect human figure. The face of it indeed was flat and broad, the nose depressed; the lips large, and the mouth wide. The fore-feet of the Yahoo differed from my hands in nothing else but the length of the nails, the coarseness and brownness of the palms, and the hairiness on the backs. There was the same resemblance between our feet, which I knew very well, though the horse did not, because of my shoes and stockings.

TOTAL READING TIME _____

Immediately answer the following questions without referring to the selection.

1. Choose the statement that best expresses the thesis.
   (a) The traveler hated the horses and loved the manlike beasts.
   (b) He soon tamed both groups of animals.
   (c) He hated the manlike beasts and respected the horses.
   (d) He remained frightened of both groups of animals.
2. The first animals were afraid of the horses.   T   F
3. The first animals clawed viciously at the man.   T   F
4. The man was surprised to see
   (a) the horses behaving like people. **(b)** such friendly horses.
   (c) such fierce horses. **(d)** horses speaking good English.
5. The two horses seemed to be able to talk to each other.   T   F
6. The horse liked to have his neck stroked by the man.   T   F
7. The horses were called *Houyhnhnms* and the manlike beasts were called *Yahoos*.   T   F
8. The horses were surprised that the man could imitate them.   T   F
9. Why did the man become so mortified when the horses referred to him

   as a "Yahoo"? _____

   _____

10. Who seemed most intelligent and respected?
    (a) the man **(b)** the Houyhnhnms **(c)** the Yahoos

Turn to the Rate Chart in the Appendix to get your words per minute. Then record your scores below and on the progress chart in the Appendix.

WORDS PER MINUTE _____

% COMPREHENSION _____

Bonus Question. Describe in detail the manlike beast.

_____

_____

_____

_____

WRITING AND DISCUSSION ACTIVITIES

1. Which animal, wild or tame, seems to you most human? State your choice in a topic sentence. Then write a paragraph giving the details about what this animal and human beings have in common. (You are writing a paragraph organized by comparison.)

2. Choose a pet you or someone in your family has owned. Draw a line down the middle of a page. On the left side of the line, list the advantages of having the pet. On the right, list the disadvantages. When you have finished, you will have done the first rough step to outlining (to be introduced in Lesson 6).

5

Recognizing Transitions

IN THIS LESSON, YOU WILL

1. continue perception and comprehension exercises;
2. learn some common *transitions,* clues to how writers organize their ideas;
3. learn to tell levels of detail;
4. apply the skills you have learned to practice paragraphs and articles.

► *Exercise 5A—Phrase Perception*

Pick out the phrase identical to the key phrase.

Key Phrase

1. broken doll	bristling dog	broken doll	broken branch
2. off the horse	for the house	on the hat	off the horse
3. puzzled student	parched peanut	puzzled student	partial payment
4. seeming concerned	seeming concerned	teeming crowd	left behind
5. capital letter	become better	cold winter	capital letter
6. having fallen	having fallen	having stolen	has fallen
7. cotton stockings	rotten boards	cotton stockings	rocking cradle
8. heated argument	hanging meat	heated argument	hated person
9. rich mechanic	rich mechanic	reached goal	repaired machine
10. into the rift	on the raft	into the rift	in a rage
11. shifting gears	lifting weights	mowing grass	shifting gears
12. foggy night	future right	faint light	foggy night
13. polished silver	polite signal	polished silver	relished supper
14. accurate solution	accurate solution	ancient salute	solvent arsenal
15. a short fable	a small stable	a smart farmer	a short fable
16. hostile driver	hostile driver	hungry diner	horrible drivel
17. drawn dagger	cowed beggar	ragged dress	drawn dagger
18. crafty plaintiff	crafty plaintiff	plain craft	carefully placed
19. too expensive	too expansive	too expensive	total expense
20. crooked picture	cracked pistol	clean practice	crooked picture

TIME _____

ERRORS _____

► *Exercise 5B—Phrase Perception*

Pick out the phrase identical to the key phrase.

Key Phrase

1. either tray — leather strap — neither prays — either tray
2. off balance — off balance — one balloon — balky child
3. typed page — paid time — typed page — tender age
4. having grown — having flown — having grown — growing old
5. every night — every night — very light — even bright
6. good lunch — bad brunch — great crunch — good lunch
7. dark secret — secrete oil — dark secret — drab secretary
8. stiff ruffle — straight ruff — slick ruffian — stiff ruffle
9. feeling hope — feeling hope — jumping rope — feeling smooth
10. look under — loud thunder — look under — wonder book
11. human voice — vocal man — humane boy — human voice
12. bound feet — bound feet — round foot — loud fool
13. vast land — vast land — sand vat — big load
14. many fees — any fees — many fees — see many
15. calm rest — calm rest — best calf — red vest
16. mailed letter — better male — mailed letter — little mall
17. catching balls — catching balls — latching doors — patching pants
18. ever after — every rafter — after events — ever after
19. of a sale — of a tale — of a sale — off a rail
20. near nine — nearly mine — near nine — rear line

TIME _____

ERRORS _____

► *Exercise 5C—Word Comprehension*

Choose the word closest in meaning to the key word in **boldface** print.

Key Word

1.	to **curtail** activities	increase	hide	stop
2.	a **secluded** island	busy	isolated	distant
3.	a serious **malady**	illness	song	female
4.	**adept** at writing	skilled	awkward	inexperienced
5.	**frugal** with money	lavish	arrogant	economical
6.	to **elongate** her neck	shorten	lengthen	cut off
7.	to **sear** his skin	burn	smooth	pat
8.	feeling **listless**	enthusiastic	sad	inactive
9.	**ravenous** for food	hungry	indifferent	searching
10.	to **invoke** help	send	ask	refuse
11.	to **bolster** his ego	tear down	support	save
12.	to feel **slothful**	energetic	sorry	lazy
13.	a **futile** gesture	useless	significant	necessary
14.	to give **esteem**	respect	dishonor	estimates
15.	**saturated** with rain	sprinkled	sick	soaked
16.	a **lateral** movement	final	sideways	upwards
17.	a **rift** in the marriage	break	turn	bridge
18.	**boisterous** behavior	timid	noisy	dynamic
19.	to **feign** illness	cure	fear	pretend
20.	a **cryptic** message	secret	affectionate	clear

TIME _____

ERRORS _____

► *Exercise 5D—Word Comprehension*

Choose the word closest in meaning to the key word.

Key Word

1. a **plausible** lie	incredible	harmful	believable
2. to **eradicate** the evidence	destroy	uncover	evade
3. to **pulverize** the enemy	fight	crush	frighten
4. a **chagrined** look	smiling	poised	embarrassed
5. to **disintegrate** with age	decay	improve	mature
6. signed "**anonymous**"	lover	unknown	affectionately
7. to reach the **apex**	bottom	side	peak
8. during **turbulent** times	calm	agitated	terrible
9. claiming to be **indisposed**	ill	wealthy	healthy
10. speaking with **intensity**	weakness	friendship	force
11. a **mutation** in the plant	insect	alteration	wilting
12. to **cull** the best apples	reject	admire	select
13. to kiss with **ardor**	passion	affection	passivity
14. a **putrid** odor	sweet	rotten	faint
15. to **revoke** his license	cancel	issue	examine
16. a **grotesque** figure	well-shaped	clumsy	distorted
17. to worship a **deity**	human	god	statue
18. to please the **clientele**	patients	relatives	customers
19. an **eloquent** speech	well-expressed	tongue-tied	long
20. an essential **component**	group	part	division

TIME _____

ERRORS _____

Pick out the phrase that means the same as the key phrase.

Key Phrase

	Key Phrase			
1.	increase speed	go faster	go slower	keep even
2.	see the whole	perceive a unit	break it up	think carefully
3.	in the beginning	as a conclusion	at the start	with certainty
4.	absent a week	gone for good	gone seven days	sick at home
5.	can't be true	is humorous	seems incredible	very complicated
6.	reliable person	can be counted on	is often late	is irresponsible
7.	beach excursion	becalmed boat	trip to seashore	hunting shells
8.	frequent disputes	seldom seen	lecture often	often argue
9.	barren landscape	picturesque land	dull, empty scenery	colorful painting
10.	conceal evidence	assist the court	hide information	hint at truth
11.	indulge in gossip	talk about people	adore turmoil	invent alibi
12.	era of anxiety	cure for worry	period of stress	time for bliss
13.	baffle authorities	make experts wonder	break the law	go to police
14.	an aerial feat	accomplishment in air	party on a plane	fear of heights
15.	fearless retort	strong bottle	courageous reply	army attack
16.	colossal blunder	great statue	huge mistake	ear-splitting sound
17.	arouse awe	become very angry	wake a group	inspire wonder
18.	customary residence	temporary home	usual living quarters	business office
19.	feeling melancholy	liking foreign foods	being sad	loving activity
20.	probably sufficient	perhaps enough	not enough variety	too little

TIME _____

ERRORS _____

► *Exercise 5F—Phrase Comprehension*

Pick out the phrase that means the same as the key phrase.

Key Phrase

1. unclad sprinter	runner without clothes	under a bridge	coughing a lot
2. delightful vision	pleasant sight	seeing too much	dirty eyeglasses
3. false compliment	true believer	artificial praise	filmed story
4. always on time	punctual every time	every minute counts	timely remark
5. wise selection	smart choice	seldom wise	messy paper
6. to review	all the way	look over	to present
7. very happy	extremely glad	quite unexpected	an attack
8. moving slowly	rapid movements	in slow motion	mothers together
9. cautious treatment	careful handling	broken leg	rented apartment
10. haughty manner	naughty girl	towering heights	arrogant behavior
11. go down fast	fast ascent	descend rapidly	gone again
12. expensive material	hard exercise	cheap goods	high-priced cloth
13. weeping gentleman	weeded garden	crying man	seeping water
14. stopped vehicle	popped cork	tire chains	stalled car
15. frantic wave	panicky gesture	frank remark	ranting and raving
16. snake in grass	serpent on lawn	rake the leaves	picnic in woods
17. wounded knee	hurt leg	wind around	smooth kneecap
18. nervous laugh	tight nerve	loud roar	worried giggle
19. clenched hand	strong fingers	polished nail	tight fist
20. remove completely	move restlessly	disappear together	take away all

TIME _____

ERRORS _____

What is a transition?

If you've ever had the experience of driving an unknown road, you know how helpful signposts along the roadside can be. They alert you to hairpin turns, sudden sharp curves, and the nature of the road just ahead. Good writers offer a similar aid to help you navigate your way through their thoughts. The signposts they use are called *transitions*. In reading, writing, and speaking, the term "transition" means a passage from one idea to another. (The root *trans* means *cross*.) Transitions are single words or brief phrases that tell you when the "road" of an author's thoughts is about to pass from one idea to another, or to change direction.

Gives clues to author's organization

In Lesson 4, you learned the common patterns in which authors organize their thoughts: *description, process, time sequence, example or illustration, classification, cause and effect, comparison and contrast,* and *addition.* Once you train yourself to be aware of an author's signposts or transitions, you'll find it easier to recognize these patterns when you read. You'll be able to make sense of what otherwise can seem like a big muddle of details, without form or clarity. You'll see how the details explain or develop the main idea, and you'll find it easier to remember them.

You already know many transitions and are sensitive to how they signal a change in a speaker's or writer's direction. For example, consider this passage: Someone you know says to you, "You are a fantastic friend. You are dependable, trustworthy, and loyal. Also, you have a great sense of humor. In addition, you are intelligent and considerate of my feelings. But. . . ."

Words such as "also" and "in addition" were signposts that probably kept you nodding your head in pleasure as you lapped up your friend's perceptive comments. What happened when you heard the word "but"? You knew, of course, a change was coming, and you probably started to steel yourself for a list of your faults.

The following chart lists the most frequent patterns of thought and some of the transitions that can help you recognize a particular pattern. As you continue to read and become more aware of transitions, you may wish to add still more to this chart.

Organizational Pattern	Transition
Description	right, left, up, down, above, below (and other words indicating position or location)
Process	first, second, third, next, then, finally (and other words indicating stages or steps)
Example, Illustration	for example, for instance, to illustrate, that is, in other words, e.g., i.e.
Cause and Effect	as a result, thus, because, therefore, hence, consequently, the reason, subsequently, so
Comparison (points out similarities)	similarly, in comparison, like, likewise, so
Contrast (points out differences)	but, however, yet, on the other hand, though, although, nevertheless
Addition/Enumeration (list of points—can overlap other patterns)	and, also, moreover, plus, furthermore, first, second, etc., least important, more important, most important
Time Sequence	at first, later, after that, finally, once, earlier, eventually, when, now (also dates, times)

May introduce levels of detail

Transitions also help you make sense of detail in another important way. You may have already noticed that all detail is not of equal importance. Some details are more important for explaining the main idea. These are *first level* details. Other details, however, are of less or second level importance. Authors use these *second level,* or minor details, to expand upon a first level detail. These minor details further explain, develop, inform, or entertain. You may have noticed in your own writing that there are many places where you could give first level, second level, even third-level details, depending on how specific you felt it was necessary to get. (Usually, the more specific the details are, the better the writing is.) Consider this paragraph:

> What makes physical fitness important for children? First of all, it offers the same advantages it offers adults. For instance, among other things, it benefits the heart and blood vessels, increases the capacity of the lungs, and makes the bones stronger. Second, it helps children control their weight. One reason weight control is especially important is that children who are overweight will often have a problem with weight all their lives. Another benefit fitness offers is psychological strength. It relieves anxiety and tension children may feel at school. It also can be effective as a treatment for depression, more of a problem in children than many people realize. In addition to these benefits, fitness offers protection from various ailments and diseases. For example, it helps prevent heart disease and high blood pressure in children.*

The topic of this paragraph is physical fitness for children. The main idea is that physical fitness is very important for children for a number of reasons. Did you notice the transitions—*first, second, another,* and *in addition*—that help point out the "addition" pattern? They also signal the four main benefits or effects of physical fitness. These are the first level details. The author provides further information about each of these details. This additional information is the second level detail. It may help to picture the relationship between the first and second level detail this way:

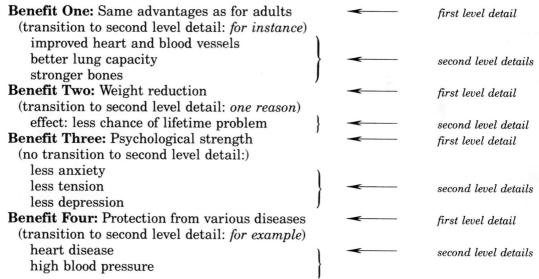

Benefit One: Same advantages as for adults ⟵ *first level detail*
  (transition to second level detail: *for instance*)
    improved heart and blood vessels
    better lung capacity   ⟵ *second level details*
    stronger bones
Benefit Two: Weight reduction ⟵ *first level detail*
  (transition to second level detail: *one reason*)
    effect: less chance of lifetime problem ⟵ *second level detail*
Benefit Three: Psychological strength ⟵ *first level detail*
  (no transition to second level detail:)
    less anxiety
    less tension   ⟵ *second level details*
    less depression
Benefit Four: Protection from various diseases ⟵ *first level detail*
  (transition to second level detail: *for example*)
    heart disease   ⟵ *second level details*
    high blood pressure

Once you begin to notice these levels of detail in what you read, your comprehension will greatly improve, as will your logic skills and your writing. But it takes patience and practice. (Start with training yourself to recognize transitions.) These skills provide the necessary foundation to organizing your thoughts in writing (or outlining)—practiced in Lessons 6 and 7.

---

*Based on information from Jane Brody, *New York Times Guide to Personal Health* (New York: Times Books, 1982), pp. 86–87, 116–117.

Theme: Tracing Our Roots

People from many different countries and backgrounds, with varied customs, have contributed their work and ideas to America. But it has not been easy for these people as they adjusted to their new homes and situations. Each group of newcomers has had to struggle with the challenge of being the "outsiders" and being different. The readings show the struggles of different people in this "melting pot" country.

Practice Paragraphs

Read these paragraphs first for the topic and the main idea. Be aware of transitions. Notice how the transitions help you see the way the details are organized.

A. (1) I was eleven before I learned we were Italian. (2) Until then, I knew we came from a real country but I didn't know what it was called—or even where it was. (3) I remember actually looking on a map of Europe for places named *Dago* and *Wop.* (4) In those days, especially if you lived in a small town, being Italian was something you tried to hide. (5) Almost everybody in Allentown was Pennsylvania Dutch, and as a kid I took a lot of abuse for being different. (6) Sometimes I got into fights with kids who called me names. . . . (7) Unfortunately, the prejudice against Italians wasn't limited to people my own age. (8) There were even a few teachers who called me "little wop" under their breath.*

1. In your own words, what is the main idea of the paragraph? (Write a complete sentence.) _____

   _____

2. Is the main idea stated in a topic sentence? _____

   If so, what is its number? _____

3. Underline the transitions in this paragraph.

4. The supporting details are organized in what type(s) of pattern(s)? __

   _____

5. Briefly list the details that prove learning he was Italian was a negative experience. _____

   _____

   _____

   Are these details first or second level? _____

B. (1) Who's the grinning Greek on the platform? (2) The man's mouth is spread so wide his teeth look like a string of taverna

___

*From *Iacocca: An Autobiography,* by Lee Iacocca with William Novak. Copyright © 1984 by Lee Iacocca. All rights reserved. Reprinted by permission of Bantam Books, Inc.

lights. (3) Now he leans over to hug someone, his thick black hair flopping over his swarthy forehead, his face flushed with feeling. (4) Then his hands go to his hips, thumbs backward and fingers splayed, the way the men do in dusty Greek villages when the dancing starts. (5) "People ask me, 'Are you tired? Is this a grind?' " he tells his audience. (6) "Are you kidding? (7) My folks came over on the boat, and I'm running for president!"*

1. In your own words, what is the main idea of the paragraph? (Write a complete sentence.) _____

_____

2. Is the main idea stated in a topic sentence? _____

If so, what is its number? _____

3. Underline the transitions in this paragraph.

4. The supporting details are organized in what type(s) of pattern(s)?

_____

5. List the physical details that illustrate his Greek heritage.

_____   _____

_____   _____

Are these details first or second level? _____

C. (1) The next morning, more toubob [white people] than usual came thundering down through the hatch [of the slave ship], and much earlier than ever before. (2) With great excitement in their words and movements, they rushed along the aisles, unchaining the men and hurriedly helping them upward. (3) Stumbling up through the hatch behind a number who were ahead of him, Kunta blinked in the early-morning light. (4) Then he saw the other toubob and the women and children standing at the rails. (5) The toubob were all laughing, cheering, and gesturing wildly. (6) Between the scabbed backs of the other men, Kunta squinted and then saw. . . . (7) Though still blurred in the distance, it was unmistakably some piece of Allah's earth. (8) These toubob really did have some place to put their feet upon—the land of toubabo doo—which the ancient forefathers said stretched from the sunrise to the sunset. (9) Kunta's whole body shook. (10) The sweat came popping out and glistened on his forehead. (11) The voyage was over.**

1. In your own words, what is the main idea of the paragraph? (Write a complete sentence.) _____

_____

_____

*Excerpts from "Jesse Jackson: The Power or the Glory" and excerpts from "The Metamorphosis of Mike Dukakis" both from Character: America's Search for Leadership by Gail Sheehy. Copyright © 1988 by Gail Sheehy. Reprinted by permission of William Morrow and Co., Inc.
**Excerpts from Roots by Alex Haley. Copyright © 1976 by Alex Haley. Reprinted by permission of Doubleday, a division of Bantam Doubleday Dell Publishing Group, Inc.

2. Is the main idea stated in a topic sentence? _____

If so, what is its number? _____

3. Underline the transitions in this paragraph.

4. The supporting details are organized in what type(s) of pattern(s)? ___

_____

5. List the details that suggest the trip was difficult for Kunta.

_____

_____

_____

Are these details first or second level? _____

Words in Context

For each *italicized* word, choose the best meaning below.

► *Short Reading 5G*

1. I tried out on Jackson an *anthropological* observation that had come to me from comparing the subculture of the segregated black South with the core culture.

study of the characteristics of **(a)** animals **(b)** mankind **(c)** the civil war **(d)** politics

2. His grandmother *cajoled* the boy, "For God's sake, Jesse, promise me you'll be somebody."

(a) scolded **(b)** bribed **(c)** coaxed **(d)** threatened

► *Short Reading 5H*

3. I see a car turn off the highway and come *lumbering* across the ruts through the sage. [Extra Clue: A huge person might *lumber* across a room.]

(a) racing **(b)** sliding downhill **(c)** moving slowly and awkwardly **(d)** moving expertly

4. Can you imagine people wanting to live this way? I for one am not going inside that *hovel*.

(a) elegant mansion **(b)** wretched shack **(c)** haunted house **(d)** singles apartment building

5. "We are here to deal with the noble leader of these people. . . ." "Deal with? Not me, not my job. They pay me to appraise, not *fraternize*." [Extra Clue: From the Latin for *fraternus,* meaning *brotherly*.]

(a) ignore **(b)** test **(c)** organize **(d)** socialize

6. "It would be very simple to go in and talk with him. . . ." "Inside in that *squalor?* Why, I'll just bet you anything that place is acrawl with black widows."

(a) miserable filth **(b)** small dwelling **(c)** dense forest **(d)** abandoned

7. I couldn't afford to get my hopes up. I was ready to *capitulate* without a groan. [Extra Clue: The root *cap* or *cep* means *to yield* or *to go.*]

    (a) give in   **(b)** go into business   **(c)** feel happiness   **(d)** feel hopeful

8. When Papa lectured, you listened. If anyone spoke up, it would be Mama, trying to *mediate.*

    (a) listen   **(b)** make a fresh start   **(c)** act quickly   **(d)** help people reach an agreement

9. I had seen those photos of Mama when she lived in Spokane, twelve years old and her round faced *blanched* with rice powder.

    (a) darkened   **(b)** whitened   **(c)** washed   **(d)** covered

10. He stood there, hands on hips, glaring at me, and not at all satisfied with this *ultimatum.* [Extra Clue: Another form of *ultimate.*]

    (a) beginning   **(b)** process   **(c)** final word or warning   **(d)** crisis

11. In Papa's glare I sometimes detected a flicker of approval, as if my streak of independence, my refusal to be shaped by him, reflected his own *obstinance.*

    (a) anger   **(b)** stubbornness   **(c)** humility   **(d)** glee

The next selection is from Gail Sheehy's new book, Character: America's Search for Leadership, *which explores how our political leaders' roots affected their character. This excerpt examines black leader Jesse Jackson, who ran for President in 1984 and 1988.*

Preview: *In 30 seconds or less, read the title and the first sentence of each paragraph. What do you think the thesis of this selection might be?*

What is one detail that helps explain Jackson's ambition?

Wait for a signal from your instructor before you begin to read. Circle your WPM after one minute. Notice the details and how they expand the thesis.

from "Jesse Jackson: The Power or the Glory?

Gail Sheehy

	WPM
I tried out on Jackson an anthropological observation that had	10
come to me from comparing the subculture of the segregated black	21
South with the core culture. A child who is gifted and receptive, who	34
picks up on everything that you give him, is singled out by the com-	48
munity to be "saved" for better things. Everyone—the neighbors on	58
the street, who will give him a licking for misbehavior in place of his	72
mother, the pastor, the coach, the teachers, even the older kids—they	84
all look out for him so that he doesn't get into trouble. No one wants	99
this child harmed, in body or reputation. Helen and Charles Jackson	110
[his parents], for instance, often went out to fight Jesse's battles for	122
him, while the boy stayed home and cried. And adults reinforced the	134
child's sense of specialness by holding him to a higher standard. They	146
boosted the boy onto their shoulders. His grandmother cajoled the	156
boy, "For God's sake, Jesse, promise me you'll be some*body.*" Soon	167
everyone knew Jesse was designated to be saved. . . .	175
He was a big, clumsy boy, pigeon-toed, and he stuttered. (When he	187
overcame the speech defect, he gave the credit to God.) . . . Jesse was	199
powerfully built.	201
"He stood head and shoulders above everybody at the age of six, and	214
he could talk," says Coach Mathis, smiling. "I told him he was going	227
to be the heir apparent to great things." Together, coach and starter	239
hammered Jesse's physical advantage into the competitor's iron will.	248
Jackson became a superior baseball player and the school's star quar-	259
terback. Mathis also taught the boy about "putting the bend into the	270
truth."	271
It was hard to miss young Jesse's talents. Consider a child so ver-	284
bal, often dealing with adults unable to read or write, who when the	296
first TVs arrived in the neighborhood offered to read the news off the	309
screen for the adults. "You want to know? Give me a dime." But it was	324
his willfulness that would have caught people's attention, because	333
everybody knew that only the strivers could overcome segregation	342
and racism. . . .	344

What is that thing inside that keeps you going? I asked Jackson **356**
after our first long interview. **361**

His answer was vague. **365**

Do you think your ambition started with just trying to get out, to **378**
make yourself worthy, and then began to feed on itself? **388**

"At one level it starts as survival." He began stuttering uncomfort- **399**
ably. "In my instance, it started from personal denial. Then group **409**
denial." He sounded like a man thirsting, his pitcher needing to be **421**
constantly refilled, but the pitcher bottomless. "I've always been **430**
loved," he affirmed. "But there's always been an air of expectation, a **442**
higher demand of me than from other people." **450**

Long after Jesse Louis Jackson had convinced others of his worth, **461**
he would, and always will, face that most disparaging of taunters— **472**
himself—demanding new and more dazzling forms of proof.* **481**

Immediately answer the following questions without referring to
the selection.

1. Jesse Jackson was ambitious mostly because
   (a) he didn't want to be poor any more.
   (b) he wanted to overcome his handicaps.
   (c) other people had high expectations of him.
   (d) he wanted to be a star athlete.

2. Which of the following traits did Jackson *not* have?
   (a) modesty (b) willfulness (c) verbal ability (d) athletic ability

3. What was the negative trait that Coach Mathis taught Jackson? _____

4. Young Jesse offered to read to the adults for free.   T   F

5. Which pattern best describes how the details are organized around the
   main idea?
   (a) classification (b) cause and effect (c) time sequence (d) addition

Record your scores below and on the progress chart in the Appendix.

WORDS PER MINUTE _____

% COMPREHENSION _____

Bonus Question. Which sentence in the first paragraph is the topic
sentence?

_____

List the transitions in the first paragraph.

_____

*Excerpts from "Jesse Jackson: The Power or the Glory" and excerpts from "The Metamorphosis of
Mike Dukakis" both from *Character: America's Search for Leadership* by Gail Sheehy. Copyright © 1988
by Gail Sheehy. Reprinted by permission of William Morrow and Co., Inc.

The next selection is from the novel One Flew Over the Cuckoo's Nest, *which was made into a film. The narrator, an Indian who appears to be a deafmute, tells what it's like not to exist in the eyes and ears of others.*

Preview: *In 20 seconds or less, read the title, the first paragraph and the last paragraph. Write what you think is the narrator's reason for pretending to be a deafmute:* _____

_____

Wait for a signal before you begin. Notice how the details expand the thesis. Also pay attention to the transitions.

from One Flew Over the Cuckoo's Nest

Ken Kesey

WPM

I lay in bed the night before the fishing trip and thought it 13
over, about my being deaf, about the years of not letting on I heard 27
what was said, and I wondered if I could ever act any other way again. 42
But I remembered one thing: it wasn't me that started acting deaf; it 55
was people that first started acting like I was too dumb to hear or see 70
or say anything at all. 75

Lying there in bed, I tried to think back when I first noticed it. 89
I think it was once when we were still living in the village on the 104
Columbia. It was summer. . . . 108

. . . and I'm about ten years old and I'm out in front of the 121
shack sprinkling salt on salmon for the racks behind the house, 132
when I see a car turn off the highway and come lumbering across the 146
ruts through the sage. . . . 150

The doors of the car open all at once and three people get out. 164
The first man stops and looks the village over. . . . 173

"Can you imagine people wanting to live this way? Tell me, 184
John, can you? I for one am not going inside that hovel," the fat 198
guy says. 200

"That hovel," John says through his mustache, "is where the 210
Chief lives, Brickenridge, the man we are here to deal with, the noble 223
leader of these people." 227

"Deal with? Not me, not my job. They pay me to appraise, not 240
fraternize." 241

This gets a laugh out of John. 248

"It would be very simple to go in and talk with him." 260

"Inside in that squalor? Why, I'll just bet you anything that 271
place is acrawl with black widows. They say these 'dobe shacks always 283
house a regular civilization in the walls between the sods. And *hot*, 295
lord-a-mercy, I hope to tell you. I'll wager it's a regular oven in there. 309
Look, look how overdone little Hiawatha is here. Ho. Burnt to a fair 322
turn, he is." 325

What he said makes me madder the more I think about it. He 338
and John go ahead talking about our house and village and property 350
and what they are worth, and I get the notion they're talking about 363
these things around me because they don't know I speak English. 374

They are probably from the East someplace, where people don't   384
know anything about Indians but what they see in the movies. I think   397
how ashamed they're going to be when they find out I know what   410
they are saying.   413

I let them say another thing or two about the heat and the   426
house; then I stand up and tell the fat man, in my very best school-   441
book language, that our sod house is likely to be cooler than anyone   453
of the houses in town, *lots* cooler! . . .   460

And I'm just about to go and tell them, how, if they'll come on   474
in, I'll go get Papa, when I see that they don't look like they'd heard   489
me talk at all. . . . Not a one of the three acts like they heard a thing I   506
said; in fact, they're all looking off from me like they'd as soon I   520
wasn't there at all.*   524

Immediately answer the following questions without referring to the selection.

(1.) State the thesis of the article in a complete sentence.

_____

_____

2. The fat man thought the chief's house would be

   (a) cold. **(b)** expensively furnished. **(c)** filled with insects.

3. At the time of this story, the narrator spoke no English.   T   F

4. The visitors were embarrassed when they realized the Indian boy had heard what they were saying.   T   F

5. What do you think the narrator did the next time he saw white people?

_____

Record your scores below and on the progress chart in the Appendix.

WORDS PER MINUTE _____

% COMPREHENSION _____

Bonus Question. Check the pattern that best describes the way in which the details in the third to last paragraph are organized.

description _____   cause and effect _____

classification _____   space relationship _____

What is the most important transition in this paragraph? _____

___

*From *One Flew Over the Cuckoo's Nest* by Ken Kesey. Copyright © 1962 by Ken Kesey. All rights reserved. Reprinted by permission of Viking Penguin, a division of Penguin Books USA, Inc.

This last selection presents a Japanese girl who struggles to be accepted in a modern American world that conflicts with her family's traditional values. As you read, think back to some time in your life when you have felt different and like an outsider.

Preview: *In 30 seconds or less, read the title and first and last paragraphs of the selection. Then write what you think will be the source of conflict between the girl and her parents:*

_____

Wait for a signal from your instructor before you begin reading the entire selection. As you read, notice the details and try to picture the conflict and how it is resolved.

Carnival Queen

Jeanne Wakatsuki Houston and James Houston

By the spring of that year, when it came time to elect the annual carnival queen from the graduating seniors, my homeroom chose me. I was among fifteen girls nominated to walk out for inspection by the assembled student body on voting day.

I knew I couldn't beat the other contestants at their own game, that is, look like a bobbysoxer. Yet neither could I look too Japanese-y. I decided to go exotic, with a flower-print sarong, black hair loose, and a hibiscus flower behind my ear. When I walked bare-footed out onto the varnished gymnasium floor, between the filled bleachers, the howls and whistles from the boys were double what had greeted any of the other girls. It sounded like some winning basket had just been made in the game against our oldest rivals.

It was pretty clear what the outcome would be, but ballots still had to be cast and counted. The next afternoon I was standing outside my Spanish class when Leonard Rodriguez, who sat next to me, came hurrying down the hall with a revolutionary's fire in his eye. He helped out each day in the administration office. He had just over-heard some teachers and a couple of secretaries counting up the votes.

"They're trying to stuff the ballot box," he whispered loudly. "They're fudging on the tally. They're afraid to have a Japanese girl be queen. They've never had one before. They're afraid of what some of the parents will say."

He was pleased he had caught them, and more pleased to be telling this to me, as if some long-held suspicion of conspiracy had finally been confirmed. I shared it with him. Whether this was true or not, I was prepared to believe that teachers would stuff the ballot box to keep me from being queen. For that reason I couldn't afford to get my hopes up.

I said, "So what?"

He leaned toward me eagerly, with final proof. "They want Lois Carson to be queen. I heard them say so."

If applause were any measure, Lois Carson wasn't even in the running. She was too slim and elegant for beauty contests. But her father had contributed a lot to the school. He was on the board of trustees. She was blond, blue-eyed. I was ready to capitulate without a groan.

"If she doesn't make carnival queen this year," Leonard went on smugly, "she'll never be queen of anything anywhere else for the rest of her life."

"Let her have it then, if she wants it so much."

"No! We can't do that! *You* can't do that!"

I could do that very easily. I wasn't going to be caught caring about this, or needing it, the way I had needed the majorette position. I already sensed, though I couldn't have said why, that I would lose either way, no matter how it turned out. My face was indifferent.

"How can I stop them from fudging," I said, "if that's what they want to do?"

He hesitated. He looked around. He set his brown face. My champion. "You can't," he said. "But I can."

He turned and hurried away toward the office. The next morning he told me he had gone in there and "raised holy hell," threatened to break this news to the student body and make the whole thing more trouble than it would ever be worth. An hour later the announcement came over the intercom that I had been chosen. I didn't believe it. I couldn't let myself believe it. But, for the classmates who had nominated me, I had to look overjoyed. I glanced across at Leonard and he winked, shouting and whooping now with all the others.

At home that evening, when I brought this news, no one whooped. Papa was furious. I had not told them I was running for queen. There was no use mentioning it until I had something to mention. He asked me what I had worn at the tryouts. I told him.

"No wonder those *hakajin* [Caucasian] boys vote for you!" he shouted. "It is just like those majorette clothes you wear in the street. Showing off your body. Is that the kind of queen you want to be?"

I didn't say anything. When Papa lectured, you listened. If anyone spoke up, it would be Mama, trying to mediate.

"Ko," she said now, "these things are important to Jeannie. She is. . . ."

"Important? I'll tell you what is important. Modesty is important. A graceful body is important. You don't show your legs all the time. You don't walk around like this."

He did an imitation of a girl's walk, with shoulders straight, an assertive stride, and lips pulled back in a baboon's grin. I started to laugh.

"Don't laugh! This is not funny. You become this kind of woman and what Japanese boy is going to marry you? Tell me that. You put on tight clothes and walk around like Jean Harlow and the *hakajin* boys make you the queen. And pretty soon you end up marrying a *hakajin* boy. . . ."

He broke off. He could think of no worse end result. He began to stomp back and forth across the floor, while Mama looked at me cautiously, with a glance that said, "Be patient, wait him out. After he has spoken his piece, you and I can talk sensibly."

He saw this and turned on her. "Hey! How come your daughter is seventeen years old and if you put a sack over her face you couldn't tell she was Japanese from anybody else on the street?"

"Ko," Mama said quietly. "Jeannie's in high school now. Next year she's going to college. She's learning other things. . . ."

"Listen to me. It's not too late for her to learn Japanese ways of movement. The Buddhist church in San Jose gives *odori* [Japanese dance] class twice a week. Jeannie, I want you to phone the teacher and tell her you are going to start taking lessons. Mama has kimonos you can wear. She can show you things too. She used to know all the dances. We have pictures somewhere. Mama, what happened to all those pictures?"

I had seen them, photos of Mama when she lived in Spokane, twelve years old and her round face blanched with rice powder.

"Papa," I complained.

"Don't make faces. You want to be the carnival queen? I tell you what. I'll make a deal with you. You can be the queen if you start *odori* lessons at the Buddhist church as soon as school is out."

He stood there, hands on hips, glaring at me, and not at all satisfied with this ultimatum. It was far too late for *odori* classes to have any effect on me and Papa knew this. But he owed it to himself to make one more show of resistance. When I signed up, a few weeks later, I lasted about ten lessons. The teacher herself sent me away. I smiled too much and couldn't break the habit. Like a majorette before the ever-shifting sidewalk crowd, I smiled during performances, and in Japanese dancing this is equivalent to a concert violinist walking onstage in a bathing suit.

Papa didn't mention my queenship again. He just glared at me from time to time, with great distaste, as if I had betrayed him. Yet in that glare I sometimes detected a flicker of approval, as if this streak of independence, this refusal to be shaped by him, reflected his own obstinance. At least, these glances seemed to say, she has inherited *that*.*

TOTAL READING TIME _____

Immediately answer the following questions without referring to the selection.

1. Choose the statement that best expresses the thesis.
   (a) Jeannie's papa thinks she smiles too much.
   (b) The school staff was afraid to have a carnival queen who was Japanese.
   (c) While Jeannie struggles for acceptance at school, her papa fears she is becoming more American than Japanese.
   (d) Jeannie is excited about being chosen queen.

2. Jeannie's becoming queen was a sign of her acceptance.   T   F

3. What did Jeannie wear during the contest for queen?
   (a) a long white gown (b) a formal black dress (c) a flower-print sarong (d) a tuxedo

4. What other school event had Jeannie participated in that made her father angry? _____

5. Leonard Rodriguez kept the contest honest.   T   F

_____

*From *Farewell to Manzanar* by Jeanne Wakatsuki Houston and James D. Houston. Copyright © 1973 by James D. Houston. Reprinted by permission of Houghton Mifflin Company.

6. Jeannie's father wanted her to marry a *hakajin* boy. **T** **F**

7. Jeannie's mother quietly took her side. **T** **F**

8. Jeannie's papa was secretly proud of her independence. **T** **F**

9. What compromise did Jeannie make with her father so he would allow her to be carnival queen? _____

_____

10. Jeannie became a very good *odori* dancer. **T** **F**

Turn to the Rate Chart in the Appendix to get your words per minute for this selection. Then record your scores below and on the progress chart in the Appendix.

WORDS PER MINUTE _____

% COMPREHENSION _____

Bonus Question: Look at the second paragraph of Long Reading 5I and pick out the transitions and patterns of organization. Fill in the blanks below as indicated. The first one has been filled in for you as an example.

transition	*pattern of organization*	
yet	contrast	(2nd sentence)
_____	_____	(4th sentence)
_____	_____	(5th sentence)

WRITING AND DISCUSSION ACTIVITIES

1. Write about some experience you have had as a newcomer to a group. For example, you might write about being a newcomer to a particular school, club, neighborhood, or country. (You are not limited to these examples, however.) Be sure to provide supporting details for your ideas about the experience.

2. What place do you consider your real home? Is it where you are living now or some other town or country? Write a paragraph describing the place that your heart calls home. Start with a topic sentence that tells where that place is and why, in general, it is important to you. The details in the rest of the paragraph should expand on the general statement you make in your topic sentence. Choose at least one detail in your paragraph to expand with second and third level detail (detail for the detail).

6

Organizing Thoughts

IN THIS LESSON, YOU WILL

1. continue perception and comprehension exercises;

2. learn how to progress from a rough, informal outline to a formal sentence outline;

3. apply the steps of *outlining* to the paragraphs and two long articles.

► *Exercise 6A—Phrase Perception*

Pick out the phrase identical to the key phrase.

Key Phrase

1.	coffee and cream	cream and coffee	coffee and cream	scream in rage
2.	sweep the room	wipe the broom	sweep the room	sweeten the drink
3.	sweet and low	low and sweet	sweet answers	sweet and low
4.	four foul fingers	fold five fingers	four foul fingers	four fat fowls
5.	leaves of grass	leaves of grass	leave the grass	mow the lawn
6.	ten tender tales	one bending trail	ten tender tales	tell ten tales
7.	row the boat	hoe the tow	row the boat	sow the oats
8.	awake at dawn	awake at dawn	the rooster crows	dig here again
9.	tear in eye	eye the tear	tear in eye	in near future
10.	a pretty picture	frame the picture	picture the pretty	a pretty picture
11.	a sharp retort	a sharp retort	a shorn sheep	a tart reply
12.	giving haggard looks	looking very haggard	giving haggard looks	living in huts
13.	sit on the stool	spit in the pool	sitting on the fence	sit on the stool
14.	hop up high	a high-up hop	hop up high	pop-up box
15.	hold on tight	hold on tight	fold a towel	much too bold
16.	hide in here	hide in here	abide with me	turn the tide
17.	tea and sympathy	see my symphony	tease the child	tea and sympathy
18.	take another path	rake the other yard	take another bath	take another path
19.	rest in peace	the best place	rest in peace	a peaceful guest
20.	jump over the sticks	overcome the ticks	jump over the sticks	pull over the stump

TIME _____

ERRORS _____

► *Exercise 6B—Phrase Perception*

Pick out the phrase identical to the key phrase.

Key Phrase

1. dirty kitchen sink   dirt in kitchen sink   sink in dirt, Kit   dirty kitchen sink

2. in the garden alone   alone in the garden   in the lone garden   in the garden alone

3. this hunting trophy   they hunt trophies   this hunting trophy   hunt this trophy

4. sing the unsung hero   sing the unsung hero   the unsung hero sings   sing a song, Hero

5. prophet of doom   prophet of doom   a doomed prophet   prophesy doom

6. rose by another name   name my other rose   rose has another name   rose by another name

7. the worm turns   the turned worm   turn the worm   the worm turns

8. talk to your plants   plant one more kiss   talk to your plants   walk to your plants

9. heaven only knows   know only heaven   heaven only knows   known in heaven

10. a goose-feather pillow   a feather pillow   feather the pillow   a goose-feather pillow

11. gather ye rosebuds   ye rosebuds gathered   gather ye rosebuds   rosebuds get gathered

12. make hay in sunshine   make hay in sun   hayride in sunshine   make hay in sunshine

13. one more record crop   more one-record crops   count one more record   one more record crop

14. wrinkled red raincoat   red wrinkled raincoat   wring the raincoat   wrinkled red raincoat

15. magnificent obsession   magnificent obsessions   magnificent obsession   magnified object

16. policeman's whistle   the policeman's whistle   policemen's whistle   policeman's whistle

17. gun of the murderer   gum of the murderer   gun of the murderer   grab for the murderer

18. jail for the guilty   jail for the guilty   pail for the guilty   wail for his guilt

19. tools of the thief   tools of the thief   tell the thief off   of the thief's tools

20. the judge's white hair   white-haired judge   judge the hare   the judge's white hair

TIME _____

ERRORS _____

► Exercise 6C—Word Comprehension

Choose the word closest in meaning to the key word in **boldface** print.

Key Word

1. **fallacious** reasoning	sound	indirect	false
2. to **froth** at the mouth	foam	grin	bite
3. a **glib** excuse	unbelievable	too-smooth	awkward
4. to arouse her **ire**	anger	passion	admiration
5. a **dynamic** duo	listless	new	energetic
6. to **glean** information	spread	gather	falsify
7. an **imperative** act	urgent	needless	interesting
8. the **deficient** essay	efficient	flawless	defective
9. **invigorating** exercise	stimulating	calming	insufferable
10. **superlative** wisdom	underrated	supreme	modest
11. a **vigilant** guard	violent	sleepy	watchful
12. the **pinnacle** of success	apex	struggle	ease
13. a **phenomenal** performer	ordinary	extraordinary	vulgar
14. the **invincible** hero	unbeatable	brave	defeated
15. to **enthrall** the audience	bore	irritate	captivate
16. **proficient** at sports	inexperienced	skilled	aggressive
17. **exuberant** compliments	lavish	lukewarm	sincere
18. to **delve** for answers	beg	pay	search
19. **spontaneous** applause	forced	unplanned	enthusiastic
20. to **dispel** the rumor	disperse	encourage	start

TIME _____

ERRORS _____

► *Exercise 6D—Word Comprehension*

Choose the word closest in meaning to the key word in **boldface** print.

Key Word

1. a **dogged** effort	inhuman	persistent	weak
2. a **communicable** disease	stoppable	incurable	catchable
3. an **illegitimate** act	illegal	legal	insane
4. an **alluring** woman	fascinating	fishing	repulsive
5. to **reimburse** the money	steal	earn	pay back
6. a **gala** event	important	festive	boring
7. **fraught** with danger	filled	free from	overcome
8. women's **intuition**	rights	poverty	instinct
9. a **portly** figure	thin	shadowy	stout
10. a **pessimistic** outlook	gloomy	positive	logical
11. keeping a **vigil**	pet	watch	budget
12. a **prelude** to the opera	ticket	conclusion	introduction
13. to **exasperate** his friends	irritate	soothe	lose
14. a **patron** for his art	critic	supplier	sponsor
15. **havoc** in the classroom	learning	commotion	order
16. a **torrid** romance	hot	cold	new
17. the building's **demolition**	site	construction	destruction
18. the **nucleus** of power	edge	center	outside
19. to **dilate** the eye	expand	narrow	brighten
20. the **betrothed** couple	married	divorced	engaged

TIME _____

ERRORS _____

► *Exercise 6E—Sentence Comprehension*

Check the sentences that express the same idea as the key sentence.

Key Sentence: Reading for ideas instead of words will increase reading rate.

1. Reading rate is increased by reacting to ideas, not single words. _____

2. It is more difficult to grasp ideas than to merely recognize words. _____

3. How well one understands ideas in reading material is often related to how well one understands the vocabulary used in the material. _____

4. Ideas are more important than isolated words. _____

5. In increasing speed, reading word for word is not as effective as reading for ideas. _____

6. A poor vocabulary often means a slower reading rate. _____

7. It is easier to read faster when reading interesting material. _____

8. One can read faster when one stops reading word for word and starts reading for ideas. _____

9. Wordy sentence structure sometimes obscures the meaning of a reading passage. _____

10. The rate of understanding ideas can be dependent on the rate of reading. _____

TIME _____

ERRORS _____

► *Exercise 6F—Sentence Comprehension*

Check the sentences that express the same idea as the key sentence.

Key Sentence: Our life is frittered away by detail. (Henry David Thoreau)

1. We should not spend our valuable time regretting past mistakes. _____
2. We waste our lives, little by little, attending to small, unimportant tasks. _____
3. Our breakfast tables are enriched by the sight of corn fritters. _____
4. A man who spends his time wisely achieves more. _____
5. Many people spend hours looking for better ways to occupy their time. _____
6. Insignificant matters take up so much of our time that our lives seem to go by without meaning. _____
7. One should pay more attention to important problems and ignore unimportant matters. _____
8. Our ambitions are frustrated by the interference of petty employers. _____
9. Advance planning saves much wasted time. _____
10. The days of our lives seem needlessly spent in taking care of minor details. _____

TIME _____

ERRORS _____

An outline is simply a chart or map of the ideas in a piece of writing. Many people find it easier to understand and remember the important ideas in a reading selection if they put them in some kind of outline. Outlines are especially helpful if the reading material is difficult. In fairly few words, an outline or chart shows how the main ideas and their details relate to each other.

Mapping

There are many ways to make this outline. Some students find it helpful to use a system of circles (or squares) and arrows to show the connections between main ideas and details. To see how this system works, read the following paragraph, then examine the map of its ideas that follows.

> Even longtime smokers who finally manage to quit gain a number of benefits. Some of these are important and long-term. Others are less dramatic but more immediate. The most important benefits are the lower risks of having a heart attack or of getting lung cancer. In addition, life expectancy in general increases. Other, more immediate, benefits include ridding the blood of carbon monoxide, which robs it of oxygen. The ex-smoker will also get better sleep and have more energy. The senses, especially taste and smell, will sharpen. And smoker's cough will begin to disappear.*

A map of this paragraph's more important ideas and supporting details could look like this:

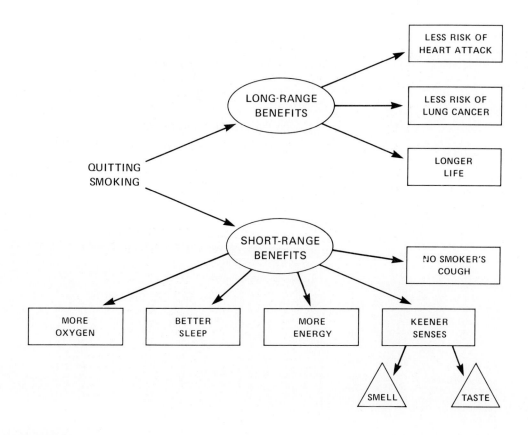

---

*Based on information in Jane Brody, *The New York Times Guide to Personal Health* (New York: Times Books, 1982), p. 255.

This system of circles and arrows to show the level of importance of major ideas and supporting details can be a fast and easy way to chart the points in a lecture or a short reading. But it's not suited for longer, more involved reading selections. You will find it useful throughout your college career to know another; more traditional way of charting an author's ideas. This method of making an outline is valuable not only as a way of organizing and understanding what you read, but also as a tool to help you plan an essay or report that you are going to write.

Outlining

To make a formal outline, you start with a simple list. As you make this list, indent details just under the ideas they explain or support. Then, instead of circles and arrows, you use a system of numbers and letters to further separate important ideas and details. The letters and numbers indicate the importance of the ideas and show their relationship to each other.

Follow these steps:

Let's go through this method step by step. To outline the paragraph about the benefits of quitting smoking, for example, *write a heading that sums up the topic.* This heading is the title for the outline. Then write a main idea statement. Now

1. List first level details.

start with a list of the first level details, that is, the most important points you found in the paragraph:

Title: **Benefits of Quitting Smoking**
Main Idea: Smokers who break the habit will gain certain benefits.
There are important, long-range benefits.
There are also less dramatic but immediate benefits. } *first level details*

2. Assign Roman numerals to first level details.

Now give Roman numerals to these first level details in your list. Remember that Roman numerals in an outline always indicate the more important points an author is making, not the less important supporting details. Your outline now looks like this:

Title: **Benefits of Quitting Smoking**
Main Idea: Smokers who break the habit will gain certain benefits.
I. Important long-range benefits.
II. Less dramatic, but immediate benefits.

3. Use capital letters for second level details.

You're ready now to add the second level details to your list. Be sure to indent those details under the first level details they explain and use capital letters to identify them. Your outline will look like this:

Title: **Benefits of Quitting Smoking**
Main Idea: Smokers who break the habit will gain certain benefits.
I. Important, long-range benefits
   A. Less risk of a heart attack
   B. Less risk of lung cancer   *second level details*
   C. Greater life expectancy
II. Less dramatic, but immediate benefits
   A. More oxygen in the bloodstream
   B. Better sleep
   C. More energy
   D. Keener senses
      1. Smell
      2. Taste   *What level of detail are these?*
   E. Disappearing smoker's cough

As you look back at the second level details in the paragraph, you may wish to expand on them and *list the third level details in your outline too.* Indent under the second level detail you want to expand upon, and use Arabic numbers (1,2,3,4, . . .) for this kind of further detail. We've already placed the third level details in the outline you just examined. Did you see where? What second level detail did we expand upon?

How much detail should you give in your outline? That depends on the size of the original reading selection and your purpose in making the outline. An outline for a short piece of writing such as a paragraph obviously won't list a great deal of second or third level detail. An outline of a chapter in a book, though, would have to give much more in order to be comprehensive and of any value if you were to use it to review for a test.

The type of outline you have just learned is called a *topic outline,* made up of sentence fragments. Many instructors prefer the more formal *sentence outline,* made up of complete sentences. Contrast the sentence outline that follows with the topic outline you have just studied. Then complete the second part:

Title: **Benefits of Quitting Smoking**
Main Idea: Smokers who break the habit will gain certain benefits.
   I. There are important, long-range benefits.
     A. They will have less risk of a heart attack.
     B. They will have less risk of lung cancer.
     C. They will have a greater life expectancy.
  II. There are also less dramatic, but immediate benefits.
     A. There will be more oxygen in the bloodstream.
     B. _____
     C. _____
     D. _____
       1. _____
       2. _____
     E. _____

Did you use complete sentences, not fragments? If not, you have written a topic outline. You may wish to check with your instructors to see which kind they prefer for class assignments.

So far, we have outlined just a paragraph. To outline a long reading selection, use this system to separate important ideas from the various levels of details:

Use Roman numerals for first level details: I, II, III, IV, V

Use capital letters for second level details supporting the first level details: A, B, C

Use Arabic numbers for third level details that expand the second level details: 1, 2, 3

Use small letters for fourth level details: a, b, c

Use Arabic numbers in parentheses for fifth level details: (1), (2), (3), (4), (5)

Outlining is 100 percent easier and more accurate if you look for the patterns in which the authors have organized their thoughts (Lessons 4 and 5). For instance, has the author organized his or her thoughts according to classification? If so, as you read, make a mental or written note of each class or category. These classes will become the Roman numerals, indicating first level details (or the most important points), in your outline. Did you notice that the author of "Benefits of Quitting Smoking" used contrast for first level details and addition for second level details?

This ability to organize your thoughts is guaranteed to help you read faster and comprehend more.

Theme: Study Skills

The three practice paragraphs offer you outlining practice with three very different subjects, written in different styles. The two Long Readings in this Lesson should be useful for any student. They offer practical suggestions to help you with a skill that every successful student masters.

Practice Paragraphs

Outline the main ideas and details in the following paragraphs. To help you get started, we've provided the outline form for the first one. Use it as a guide when you outline the other two paragraphs.

A. I have a friend who will go to any lengths to achieve what she calls Total Beauty. Three years ago, when she first moved to Los Angeles, land of many Total Beauties, she had rhinoplastic surgery (a nose job). She had a distinctive Roman nose that perfectly suited her rather long, thin face. Now she has a cute little snub nose which seems to belong to someone else's cute little pixie face. Last year she decided she must have Inner Peace to achieve Outer Beauty. She, in turn, immersed herself in Transcendental Meditation, Yoga, EST, Bio-Energetics, and Bio-feedback. She became so peaceful, as a result, that she lost her high pressure sales job—thereby suspending funds for other important beauty projects like facials and manicures. Finally, this year she abandoned Inner Peace to look like Madonna, one of the media's favorite sex kittens. She tortured her lovely, shiny, straight brown hair through two permanents (the first wasn't curly enough), a bleaching, and a streaking. Her fine hair overreacted, and she appears most of the time these days with a colorful peasant scarf over her frizzled blond hair. If the fashion this summer calls for a tranquil, snub-nosed gypsy with yellow Brillo-pad hair, she is definitely *in*.

1. The ideas in this paragraph are organized according to which paragraph patterns? _____

_____

Underline the transitions that reinforce one of those patterns.

2.   Title: _____

Main Idea: _____

_____

I. _____ (1st project)

    A. _____

    B. _____

II. _____ (2nd project)

    A. _____

    B. _____

III. _____ (3rd project)

    A. _____

    B. _____

    Conclusion: _____

                       _____

B. It would be difficult to find anyone who has not suffered from a severe headache. However, not many people know there are three different types of headaches. Of these three types, the *tension* headache is the most common and least painful. This muscular headache is usually described as a dull ache in the scalp, jaw, neck, or shoulders. The second, more severe type, the *migraine* headache, affects twice as many women as it does men. The migraine, a combination of muscular and vascular contractions, is described as a throbbing pressure. Some sufferers see flashing lights or dots or lines just before their migraine strikes. Others have nausea and vomiting. The most severe and least common, the *cluster* headache, affects only 1.5 percent of the population, but it makes a person unable to function. The cluster headache focuses on eyes, neck, and temples. It is described as a hot branding poker rammed into the head. Its name comes from its tendency to hit quickly, one after the other.*

1. The ideas in this paragraph are organized according to which paragraph patterns?

    _____

2.   Title: _____

3.   Main Idea: _____

    _____

    _____

    _____

    _____

    _____

    _____

    _____

    _____

    _____

    _____

    _____

    _____

*From "Oh, My Aching Head" by Nancy Gottesman. *Los Angeles Magazine,* April 1984. Reprinted by permission.

C. There is good news for the 40 million American victims of killer headaches. In the past, headache sufferers, like Job, have usually resigned themselves to enduring their affliction. They assumed their headaches were caused by stress or a genetic weakness. Many thought their only choices of escape were overmedication or suicide. Better choices are now available. Pain-control clinics have sprung up all over the country to diagnose the type and cause of the headache before treatment is prescribed. The specialists in the clinics first diagnose the type. Is it a tension, migraine, or cluster headache? Kareem Abdul-Jabbar, the basketball star, suffered from excruciating headaches beginning at age 14. As an adult, he was afraid to drive more than 40 minutes from his home because, if a headache struck his optic nerve, he became unable to drive. His headaches were diagnosed as the most severe type, the cluster. Joan Didion, a well-known author, even wrote an essay, "The Bed," about her migraine headaches. After the type has been determined, tests are made to detect cause. Stress is thought to be a trigger rather than a cause for the headache. More likely causes are food allergies such as chocolate, red wine, milk products, or wheat. Other headaches are caused by dental problems (off-center bite or teeth clenching) or a hypoglycemic state (abnormally low blood-sugar count). Migraines in women are believed to be related to estrogen levels. Even smog is being investigated as a possible cause. Finally, treatment is based on the diagnosis of type and cause. Kareem Abdul-Jabbar's cluster headaches were relieved when he was found to be allergic to MSG (monosodium glutamate) and he simply avoided this food seasoning.*

1. The ideas in this paragraph are organized according to which paragraph patterns?

   _____

2.   Title: _____

   Main Idea: _____

   _____

   _____

   _____

   _____

   _____

   _____

   _____

   _____

---

*From "Oh, My Aching Head" by Nancy Gottesman. *Los Angeles Magazine,* April 1984. Reprinted by permission.

For each *italicized* word, choose the best meaning below.

► Long Reading 6G

1. But the average student is probably motivated by a more *tangible,* immediate, and pressuring reason—the requirement to take and pass tests.

   (a) indefinite **(b)** rewarding in money **(c)** definite **(d)** puzzling

2. This stimulation produces the energy needed to think clearly and to act with *precision* over a longer period of concentration than the daily recitation requires.

   (a) exactness **(b)** enthusiasm **(c)** quickness **(d)** sleepiness

► Long Reading 6H

3. As in objective questions, qualifying words give the question its *explicit* meaning.

   (a) vague **(b)** crude **(c)** most important **(d)** clearly stated

Do you have a negative attitude about tests? The next article offers some useful tips on preparing for a test.

Preview: *In 60 seconds or less, read the title, about half the first paragraph, all the headings and subheadings, and the last sentence.*

(1) What is the thesis? _____

_____

(2) How many major steps does this article present? _____

(3) How many minor steps? _____

Wait for a signal from your instructor. Then start reading the article from the beginning. As you read, notice the organization of the article and how the parts explain the thesis.

Preparing for Tests

William H. Armstrong

Ideally it should be love of learning, achievement, and self-improvement that prompts all learning. But the average student is probably motivated by a more tangible, immediate, and pressuring reason—the requirement to take and pass tests. Few high school students are not concerned with the aptitude and achievement tests that they must take to get into college. Even students not planning to attend college will take placement, adaptability, and promotion tests if they are to succeed in their field. Promotion in the armed services does not depend on physical prowess and length of service. It depends, instead, on the ability to study and pass promotional tests. You need to understand the importance of tests, the best methods of preparation, the common sense required for both a physical and mental approach to them, how to read instructions and questions correctly, and how to answer the way the test or teacher expects you to answer. Then you will have acquired the meaning and feeling for tests. This is one of the most valuable psychological benefits that can come from your education.

Attitude Toward Tests

Dr. Francis P. Robinson in his book, *Effective Study*, poses this question: "Did you ever thank a teacher for giving a test?" At first glance you are not likely to find much in your thinking that would help inspire a "yes." The teacher spends a lot of time preparing the test questions. After you have taken the test, the teacher spends many hours carefully evaluating your paper. Mistakes are marked so that when your paper is returned you can go over them and perhaps write in corrections. Then you will not make the same mistakes again.

Tests as a Personal Battle

Do you, like many of your fellow students, consider the test or examination as a personal battle which the teacher wages in an attempt to defeat you, or do you see it as a contest in which one tries to outwit the other? If this is your attitude toward tests, you probably do one of two things when the teacher returns your paper to you. One, you throw it away without bothering to do more than glance through it to see where points were taken off. Or two, without checking an incomplete answer against the facts as studied, you approach the teacher and demand to know why points were taken off. This is the most negative of approaches. The difference in attitude can be seen in the difference between two questions: "Why did you take off points on this question?" and "What should I have included that I did not?"

Fear of Taking Tests

Another attitude that you should avoid is that of fear. Fear of taking tests results in tension and disturbed thinking. These, in turn, produce blind spots (not being able to remember answers that you knew ten minutes before the test) and careless mistakes. This fear also keeps people from venturing into new areas in life. They may visualize the new method, the better tool, or the strong bridge, but they hesitate until someone else realizes their dreams.

Fear prevents success on tests and examinations because fear conditions the mind for failure. Students who are afraid start in a state of confusion and disorder. Thus they throw away the advantages they have gotten by preparation. Students who approach tests with fear are almost always characterized by the following: (1) Their grade is considerably lower than their daily recitation grades, sometimes as much as twenty points lower. (2) They complain about the teacher—insufficient explanation, lack of detailed review, etc. (3) They find fault with the test material—too long, not the type of questions expected and studied for, didn't understand the wording of questions. For example, they read the word *muckrakers* instead of *mugwumps* and missed the whole point. (4) Their preparation consists of a frantic last-ditch effort. They suffer from loss of sleep almost to the point of total exhaustion, and often loss of important notes or review material just when they were needed most. (5) Fear drives these students to study for the test with another student. Invariably they choose a study companion who has the same attitude of fear. Often the other student's knowledge of the subject is only equal to, or perhaps less than, their own.

If you recognize two or more of these characteristics as behavior patterns which you practice at test and examination time, you should change your attitude as quickly as possible. To continue them is to subject yourself to a climate of tension and fear and to condition yourself for defeat.

A Positive Approach to Tests

A third attitude is wholly positive. It is the attitude of challenge, self-confidence, and content-reliability. Students who accept a test as a challenge to show the teacher the extent of their knowledge of the subject and to improve their grades are stimulated. This stimulation produces the energy needed to think clearly and to act with precision over a longer period of concentration than the daily recitation requires. The attitude of challenge is reflected by enterprising rather than burdensome preparation. Self-confidence develops from this adequate preparation. There is no room for tension and fear. Even a questionable answer is approached by a calculated reliability. The belief is that a worthwhile answer, although perhaps only partially correct, can be worked out. This attitude requires the relationship between student and teacher, and question and answer, always to be one of cooperative production rather than competitive destruction.

To adopt an attitude of challenge and self-confidence toward tests and examinations, you must first understand the real purposes of tests.

Reasons for Tests

Motivation

From the student's point of view, the first reason for tests is motivation. Few of us are self-disciplined and motivated enough to educate ourselves without direction and requirement. Being tested periodically on accumulated knowledge is a strong motivating force.

Chance to Show Knowledge

A second reason for tests is that they provide students with a chance to show how much they have learned. Daily recitation does not provide such an opportunity. A test gives the students a chance to show their ability to organize and unify large volumes of material. This is not possible in preparing for day-to-day assignments.

Prediction of Future Tests

A third reason is that students gain insight into what the teacher considers most important. If test questions deal with main topics and essential principles, the student can accurately estimate the nature of future and larger tests.

Discovery of Weaknesses and Progress

A fourth important reason is that students can discover both their shortcomings and the extent of their progress. They can carefully study their errors and the general areas in which they occur. They can see a pattern to their errors. Do they have difficulty in reading questions? Do they take sufficient notes? Do they catch important review hints in class? Then they can take steps to correct their weaknesses. They can also measure their progress in writing, their ability to organize ideas and record them rapidly. And, most significant of all, they can measure whether or not their mental growth is keeping up with the demand of the subject.

Experience in Making Decisions

The fifth reason for tests is that they form one of the most important learning processes. They require students to make decisions on how to use time, interpret facts, discriminate between essential and supporting ideas, and reasonably distribute time and ideas. Indeed, we may call tests mind-stretchers. . . .

Now that you understand the reasons for tests and examinations, and how they benefit both student and teacher, you should not groan when a test is announced. Do not approach it as a burdensome chore or with light indifference. Approach it with an honest and determined effort for self-improvement. If you manage this, your grade will manage itself.*

TOTAL READING TIME _____

Immediately answer the following question without referring to the selection.

1. Of the four following points, one is first level (important) detail, and three are second level (supporting) details. Which is the first level detail?

    (a) Students need to overcome the fear of taking tests.

    (b) Taking tests helps motivation to learn.

    (c) Students need to understand the reasons for taking tests.

    (d) Taking tests provides experience in making decisions.

2. Write a sentence outline reflecting the organization and most important points of the article. You may refer to the reading selection, but use your own words as much as possible.

    _____

    _____

    _____

    _____

    _____

    _____

    _____

    _____

    _____

    _____

    _____

---

*From *Study Tips: How to Study Effectively and Get Better Grades,* Armstrong and Lampe II © 1975, 1983, Barron's Educational Series, Inc., Hauppauge, N.Y. Reprinted by permission.

_____

_____

_____

_____

_____

_____

_____

_____

_____

_____

_____

_____

_____

Check your answer for the question and your outline with the key in the back of the book. (There will be no comprehension score.) Then turn to the Rate Chart in the Appendix to find your words per minute for this selection. Finally, record your WPM score below and on the progress chart in the Appendix.

WORDS PER MINUTE _____

Do you get a mental block when you take a test? Are you confused by the different types of tests? If so, the test-taking tips in the next article should give you confidence.
Preview: *In one minute or less, read the title, the headings, the first paragraph under each heading, and the first sentence to the right of each number.*

(1) Define objective tests: _____

_____

(2) Define subjective tests: _____

_____

Wait for a signal from your instructor. Then start reading the article from the beginning. As you read, notice again how it is organized, and concentrate on remembering the suggestions.

Taking Tests

William H. Armstrong

Tests are generally two kinds: objective and subjective.

Objective Tests

Objective, or short-answer, tests require you to recognize correct answers among incorrect ones, or true statements set beside false ones. Objective tests also measure your ability to recall details. Objective questions are usually one of the following types: (1) Recall (filling in blanks); (2) Recognition (multiple choice, true and false, and matching). . . .

Here are some things that you should consider in approaching objective tests:

1. Pay particular attention to mechanical instructions; that is, instructions which tell you *where* and *how* to answer questions. Wrong position may result in wrong answers. In any case, answering in ways other than that required may cause the teacher difficulty in grading your paper. Some teachers take off points for not following instructions.

2. The questions are usually numerous; sometimes you do not have to answer all of them. Always answer the questions that you know first and come back to any that you wish to spend time on.

3. Read certain types of objective questions (particularly True-False) so that you observe all qualifying words. These words—*usually, always, most, never, some*—give insight into when and under what conditions a statement is or is not correct. Modifiers play their most important role in True-False questions.

4. All objective questions require correct reading. Don't let your own opinions cause you to read into the question a word that is not

there. This results in wrong answers, and after the examination you say, "But I thought the question was."

5. Do not change answers too quickly as you check your test before turning it in. Your first answer is the more reliable unless you are absolutely sure you have made a mistake. If there is any doubt, leave the first answer.

6. Do not think that neatness and order can be ignored on objective tests. Words and numbers can be written sloppily or neatly. Neatness begins with the first blank you fill and ends with the way you sign your name.

Subjective Tests

The second kind of test, the subjective, demands more of the student in both recalling and organizing subject matter. These are usually called "essay" tests. They may be short-answer questions (a paragraph) or discussion questions (a lengthy essay that measures the student's entire scope of knowledge on a particular part of the course). The word "subjective" implies that this kind of examination is more personal than the objective test. It provides students with a greater opportunity to show the extent of their preparation. It also provides the teacher with a chance to make more personal judgments in evaluating the paper. For this reason you should think in terms of what judgment you would make of your answers if you were the teacher.

Essay tests measure your ability to recall what you have learned and organize it intelligently. You must write clearly and with meaningful interpretation, selection, or application, depending upon what is asked for by the question. The first and most important thing to remember about essay examination questions is that there is no such thing as a *general answer.*

You can write successful essay tests by practicing a few *must* requirements:

1. Read through all the essay questions before you start to write. Essay tests demand a rather precise allotment of time for each question. On many discussion questions you can write much more than time allows. Therefore, a sketchy outline is almost a necessity in alloting the time needed for each question. If you recognize key words pertaining to the answer at the first reading, write them in the margin as future aids to recall.

2. When you are ready to answer the first question, write the time alloted to it in the margin of your paper. Then read the question to determine exactly what it asks you to do and what instructions are included for doing it. If the question asks for Alexander's spiritual legacy, it is a waste of time to describe the physical legacy. That is, do not discuss the army, devoted generals, etc., he received from his father. As in objective questions, qualifying words give the question its explicit meaning. Yet some students read words which are not there into questions. The student who reads *muckrakers* instead of *mugwumps* may write a beautiful answer, but he will get no credit. He answered a question that wasn't asked. The qualifying words of a question are really the directions

for answering it. A record of careless mistakes on tests and examinations made by students at Kent School over a five-year period showed that carelessness in reading the question was responsible for 64% of all careless mistakes.

3. Read the question a second time to determine the steps you will take in writing a quality answer. Decide what amount of material is needed to produce a complete answer. Be sure your answer is not so brief that you exclude important details nor so wordy that you make rambling generalizations. This is the time to complete the mental or key-word outline that you began at your initial reading of the tests. Mentally blueprint the arrangement, significance, and accuracy of topics and accompanying details. Visualize an effective opening statement. If possible, restate part of the question. Never start an answer with a pronoun without an antecedent. Two such beginnings, fatal to a good mark but often used, are: "It is when" and "It is because." Always make the subject of the question the subject of your answer. As you read the question for the second time you must constantly watch for anything that will give your answer an element of vagueness.

4. As you write your answer keep in mind the teacher's preference for style of presentation and use of illustrations to show understanding. What would the teacher consider a model answer? If the teacher has complimented you on earlier test papers for the way you handled an answer, try to apply this method to as many questions as possible. Ask yourself the question, "What is the teacher's aim in this particular question?" Make your paper easy to grade. Use signal words and numerals to introduce important facts and series. Number questions to the left of the red margin and skip one or two lines between answers. Remember that the neatly written paper has fewer mistakes and is easier for the teacher to grade.

5. Concentrate on one question at a time and use a mental system of numbering important points in your answer. Students often "overwrite" or "write away from" questions because they jump ahead and are thinking of a question to come. The teacher has not asked questions which require repeating subject matter, so be careful to keep all answers within the limits set by the questions. An excellent method for avoiding generalizations and worthless "padding" is to mentally number important points as you write them down. Illustrations, specific elaboration, important facts, and explanations to clarify your understanding of a definition or event are all necessary parts of a good essay answer. If you number important items mentally as you write, you will see the difference between what has value (and will add to your grade) and what is worthless.

6. Check over the completed examination paper before you turn it in and after it has been graded and returned to you. You should reserve ten minutes of each examination hour for checking after you have completed the writing. Check for mechanical errors and obvious factual mistakes such as wrong words, incorrect conclusions, transposed characters, etc. As with objective tests, do not change anything in an answer unless you are absolutely sure it is wrong. Rely on your first impression.

You can learn much about writing better examinations and using better methods of study by going over the graded paper after it has been returned. By checking against your book you can see what you omitted that the teacher considered important. You can see how you misinterpreted the qualifying word in a question. If you note such errors carefully, you will not repeat them on the next test.*

TOTAL READING TIME _____

Answer question 1 without referring to the selection.

1. One of the four following points is a first level (important) detail, and three are second level (supporting) details. Which is the first level detail?

   (a) Do not change answers too quickly before turning in your test.

   (b) Read through all essay questions before you start to write.

   (c) When questions are numerous, first answer the questions you know.

   (d) Subjective tests require both recalling and organizing the subject matter.

2. Write a sentence outline reflecting the organization and most important points of the article. You may refer to the reading selection, but use your own words as much as possible.

   _____

   _____

   _____

   _____

   _____

   _____

   _____

   _____

   _____

   _____

   _____

   _____

   _____

   _____

   _____

   _____

   _____

   _____

*From *Study Tips: How to Study Effectively and Get Better Grades,* Armstrong and Lampe II © 1975, 1983, Barron's Educational Series, Inc., Hauppauge, N.Y. Reprinted by permission.

_____

_____

_____

_____

_____

_____

_____

_____

_____

_____

_____

_____

_____

_____

_____

_____

_____

Check your answer for the question and your outline with the key in the back of the book. (There will be no comprehension score.) Then turn to the Rate Chart in the Appendix to find your words per minute for this selection. Finally, record your WPM score below and on the progress chart in the Appendix.

WORDS PER MINUTE _____

Another key skill in reading and writing is the ability to summarize accurately. A summary is a brief restatement of the main points in something you read or hear. In certain ways, a summary is like an outline. It contains the author's most important points about a topic. It also has supporting details where necessary to clarify a point. But a summary appears in the form of a paragraph or essay, not in the numbered form of an outline.

1. Working as a team with the person sitting next to you, first list the important points in one of the reading selections in this Lesson. Then, working by yourself, use this list to write a one-page summary in your own words. Use supporting details if a point is not clear without it. **Writing tip:** to keep your sentences from sounding choppy, use transitions as you move from one point to the next. (Examples of transitions you may need to use include: *also, in addition, second, next, however, for example.*)

2. Reread any of the selections in Lessons 1 through 6, and write a one-half to one-page summary.

7

Using P R O— How the Pros Study–Read

IN THIS LESSON, YOU WILL

1. continue perception and comprehension exercises;

2. learn a method for active and aggressive study-reading (*PRO* = prepare-read-organize);

3. Using the previewing and outlining steps, apply the *PRO* method to two long articles.

► *Exercise 7A—Phrase Perception*

Pick out the phrase identical to the key phrase.

Key Phrase

1.	a big mouth	an ugly mule	a birch tree	a big mouth
2.	to commence	to comprehend	to commence	too common
3.	a sweet child	a sweet child	a crafty swindle	a black phone
4.	in a circle	inner circle	in a circle	on the clock
5.	the valley below	below the rail	the vast lot	the valley below
6.	bright metal	bright metal	right pedal	night patrol
7.	pack a lunch	poke a bunch	punch a back	pack a lunch
8.	the center ring	the ringing bell	the center ring	the round cell
9.	long road	right load	long road	large reed
10.	the white rose	the wheat roll	the long wait	the white rose
11.	a good life	a good life	a dog's life	a loud ghoul
12.	five fingers	four ringers	live stingers	five fingers
13.	vanity fair	valiant four	vanity fair	vain fear
14.	make sad	make sad	make mad	fake size
15.	rather thin	rather thin	neither tin	rather tan
16.	to be prompt	to see beans	to be fast	to be prompt
17.	really famished	really finished	really famished	real family
18.	to remain home	to remain home	the real hustle	to sail away
19.	given a box	given a fox	liven a room	given a box
20.	insert something	omit something	serve things	insert something

TIME _____

ERRORS _____

► *Exercise 7B—Phrase Perception*

Pick out the phrase identical to the key phrase.

Key Phrase

1. beneath contempt   beneath contempt   corrupt benefactor   bent cantilever

2. written orders   white orbs   written orders   bitten partner

3. catching fish   scratching dishes   catching fish   matching wish

4. around ten   arid land   round fin   around ten

5. near distraction   near distraction   traction gears   need affection

6. in the dark   in the dark   on a lark   in a shark

7. typed letter   typical setter   typed letter   better types

8. having been right   being half bright   have frightened   having been right

9. neither vase   either face   neither vase   nether regions

10. every airline   very aimless   every airline   level airfield

11. thrifty husband   thrifty husband   shifty human   mighty hungry

12. sounding the alarm   selling the alcohol   pounding the album   sounding the alarm

13. frustrated teacher   frustrated teacher   fraternity brother   frumpish dresser

14. tea for three   two for tea   for the tease   tea for three

15. knitted sweater   knitted sweater   swift kite   knifed swine

16. running fawn   ruining fast   running fawn   routine feast

17. losing the pen   losing the pen   loading the wren   penning the letter

18. take the plunge   lunge at cake   rake the plume   take the plunge

19. of another planet   of another planet   the onerous plot   to smother ants

20. frantic searcher   fast runner   funny antics   frantic searcher

TIME _____

ERRORS _____

► *Exercise 7C—Word Comprehension*

Choose the word closest in meaning to the key word in **boldface** print

Key Word

1.	its **myriad** colors	visible	few	many
2.	his **erratic** behavior	irregular	evil	conforming
3.	to be **oriented** to school	turned off	adjusted	confused
4.	to **concur** with the choice	disagree	approve	agree
5.	to **peruse** the book	scrutinize	pursue	ignore
6.	**inherent** in people	accidental	educated	inborn
7.	to reach his **aspiration**	shelf	goal	high note
8.	a strict **regime**	parent	ruler	system
9.	a **tentative** date	conditional	definite	later
10.	an **affable** manner	disagreeable	friendly	crude
11.	a **fervent** courtship	listless	romantic	intense
12.	a clever **ruse**	trick	thought	reply
13.	to **replenish** the food	remove	resupply	devour
14.	a **virile** mate	masculine	feminine	virginal
15.	the **vanguard** of the army	rear	middle	front
16.	the **zenith** of her career	high point	bottom	satisfaction
17.	feeling **distraught**	unruffled	troubled	distant
18.	a **bizarre** story	commonplace	market	grotesque
19.	a **gullible** listener	trusting	suspicious	inattentive
20.	to **deter** from proceeding	encourage	prevent	observe

TIME _____

ERRORS _____

► *Exercise 7D—Word Comprehension*

Choose the word closest in meaning to the key word in **boldface** print.

Key Word

1.	to **diffuse** the dye	erase	disperse	darken
2.	a **rigorous** schedule	difficult	useless	relaxed
3.	a **versatile** device	limited	many-sided	useless
4.	a creative **innovation**	result	tradition	change
5.	a grassy **knoll**	small hill	large yard	hole
6.	a **flagrant** sin	subtle	condemned	bold
7.	a **regimen** of exercise	need	system	place
8.	to **perpetrate** a crime	stop	assist	commit
9.	a **lethal** weapon	deadly	illegal	hidden
10.	an **ominous** sign	promising	grim	confusing
11.	to be **condescending**	calculating	praiseworthy	patronizing
12.	an **incredulous** crowd	unbelieving	trusting	rowdy
13.	to **deviate** from the point	look	digress	measure
14.	a wise **mentor**	slave	employer	adviser
15.	to **accost** a stranger	approach	avoid	fear
16.	**derelict** in one's duty	careful	neglectful	dangerous
17.	an **inane** remark	animated	profound	foolish
18.	an **ambiguous** answer	clear	obscure	blasphemous
19.	a **candid** interview	frank	evasive	ill-humored
20.	acting with **propriety**	bad manners	suitability	unfitness

TIME _____

ERRORS _____

► *Exercise 7E—Phrase Comprehension*

Pick out the phrase that means the same as the key phrase.

Key Phrase

1.	endorsing someone	acquired holiday	giving approval to	red sails in sunset
2.	making a living	by hook or crook	something unknown	earning income
3.	a pile of debris	a stack of wastes	a nursery for children	cruel judge
4.	denied the privilege	overly dressed	barred opportunity	is equal to
5.	a loving caress	a good human	highly concentrated	an affectionate hug
6.	his greatest error	perhaps others do	locked in the barn	his biggest mistake
7.	deluged by gifts	off the side	glutted with presents	never alone
8.	an array of food	a variety of edibles	lovely tablecloth	let do
9.	an inoculation	for the aged	to set free	measles shot
10.	a lofty human	the story of	a noble person	in every way
11.	be flustered	be confused	bright luster	chair backs
12.	wretched behavior	empty out	awful conduct	experience pain
13.	a probing mind	a searching intelligence	run for your life	body and soul
14.	perturbing episode	in low esteem	a great outcry	unsettling experience
15.	a happy jaunt	pleasant and cheerful	a gay journey	more later
16.	raging controversy	arena in which	a motive for	a serious conflict
17.	guilty culprit	the offender	display kindness	bravery and faith
18.	anticipated wedding	running for office	foreseen marriage	one day
19.	hectic party	in all events	hallowed grounds	wild get-together
20.	extinct creature	vanished dinosaur	down the hatch	large animal

TIME _____

ERRORS _____

► Exercise 7F—Phrase Comprehension

Pick out the phrase that means the same as the key phrase.

Key Phrase

1. harboring guilts	free parking	feeling of remorse	a safe port
2. a positive answer	to reply yes	a double negative	a light statement
3. to quench thirst	to squeeze hard	satisfy need for drink	rain water
4. to happen biannually	late blooming flower	a year of accidents	twice-a-year event
5. a supplementary note	a friendly letter	additional statement	vagabond lover
6. accumulating wealth	losing one's money	becoming rich	birds flying south
7. potentially explosive	might blow up	the fertile land	a wet firecracker
8. an array of flowers	ring around the rosy	an army of soldiers	abundance of flora
9. a soft caress	a light stroke	a rough touch	the right handle
10. a biographical novel	a scientific lecture	book about someone else	the study of bugs
11. survival of the fittest	tight-fitting sweater	endurance of the best	gasping for breath
12. a haughty manner	a high position	a good etiquette	snobbish behavior
13. inquisitive glance	facial masque	questioning look	poker face
14. unexpected betrayal	southern exposure	surprise treachery	unlocked gate
15. uncanny power	extraordinary ability	not often right	a penthouse suite
16. toeing the line	behaving properly	a sore foot	parallel bars
17. a loud uproar	a roaring lion	a noisy disturbance	out with a bang
18. boost the morale	a booster shot	a moral dilemma	uplift mental condition
19. eating with relish	a clean radish	a good appetite	a picky eater
20. horrid disease	case of measles	under the sickbed	disgusting illness

TIME _____

ERRORS _____

1. **Prepare**

2. **Read**

3. **Organize**

The two readings in this Lesson are different from others in this book in that they are to be "studied," not read to build speed. They were chosen to give you practice in an effective method of studying a textbook: PRO. This method provides more flexibility than most study formulas because you can modify it to fit your purpose and time limits.

Studying passively — Most untrained students begin a reading assignment in a textbook "cold." By that we mean they begin reading the first word of the material and continue passively, until they reach the last word. They read without system, without questioning, without much interest. Result: They often finish reading without any idea of what they have read.

So they reread, again passively. Or they may this time mark everything they guess is important with a felt-tip pen. We have all seen these "yellow pages"; almost every line has been highlighted. No distinction has been made between major and minor points. They still cannot recite the content in any organized way. Perhaps they cannot recite any point because it has no meaning for them. Usually they complain, "I just can't get into this subject" or "I study and study but I can't remember any of it."

Studying actively — If this sounds like you, then try the PRO method. It forces you to study actively, to test yourself. It forces you to organize your thoughts before, during, and after you read—to organize in your own words.

Before you begin study-reading, set your goals. Select a study unit that you know you can "read and absorb" in the time available. A unit should be any clearly marked section of your book, such as one chapter or the pages between two large headings. You must allow time for all three steps in this study period.

Now for the PRO method itself. Learn the steps and practice them on the two readings in this Lesson. Much of what you have already learned in the first six Lessons (particularly about finding the main idea and outlining) will be useful in this study technique. Remember that you will be a PRO—a professional student— only if you learn to use the method with your other course work. Naturally, you should use common sense in adapting it to fit various fields, types of textbooks, and time limitations.

Step 1. P = Prepare

This step will bring to light the topic and main ideas. Some experts call this first step *prereading, preview, survey,* or *overview.* You have been practicing this on every Short and Long Reading. Whatever you call it, it means to read selectively and aggressively—and to skip selectively. Preparing gives you some background on your reading material so you don't have to read it "cold." It makes you think. It arouses your interest and makes your mind receptive. The idea is to "start with the large" before you "fill in the small." See the skeleton, the major patterns. What logic pattern holds the ideas together? Is it "addition"? Is it "cause and effect"? See the whole so the parts will have meaning for you.

Steps for preparing — First, **look over the unit to be studied.** Consider carefully the title or chapter heading, the author, and subheadings (or subtitles—used to indicate divisions within the unit). Become familiar with any system of print or numbering used to show the importance and relationships of the subheadings. Note size, color, and position of subheadings. Are they in boldface print or italics? (Examine the system used in this article.) Next, read the introduction or first paragraph. Then read the first one or two sentences underneath each subheading (or in each paragraph if you have time). Remember that these first sentences usually contain the topic sentences. Finally, read the summary or last paragraph. If time permits, look over illustrations, charts, graphs, and questions at the end of the unit.

Second, **stop to digest the information you know at this point.** Think over what you have surveyed. In 70 to 90 percent of most informative prose you will have a good idea of the general content. You will know the author's topic, main idea, and important supporting ideas (or first level details). You should also have picked up some idea of the author's organization. Do you remember many details? If you do, you were not selective enough in your skipping. Don't read the details until Step 2.

Third, to prepare even more aggressively, **ask yourself questions about your preview.** What does the title or topic mean? How many subdivisions are there? How do these develop the author's main idea? How much of this do I know already? How does the knowledge fit into the course? Into my life? At the very least, mentally turn the title and subheadings themselves into questions. Or you might jot down a list of the questions—perhaps some questions that might appear on a test. For really effec-
Beginning an outline tive studying, you can write the questions down as the first stage of a rough outline. But leave room between each question for important notes you will fill in after you actually read the unit.

Step 1—Prepare—enables you to approach the actual reading with an inquiring mind. It forces you to become involved with the subject, even though you may think you have no interest in it.

Step 2. R = Read

No stopping **Read through the entire study unit without stopping,** from the title or section heading to the end. As you read, relate the main ideas to the supporting details. Allow what you know about the author's organization or framework to aid you. Keep a pencil in your hand to check quickly important ideas as you read. But do not stop to underline or take notes. This will interrupt your train of thought. Save your underlining and notetaking for Step 3.

Step 3. O = Organize

Finally, to make the most of the first two steps, you must organize the information you have previewed and read.

First, **digest what you have read** to firmly implant the most important ideas in your memory. "How" you digest depends on the subject matter and your needs. It also depends on your ability to organize your thoughts mentally, orally, or on paper. At the very least, go over in your thoughts what you have read; that is, repeat the main points to yourself. A more effective way is to tell someone else, perhaps another student with whom you are studying. This forces you to clarify your thoughts even more.

Finishing the outline Second, the most effective way to organize your thoughts is to **take notes or write an outline.** If you started the framework of an outline in Step 1, you might now fill in the supporting details. How many of your questions from Step 1 were answered? Show by labeling and indenting the difference between first, second, third (and fourth, if necessary) level details. (Use the size and type of print of the subheadings as clues to what you should label and indent.) Do not use the author's words; use your own. You have not learned anything unless you can tell it in your own words. The key to a good study outline is to be brief but specific. (Hint: in your notebook, save a blank page opposite your outline for the teacher's lecture notes on that unit.)

Third, immediately review the material you have organized. This can make the difference between a B or an A on a test. Skim (but do not reread) quickly through the study unit again. Look for any important material you may have remembered wrong or forgotten entirely. Change or add to your outline. Stress what the author seems to stress. Add the teacher's notes to your outline. (If you want to be a model student, retype your outline and incorporate the teacher's lecture notes.) Since by now you really know what is important and what is not, this is the time to underline or mark in your text or notes. Mark sparingly, no more than once per paragraph (and often less). Make flash cards for any facts, terms, or names you need to memorize. Try answering the questions you formulated in Step 1. Or formulate new questions and practice answering them.

As a way of organizing what you have just read, try to outline these few pages explaining the PRO method. Note how easily it lends itself to outlining.

When you try the PRO method on the two reading selections in this Lesson, follow the directions exactly, even if they seem slow and awkward at first. You need to be aggressive, intelligent, and directed in this hardest reading task of all—study-reading.

Theme: The Sciences

The root of the word "science" means *to know.* The word still carries that original idea of seeking knowledge. It implies a curiosity in the world around us and a desire to know and understand. The two Long Readings in this Lesson, taken from a college communications text book, are typical of those you might be asked to study-read in social science courses.

Words in Context

For each *italicized* word, choose the best meaning below.

▶ *Long Reading 7G*

1. If your health is being *jeopardized* by the cigarette smoke from someone nearby, you are clearly punishing yourself by remaining silent.

   (a) improved **(b)** endangered **(c)** irritated **(d)** changed

2. This *amiable* façade or appearance eventually crumbles, leaving the crazy-maker's victim confused and angry at having been fooled. [Extra Clue: *Ami* means *friend.*]

   (a) grouchy **(b)** tricky **(c)** beautiful but evil **(d)** pleasant and friendly

▶ *Long Reading 7H*

3. In a less admirable way, indirectly aggressive crazymakers can defeat their partners by inducing guilt, avoiding issues, withholding desired behaviors, *pseudo-accommodating,* and so on. [Extra Clue: *Pseudo* means *false.*]

   (a) being secretive **(b)** pretending to be helpful **(c)** pouting **(d)** damaging someone's reputation

4. It would seem only justifiable to *coerce* others into behaving as we think they should in the most extreme circumstances.

   (a) force **(b)** persuade **(c)** bribe **(d)** tease

Apply the PRO Method to the Next Long Reading

▶ Step 1. P = Prepare

Preview or survey the title, author's name, and subheadings. (You might want to copy them in the space on page 171, as if you were beginning an outline. If so, skip a couple of lines between each subheading to leave room for details to be filled in after reading the selection.) Next, read the first and last sentences following each subheading. Think over the first level details and the organization of the article. Finally, ask yourself how the subheadings explain the topic of the articles. Formulate at least one question for each subheading—a question you think will be answered in the reading selection. Jot down the questions on some scratch paper. (Or you might make the questions a part of your outline on page 172 by writing them indented below the appropriate subheadings.) Now you are prepared to read the selection.

This first social science article explains how people react to conflicts with other people.

Study-read the selection carefully, continuing to use the PRO method. Do not stop to underline or take notes. Wait for a signal from your instructor before you begin reading.

Interpersonal Conflict

Ronald B. Adler and Neil Towne

Conflict is Natural

Without exception *every* relationship of any depth at all has conflict. No matter how close, how understanding, how compatible you are, there will be times when your ideas or actions or needs or goals won't match those of others around you. You like rock music, but your companions prefer Beethoven. You want to date other people, but your partner wants to keep the relationship exclusive. You think a paper you've done is fine, but your instructor wants it changed. You like to sleep in on Sunday mornings, but your roommate likes to play the stereo—loudly! There's no end to the number or kinds of disagreements that are possible. . . .

How can facing up to problems and disagreements bring people together? How can feelings like anger and hurt make a relationship stronger? . . . The first step is to take a look at some of the present ways you handle conflict.

Styles of Conflict

There are four ways in which people can act when their needs aren't met. Each one has very different characteristics, as we can show by describing a common problem. At one time or another almost everyone has been bothered by a neighbor's barking dog. You know the story. Every passing car, distant siren, pedestrian, and falling leaf seems to set off a fit of barking that leaves you unable to sleep, socialize, or study. By describing the possible ways of handling this kind of situation, the differences between *nonassertive, directly aggressive, indirectly aggressive,* and *assertive behavior* should become clear.

Nonassertive Behavior

There are two ways in which nonasserters manage a conflict. *Sometimes they ignore their needs.* Faced with the dog, for instance, a nonassertive person would try to forget the barking by closing the windows and trying to concentrate even harder. Another form of denial would be to claim that no problem exists—that a little barking never bothered anyone. To the degree that it's possible to make problems disappear by ignoring them, such an approach is probably advisable. In many cases, however, it simply isn't realistic to claim that nothing is wrong. For instance, if your health is being jeopardized by the cigarette smoke from someone nearby, you are clearly punishing yourself by remaining silent. In all these and many more cases simply pretending that nothing is the matter when your needs continue to go unmet is clearly not the answer.

A second nonassertive course of action is to acknowledge your needs are not being met and simply to accept the situation. The hope is that it might clear up without any action on your part. You could, for instance, wait for the neighbor who owns the barking dog to move. You could wait for the dog to be run over by a passing car or to die of old age. You could hope that your neighbor will realize how noisy the dog is and do something to keep it quiet. Each of these is a possibility, of course, but it would be unrealistic to count on one of them to solve your problem. And even if by chance you were lucky enough for the dog problem to be solved without taking action, you couldn't expect to be so fortunate in other parts of your life.

In addition, while waiting for one of these outcomes, you would undoubtedly grow more and more angry at your neighbor. A friendly relationship between the two of you would be impossible. You would also lose a degree of self-respect, since you would see yourself as the kind of person who can't cope with even a common everyday irritation. Clearly, nonassertion is not a very satisfying course of action—either in this case or in other instances.

Direct Aggression

Where the nonasserter underreacts, *a directly aggressive person overreacts.* The usual consequences of aggressive behaviors are anger and defensiveness or hurt and humiliation. In either case aggressive people build themselves up at the expense of others.

You could handle the dog problem with direct aggression by loudly confronting your neighbors. You could call them names and threaten to call the dogcatcher the next time you see their hound running loose. If the town in which you live has a leash law, you would be within your legal rights to do so.

Thus you would gain your goal of bringing peace and quiet to the neighborhood. Unfortunately, your direct aggression would have other, less productive results. Your neighbors and you would probably cease to be on speaking terms. You could expect a complaint from them the first time you violated even the most minor city ordinance. If you live in the neighborhood for any time at all, this state of hostilities isn't very appealing.

Indirect Aggression

In several of his works psychologist George Bach describes behavior that he terms "crazymaking." *Crazymaking occurs when people have feelings of resentment, anger, or rage that they are unable or unwilling to express directly.* Instead of keeping these feelings to themselves, the crazymakers send these aggressive messages in subtle, indirect ways, thus maintaining the front of kindness. This amiable façade eventually crumbles, however, leaving the crazymaker's victim confused and angry at having been fooled. The targets of the crazymaker can either react with aggressive behavior of their own or retreat to nurse their hurt feelings. In either case indirect aggression seldom has anything but harmful effects on a relationship.

What's your conflict style? To give you a better idea of some unproductive ways you may be handling your conflicts, we'll describe some typical conflict behaviors that can weaken relationships. In our survey we'll follow the fascinating work of George Bach, a leading authority on conflict and communication.

Bach explains that there are two types of aggression—clean fighting and dirty fighting. Either because they can't or won't express their feelings openly and constructively, dirty fighters sometimes resort to "crazymaking" techniques to vent their resentments. Instead of openly and caringly expressing their emotions, crazymakers (often unconsciously) use a variety of indirect tricks to get at their opponent. Because these "sneak attacks" don't usually get to the root of the problem, and because of their power to create a great deal of hurt, crazymakers can destroy communication. Let's take a look at some of them.

Types of Crazymakers

a. The *avoider* refuses to fight. When a conflict arises, he'll leave, fall asleep, pretend to be busy at work, or keep from facing the problem in some other way. This behavior makes it very difficult for the partner to express his feelings of anger, hurt, etc., because the avoider won't fight back. Arguing with an avoider is like trying to box with a person who won't even put up his gloves.

b. Instead of saying straight out that she doesn't want or approve of something, the *guiltmaker* tries to change her partner's behavior by making him feel responsible for causing pain. The guiltmaker's favorite line is, "It's o.k., don't worry about me...." (with a big sigh).

c. Rather than come out and express his feelings about the object of his dissatisfaction, the *distracter* attacks other parts of his partner's life. Thus he never has to share what's really on his mind and can avoid dealing with painful parts of his relationship.

d. This person doesn't respond immediately when she's angry. Instead, she puts her resentment into her gunnysack. After a while it begins to bulge with large and small gripes. Then, when the sack is about to burst, the *gunnysacker* pours out all her pent-up aggressions on the overwhelmed and unsuspecting victim.

e. Instead of honestly sharing his resentments, the *trivial tyrannizer* does things he knows will get his partner's goat—leaving dirty dishes in the sink, clipping his fingernails in bed, belching out loud, turning up the television too loud, and so on.

f. Because she's afraid to face conflicts squarely, the *joker* kids around when her partner wants to be serious, thus blocking the expression of important feelings....

g. The *contract tyrannizer* will not allow his relationship to change from the way it once was. Whatever the agreements the partners had as to roles and responsibilities at one time, they'll remain unchanged. "It's your job to . . . feed the baby, wash the dishes, discipline the kids. . . ."

h. The *kitchen sink fighter* is so named because in an argument he brings up things that are totally off the subject ("everything but the kitchen sink"): the way his partner behaved last New Year's Eve, the unbalanced checkbook, bad breath—anything.

Assertion

Assertive people handle conflicts skillfully by expressing their needs, thoughts, and feelings clearly and directly. But they do not need to judge others or dictate to them. They have the attitude that most of the time it is possible to resolve problems to everyone's satisfaction. Possessing this attitude and the skills to bring it about doesn't guarantee that assertive people will always get what they want. It does, however, give them the best chance of doing so. An additional benefit of such an approach is that whether or not it satisfies a particular need, it maintains the self-respect of both the asserters and those with whom they interact.

An assertive course of action in the case of the barking dog would be to wait a few days to make sure that the noise is not just a fluke. If things continue in the present way, you could introduce yourself to your neighbors and explain your problem. You could tell them that although they might not notice it, the dog often plays in the street and keeps barking at passing cars. You could tell them why this behavior bothers you. It keeps you awake at night and makes it hard for you to do your work. You could point out that you don't want to be a grouch and call the pound. Rather than behaving in these ways, you could tell them that you've come to see what kind of solution you can find that will satisfy both of you. This approach may not work. You might then have to decide whether it is more important to avoid bad feelings or to have peace and quiet. But the chances for a happy ending are best with this assertive approach. And no matter what happens, you can keep your self-respect by behaving directly and honestly.*

TOTAL READING TIME _____

► Step 3. O = Organize

Write a sentence outline of the article using the method you learned in Lesson 6. (Or fill in the outline you started in Step 1 with any additional details you think are important.) The labels and certain items have been provided as a clue to the organization.

Title: _____

Thesis: _____

_____

I. _____

---

*Adapted from "Interpersonal Conflict" and "Resolving Interpersonal Conflict" from *Looking Out/ Looking In,* Third Edition by Ronald Adler and Neil Towne, copyright © 1981 by Holt, Rinehart and Winston, Inc., reprinted by permission of the publisher.

II. _____

    A. _____

        1. _____

        2. _____

    B. _____

        1. _____

        2. _____

    C. _____

        1. _____

        2. _____

            a. _____   e. _____

            b. _____   f. _____

            c. _____   g. _____

            d. _____   h. _____

    D. _____

        1. _____

        2. _____

NOTE: Ask your instructor for a model outline from the *Instructor's Manual.*

Now review the article as if you were preparing for a test. Repeat your preview of the article, underlining important points. Study your outline until you are ready to take the following quiz.

► *How well did you apply the PRO method?*

Answer the questions without referring to the selection or to your outline. (Pretend that this is an important test for which you have studied.)

1. Choose the statement that best expresses the thesis.

    (a) Conflict between people cannot be avoided or satisfactorily resolved.

    (b) Of the four ways to handle conflict, assertion is the best.

    (c) Direct aggression is the best way to solve problems.

    (d) The best way to handle conflict is to keep the peace at any cost.

2. The example used in all four methods of reacting to conflict is the one involving

    (a) frequent loud parties.

    (b) people dropping by without calling.

    (c) a neighbor's barking dog.

    (d) people owing you money.

3. Nonassertive people would be most likely to call the police.   **T**   **F**

4. The directly aggressive person tends to overreact.   **T**   **F**

5. An example of direct aggression is to leave dirty dishes in the sink to show resentment.   **T**   **F**

6. An indirectly aggressive person is so kind and tactful that a relationship is usually improved by his tactics.   **T**   **F**

Name and define two types of crazymakers:

7. _____

8. _____

9. Explain how an assertive person would handle the barking dog conflict.

_____

_____

10. The assertive approach maintains the self-respect of all parties involved.   **T**   **F**

Turn to the Rate Chart in the Appendix to find your words per minute for this selection. Then, record your WPM score below and on the progress chart in the Appendix.

WORDS PER MINUTE _____

% COMPREHENSION _____

Apply the PRO Method to the Next Long Reading

► Step 1. P = Prepare

Preview or survey the title, author's name, and subheadings. (You might want to copy them in the space on page 171, as if you were beginning an outline. If so, skip a couple of lines between each subheading to leave room for details to be filled in after reading the selection.) Next, read the first and last sentences following each subheading. Think over the first level details and the organization of the article. Finally, ask yourself how the subheadings explain the topic of the article. Formulate at least one question for each subheading—a question you think will be answered in the reading selection. Jot down the questions on some scratch paper. (Or you might make the questions a part of your outline on page 171 by writing them indented below the appropriate subheadings.) Now you are prepared to read the selection below.

The next article explains how people resolve social conflicts. Study-read the following selection carefully without stopping to underline or take notes. Wait for a signal from your instructor before you begin reading.

Resolving Interpersonal Conflict

Ronald B. Adler and Neil Towne

So far, we've looked at individual styles of communication. While assertive problem-solving may be the best of these, it's obvious that not everyone uses it. Even when one person behaves assertively, there's no guarantee that others will do so. There are three quite different outcomes of the conflicts between nonassertive, indirectly aggressive, directly aggressive, and assertive people. By looking at each of them, you can decide which ones you'll seek when you find yourself facing a conflict with another person.

Win-Lose

Win-lose conflicts are ones in which one party gets what he or she wants while the other comes up short. People resort to this method of resolving disputes when they perceive a situation as being an "either-or" one. Either I get what I want or you get your way. The most clear-cut examples of win-lose situations are certain games such as baseball or poker in which the rules require a winner and a loser. Some interpersonal issues seem to fit into this win-lose framework. Examples are two coworkers seeking a promotion to the same job or a couple who disagree on how to spend their limited money.

Power is the main feature in win-lose problem solving, for it is necessary to defeat an opponent to get what you want. The most obvious kind of power is physical. Some parents threaten their children with warnings: "Stop misbehaving or I'll send you to your room." Adults who use physical power to deal with each other usually aren't so blunt, but the legal system is the implied threat: "Follow the rules or we'll lock you up."

Real or implied force isn't the only kind of power used in conflicts. People who rely on authority of many types engage in win-lose methods without ever threatening physical force. In most jobs supervisors have the potential to use authority in the assignment of working hours, job promotions, desirable or undesirable tasks. And, of course, they have the power to fire an unsatisfactory employee. Teachers can use the power of grades to coerce students to act in desired ways.

Intellectual or mental power can also be a tool for conquering an opponent. Everyone is familiar with stories of how a seemingly weak hero defeats a stronger enemy through cleverness. He shows that brains are more important than brawn. In a less admirable way, indirectly aggressive crazymakers can defeat their partners by inducing guilt, avoiding issues, withholding desired behaviors, pseudoaccommodating, and so on.

Even the usually admired democratic principle of majority rule is a win-lose method of resolving conflicts. However fair it may be, this system results in one group getting its way and another being unsatisfied.

There are some circumstances when the win-lose method may be necessary, as when there are truly scarce resources and where only one party can achieve satisfaction. For instance, if two suitors want to marry the same person, only one can succeed. And to return to an earlier example, it's often true that only one applicant can be hired for a job. But don't be too willing to assume that your conflicts are necessarily win-lose. As you'll soon read, many situations that seem to require a loser can be resolved to everyone's satisfaction.

There is a second kind of situation when win-lose is the best method. Even when cooperation is possible, the other person may insist on trying to defeat you. Then the most logical response might be to defend yourself by fighting back. "It takes two to tango," the old cliché goes, and it also often takes two to cooperate.

A final and much less frequent justification for trying to defeat another person occurs when the other party is clearly behaving in a wrong manner, and where defeating that person is the only way to stop the wrongful behavior. Few people would deny the importance of restraining a person who is deliberately harming others, even if the aggressor's freedom is sacrificed in the process. The danger of forcing wrongdoers to behave themselves is the wide difference in opinion between people about who is wrong and who is right. Given this difference, it would only seem justifiable to coerce others into behaving as we think they should in the most extreme circumstances.

Lose-Lose

In lose-lose methods of problem solving, neither side is satisfied with the outcome. While the name of this approach is so discouraging that it's hard to imagine anyone could willingly use the method, in truth lose-lose is a fairly common approach to handling conflicts.

Compromise is the most respectable form of lose-lose conflict resolution. In it, all the parties are willing to settle for less than they want because they believe that partial satisfaction is the best result they can hope for.

In his valuable book on conflict resolution, Albert Filley points out an interesting observation about our attitudes toward this method. Why is it, he asks, that if someone says, "I will compromise my values," we view the action unfavorably, yet we talk admiringly about parties in a conflict who compromise to reach a solution? While compromises may be the best obtainable result in some conflicts, it's important to realize that both parties in a dispute can often work together to find much better solutions. In successes *compromise* is a negative word.

Most of us are surrounded by the results of bad compromises. Consider a common example, the conflict between one person's desire to smoke cigarettes and another's need for clean air. The win-lose outcomes on this issue are obvious. Either the smoker abstains or the nonsmoker gets polluted lungs—neither very satisfying. But a compromise in which the smoker only gets to enjoy a rare cigarette or must retreat outdoors and in which the nonsmoker still must inhale some fumes or feel like an ogre is hardly better. Both sides have lost a considerable amount of both comfort and goodwill. Of course the costs involved in other compromises are even greater. For example, a divorced couple might compromise on child care by haggling over custody. Then if they finally grudgingly agree to split the time with their youngsters, it's hard to say that anybody has won.

Compromises aren't the only lose-lose solutions, or even the worst ones. There are many instances in which the parties will both strive to be winners, but as a result of the struggle, both wind up losers. On the international scene many wars illustrate this sad point. A nation that gains military victory at the cost of thousands of lives, large amounts of resources, and a damaged national consciousness hasn't truly won much. On an interpersonal level the same principle holds true. Most of us have seen battles of pride in which both parties strike out and both suffer. It seems as if there should be a better alternative. Fortunately there often is.

No-Lose

In this type of problem solving the goal is to find a solution that satisfies the needs of everyone involved. Not only do the partners avoid trying to win at the other's expense, there's a belief that by working together it's possible to find a solution in which everybody reaches his goals without needing to compromise. One way to understand how no-lose problem solving works is to look at a few examples.

> Gordon was a stamp collector; his wife Elaine loved to raise and show championship beagles. Their income didn't leave enough money for both to practice their hobbies. Plus, splitting the cash they did have wouldn't have left enough for either. Solution: Put all the first year's money into the puppies. Then after they were grown use the income from their litters and show prizes to pay for Gordon's stamps.
>
> Mac loved to spend his evenings talking to people all over the world on his ham radio set. However, his wife Marilyn felt cheated out of the few hours of each day they could spend together. Mac didn't want to give up his hobby. Marilyn wasn't willing to sacrifice the time she needed alone with her husband. Solution: Three or four nights each week Mac stayed up late and talked on his radio after spending the evening with Marilyn. On the following mornings she drove him to work instead of his taking the bus. This allowed him to sleep later.
>
> Wendy and Kathy were roommates who had different studying habits. Wendy liked to do her work in the evenings, which left her days free for other things. Kathy felt that nighttime was party time. Solution: Monday through Wednesday evenings Wendy studied at her boyfriend's place, while Kathy did anything she wanted. Thursday and Sunday Kathy agreed to keep things quiet around the house. Then Friday and Saturday they both partied together.

The point here isn't that these solutions are the correct ones for everybody with similar problems. The no-lose approach doesn't work that way. Different people might have found other solutions that suited them better. What the no-lose method does is give you an approach—a way of creatively finding just the right answer for your unique problem. By using it you can tailor-make a way of resolving your conflicts that everyone can live with comfortably.

You should understand that the no-lose approach doesn't call for compromises in which the participants give up something they really want or need. Sometimes a compromise is the only choice. But in the method we're talking about you find a solution that satisfies everyone—one in which nobody has to lose.*

TOTAL READING TIME _____

► Step 3. O = Organize

Write an outline (either sentence or topic) of the article using the method you learned in Lesson 6. (Or fill in the outline you started in Step 1 with any additional details you think are important.)

_____

_____

_____

_____

_____

_____

_____

_____

_____

_____

_____

_____

_____

NOTE: Ask your instructor for a model outline from the *Instructor's Manual.*

---

*Adapted from "Interpersonal Conflict" and "Resolving Interpersonal Conflict" from *Looking Out/ Looking In,* Third Edition by Ronald Adler and Neil Towne, copyright © 1981 by Holt, Rinehart and Winston, Inc., reprinted by permission of the publisher.

Now review the article as if you were preparing for a test. Repeat your preview of the article, underlining important points. Study your outline until you are ready to take the quiz.

► *How well did you apply the PRO method?*

Answer the following questions without referring to the selection or to your outline. (Pretend that this is a test for which you have studied.)

1. Choose the statement that best expresses the thesis.
 (a) Of the three methods, the no-lose approach is the most desirable approach to resolving conflict.
 (b) Compromise is the only fair way to resolve conflict.
 (c) Winning through power is the favorite way to resolve conflict.
 (d) The best way to resolve conflict is to avoid it.

2. The democratic principle of majority rule is a win-lose method.　　　　T　　F

3. There are times when the win-lose method is unavoidable. Name one of those times:

_____

_____

4. The use of power is typical of which method?
 (a) win-lose **(b)** lose-lose **(c)** no lose

5. The authors suggest that the lose-lose method of resolving conflict is the least desirable of the three.　　　　T　　F

6. The lose-lose method is also the least commonly used approach to handling conflicts.　　　　T　　F

7. The example of the two roommates who resolved a conflict over studying versus partying illustrates which of the three methods? _____

8. The authors imply that the no-lose method is the best solution to *any* situation.　　　　T　　F

9. The point of the no-lose method is that nobody loses.　　　　T　　F

10. Define the no-lose method. _____

Turn to the Rate Chart in the Appendix to find your words per minute for this selection. Then record your WPM score below and on the progress chart in the Appendix.

WORDS PER MINUTE _____

% COMPREHENSION _____

1. Look over the two outlines you wrote on the Long Readings in this Lesson. Choose the one on the subject about which you know more. Now pick one major point (represented by a Roman numeral and all the points indented underneath it) from the outline and write a paragraph expanding that portion of the outline. You may draw on your memory of the Long Reading and/or from your own knowledge of the subject.

2. Discuss a situation in which you or someone you know used the win-lose, the lose-lose, or the no-lose method of resolving a conflict. How effective was the method? If you were unsuccessful, what method would have been better—and why?

3. Apply the PRO study-reading method to a textbook chapter you have been assigned in another class.

8

Skimming for Overview

IN THIS LESSON, YOU WILL

1. continue to improve perception and comprehension in timed exercises;
2. know when to skim for general idea;
3. learn to incorporate the preview technique into skimming for overview;
4. *skim* for general idea in the three reading selections.

► *Exercise 8A—Phrase Perception*

Pick out the phrase identical to the key phrase.

Key Phrase

1.	shoes and socks	socks and shoes	shoes and socks	shoe the horse
2.	red schoolhouse	read schoolbook	red schoolhouse	red poolhouse
3.	sit quietly there	sit quietly there	sit quietly here	sit quite quietly
4.	a good purpose	a good purpose	a purple food	a hidden purpose
5.	fly away now	fly away now	now fly away	fly that way
6.	fields and streams	field that hit	streams and fields	fields and streams
7.	big soft pillow	soften big pillow	big soft pillow	dig soft ridges
8.	the quick defeat	the quiet defeat	the quick defeat	the queer defect
9.	isolate the town	the brown insole	the round isobar	isolate the town
10.	eat with relish	eat with relish	beat with relish	eat the radish
11.	caught in a maze	caught in a maze	caught in a haze	caught with a mate
12.	this superb dinner	this superb dinner	this inner stupor	this winning suburb
13.	a conscious effort	a consecrated fort	a formed conscience	a conscious effort
14.	strike the knave	stroke the slave	strike the knave	the grave knack
15.	those precious few	these precise few	those precious few	these few luscious
16.	reverse the trend	reverse the trend	review the trick	the reversed trend
17.	the mangled body	mangle the body	the mangled body	the tangled web
18.	that gentle person	fat genteel person	that genuine person	that gentle person
19.	figure the fraction	figure the fraction	the figured fraction	puncture the fragment
20.	throughout infinity	through infinity	thoroughly infirm	throughout infinity

TIME _____

ERRORS _____

► *Exercise 8B—Phrase Perception*

Pick out the phrase identical to the key phrase.

Key Phrase

1. an open book	an open door	open a book	an open book
2. be always gay	be almost gay	be always gay	be another guy
3. pitch the tent now	pitch the tent now	pinch the red cow	watch the rent grow
4. reading fiction	reading fiction	working fractions	reading non-fiction
5. built like a brick	like a built brick	built like a bat	built like a brick
6. very bruised ego	very bruised ego	very broken ego	very bruised skin
7. lovely green lamp	lovely green ramp	lovely green lamp	lovely damp stream
8. navy blue suit	navy blue blouse	blue-suited navy	navy blue suit
9. twice seen film	twice seen film	seen two films	wind the filmstrip
10. catch the ball fast	catch the ball fast	snatch ball fast	watch the ball fall
11. cover the bed	cover the bad	cover the beds	cover the bed
12. estimate damage	estimate the profit	estimate damage	estimate the danger
13. good baked potato	bake good potatoes	good baked potato	baked potatoes
14. snakes in a pen	snakes in a pen	snake in a pen	snakes in a bin
15. twist and shake	twisted and shaken	twist a snake	twist and shake
16. pick a pretty posy	pick a pretty pose	pick pertinent point	pick a pretty posy
17. turn page slowly	slowly turn page	turn cheek slowly	turn page slowly
18. hunt with hounds	hunt for pound	hunt with hounds	hunt without hound
19. a shattered pot	a shattered pot	shatter the pot	a flattened pot
20. the first circle	the first circus	the fast circuit	the first circle

TIME _____

ERRORS _____

▶ Exercise 8C—Word Comprehension

Choose the word closest in meaning to the key word in **boldface** print.

Key Word

1.	a **placid** smile	excited	calm	well-placed
2.	an **eminent** lecturer	distinguished	pompous	brilliant
3.	a **precarious** position	safe	precious	risky
4.	an **aversion** to snakes	fascination	hatred	fear
5.	**disdainful** of foreigners	distrustful	scornful	friendly
6.	a **tranquil** mood	upset	terrible	peaceful
7.	an **erroneous** remark	wrong	radical	correct
8.	a **jubilant** celebration	quiet	joyful	frenzied
9.	to **rejuvenate** his health	jeopardize	justify	restore
10.	a **dubious** honor	prized	double	doubtful
11.	an **incendiary** speech	inflammatory	senseless	casual
12.	a **rampant** disease	incurable	widespread	unpopular
13.	a **premonition** of danger	forewarning	knowledge	absence
14.	to **interrogate** witnesses	entrap	coach	question
15.	a **brusque** answer	gracious	lengthy	curt
16.	a **profane** act	Biblical	blasphemous	profound
17.	to **fetter** with rules	improve	set free	restrain
18.	a **doleful** expression	mournful	angry	cheerful
19.	a **revulsion** for rats	fondness	disgust	indifference
20.	a **resolute** plan	flexible	agreeable	determined

TIME _____

ERRORS _____

► *Exercise 8D—Word Comprehension*

Choose the word closest in meaning to the key word in **boldface** print.

Key Word

1. military **reconnaissance**	attack	defeat	survey
2. a **primeval** time	ancient	troubled	recent
3. to **encumber** with debts	charge	burden	bankrupt
4. an **impassive** expression	emotionless	lively	passionate
5. to sing with **gusto**	boredom	off-key	enthusiasm
6. **invocation** for help	disregard	prayer	demand
7. an **inadvertent** error	deliberate	harmful	accidental
8. deserving **retribution**	revenge	praise	rewards
9. a **loathing** for beans	desire	aversion	recipe
10. to become **exhilarated**	elated	depressed	horrified
11. a weak **hypothesis**	assignment	personality	theory
12. a **sensory** experience	sordid	sensual	sensible
13. to **vie** for attention	compete	pay	dance
14. an **irrepressible** cough	annoying	loud	uncontrollable
15. a **deranged** mind	changeable	disturbed	decent
16. an **opportune** moment	timely	rare	inconvenient
17. to **nullify** the law	support	enact	abolish
18. to **ascribe** with virtue	deny	credit	describe
19. a **subsequent** memo	later	overbearing	sudden
20. from his **vantage** point	weaker	uncertain	better

TIME _____

ERRORS _____

► *Exercise 8E—Sentence Comprehension*

Check the sentences that express the same idea as the key sentence.

Key Sentence: Who can protest and does not is an accomplice in the act. (The Talmud)

1. If you do not protest about some wrongful act, you are as guilty as the actor. _____

2. Ignorance of the law is no excuse. _____

3. Silence is golden. _____

4. Protest and dissent are seldom useful to society. _____

5. Silent disagreement is one good way to combat evil. _____

6. Free speech and dissent can act as curbs on unlawful acts. _____

7. Indifference or silence about a crime is the same as helping the criminal. _____

8. A responsible person does not keep quiet about injustice. _____

9. Group protest is more effective than individual protest. _____

10. Good always wins out over evil. _____

TIME _____

ERRORS _____

► *Exercise 8F—Sentence Comprehension*

Check the sentences that express the same idea as the key sentence.

Key Sentence: There is a strong correlation in reading between concentration and comprehension.

1. Ability to concentrate in reading is closely related to understanding what is read. _____

2. Paying careful attention when reading increases comprehension. _____

3. Concentrating on punctuation makes oral reading more effective. _____

4. The ability to comprehend long, difficult passages correlates directly to intelligence. _____

5. Reading rapidly improves both comprehension and concentration. _____

6. Reading comprehension is improved by good concentration. _____

7. Many corporations have encouraged executives to learn speed reading. _____

8. The challenge of reading every other line improves concentration. _____

9. Good readers choose a reading environment without distracting noises and sights. _____

10. Retention of factual detail is dependent upon reading the material twice. _____

TIME _____

ERRORS _____

What is skimming?

The terms "skimming" and "scanning" are often used interchangeably. Both involve selective skipping at high speeds. *Skimming is reading for the general idea or the big picture. Scanning* is looking for exact answers to specific questions. (See more on scanning in the Appendix.)

How fast?

Some reading experts make a big point of skimming, and their estimates of 800 words per minute and up may frighten you. You may feel, "I can just barely read and comprehend at 200 wpm. How can I possibly read at 800 wpm?"

There are three good answers to that question. (1) You already have skimmed reading material at 800 wpm or faster. (2) Skimming is not the same as careful reading. It's skipping. You read only the most important parts. (3) For your first skimming goal, you will try to at least double your present reading speed. With frequent practice, you'll soon draw closer to your long-term goal of 800 wpm.

You will not always want or need to read everything. Instead, you should skim if your purpose is one of the following:

Examples—when to skim

1. to reread material you have already studied;

2. to sort out and discard, as with the junk mail in your home or office;

3. to "try before you buy"—or really read—a new book or magazine;

4. to pass over minor or uninteresting sections when you are reading for pleasure—for example, to follow the major plot in a light, easy novel;

5. to keep informed in a general way about the news;

6. to review your lecture notes after class;

7. to see which reference materials might be useful to your term paper;

8. to be able to discuss the general content of a reading assignment in class when you didn't have time to really read and study it.

Skimming should give you a general overview, not detailed knowledge. Good skimmers read selectively, skipping over some sentences, paragraphs, and even whole pages. They know they can always come back and read for details, if they wish. To skim, follow these steps:

How to skim

1. Survey first for the topic, length of the material, and its organization. Note any subdivisions or spaces with headings or subheadings. Also look for any numbered lists, capital letters, italics, or boldfaced print.

2. Read the title and the first paragraph, looking for the thesis. If the thesis is not in the first paragraph, read the second paragraph. Also read the last paragraph. The thesis or main points may be restated there.

3. Now look for main ideas in the first, and if necessary, second sentence of each paragraph. (If the material is too long or you don't have much time, read the first sentence under each heading or division. Usually it's a topic sentence.)

4. Look for important transitions, e.g. *but,* a *second* reason, *the result is....*

5. Decide the article's main pattern of organization.

6. Resist the temptation to read everything.

Theme: Stories of Famous People

Before you read the selections in this Lesson, think about what kind of person becomes a public figure—whether politician or social reformer. What motivates people to go beyond the limits expected of them and become public figures?

Words in Context

For each *italicized* word, choose the best meaning below.

► *Short Reading 8G*

1. *Silent Spring,* published in 1962, showed quite clearly that man was endangering himself and everything else on this planet by his *indiscriminate* use of chemical pesticides.

   (a) expensive **(b)** careless and random **(c)** infrequent **(d)** carefully planned

2. Prince Hamlet [from Shakespeare's play] used revoltingly *grisly* images in vicious baiting of his hated uncle: "Your worm is your only emperor for diet. . . ." [Extra Clue: A mass murder scene would be grisly.]

   (a) horrible **(b)** poetic **(c)** mildly unflattering **(d)** false

► *Short Reading 8H*

3. When Golda graduated as valedictorian of her class, her mother was *elated.*

   (a) relieved **(b)** calm **(c)** joyful **(d)** determined

4. Papa had, for once, sided with her—*albeit* rather faintly.

   (a) even though **(b)** in addition **(c)** since **(d)** therefore

5. And with the war came dire reports of increased *pogroms.* [Extra Clue: From Russian meaning *desolation.]*

   (a) injuries **(b)** draft calls **(c)** economical hardship **(d)** organized massacres

6. Her mission: to try to stir the *complacent* American Jewish youth, awaken them to the philosophies and the necessities of Labor Zionism. [Extra Clue: The middle class is said to be complacent.]

   (a) selfish **(b)** self-satisfied **(c)** wealthy **(d)** excitable

7. His daughter, to stand on a soap box *exhorting* people on the street!

   (a) pleading with **(b)** singing to **(c)** urging strongly **(d)** shouting at

► *Long Reading 8I*

8. She had her own way of showing her displeasure—not to yell or even to scold, but to greet her son at all times with an *impassive* stare.

   (a) showing no emotions **(b)** hostile **(c)** angry **(d)** deceptively sweet

9. She inquired scrupulously into his plans for the future and, *eliciting* no assurance that he was even willing to entertain the notion of college, she closed him out completely.

(a) forcing   (b) drawing forth   (c) begging for   (d) winning

10. Johnson saw the trip, when he talked about it later, in cartoon *imagery.*

(a) lies   (b) drawings   (c) mental pictures   (d) funny stories

The first reading is about Rachel Carson, who wrote two important books warning us to protect our environment. Because of the dangerous "greenhouse" effect, we are finally heeding that warning.

Preview: *In one minute or less, read the title, headings, first sentence under each heading, and last sentence in the article. Then write below (1) what you think the thesis might be and (2) any questions you have about the article from doing the preview.*

(1) _____

(2) _____

Wait for a signal from your instructor. Then skim *the article in one minute by looking only for the main idea in each paragraph, or at least try to double your usual reading speed. This exercise is nearly twice the length of the earlier Short Readings; so skim as rapidly as you can. Circle your WPM after one minute.*

A Friend of the Environment

John Hartley

WPM

Early Kinship with Nature

 4

A little girl tramping around in the Pennsylvania woods near her home senses a pleasant kinship with the birds and plants and animals. She is at ease with them. They are, in a way, her close friends. The little girl, like many people, feels that these wonders of Nature are precious and permanent. | 13 / 25 / 39 / 52 / 57

Rachel Carson continued to feel that way for much of her life. "It was pleasant to believe," she wrote later, "that much of Nature was forever beyond the tampering reach of man. He might level the forests and dam the streams, but the clouds and the rain and the wind were God's. It was comforting to suppose that the stream of life would flow on through time in whatever course God had appointed for it—without interference by one of the drops in that stream—man." | 69 / 82 / 94 / 107 / 119 / 130 / 142 / 143

Silent Spring—a Warning to Mankind

149

But she found out that she was wrong. As a scientist, she learned with sadness that little in Nature is truly beyond the "tampering reach of man." Then, angrily aware of the harsh facts concerning the present and future dangers to the environment, she used her great skills as a writer to sound a startling warning to mankind. *Silent Spring,* published in 1962, showed quite clearly that man was endangering himself and everything else on this planet by his indiscriminate use of chemical pesticides. As her title suggests, Miss Carson was saying that there might come a springtime that would indeed be silent. It would be silent because the birds, as well as other creatures and plants, would have been destroyed by the man-made poisons used to kill crop-threatening insects. | 161 / 172 / 183 / 193 / 207 / 217 / 228 / 238 / 249 / 263 / 273 / 279

Her Desire to be a Poet

When she was that little girl in Pennsylvania, Rachel Carson never would have believed that years later she would write a scientific book that would stir up so much controversy. The book created the fervor for "protecting the environment" that has become so commonplace today. Because she had always been such an avid and appreciative reader, her dream when she started college was to become an imaginative writer. She wanted to be one perhaps like the English poet John Masefield. His fine words had fired her imagination about the sea, which she had never seen. When she was a sophomore, though, she took a course in biology. It was there she discovered the wonder and excitement of scientific study of those animals she had learned to know and admire as a child tramping through the woods.

Redirected Toward Science

After finishing college, she did research and taught in various universities and government agencies. At the same time, she did indeed become acquainted with the sea that Masefield had written about. She learned "the gull's way and the whale's way where the wind's like a whetted knife." Like any good scientist, she took extensive notes about her studies, whether her focus of the moment was a crab in Chesapeake Bay or a turtle in the Caribbean. Ultimately she wrote about the sea. She wrote about it not only in formal academic reports but also in a book that informed and thrilled laymen around the world. *The Sea Around Us*, published in 1951, has been translated into more than thirty languages and was on the best-seller list for more than eighty consecutive weeks. Rachel Carson, a scientist with the magic touch of a poet, shared her love of the ocean and its creatures with all mankind. Her style was clear but lively, informative but not preachy, and for most readers truly exhilarating. Although the oceans may cover seven-tenths of the earth's surface, few of us know much about them. *The Sea Around Us* was a delightful antidote to our ignorance.

Her Concern over Pesticides

In the decade after publication of *The Sea Around Us* she continued with her research and writing. There were other books and numerous magazine articles. Most of them dealt with the major love of her life—the sea. However, because she was a true scientist and an aware human being, she knew that everything on this planet is connected to everything else. Thus, she became increasingly alarmed by the development and use of DDT and other pesticides of its type. These chemicals, she knew, do not break down in the soil. Instead, they tend to be endlessly recycled in the food chains on which birds and animals and man himself are completely dependent.

The Poisonous Cycle

One might guess that at this time Carson the reader might have reminded Carson the scientist of some passages in Shake-

285
295
306
317
327
338
349
361
372
384
396
406
418
421

424

434
444
454
466
478
490
502
515
527
539
551
561
576
587
597
609
622
623

627

639
649
660
674
686
695
707
719
732
740

743

754
764

speare's most famous play. Prince Hamlet used revoltingly grisly 772
images in vicious baiting of his hated uncle: "Your worm is your only 785
emperor for diet. We fat all creatures to fat us, and we fat ourselves 799
for maggots. Your fat king and your lean beggar is but variable ser- 812
vice, two dishes, but to one table. . . . A man may fish with the worm 825
that hath eat of a king, and eat of the fish that hath fed of that worm. 842
. . . A king may go a progress through the guts of a beggar." 854

Rachel Carson knew of this poisonous cycle. And she knew 864
now, as her own observations were confirmed by fellow scientists all 875
over the country, that this "worm" now carried a heavy concen- 886
tration of poison. It could be passed on to fish, to other animals, to 889
their food supply, and to men and women and children throughout 910
the earth. In spite of fierce opposition from the chemical industry, 921
from powerful government agencies, and from farmer organiza- 929
tions, she persisted in her research and writing. Then in 1962 939
she published *Silent Spring.* The book exploded into the public 949
consciousness. It received great praise from some, great criticism 958
from others. The little girl from the Pennsylvania woods, now 968
approaching middle age, had fired a major salvo in the battle for 980
the environment.* 982

Immediately answer the following questions without referring to
the selection.

1. When Rachel Carson became an adult, she
  (a) became a poet because of her love for nature.
  (b) never lost her belief that nature is permanent and incapable of really being harmed.
  (c) wrote books as a result of her concern for the dangers to nature.
  (d) passed her love of nature's wonders on to her children.
2. Carson's first ambition was to be a
  (a) poet. **(b)** scientist. **(c)** housewife. **(d)** forest ranger.
3. What is the title of her first book? _____
4. Explain the poisonous cycle Carson saw happening in nature.

_____

_____

5. Her books were well written but not widely read.   T   F

Record your scores below and on the progress chart in the Appendix.

WORDS PER MINUTE _____

% COMPREHENSION _____

---

*John Hartley, "A Friend of the Environment." Reprinted by permission of the author.

In the next article, look for the reasons that caused Golda Meir to break with Jewish tradition for women and become one of the first women to be elected a head of state.
Preview: *Read the title, headings, first sentences under each heading, and the last two paragraphs. Write the questions you have from doing the preview:*

_____

_____

_____

Wait for a signal from your instructor before you start. Then skim *the article at double your usual reading speed, looking for main ideas. Circle your WPM after one minute.*

from Golda: The Life of Israel's Prime Minister

Peggy Mann

WPM

The Struggle with Her Parents Over Her Education   8

When Golda graduated as valedictorian of her class, her   17
mother was elated. Now the girl could work full time in the grocery   30
store. Even in America girls were not expected to go to *high* school! 43
Golda, however, expected to go. And after some tearful argu-   53
ments, her parents agreed. Papa had, for once, sided with her—   63
albeit rather faintly. Perhaps he felt guilty that he, the breadwinner, 74
actually earned so little. He was a wise, gentle, and scholarly man,   86
but not cut out for business. . . .   92
She had decided to become a teacher because such a pro-   103
fession was "intellectually and socially useful." Mama, however, had 111
found out that married women were not permitted to teach in the   123
local schools. "You want to be an old maid?" she screamed at Golda.   136
"*That's* what you're studying for?"   141
Papa now sided strongly with Mama. Either Golda must quit   151
school and go to work like other sensible girls her age, or she must 165
transfer to a business school to be trained in subjects which would   177
help her get a job and, who knows, a husband too. . . .   188
[After running away from home and living with her married   198
sister in Denver for two years, Golda won this battle too. She re-   210
turned to Milwaukee to finish high school.]   217

Golda's Determination for a Jewish Homeland   223

Golda was still in high school when the First World War broke   235
out in Europe. And with the war came dire reports of increased   247
pogroms. The Jewish Pale of Settlement lay, unfortunately, in the   257
very territory where Russian and German-Austrian armies clashed   265
most often in violent battle. When the White Russian Army fled in   277
retreat, they slaughtered Jews in that section for being German sym- 288

pathizers. When the Russians swept back and Germans fled from the 298
same section, *they* murdered Jews for being Russian spies. 307

The White Russian armies and their bitter opponents, the 316
Germans, seemed to agree on one tenet only: anti-Semitism. And 326
they had ample opportunity for carrying out their battle cry: death 337
to the Jews. For of the ten million Jews in Europe, eight million lived 351
in the Russian and Austro-Hungarian empires. 357

Millions of Jews were rendered homeless. Committees were 365
organized to raise funds for the ever-swelling ranks of Jewish refu- 376
gees who fled from one town to the next, trying to keep out of the 390
way of the armies. Golda worked with People's Relief and with an 402
organization called Aid in Need, formed by Jewish workers in Mil- 413
waukee to help hungry and homeless European Jews. . . . 420

She felt broken apart inside. For nights she could not sleep. 431
What *good* did it do, running around, making speeches, collecting 441
money for a new generation of suffering, displaced, wandering Jews? 451
There had to be a better answer than this. There *had* to be one place 466
in the world where Jews could at last be free from persecution. There 479
had to be a Jewish homeland. And it must be created as soon as 493
possible. All her beliefs suddenly solidified into one single purpose. 503
As soon as she could she would go to Palestine and devote her life to 518
this goal. She joined Poale Zion, the Labor Zionist Party. . . . 528

Golda's Talent as a Speaker 533

She set about making money for her passage to Palestine. She 544
worked part time at the Sixteenth Street and North Avenue branch 555
of the Milwaukee Public Library. In the spring of 1916 she graduated. 567
. . . She entered Milwaukee Normal School for Teachers and took a 577
part-time job at a Yiddish-speaking folk school which advocated 586
Labor Zionism. But even this seemed too far removed from her goal. 598
So she started speaking for the Labor Zionists' Poale Zion. 608

The organization soon discovered that the eighteen-year-old 616
girl had a remarkable talent as a speaker. They sent her on speaking 629
engagements around the country. Her mission: to try to stir the com- 641
placent American Jewish youth, awaken them to the philosophies 649
and the necessities of Labor Zionism. 655

One Friday night she was scheduled to speak in Milwaukee, 665
not in a meeting room or an auditorium. She would speak on a street 679
corner. Standing on a soap box. 685

Her father heard about the plan and was horrified. Women, 695
he thundered at Golda, did not *do* such things! His daughter, to stand 708
on a soap box exhorting people on the street! "If you dare to go 722
ahead with that speech," he threatened, "I'll come down there and 733
pull you off home by your braids!" 740

"I'm sorry, Papa," Golda said, firmly, "but the speech has 750
already been announced." 753

She took the precaution of telling members of Poale Zion 763
that her father might create a scandal that evening, and since she did 776
not cherish the notion of being dragged off the soap box, she asked 790
that they form a protective circle around her as she spoke. 801

This was done. But it was almost unnecessary, for the crowd 812
which gathered on the street corner that night was so large that 824

Moshe Mabovitch would have had a hard time shoving his way 835
through. Most of the bystanders had stopped out of curiosity. It was 847
not every day that one saw an attractive young girl standing on a 860
soap box and talking about a faraway land called Palestine. They 871
soon found themselves spellbound, caught up by Golda's impas- 880
sioned oratory. 881

As she spoke, Golda noticed her father at the edge of the 893
crowd; noticed thankfully that he did not, after all, seem bent on 905
making a scene. 908

Afterward, Poale Zion members gathered around her with 916
congratulations. It was a fine speech. One of the best she had ever 929
made. . . . 930

When she got home, her mother was sitting at the kitchen 941
table sewing. 943

"Where's Papa?" 945

"In bed." 947

Bluma looked up. She was smiling a little. "He came in. He sat 960
down. He shrugged. He said, 'Where did she get this talent for speak- 973
ing?' Then he stood up. He said, 'God knows what this girl may be 987
able to do!' And he went to bed." 995

From that night onward the Mabovitches offered no more 1004
objections to anything Golda wanted to do. They seemed to realize 1015
that they had somehow bred a very special child. Their best contri- 1027
bution now would be not to interfere. . . . 1033

Many years later, when the new country called Israel was 1043
about to be born, its leader, David Ben-Gurion, would proclaim: 1053
"Some day when our history is written it will say that there was a 1067
Jewish woman who raised the money which made this nation 1077
possible." 1078

The Jewish woman he referred to was Golda.* 1086

Answer the following questions without looking back at the selection.

1. State the thesis of the selection in a complete sentence.

____

____

2. Golda's father always supported her—even against her mother's wishes. **T** **F**

3. Why did Golda's mother object to her daughter becoming a teacher? ___

____

4. Golda started working for a Jewish homeland during World War I. **T** **F**

5. Her father became reconciled to her
(a) getting an education. **(b)** marriage. **(c)** public speaking talent. **(d)** helping Jews.

Record your scores below and on the progress chart in the Appendix.

WORDS PER MINUTE _______

% COMPREHENSION _______

*From *Golda: The Story of Israel's Prime Minister* by Peggy Mann. Copyright © 1971, 1973, by Peggy Mann. Reprinted by permission of Curtis Brown Ltd.

In this last article, look for the forces, both internal and external, that drove our late President, Lyndon Johnson, who hated school, to continue his education and go into politics.

Preview: *In one minute or less, read the title, headings, first sentence under each heading, and last sentence in the article. Then write the questions you formed as you previewed:*

_____

_____

_____

Wait for a signal from your instructor before you start. Then skim *the article at double your usual reading speed (or faster, if you can), looking only for main ideas.*

from Lyndon Johnson and the American Dream

Doris Kearns

Lessons from His Father

"One of the first things I remember about my daddy," Johnson said, "was the time he cut my hair. When I was four or five, I had long curls. He hated them. 'He's a boy,' he'd say to my mother, 'and you're making a sissy of him. You've got to cut those curls.' My mother refused. Then, one Sunday morning when she went off to church, he took the big scissors and cut off all my hair. When my mother came home, she refused to speak to him for a week. . . ."

The . . . tension between father and son reveals itself in a story Johnson later told about his first experience killing an animal. "In the fall and the spring, I spent every moment when I wasn't in school out in the open. With the other boys, I went hunting squirrels and rabbits. I carried a gun and every now and then I pointed it at the animals but I never wanted to kill any of them. I wanted only to know that I could kill if I had to. Then one day my daddy asked me how did it happen that I was the only boy in the neighborhood who had never shot an animal. Was I a coward? The next day I went back into the hills and killed a rabbit. It jumped out at me from behind a bush and I shot it in between the eyes. Then I went to the bathroom and threw up. . . ."

Conflict with His Mother

Just the same, Johnson seemed to endure his father's testing far better than his mother's gloomy silence. . . . Indeed, she had refrained for months from commenting about his mediocre performance in school or his frequent evenings on the town with his friends. She had her own way of showing her displeasure—not to yell or even to scold, but to greet her son at all times with an impassive stare. She made no secret of the fact that his drinking, fast driving, and generally aggressive behavior displeased her. Nor did she conceal the repugnance she felt at the reputation he had established in school as a sluggish student who treated everything as a joke. Johnson knew by his mother's withdrawal that he had not lived up to the splendid vision she had held of him as a boy.

When Johnson graduated from high school in May 1924, Rebekah allowed her quarrel with her son to surface at last. When she spoke, daily taking him to task for his slovenly manner, she had, as Johnson later described it, "a terrible knifelike voice."

She inquired scrupulously into his plans for the future and, eliciting no assurance that he was even willing to entertain the notion of college, she closed him out completely. During supper she would direct her remarks to her husband and her younger children, never so much as confirming Lyndon's existence. Directly after supper, she went to bed.

"We'd been such close companions, and, boom, she'd abandoned me. I wanted to please her, but something told me I'd go to pieces if I went to college. I'd just finished ten years of sitting inside a school; the prospect of another four years was awful. It would make me a sissy again and I would lose my daddy's respect. . . ."

Trip to California

Yet our concern here is not simply with the conflicts from which Lyndon Johnson suffered, but with how he surmounted or utilized these conflicts, adapting them to the realities of his life. And here the interesting biographical fact is that Johnson knew enough at the age of fifteen to know that he simply had to get away.

That summer—the summer of 1924—the opportunity arrived. A group of Johnson's friends had decided to leave home and go to California. For each of the boys the trip no doubt meant something different—adventure, the hope of work. There was a report, one of the boys later recollected, that money out there grew on trees and that a person had but to reach up and get it. Lyndon, youngest of the group, listened in as they made their plans; he watched as they fixed up the old Model T that would carry them West. He wanted desperately to go along, but he knew that his parents would never allow him to leave. "Going was one hell of a problem," he said. "I decided I'd just say to my mother and father that I was going West with the boys. I knew it would be an emotional scene, but one night I decided to look them straight in the eye and reveal my plans. But when I reached the front door of my house, I began to shiver uncontrollably. At last, I went in. They sat opposite one another at the kitchen table. My sisters and brother were there. I tried to speak, but I couldn't say a goddamn word. I lost my nerve."

One week later, before the sun came up on a Monday morning, the boys took off in their Model T. At the last minute, Johnson decided, without asking or telling anyone, to go with them. He jumped into the car. "Here I am," he said. "Let's hurry along and be on our way."

During the entire trip Johnson walked around carrying his suitcase as though it were incredibly heavy and had within it enough clothes to last a family of twenty for fifteen years. His companions could not imagine why Johnson took so much along and yet wore the same clothes day after day. Then one afternoon the baling wire that Johnson had used to tie up the suitcase came loose and it opened on the street. Out rolled the sum of Johnson's worldly possessions—a straw hat!

The Vagabond

Johnson saw the trip, when he talked about it later, in cartoon imagery. He recounted brushes with gruff poker players, scenes of burying money in underground holes, and fancies of reliving his grandfather's life on the frontier.

But the old frontier had promised economic and spiritual independence, and in California, in 1924, that independence was not easy to secure. Indeed, Johnson was barely able to survive on the grapes he picked, the dishes he washed, and the cars he fixed. Just the same, he remembered living happily for a time in different places. Free of both his mother and his father, he found he had an immense curiosity about the different kinds of people with whom he worked—the field hands in the Imperial Valley, the cooks in the all-night cafés, the garage mechanics in the big cities. He found himself constantly entertaining his fellow workers with stories and jokes. People seemed to like him; they admired his quickness.

Johnson lived the vagabond life for nearly a year; then, when his money dried up completely, he took a job in Los Angeles as a clerk to a criminal lawyer. The job was no accident. The lawyer was a cousin of Rebekah's. There Lyndon stayed for another year, until one August day in 1926 when, suddenly, faced with an offer of a ride to Texas, he decided that after two years' absence he was ready to return.

The Decision

Johnson would long remember this trip back home; he later theatrically designated it *the* moment when he found his vocation of politics. On the trip, as Johnson recounted it, he thought a great deal about his parents. "I still believed my mother the most beautiful, sexy, intelligent woman I'd ever met and I was determined to recapture her wonderful love, but not at the price of my daddy's respect. Finally, I saw it all before me. I would become a political figure. Daddy would like that. He would consider it a manly thing to be. But that would be just the beginning. I was going to reach beyond my father. I would finish college; I would build great power and gain high office. Mother would like that. I would succeed where her own father had failed; I would go to the Capitol and talk about big ideas. She would never be disappointed in me again."

Johnson reached his boyhood home on a Sunday afternoon. When he walked inside the door, he carried with him an air of pride and self-respect. At supper that night, there was, as he remembered it, much conversation. Later, left in his room, he knew that somehow things were different. He was ready to embark on his future career.

Perhaps the trip was, as Johnson believed, a turning point, marking the transition from childhood to adulthood. The separation from home obviously helped to distance Lyndon in a positive way from his mother's ceaseless pressure. And the resolve he felt that night he returned certainly showed up in the rapid successes he achieved once he entered college. But turning points are rarely as dramatic as we remember them to be. Despite his resolution, Lyndon stayed away from the study of books for another six months, taking, instead, a job with a road gang. Finally, one hot afternoon in February 1927, he went to his mother and said: "All right, I'm sick of working just with my hands and I'm ready to try and make it with my brain."*

TOTAL SKIMMING TIME _____

Immediately answer the following questions without referring to the selection.

1. Choose the statement that best expresses the thesis.
    (a) Johnson's parents' conflicting expectations of him helped shape his personality and career goals.
    (b) Johnson's decision to become a politician was primarily to please his mother.
    (c) His decision to become a politician was primarily to please his father.
    (d) After much difficulty, Johnson finds his true vocation.

2. One might infer that Johnson's drinking, running around, and neglecting school was partly to keep his father from thinking he was a sissy.   T   F

3. What was one of the first things Johnson remembered about his father?

   _____

4. Johnson liked to go hunting and bring in game for the family.   T   F

5. Johnson's mother habitually nagged her son about his behavior.   T   F

6. Which of the following best describes the method Johnson's mother used to influence him?

    (a) warm, loving advice (b) the cold, silent treatment (c) pretending to be ill (d) severe whippings

7. Johnson initially did not want to go to college.   T   F

8. He took a suitcase full of clothes and books with him to California.   T   F

9. In California, he worked at various jobs for a year, then as a clerk for a lawyer for another year.   T   F

10. He claimed that it was on his trip back from California that he decided to become a politician.   T   F

Turn to the Rate Chart in the Appendix to get your words per minute for this selection. Then record your scores below and on the progress chart in the Appendix.

WORDS PER MINUTE _____

% COMPREHENSION _____

---

*Excerpts from *Lyndon Johnson and the American Dream* by Doris Kearns. Copyright © 1976 by Doris Kearns. Reprinted by permission of Harper & Row, Publishers, Inc.

1. Who is a famous person that inspires you in some way? Compose a topic sentence that makes a general statement about the area of your life this person affects. The body of your paragraph will give the details.

2. Examine your life as it relates to your own ambition. Draw a line down the middle of a sheet of paper. To the left of the line list your positive traits that might help you get what you want. To the right of the line list the negative traits that might prevent you from getting what you want. Choose a point of view (stress the negative traits, the positive traits, or both contrasting traits) that could be interesting for an essay. Eliminate items on the list that don't fit and add others. Now write a main idea statement (or thesis statement) and an outline based on the list as if you were planning to write an essay on the subject.

9

Reading Critically

IN THIS LESSON, YOU WILL

1. continue perception and comprehension exercises;
2. learn to recognize an author's purpose;
3. learn to tell facts from opinions;
4. judge how reliable an author's facts and opinions might be.

► *Exercise 9A—Phrase Perception*

Pick out the phrase identical to the key phrase.

Key Phrase

1. plush velvet lining	lush velvet lining	plush velvet lining	very plush living
2. speaking to group	speaking to group	speeding to place	reaching group
3. pasting gold parts	pasting partial gold	pasting gold parts	partial gold paste
4. holding hands high	holding hands high	holding high hands	holding high hand
5. say nothing to him	nothing said to him	say more to him	say nothing to him
6. long slender legs	long spending days	along slender lines	long slender legs
7. place for dinghy	place for dinghy	place for dimple	a dingy place
8. eating good jerky	eating food jerkily	wearing good jerseys	eating good jerky
9. left-handed batter	left-handed batter	left-handed batters	right-handed batter
10. dealing with pathos	dealing with pathos	dealing with bathos	dealing with patience
11. has the button	has the butter	was the button	has the button
12. spoken with candor	spoken with candor	spoken candidly	poke the canine
13. that pungent odor	punctured motor	that pungent odor	the pungent odor
14. an obscure person	an obsessed person	an obscure person	an observed person
15. two in the dark	two in the dark	ten in the dark	two in the park
16. one forlorn girl	one forlorn curl	one foreign girl	one forlorn girl
17. sleeping dogs lying	sleeping dogs lying	the dogs lying	creeping dogs lying
18. taking out garbage	taking out garbage	taking out baggage	taking in garbage
19. more narrow minds	more national binds	more narrow minds	more rational minds
20. carrying crates	carrying crates	parrying cracks	raising rates

TIME _____

ERRORS _____

► *Exercise 9B—Phrase Perception*

Pick out the phrase identical to the key phrase.

Key Phrase

1. eating ice cream   making ice cream   eating ice cream   heating ice cream

2. picking up sticks   picking up sticks   picking dead sticks   packing up stacks

3. gnawing the bone   gnawing the bones   throwing the stone   gnawing the bone

4. empty the basket   empty the waste basket   empty two baskets   empty the basket

5. filling the tooth   filling the tooth   filling the teeth   filing the tooth

6. shoes all shined   sun all shining   shores all shiny   shoes all shined

7. the Monkey Trial   the Monkey Trial   the Monkey Trail   the Monkey's Trial

8. a chilling frost   a chilled frosting   a chilling frost   a killer frost

9. pen on the table   pen in the table   pencil on the table   pen on the table

10. news of the week   news of the weak   blues of the bleak   news of the week

11. sat in the sun   sat in the sun   seat with your son   not in the sun

12. drinking the coffee   drinking the coffee   drinking the coke   blinking an eye

13. viewing a bad film   viewing a sad film   viewing a bad film   viewing bad films

14. under milkwood   under milkwoods   under milkworm   under milkwood

15. spared a dime   spared a dame   a spared dime   a dim space

16. lightning flash   lightning splash   lighter flash   lightning flash

17. my older brother   my old mother   my old brother   my older brother

18. peace with honor   peaceful honor   peace with honesty   peace with honor

19. evaded the draft   evaded the draft   avoided the draft   invaded the draft

20. different drummer   diffident drummer   different drummer   difficult drummer

TIME _____

ERRORS _____

► *Exercise 9C—Word Comprehension (Variation)*

Choose the **antonym** (opposite word) of the key word among the words on the right. Most of the words in these exercises have appeared before in other Word Comprehension exercises.

NOTE: Use the synonyn, included in the three choices, as a clue.

Key Word

1.	an **ornate** room	plain	beautiful	elaborate
2.	a **surly** reply	tender	bad-tempered	pleasant
3.	to **spurn** your betrothed	reject	accept	help
4.	**superfluous** friends	numerous	extra	necessary
5.	to **idolize** a teacher	degrade	worship	introduce
6.	the storm to **abate**	pour	subside	increase
7.	an **aptitude** for math	hatred	inability	ability
8.	to **stifle** a laugh	smother	hear	let out
9.	to **delete** verbs	add	replace	omit
10.	her **nimble** fingers	agile	stiff	broken
11.	to **pilfer** the jewels	give	borrow	steal
12.	to **deplore** violence	witness	approve	disapprove
13.	to **reprimand** students	scold	lecture	compliment
14.	to **redeem** his honor	forget	ruin	recover
15.	a **tedious** job	interesting	well-paid	boring
16.	to **comply** with rules	argue	defy	agree
17.	a **renowned** author	foreign	unknown	famous
18.	**illegible** signatures	neat	unreadable	readable
19.	to **sever** a relationship	cut off	bind	treasure
20.	an **ecstatic** moment	fearful	joyful	depressing

TIME _____

ERRORS _____

► *Exercise 9D—Word Comprehension (Variation)*

Choose the **antonym** (opposite word) of the key word in **boldface** print.

Key Word

1. an **obstinate** child	stubborn	shy	agreeable
2. to **abhor** cruelty	witness	approve	detest
3. an **extravagant** price	cheap	unknown	excessive
4. to **secrete** the story	hide	enjoy	uncover
5. seen to be **sham**	nude	genuine	fake
6. a **valiant** attempt	cowardly	pretentious	brave
7. to **imply** a compliment	refer	infer	suggest
8. to remain **destitute**	rich	poor	humble
9. to **wane** in health	decline	glory	increase
10. to become **mute**	married	talkative	silent
11. **famished** at dinner	drunk	starved	satisfied
12. a **trivial** point	dangerous	important	petty
13. an **obscure** law	clear	vague	interesting
14. a **sublime** time	subtle	ordinary	noble
15. a **fabulous** meal	wonderful	expensive	common
16. to **forgo** the bonus	give in	take	give up
17. to **concede** the argument	win	give up	give in
18. the **expired** patient	dead	neglected	living
19. to **amputate** an arm	break	sew on	cut off
20. a **tangible** improvement	abstract	useless	concrete

TIME _____

ERRORS _____

► Exercise 9E—Phrase Comprehension (Variation)

Mark every *noun* in the phrases below. (A noun expresses person, place, thing, or idea.) Each phrase has at least one noun; some have more than one. (Do not mark nouns used to modify other nouns. Example: in "*car* coat," *car* is used as an adjective and *coat* is the noun.) Try to follow the action in the list even though you are reading only sentence fragments.

1. international airport
2. cars swarming like flies
3. palm-tree-lined streets
4. concrete parking structures
5. monotonous recorded voice
6. droning the same words
7. "no parking"
8. "for loading and unloading"
9. "of passengers only"
10. taxi driving up
11. passenger in mink coat
12. baggage unloaded
13. porter receiving tip
14. doors swinging wide
15. checked-in at ticket counter
16. going through security check
17. rushing down concourse
18. high heels clicking
19. running up escalator
20. arrival at gate
21. a scramble for ticket
22. seat assignment by window
23. flight delayed
24. tension in voices
25. police rushing by

26. rumors of bomb
27. the waiting in lobby
28. eyes staring at mink
29. cold plastic cushions
30. cigarette butts underfoot
31. smell of stale smoke
32. spilled soft drinks
33. paper-thin hamburgers
34. grease on chins
35. children running by
36. soldier kissing wife
37. the chatter in foreign languages
38. another flight announcement
39. passengers boarding plane
40. smiling stewardess
41. settled in first class
42. near a window
43. sipping on champagne
44. fastening seat belt
45. no smoking
46. demonstration by stewardess
47. captain's voice on speaker
48. apology for delay
49. smooth take-off
50. explosion in air

NOTE: Picking out the *nouns* (and the *verbs* in later exercises) gives you practice in focusing on the most important words in a sentence. These words carry the core idea.

TIME _____

ERRORS _____

► *Exercise 9F—Phrase Comprehension (Variation)*

Mark every *noun* in the phrases below. Each phrase has at least one noun; some have more than one. Try to get an impression of the setting as you work through the list.

1. quiet rural scene
2. narrow dirt road
3. four-room sharecropper shack
4. outhouse in back
5. with no door
6. big shade trees
7. used tires in yard
8. patches of grass
9. chickens scratching around
10. tin roof shining
11. porch falling down
12. big cracks in walls
13. faint smell of urine
14. rain-stained wallpaper
15. straight-backed chairs
16. with cowhide bottoms
17. wood-burning stove
18. iron bedstead
19. chipped green paint
20. old feather mattress
21. with split seams
22. homemade kitchen table
23. wooden bench underneath
24. peas boiling on stove
25. cut green onions

26. pork frying in pan
27. biscuits in oven
28. sunset over pine trees
29. milking time near
30. the farmer's daughter
31. milkbucket swinging
32. carefully unwiring gate
33. walking through cowpen
34. rain-soaked ground
35. boots burying in mud
36. pigs grunting low
37. plow mules blinking
38. ramshackle barn
39. cow in stall chewing cud
40. and flicking flies
41. head against cow's belly
42. hands working like machines
43. hound dog watching
44. squirt on dog's head
45. hound dog leaping
46. milkbucket full
47. back in the kitchen
48. milk through strainer
49. biscuits done
50. supper on table

TIME _____

ERRORS _____

NOTE: You have been using your *skimming* skills to follow the story and your *scanning* skills to look for a specific answer.

So far in this book you have tried to find the main idea and important details of each reading. You have also learned how to organize those ideas and details. In the remaining Lessons, you will work on another essential skill: reading critically.

What does it mean to read critically? You probably recognize the word "critic" as the root of "critical." When you read as a critic, you question what you read. You evaluate the merits and faults of what an author is saying. You learn to see if the author presents the subject in a fair and trustworthy way. You also learn to read "between the lines" and notice the things an author hints at or implies instead of saying directly. In other words, you learn to infer and draw conclusions, skills that are important in every job or social activity.

Benefits of reading criticallyAs your ability to read critically grows, you reap three rewards. First, you recognize and better understand ideas that are well presented. Second, you gain a valuable ability to question those ideas that are not fairly or accurately presented. Thus you can protect yourself against misleading claims or ideas. Third, you have a tool that you can use in your own writing and speaking so you will sound informed and believable.

In this Lesson we will focus on (1) how to determine a writer's purpose; (2) how to tell facts from opinions; (3) how to judge the value of a writer's facts and opinions. (Later Lessons will introduce inference, another skill of a good critical reader.)

Determining an Author's Purpose

The first thing a good critical reader does is determine the author's purpose for writing. Usually a writer's purpose is one of these three possibilities:

1. *to inform* (Most textbook chapters, news articles, and instructions explain or inform.)

2. *to persuade* (Most advertising and newspaper editorials argue a particular point of view. They want to convince or persuade you to agree.)

3. *to entertain* (This is the main purpose of many stories, humorous essays and biographies. But sometimes writers want to entertain at the same time they try to persuade and inform you, so these purposes can overlap.)

Why you should know an author's purpose.You need to know a writer's purpose so you can judge how well facts and opinions are used. Writers who inform usually have the most facts and opinions from experts. Selections written to entertain usually have less need of facts and expert opinions.

Telling Facts From Opinions

A mistake some inexperienced readers make is thinking an opinion is a fact, especially when they read it in print. We need to know the difference between facts and opinions because we evaluate them in different ways. *Factual statements can be proven to be true or false. An opinion statement, on the other hand, is someone's judgment.* It often shows someone's approval or disapproval of something.

► *Exercise*

Place a check before the following statements that are facts. You do not have to know if a fact is true or false. Decide if it's possible to *prove* it as true or false.

_____ 1. The capital of Florida is Tallahassee.

_____ 2. Cornbread sopped in gravy is more delicious than fried catfish.

_____ 3. We should learn to tell the difference between right and wrong before the age of seven.

_____ 4. Former President Reagan, when he was Governor of California, said "If you have seen one redwood tree, you've seen them all."

_____ 5. Steve Martin is one of the funniest comedians starring in movies today.

_____ 6. Putting a man on the moon was a noble and uplifting act.

_____ 7. It rains daily in the Sahara Desert.

_____ 8. People who hold public office must be proper and respectable in their sexual conduct.

Did you notice that one part of statement number 4 is a fact, and the other part an opinion? It's a fact that Reagan said what he did, but the quotation is Reagan's opinion. The only other facts are numbers 1 and 7. Did you notice that words like "should" and "must be" usually signal an opinion?

Evaluating the Evidence

Once you are able to tell the difference between a fact and an opinion, you can judge how well a writer is using each.

Ask these questions about facts:

How good are the facts?

1. Are they recent? In some fields, such as computers, new developments occur fast, so facts from even three years ago may be outdated.

2. Are they from a reliable source? When you get more knowledge of your field, you will learn which sources you can trust. With your instructor or class, you may wish to decide the organizations and publications whose facts you would trust in various fields. For example, consider: To what extent is your college newspaper reliable? Your city's daily newspaper? Radio and television newscasts? How about a university's published research in science? Word of mouth from your neighbor? Word of mouth from a political lobbyist? Word of mouth from a radio phone-in talk show? What other sources can you think of whose information may or may not be reliable, and why?

Ask these questions about opinions:

How good are the opinions?

1. Are they reliable, meaning do they come from an expert in the field? When you see baseball players talking about car insurance or famous actors talking about health, some advertiser has found a way to catch your attention. But those actors and baseball players are probably not experts in the areas of car insurance or health.

2. Are these opinions based on any facts?

Lesson Summary

1. First decide an author's purpose.

2. Notice which statements are facts and which are opinions.

3. Check to see that the facts and opinions are reliable and that they fit the author's purpose. Articles written to inform or persuade require more facts and reliable opinions than articles written to entertain.

Theme: Current Problems

These readings examine two serious problems that stir up a great deal of public controversy. The Practice Paragraphs present recent articles from newspapers and magazines on what to do about the decrease in adequate child care, a problem made worse by an increase in working women. The two Long Readings give both sides of the hotly debated gun control issue.

Practice Paragraphs

As you do with all readings, first find the topic and main idea of each paragraph. Look for the author's purpose, and notice the facts and opinions. How reliable are they? Do they fit the author's purpose?

A. (1) Older children—three- and four-year-olds—seem to do fine in quality day care. (2) But recent studies are far from encouraging for new parents returning to work. (3) "There is rather robust evidence that children who've been in more than 20 hours of non-parental care a week in the first year of life are at greater risk of being insecure in their relationships with mothers," says Dr. Jay Belsky, a Penn State authority on child care. (4) "Later in child-hood, these kids are also likely to have more temper tantrums, be more disobedient and do less well in school."*

1. In your own words, what is the main idea of this paragraph? (Write a complete sentence.)

   _____

   _____

2. What is the author's main purpose? _____

3. What is Dr. Jay Belsky's main purpose? _____

   _____

4. Is this paragraph mostly fact or mostly opinion? _____

5. How well do the facts and opinions fit the author's purpose? _____

B. (1) Child-support payments should be as easy to make as car payments. (2) Employers help their workers repay credit-union loans with voluntary payroll deductions. (3) Now the city of Los Angeles is encouraging companies to follow suit in order to improve the compliance with child-support orders. (4) It doesn't cost much to do. (5) It can actually save time and money by avoiding the hassle that occurs when an employee's wages are garnished. (6) And, most important, it makes sure that children's needs for food, shelter and clothing can be met. (7) Many divorced parents do pay to support their children, but others have problems disciplining themselves to do so. (8) Studies show that fewer than half the parents who are awarded child support receive the full

---

*From "The Day Care Dilemma" by Hal Straus, *American Health Magazine* © 1988 (September). Reprinted by permission.

amount that their children are owed; one-fourth get no support at all.*

1. In your own words, what is the main idea of this paragraph?

   _____

2. What is the author's main purpose? _____

3. Where is an example of fact? Sentence number: _____

   Where is an example of opinion? Sentence number: _____

   Is this paragraph mostly fact or mostly opinion? _____

4. Are the author's facts and opinions reliable? _____ Why?

   _____

5. How well do the facts and opinions fit the author's purpose?

   _____

   _____

C. (1) Sweden, unlike America, has a comprehensive early child-care program, available as a right to all parents. (2) High fractions of mothers now work in both nations (84% in Sweden, 64% in America). (3) But in Sweden parents have assurance that someone dependable is caring for the kids during work hours. (4) More fundamentally, Sweden has decided that even single mothers (and their children) are entitled to a decent standard of living. (5) In the United States the typical public-assistance grant provides an income well below the poverty line. (6) It locks welfare mothers into a cycle of dependency. (7) It offers nothing to struggling single parents whose earnings place them slightly above welfare limits. (8) By contrast, in Sweden, as in most of Western Europe, payments to single mothers are sufficient to provide a modestly decent standard of living, and society offers other family supports as well.**

1. In your own words, what is the main idea of this paragraph?

   _____

2. What is the author's main purpose? _____

3. Where is an example of fact? Sentence number: _____

   Where is an example of opinion? Sentence number: _____

   Is this paragraph mostly fact or mostly opinion? _____

4. Are the author's facts and opinions reliable? _____ Why?

   _____

5. How well do the facts and opinions fit the author's purpose?

   _____

---

*From "Support for Child Support," *Los Angeles Times,* August 3, 1988. Copyright © 1988 Los Angeles Times. Reprinted by permission.

**From "Single-Parent Family Needn't Mean Disaster" by Robert Kuttner. Reprinted by permission of the author.

Words in Context

For each *italicized* word, choose the best meaning below.

► *Long Reading 9G*

1. Any unauthorized citizen found with guns in his home by the OGPU or the KGB is automatically suspected of *subversive* intentions and subject to severe penalties. [Extra Clue: The prefix *sub* means *under.*]

   (a) planning a bank robbery **(b)** suicidal **(c)** plotting to overthrow the government **(d)** being an escaped convict

2. An armed citizenry is the first defense, the best defense, and the final defense against *tyranny.*

   (a) cruel use of authority **(b)** a revolution **(c)** overthrow of the king **(d)** communism

► *Long Reading 9H*

3. The handgun . . . is the preferred weapon of crime, because it is both so *lethal* and so easily concealed.

   (a) cheap **(b)** deadly **(c)** lightweight **(d)** well-known

4. Thus, *inadvertently* the solid citizen is helping to arm the criminal class.

   (a) fully intending to **(b)** without meaning to **(c)** subconsciously **(d)** without being paid to

5. Yet few of these present-day tough guys know that Earp was in fact an early *proponent* of handgun control.

   (a) opponent **(b)** supporter **(c)** indifferent to **(d)** researcher

The following argument, in favor of owning guns, was written by Edward Abbey, who writes novels about the West.

Preview: *In 40 seconds or less, read the title, first paragraph, first sentence of each paragraph, and the last paragraph. Then write what you think the thesis is.*

_____

_____

Now wait for a signal from your instructor before you begin reading. Read carefully to see if your idea of the thesis is correct. Also be aware of the appeals made by the author to your emotions.

The Right To Arms

Edward Abbey

If guns are outlawed
Only outlaws will have guns.
(True? False? Maybe?)

Meaning weapons. The right to own, keep, and bear arms. A sword and a lance, or a bow and a quiverful of arrows. A crossbow and darts. Or in our time, a rifle and a handgun and a cache of ammunition. Firearms.

In medieval England a peasant caught with a sword in his possession would be strung up on a gibbet and left there for the crows. Swords were for gentlemen only. *(Gentlemen!)* Only members of the ruling class were entitled to own and bear weapons. For obvious reasons. Even bows and arrows were outlawed—see Robin Hood. When the peasants attempted to rebel, as they did in England and Germany and other European countries from time to time, they had to fight with sickles, bog hoes, clubs—no match for the sword-wielding armored cavalry of the nobility.

In Nazi Germany the possession of firearms by a private citizen of the Third Reich was considered a crime against the state; the statutory penalty was death—by hanging. Or beheading. In the Soviet Union, as in Czarist Russia, the manufacture, distribution, and ownership of firearms have always been monopolies of the state, strictly controlled and supervised. Any unauthorized citizen found with guns in his home by the OGPU or the KGB is automatically suspected of subversive intentions and subject to severe penalties. Except for the landowning aristocracy, who alone among the population were allowed the privilege of owning firearms, for only they were privileged to hunt, the ownership of weapons never did become a widespread tradition in Russia. And Russia has always been an autocracy—or at best, as today, an oligarchy.

In Uganda, Brazil, Iran, Paraguay, South Africa—wherever a few rule many—the possession of weapons is restricted to the ruling class and to their supporting apparatus: the military, the police, the secret police. In Chile and Argentina at this very hour men and women are being tortured by the most up-to-date CIA methods in the effort to force them to reveal the location of their hidden weapons. Their guns, their rifles. Their arms. And we can be certain that the Communist masters of modern China will never pass out firearms to *their* 800 million subjects. Only in Cuba, among dictatorships, where Fidel's revolution apparently still enjoys popular support, does there seem to exist a true citizen's militia.

There must be a moral in all this. When I try to think of a nation that has maintained its independence over centuries, and where the citizens still retain their rights as free and independent people, not many come to mind. I think of Switzerland. Of Norway, Sweden, Denmark, Finland. The British Commonwealth. France, Italy. And of our United States.

When Tell shot the apple from his son's head, he reserved in hand a second arrow, it may be remembered, for the Austrian tyrant Gessler. And got him too, shortly afterward. Switzerland has been a free country since 1390. In Switzerland basic national decisions are made by initiative and referendum—direct democracy—and in some cantons by open-air meetings in which all voters participate. Every Swiss male serves a year in the Swiss Army and at the end of the year takes his government rifle home with him—where he keeps it for the rest of his life. One of my father's grandfathers came from Canton Bern.

There must be a meaning in this. I don't think I'm a gun fanatic. I own a couple of small-caliber weapons, but seldom take them off the wall. I gave up deer hunting fifteen years ago, when the hunters began to outnumber the deer. I am a member of the National Rifle Association, but certainly no John Bircher. I'm a liberal—and proud of it. Nevertheless, I am opposed, absolutely, to every move the state makes to restrict my right to buy, own, possess, and carry a firearm. Whether shotgun, rifle, or handgun.

Of course, we can agree to a few commonsense limitations. Guns should not be sold to children, to the certifiably insane, or to convicted criminals. Other than that, we must regard with extreme suspicion any effort by the government—local, state, or national—to control our right to arms. The registration of firearms is the first step toward confiscation. The confiscation of weapons would be a major and probably fatal step into authoritarian rule—the domination of most of us by a new order of "gentlemen." By a new and harder oligarchy.

The tank, the B-52, the fighter-bomber, the state-controlled police and military are the weapons of dictatorship. The rifle is the weapon of democracy. Not for nothing was the revolver called an "equalizer." *Egalité* implies *liberté*. And always will. Let us hope our weapons are never needed—but do not forget what the common people of this nation knew when they demanded the Bill of Rights: An armed citizenry is the first defense, the best defense, and the final defense against tyranny.

If guns are outlawed, only the government will have guns. Only the police, the secret police, the military. The hired servants of our rulers. Only the government—and a few outlaws. I intend to be among the outlaws.*

TOTAL READING TIME _____

Answer the following questions without referring to the article.

1. Write a sentence that gives the thesis for this article.

_____

_____

2. In the sentence, "swords were for gentlemen only," the author's use of *gentlemen* is meant to be

(**a**) positive. (**b**) negative. (**c**) neutral.

3. What is the author's purpose in using historical references to restrictive societies such as medieval England and Nazi Germany?

_____

4. What is the author's purpose in referring to William Tell, the legendary Swiss hero? _____

_____

5. The claim that the punishment for "possession of firearms by a private citizen of the Third Reich" was death is a statement of

(**a**) fact. (**b**) opinion. (**c**) a mixture of both.

6. "The registration of firearms is the first step toward confiscation." This statement is (**a**) fact. (**b**) opinion. (**c**) a mixture of both.

7. The author would place no limitations on owning a gun.   T   F

8. How does author, calling himself a liberal and saying he is not a John Bircher, give himself more credibility on the gun control issue? _____

_____

9. This article is mostly (**a**) fact. (**b**) opinion. (**c**) a balanced mixture of the two.

10. In this article, the author's main purpose is to (**a**) inform. (**b**) persuade. (**c**) entertain.

Turn to the Rate Chart in the Appendix to get your words per minute for this article. Then record your scores below and on the progress chart in the Appendix.

WORDS PER MINUTE _____

% COMPREHENSION _____

This next longer reading, by Pete Shields, gives a rebuttal to the reasons people give for owning guns. He has been an effective advocate for gun control since 1974, when his son was murdered by a man with a handgun. He is chairman of Handgun Control, Inc.

Preview: *In 40 seconds or less, read the title, headings, and first and last paragraphs, looking for the thesis. Then write what you think the thesis is:* _____

_____

Wait for a signal from your instructor before you begin reading. As you read, carefully examine the author's point for reliability.

Why Do People Own Handguns?

Pete Shields

Answers to the question "Why do people own or acquire *handguns?*" are entirely different from answers to the question "Why do people own rifles and shotguns?"

It is not at all difficult to explain why people own firearms other than handguns. From southern Florida to northern Michigan, and from Portland, Oregon, to Portland, Maine, men and women have been using rifles and shotguns for hunting and for sport for as long as this country has been a country—and before. Their use of firearms—rifles and shotguns—is not part of the problem. . . .

It is important to understand that our organization, Handgun Control, Inc., does not propose further controls on rifles and shotguns. Rifles and shotguns are not the problem; they are not *concealable.*

Why do people own and acquire handguns? That's the hard question. There are many answers to it. Some are perfectly logical, others questionable, and a few downright hard to figure.

Criminal Activity

After the handgun, the criminal's next weapon of choice is the knife, but it is such a far second that guns used in crime outnumber knives used in crime by *at least* three to one. The handgun, especially one with a relatively short barrel, is the preferred weapon of crime because it is both so lethal and so easily concealed. Stuck inside the belt, only the grip or handle is visible, and a jacket or suitcoat or sweater can easily cover that small bulge. Also, the handgun slips easily into a coat, jacket pocket or purse. The inside of an automobile offers any number of handy hiding spots. . . .

In the American Handgun War, the small, easily concealable handgun in the wrong hands is the *enemy.* For despite what the pro-pistol lobby says, guns *do* kill people. One person every fifty minutes.

Self-Defense

The frightening rise in crimes of violence throughout the country has caused more and more well-intentioned people to arm themselves. They buy guns to protect their homes and to carry with them for personal protection when traveling. Many, many people now carry handguns in their cars. Perhaps we should not have been so startled by an incident at the height of the gasoline crisis a few years ago, when one motorist shot and killed another who had cut in front of him in a filling-station line.

Unfortunately, instead of protection, what the new handgun owner too often gets is personal tragedy. As I found out in my original reading, and as research in the area of self-defense has borne out ever since, a handgun does not protect the American home very well.

The home handgun is far more likely to kill or injure family members and friends than anyone who breaks in, and is especially harmful to young adults and to children.

Because 90 percent of burglaries take place when no one is home, the handgun bought for self-defense is very often stolen. According to law-enforcement authorities, each year an estimated 100,000 handguns are stolen from law-abiding citizens. These guns then enter the criminal underworld and are used in more crimes. Thus, inadvertently, the solid citizen is helping to arm the criminal class.

As a New York City police sergeant recently pointed out to a homeowner who asked if he should buy a handgun to protect his home, too often it is the homeowner *himself* who ends up getting shot and killed, because he most often *warns* the robber by saying something like "Stop!" or "What do you think you're doing?" Alerted, the thief turns and fires.

Another reason the handgun is not essential for home protection is that citizens in their homes don't need the one feature which most appeals to and attracts the criminal to the handgun—its concealability. The shotgun is far more intimidating to the intruder.

In street crime, the use of the handgun for self-defense is extremely risky, with the defender often losing the weapon and having it used against him. The handgun owner seldom even gets the *chance* to use his or her weapon because the element of surprise is always with the attacker. In fact, trying to use a handgun to ward off someone bent on aggravated assault makes the risk of death quite a bit higher.

For the ordinary citizen, using a handgun is seldom helpful for self-defense on the street. And, in the home, about the only way to get real protection from a personal handgun would be to have it always at the ready, perhaps in hand every time there is a knock on the door, loaded and ready to fire. That is not exactly the American way. Or my idea of a civilized society. . . .

Hunting and Target-Shooting

In my opinion, there is only one legitimate handgun sport and that is target-shooting. It is practiced at target ranges which are properly supervised and usually quite safe. Only certain handguns are true "sporting weapons," recognized as such by the sport's adherents.

On the other hand, "plinking"—shooting at tin cans and other small targets—in one's backyard is not and should not be considered a serious sport. When uncontrolled and unsupervised, it can be a very dangerous practice.

Some opponents of handgun control have claimed that we are out to stop all hunting and that controlling the handgun would severely affect hunting. That is simply untrue. Handgun control would in no way abridge the freedom of the true hunter. Few if any knowledgeable hunters consider the handgun an effective hunting weapon.

There *are* a few hunters who do hunt with handguns, but most states place restrictions on the type of guns that can be used in hunting, the reason being that killing of game should be done in as humane a manner as possible. Small-caliber handguns are more likely to wound the animal rather than kill it outright. Realistically, only long guns, rifles and shotguns are effective firearms for hunting.

People must understand that handguns and hunters are distinctly separate issues. Because the vast majority of hunters use a rifle or a shotgun, there is no reason why their pursuit of game (and sport) should be affected by handgun control. Mixing anti-hunting sentiment with the handgun issue confuses the killing of animals with the killing of people. . . .

The Second Amendment Argument

To understand the supposed constitutional argument it is essential that the reader be familiar with the *full and complete* wording of the Second Amendment to the Constitution of the United States. It reads: "A well-regulated Militia, being necessary to the security of a free State, the right of the people to keep and bear Arms, shall not be infringed." It would be interesting to take a poll of Americans and see how many have forgotten, or never knew, the Amendment's initial twelve words. Certainly, the pro-pistol lobby has not seen fit to clarify that point. The "militia" of the Amendment is what we all know today as the National Guard.

On five separate occasions, the Supreme Court of the United States has ruled that the Second Amendment was intended to protect members of a state militia from being disarmed by the federal government. In addition to those five Supreme Court decisions, the American Bar Association stated, in 1975, at its annual convention, that "every federal court decision involving the amendment has given the amendment a collective, militia interpretation and/or held that firearms-control laws enacted under a state's police power are constitutional."

The five cases in which the U.S. Supreme Court has ruled on the Second Amendment are: *U.S. v. Cruickshank* (1875); *Presser v. Illinois* (1886); *Miller v. Texas* (1894); *U.S. v. Miller* (1939); and *U.S. v. Tot* (1942). . . .

The "Macho" Image Argument

To many handgun buyers, owning a gun is a carry-over from the days of the Wild West, the frontier days, when the six-shooter made might, and might made the man. And in that era, one of the mightiest or most macho of men was Wyatt Earp—at least that is what many of today's handgun owners believe. Yet few of these present-day tough guys know that Earp was in fact an early proponent of handgun control. He went so far as to *ban* them inside the city limits. There was a law in Dodge City that no one but law-enforcement officers was allowed to carry a six-shooter in public. Earp arrested anyone who broke this law.

Psychiatrists tell us that the great frontier still lives in the minds of men who buy handguns believing the weapon will give them a stronger sense of masculinity. The deadly nature of a handgun can make the smallest man bigger than the biggest *unarmed* man.

As we have seen time and time again, a loaded handgun in the possession of someone driven by emotion is a time bomb ready to explode. Examples are provided by almost any newspaper on almost any day.

Clarksville, Tennessee: "RUSSIAN ROULETTE GAME PROVES FATAL"

Austin, Texas: "FRIENDS TRIED TO STOP HIM, HE TRIED RUSSIAN ROULETTE—AND HE LOST"

Chicago, Illinois: "CHICAGO BOY, 9, DIES IN CLUB'S 'RUSSIAN ROULETTE' INITIATION"

Indianapolis, Indiana: "DRIVER SHOT TO DEATH ON FREEWAY FOLLOWING RIGHT-OF-WAY DISPUTE," . . .

It is said, and certainly my own experience bears it out, that until the violence touches you, no matter how great your concern may be, it still remains *concern* and not *action*.

We all deplore the statistics, and we shudder as we read the latest horror story in the newspaper or see the interview with the grieving survivors, but until we are touched personally we seldom take action.

But the point is we already *are* personally touched by the amount of violence in this country.

If you love to walk in the evening but aren't doing so because your neighborhood isn't "as safe as it once was," or you avoid seeing certain old friends because of where they live, or if you find yourself getting up in the middle of the night to double-check doors and windows, then you are already a casualty, already a victim of the American Handgun War.*

TOTAL READING TIME _____

Answer the following questions without referring to the article.

1. Write a sentence that gives the thesis for the article.

_____

_____

2. The author is against the private use of *all* firearms.　　　　　　　T　　F

3. Is the statement, "guns used in crime outnumber knives used in crime by *at least* three to one," an effective fact to support his arguments for gun control? _____

4. "Inadvertently, the solid citizen is helping to arm the criminal class." This statement is **(a)** fact. **(b)** opinion. **(c)** a mixture of the two.

5. What does the author consider to be the only legitimate handgun sport? _____

6. What is the author's rebuttal to the claim that controlling the handgun would severely affect hunting? _____

_____

7. The author's rebuttal to the Second Amendment argument is mostly **(a)** fact. **(b)** opinion. **(c)** a mixture of the two.

_____
*From "Why Do People Own Handguns?" from *Guns Don't Die—People Do* by Pete Shields with John Greenya. Copyright © 1981 by Pete Shields and John Greenya. Reprinted by permission of Arbor House/ William Morrow and Co., Inc.

8. The author's rebuttal to the "Macho" image argument is mostly **(a)** fact. **(b)** opinion. **(c)** a mixture of the two.

9. Does the author's tragic personal experience make his arguments unreliable?

_____

10. The author's major purpose in this article is to

(a) inform. **(b)** persuade. **(c)** entertain. **(d)** both **(a)** and **(b).**

Turn to the Rate Chart in the Appendix to get your words per minute for this article. Then record your scores below and on the progress chart in the Appendix.

WORDS PER MINUTE _____

% COMPREHENSION _____

WRITING AND DISCUSSION ACTIVITIES

1. What is your solution to the problem of day care for children of working parents? Write a paragraph, stating your solution in a topic sentence. Then support your belief with opinions and/or facts. Underline any facts.

2. Cut out an article from the opinion page of your local newspaper. (a) Underline all the facts. (b) State the author's main purpose—to inform, persuade, or entertain.

10

Determining Inference

IN THIS LESSON, YOU WILL

1. continue perception and comprehension exercises;

2. learn to draw *inferences* (or conclusions) from more difficult paragraphs and articles.

► **Exercise 10A—Phrase Perception (Variation)**

Each column of twenty items has only one key phrase (in italics). Mark each repeated phrase. Work through both columns vertically before checking your time. Try to focus from dot to dot.

Key Phrase	Key Phrase
livid with fear	*singed his finger*
lived with fear	singed his finger
livid with fear	singed his fins
loved with fear	signal his finish
loved with tears	signing his finish
living with fear	signal the swingers
living with fears	singed his finger
livery of fear	singed his fingers
lively with wear	signed the singers
livid with fear	singed two fingers
alive with fear	singe her finger
livid ears	singer's fingers
lively ears	singe my fingers
in living color	singing of fingers
livid with fear	unhinged with anger
living on fear	singing of anger
lived without fear	singed his finger
lives with fear	sign this finger
livid with fear	signed with fingers
alive with fleas	singed his finger
liquid with fear	Band-aid, please!

TIME _____

ERRORS _____

NOTE: Check the Answer Key to see how many times each key phrase is repeated.

► *Exercise 10B—Phrase Perception (Variation)*

Each column of twenty items has only one key phrase. Mark each repeated phrase. Work through both columns vertically before checking your time.

Key Phrase	**Key Phrase**
tract of land	*curry favor*
track of land	curry favors
track landing	carry favors
attract land	famous curry
tractor on land	carry flavor
traction on land	the cur you favor
tract of land	cherry flavor
trace of land	carrying favors
trace island	cure favorite
tract of land	cursory favor
trace inland	curry flavoring
trace the island	curry favor
tract or land	savor the curry
race for land	hurry the favor
track the landing	curious favor
tract of land	curry for four
tracing the hand	crawl for favors
trance of mind	can I favor
race to land	care for few
tract of land	curry favor
contract for land	furry favors

TIME _____

ERRORS _____

▶ *Exercise 10C—Word Comprehension (Variation)*

Choose the **antonym** (opposite word) of the key word in **boldface** print.

Key Word

1.	to **suppress** a laugh	ridicule	let out	hold back
2.	a **swarthy** complexion	light	spotty	dark
3.	an **aggressive** advance	smart	shy	forceful
4.	to **thwart** her ambition	stop	seek	aid
5.	a **titanic** ship	tiny	huge	sunk
6.	to **verify** his alibi	confirm	doubt	dispute
7.	a **wayward** child	sickly	obedient	willful
8.	an **abominable** movie	delightful	sentimental	disgusting
9.	a **staunch** companion	selfish	weak	strong
10.	a **disciple** of Satan	law	follower	leader
11.	the **ravaged** forest	thriving	destroyed	invisible
12.	the **preface** to a book	introduction	conclusion	cover
13.	a soul in **turmoil**	commotion	change	peace
14.	a **random** selection	unplanned	planned	unwise
15.	an **indispensable** tool	useless	cheap	necessary
16.	his **dwindling** savings	changing	shrinking	growing
17.	an **ingenious** strategy	clever	workable	stupid
18.	a **complex** thought	simple	unpopular	complicated
19.	to **commend** a performance	praise	condemn	study
20.	to **amass** great wealth	accumulate	desire	lose

TIME _____

ERRORS _____

► *Exercise 10D—Word Comprehension (Variation)*

Choose the **antonym** (opposite word) of the key word in **boldface** print.

Key Word

1.	**oblivious** to pain	unaware	conscious	obvious
2.	**deficient** in friends	plentiful	lacking	lucky
3.	**tolerable** weather	welcome	unbearable	acceptable
4.	to become **dormant**	active	bored	sleeping
5.	to **segregate** the sexes	ignore	integrate	separate
6.	the **ultimate** success	minor	final	rewarding
7.	an **eccentric** old man	odd	wealthy	typical
8.	an **appalling** mistake	insignificant	costly	horrifying
9.	two **diverse** plans	unworkable	different	similar
10.	to **convalesce** after illness	recuperate	relapse	shake
11.	a **furtive** gesture	forthright	sneaky	quick
12.	a **droll** remark	dramatic	sad	amusing
13.	to **allay** suspicion	ignore	relieve	aggravate
14.	a **demure** young maid	bold	shy	ignorant
15.	to **enhance** the day	treasure	improve	worsen
16.	**bedlam** in the room	confusion	order	furniture
17.	a **mediocre** accomplishment	terrible	ordinary	exceptional
18.	a **despondent** widow	silent	happy	depressed
19.	a **naive** young boy	sophisticated	dumb	innocent
20.	an **accessible** escape	available	sensible	closed

TIME _____

ERRORS _____

► *Exercise 10E—Sentence Comprehension*

Check the sentences that express the same idea as the key sentence.

Key Sentence: A majority of the women in the United States who work do so because of real economic need, not because they want more spending money for luxuries.

1. Although it is generally believed that most American women work for extra money, the majority work out of financial need. _____

2. Too many American women neglect their homes and work for luxuries their husbands cannot buy them. _____

3. Many women work to send their children to college. _____

4. Since 1940, the number of mothers who work has increased about nine times. _____

5. Because of rising inflation, economic needs dictate that more women work now than ever before. _____

6. The majority of American women spend over half their wages for luxuries. _____

7. A woman's place is in the home, not in the office or factory. _____

8. Most wages earned by women are spent for household needs, whereas wages earned by men are spent for larger monthly bills. _____

9. Statistics prove that more working women than working men give to charities. _____

10. The main reason that most women in America work is a need for money to buy necessities, not to buy extra items. _____

TIME _____

ERRORS _____

► *Exercise 10F—Sentence Comprehension*

Check the sentences that express the same idea as the key sentence.

Key Sentence: Both heredity and environment influence students' academic successes.

1. Where students live has more influence on them than who their parents are. _____

2. Genetic characteristics and living conditions are both factors influencing students' success in school. _____

3. Atmospheric conditions affect students' ability to study. _____

4. Students' parentage is more important than environment and heredity. _____

5. Students' progress in school is affected by environment and heredity. _____

6. Making good grades is a result of a highly cultural background. _____

7. Students' surroundings while growing up and the qualities inherited from their parents affect how well they do in school. _____

8. Students have difficulty with their homework if their home is noisy. _____

9. Neither heredity nor environment greatly affects students' progress in school. _____

10. Community expectations often motivate students to make better grades. _____

TIME _____

ERRORS _____

The preceding Lesson introduced you to the practice of critical reading. In this Lesson and the following ones you will continue that training as you develop another skill: determining inferences, a skill that requires you to read *beneath the surface*.

An inference is an idea that speakers or writers do not state openly but intend you to understand anyway. Through their words or actions, they *imply* or suggest an idea. From their words or actions, you *infer* that idea. Said another way, you receive the message that the person is sending you through a hint or indirect suggestion. For example, your mother might not come right out and tell you that she would like to see you more often. Instead, she may hint or imply it by her actions or words. If you get her hint, you have *inferred* it. You have understood what she was implying.

Inferring from actions

Sometimes an implication is obvious and simple. For example, a door slammed in your face quickly tells you someone is angry with you. A simple situation such as "dogs barking all night" implies "many sleepless neighbors." "Many sleepless neighbors" can logically imply "many angry neighbors" and might lead to phone calls and perhaps police action.

Inferring from words

But other times, especially in speaking and writing, the implication may be more subtle. In these cases, you will have to read more deeply or listen carefully and to examine all the evidence. Only then can you infer accurately. Examples that require subtle inference might be found in

1. a political speech;

2. an advertisement on television or in a magazine;

3. the text of a new law;

4. the entire style, setting and character development of a novel or movie.

To make accurate inferences in these cases you need to pay close attention to the implications of words and phrases.

► *Connotations of Words*

You may have heard the saying "The pen is mightier than the sword." This generalization recognizes the power that words have. We have all been in situations when words, written or spoken, have moved us to fight, cry, run, laugh, even fall in love. This power does not come from the *literal* meaning alone of words. It comes from the power of words to suggest or imply. These other meanings of words, with the feelings or ideas they suggest, are called their *connotations*.

Recognizing neutral language

Because of the situations in which certain words are often used, they are usually associated with that situation. For example, suppose your professor asked you to come see her this afternoon about an essay you wrote. Would you say you have a *date* or *meeting* with your professor? Which word is the most *neutral*? Which word has other associations?

In the situation where you probably often find yourself—a college classroom—the kind of language that is preferred is neutral language. A "meeting" is more neutral than a "date." It's true a date might be nothing more than an appointment. But the word is often used for a meeting that has romantic possibilities—a different situation. So the word "date" in this context is not as neutral as the word "meeting" because of its romantic connotations.

► *Exercise*

How good are you at recognizing neutral language? Circle the word or phrase in each list that seems to be the most neutral, that is, without strong positive or negative connotations.

1. Your essay, Mr. Tarbrush, is (mediocre) (so so) (average).
2. The results of the experiment were (negative) (a disappointing failure) (a crushing blow).
3. My car insurance company (messes up often) (is totally inept) (makes some mistakes).
4. George is Mary's (lover) (friend) (soul mate).
5. My friend says I am (stubborn) (strong-willed) (firm).

(Answers: average; negative; makes some mistakes; friend; firm)

Using connotations

The ability to recognize and use neutral language is important in many fields, such as journalism, law, academic writing, and science. It is also important to avoid insulting people and to keep the peace in your relations with family and friends. But sometimes writers or speakers deliberately use language that is *not* neutral. Why? They may wish to use the rich connotations of words to:

1. set a mood, as in a story or a formal speech;
2. inspire you to action, as in a religious sermon or a political campaign;
3. plant ideas in your mind, as in advertising, literature and, yes, romance;
4. or simply to entertain you, as in good conversation or literature.

Whatever the reason, the ability to draw inferences depends first on a correct literal understanding of what's being written or said. Then you must interpret the implications carefully. Stay with what the author *intended you to infer.* Do not let your imagination make inferences that the facts or evidence cannot support.

As you read the following passage, notice the *actions* and the *words that describe those actions.* What is the author implying with them?

> In the living room, the grandmother sat in her usual chair. She looked down at her lap while one hand absently stroked the other. The mother pressed the drip-dry men's shirts, one after the other, and hung them on hangers with more than the usual thump of her iron and clanking of the hangers. Every few minutes she glanced at the wall clock, with a worried twitch of her eyebrows. Davey, the ten-year-old, ran into the room and turned on the television. But the mother pushed past him, snapped it off, and gritted between her teeth, "You can't have that boob tube on tonight!" He opened his mouth in surprise, then turned and ran out, slamming the door. Once again, the iron thumped, the shirt hangers clanked. To the two women, the hands of the clock seemed to be paralyzed.

1. *Stated details:* What are some of the stated details? (Look at the stated actions.)

   _____

   _____

   In what pattern are they organized? _____

2. *Connotations of words:* What feeling or emotion is implied by these phrases and words from the passage?

absently: _____

more than the usual thump: _____

pushed, snapped, gritted: _____

boob tube: _____

slamming: _____

paralyzed: _____

3. *Unstated details:* What are some of the simple unstated facts? (Example: The two women share the same feeling of anxiety.)

_____

_____

4. *Deeper inferences:* What deeper inferences can you make about this situation? _____

_____

5. Try to think of some *unsupported* inferences (in other words, guesses that go too far).

_____

_____

► *Answers*

1. *Stated details:* Three people are mentioned: a mother who is ironing silently, a grandmother who is sitting silently, and a ten-year-old boy who is not allowed to watch his usual TV program. The mother watches the clock anxiously. And so on. (The details are arranged in a chronological time sequence.)

2. *Connotations of words: absently* implies something else is on her mind; *more than the usual thump* implies anger; *pushed, snapped, gritted* implies anger; *boob tube* implies impatience and anger; *slamming* implies hurt feelings, anger, confusion; *paralyzed* implies helplessness, out of hope and patience, waiting for something important.

3. *Unstated details:* The two women share the same feeling of anxiety. The mother seems irritated by the ten-year-old's behavior. He must usually watch TV, since he seems surprised at being scolded.

4. *Deeper inferences:* Someone—the father?—is late coming home. Something is about to happen, which the women know about and expect but the ten-year-old doesn't. It is not a pleasant something—the details all express tension in the air.

5. *Unsupported inferences:* Father has lost his job and is coming home in a drunken rage to beat his family. Or the two women and the child are being held hostage by an ax murderer sleeping in the bedroom while his shirt is being ironed.

Theme: Beyond Sex Roles

These readings discuss a hot social issue: expectations that people or society might have for us because of our sex. As some of these selections suggest, even our *own* view of ourselves might be limited by how we feel we have to act just because we were born male or female.

Practice Paragraphs

Read the following paragraphs carefully for the author's implied meaning. Look beneath the surface for *unstated* details as well as for *stated*.

A. The slightest mischance in my life makes me want to fling myself into the protection of someone else's bank account. And yet I still speak of "our money" as clearly separated from "my money." Occasionally, men become liberated and it is a dreadful shock. "I'm not going to work this year; I need to think," announced a friend's husband. She had spent seven years in his care and keeping and then, as she put it, "Finally I get my own business going and *he* wants to lie around all day." Why not? Women who say, "I like my freedom—I have my day organized and I can do what I like with my time," forget that men are entitled to some of that freedom. They are also prisoners of the rigid structure of their roles and jobs.*

1. On the *surface* level, what is the author's main idea? (State your idea in a complete sentence.) _____

_____

2. Write two examples the author gives of how she and other women are unfair to men. (This unfairness is an *unstated* detail.)

_____

_____

3. What are some deeper inferences you might draw about the author's attitude on the conflict she describes?

_____

_____

_____

B. In men, good looks is a whole, something taken in at a glance. It does not need to be confirmed by giving measurements of different regions of the body. Nobody encourages a man to dissect his appearance, feature by feature. As for perfection, that is considered trivial—almost unmanly. Indeed, in the ideally good-looking man a small imperfection or blemish is considered positively desirable. According to one movie critic (a woman) who is a declared

---

*From "The Housewife's Moment of Truth" by Jane O'Reilly. Reprinted by permission of the author.

Robert Redford fan, it is having that cluster of skin-colored moles on one cheek that saves Redford from being merely a "pretty face."*

1. On the *surface* level, what is the author's main idea? (State your idea in a complete sentence.) _____

   _____

2. Explain how a woman's appearance is viewed. (This is merely *implied* in the paragraph.) _____

   _____

   _____

3. In what way are both men's and women's appearances viewed as a put-down of women? _____

   _____

   _____

   _____

C. (1) Have women come a long way, baby? (2) The answer was "no" at a teleconference held at El Camino College, in Torrance, California. (3) In this exploration of the status of women over 40, feminist lawyer, Gloria Allred, and conference organizer, Dr. Sharon Yaap made several discouraging points. (4) "Being women means they have a 60 percent greater chance than men of spending their later years in poverty. (5) Two-thirds of all women between the ages of 40 and 60 are trapped in low-paying, dead-end jobs. . . . (6) Only 7 percent of women who divorce their husbands are being awarded alimony, and then only as an economic cushion until they are able to support themselves. (7) Following divorce, a woman's income declines an average of 70 percent, while a man's income rises by an average of 40 percent. (8) Seventy-seven percent of all women are unable to collect child support three years after it's awarded. . . ."**

1. What is the author's implied main idea? (State your idea in a complete sentence.) _____

   _____

2. Which sentence, more than any other, makes the strongest implication that men are irresponsible? _____

3. What action do you infer Ms. Allred wants the women at the teleconference to take? _____

   _____

---

*From Susan Sontag, *Beauty* (New York: Farrar, Straus, & Giroux, 1975).

**From "Women over 40 in the '80s" by Verne Palmer, *The Daily Breeze*, October 4, 1988. Reprinted with permission of The Daily Breeze © Copyright 1988.

Words in Context

For each *italicized* word, choose the best meaning.

► *Short Reading 10G*

1. No one remarks *disparagingly* about the male executive who "shoots from the hip" during the day and becomes tender and affectionate with his family at home; somehow, casual observers don't see an inconsistency here. [Extra Clue: An antonym is *complimentarily.*]

   (a) angrily (b) secretively (c) belittingly (d) loudly

► *Short Reading 10H*

2. Over the years, out of an *innate* sense of respect, I imagine, I have refused to smother women with outdated courtesies [Extra Clue: from *nasci* meaning *to be born*]

   (a) learned (b) inborn (c) artistic (d) reluctant

► *Long Reading 10I*

3. She had planned a funny little story about the deeply humorous *pomposity* of executives. [Extra Clue: Politicians are often accused of being pompous.]

   (a) sophistication (b) jokes (c) mannerisms (d) self-importance

The first selection, from Men Are Just Desserts *by Sonya Friedman, points out the difficulties faced by a woman in business if she tries to step out of her traditional role. See if you agree with her point of view.*

Preview: *In 20 seconds or less, read the title, first two sentences, and last two sentences of the article. What problem do you think ambitious women in an office have with men, according to this author?* _____

_____

Wait for a signal from your instructor before you begin reading. Circle your WPM after one minute. Inference tip: Look for the author's definition of "bitch."

from *Men Are Just Desserts*

Sonya Friedman

WPM

I would like to offer another perspective on the word *bitch*.	11
The next time a man at the office spits out "Bitch!" or mumbles it	25
under his breath just loud enough for you to doubt whether you've	37
heard it at all, congratulate yourself, if he's referring to you. You've	48
received a compliment. It probably means you've demonstrated com-	56
petence, effectiveness, and assertiveness. The man is therefore feel-	65
ing inadequate or cornered. Since he's not prepared to deal with a	76
woman who knows what she's talking about, especially if she proves	87
him wrong, he's agitated and threatened. If he's threatened, his	97
power is on the line, and when that line is drawn by a woman, she is,	113
in his eyes, a bitch. As Michael Korda says in *Power! How to Get It, How*	129
to Use It, "Pushed hard enough, (men) will give way on money, titles,	142
large offices, expense accounts—anything but power. So long as a	153
man can have the final word, he is reasonably content to give up	166
anything else, though not of course without a struggle." . . .	175
A man is admired for displaying good business sense. Men	185
have long equated greatness in industry with the ability to "drive a	197
hard bargain," "rule with an iron fist," "keep an ear to the ground,"	210
"be a tough negotiator," and "tell it like it is." What of women who	224
possess such skills? Men still hold to the notion that assertiveness	235
and the ability to use logic are biologically determined traits—male	246
traits. The women who dares to defy this notion is therefore a	258
"bitch"; "she thinks she knows it all." In fact, in a man's eyes, she may	273
know too much, or she may know just enough to get his job. A man	289
who has the power to provoke feelings of inadequacy in another	300
man is one thing; a woman who has the power to arouse such feel-	314
ings in a man is the worst kind of creature . . . a bitch. . . .	325
Ideally, the qualities that draw admiring glances in the busi-	335
ness world should be redefined to include both men and women.	345
The truth is that a woman can be competitive and feminine too. No	358
one remarks disparagingly about the male executive who "shoots	367
from the hip" during the day and becomes tender and affectionate	378
with his family at home; somehow, casual observers don't see an	389
inconsistency here. But if a woman displays the same behavior, she	400
must be sexually frustrated, unnatural, fulfilling her wish to be a	411

man, relentlessly trying to prove something—a bitch. But an un-**421**
biased appraisal reveals that she's fulfilling herself by working intel-**431**
ligently and productively. And if she's called a bitch for that, her only**443**
answer should be "Thank you."***448**

Immediately answer the following questions without referring to the selection.

1. When a woman shows the same aggressiveness and competence in business that a man does, some men react with

   (a) praise and congratulations. (b) fear and hostility. (c) amusement. (d) indifference.

2. A woman in business frequently receives disapproval for displaying the qualities for which a man is admired. **T** **F**

3. What is most difficult for a man to give up in business?

   (a) power (b) money (c) a title (d) a large office

4. The author suggests that a woman's being called a bitch is positive rather than negative because it means she has been effective in her job. **T** **F**

5. The title *Men Are Just Desserts* is a play on words and could have more than one meaning. What does it mean

   (a) if you stress "desserts"? _____

   (b) if you stress "just"? _____

Record your scores below and on the progress chart in the Appendix.

WORDS PER MINUTE _____

% COMPREHENSION _____

---

*Reprinted by permission of Warner Books/New York. From *Men Are Just Desserts*. Copyright © 1983 by Sonya Friedman.

The second article, by Jack Smith, popular Los Angeles Times *columnist, expresses the confusion men have over changes in etiquette because of women's liberation.*

Preview: *Quickly read the title and first and last paragraphs. Then write what you think the thesis will be.*

_____

_____

Wait for a signal from your instructor before you begin. Circle your WPM after one minute. Try to determine from the author's language what his tone (or attitude) is. Be careful not to assume the obvious. Also, be alert to who says what.

Men's Liberation from Etiquette

Jack Smith

	WPM
One of the blessings for men in women's liberation, accord-	10
ing to the feminist magazine *Ms.*, is that men are no longer obliged	22
to pay women the stylized courtesies of the etiquette book.	32
"Goodby Emily, Goodby Amy," says Jane Trahey in an article	42
on the new manners. Ms. Trahey declares that a perfectly able	53
woman no longer has to act helpless in public. She no longer need	66
allow a man to steer her about by the elbow, pull out chairs, open	80
doors, and otherwise act as if he were dealing with a dummy.	92
Ms. Trahey points out that women do not need help getting in	104
and out of cars. "Women get in and out of cars twenty times a day	119
with babies and dogs. Surely they can get out by themselves at night	132
just as easily."	135
She also says there is no reason why a man should walk on the	149
outside of a woman on the sidewalk. "Historically, the man walked	160
on the inside so he caught the garbage thrown out of a window.	173
Today a man is supposed to walk on the outside. A man should walk	187
where he wants to. So should a woman. If, out of love and respect, he	202
actually wants to take the blows, he should walk on the inside—	214
because that's where the muggers are all hiding these days."	223
As far as manners are concerned, I suppose I've always been a	235
feminist. Over the years, out of an innate sense of respect, I imagine,	248
I have refused to smother women with outdated courtesies.	257
It is usually easier to follow rules of social conduct than to	269
depend on one's own taste. But rules may be safely broken, of course,	282
by those of us with the gift of natural grace. For example, when a	296
man and woman are led to their table in a restaurant and the waiter	310
pulls out a chair, the woman is expected to sit in the chair. That is	325
according to Ms. Amy Vanderbilt. I have always done it the other way,	338
according to my wife.	342
It came up only the other night. I followed the hostess to the	355
table, and when she pulled the chair out I sat on it, quite naturally,	369
since it happened to be the chair I wanted to sit in. I had the best view	386
of the boats.	389

"Well," my wife said, when the hostess was gone, "you did
it again."

"Did what?" I asked, utterly baffled.

"Took the chair."

Actually, since I'd walked through the restaurant ahead of my
wife, it would have been awkward, I should think, not to have taken
the chair. I had got there first, after all.

Also, it has always been my custom to get in a car first, and let
the woman get in by herself. This is a courtesy I insist on as the
stronger sex, out of love and respect. In times like these, there are
muggers lurking about. It would be foolhardy indeed to put a
woman in a car and then shut the door on her, leaving her at the
mercy of some lout who might well be crouching in the back seat.*

400
402
408
411
421
434
443
458
473
486
497
512
525

Immediately answer the following questions without referring to
the selection.

1. State the thesis of the selection in a complete sentence.

_____

_____

2. The author's attitude toward the issue of etiquette and women's liberation is one of

(a) harsh criticism of men. (b) anger at women. (c) gently poking
fun at both men and women.

3. Ms. Trahey points out that women with babies and dogs do need to be
helped in and out of cars.   T   F

4. The author says he always gets in a car first to protect his wife.   T   F

5. The purpose of the restaurant example is to show that

(a) Smith has bad manners.

(b) some rules of etiquette are foolish.

(c) his wife expects too much.

Record your scores below and on the progress chart in the Appendix.

WORDS PER MINUTE _____

% COMPREHENSION _____

*From "Men's Liberation From Etiquette" by Jack Smith in "Goodbye Amy, Hello Jane," *Los Angeles Times,* September 12, 1972. Copyright © 1972 Los Angeles Times. Reprinted by permission.

This last selection from Ms. *magazine has become a classic in the feminist movement. It describes the awakening of women to an awareness of the roles they have been forced into.*

Preview: *In 40 seconds or less, read the title, first paragraph, and last two sentences of the article. Then write what you think the thesis will be.* _____

_____

Wait for a signal from your instructor before you begin reading. (Read again the parts you just previewed.) As you read, look more closely than usual for inference.

Click!

Jane O'Reilly

Women are beginning to experience that click! of recognition—that moment of truth that brings a gleam to our eyes and means the revolution has begun. Those clicks are coming faster, and women are getting angry. Not redneck-angry from screaming because we are so frustrated and unfulfilled, but clicking-things-into-place-angry. We have suddenly and shockingly seen the basic lack of order in what has been believed to be the natural order of things.

One little click turns on a thousand others.

In Houston, Texas, a friend of mine stood and watched her husband step over a pile of toys on the stairs, put there to be carried up. "Why can't you get this stuff put away?" he mumbled. Click! "You have two hands," she said, turning away.

Last summer I got a letter from a man who wrote: "I do not agree with your last article, and I am cancelling my wife's subscription." The next day I got a letter from his wife saying, "*I* am not cancelling *my* subscription." Click!

On Fire Island my weekend hostess and I had just finished cooking breakfast, lunch, and washing dishes for both. A male guest came wandering into the kitchen just as the last dish was being put away and said, "How about something to eat?" He sat down, expectantly, and started to read the paper. Click! "You work all week," said the hostess, "and *I* work all week, and if you want something to eat, you can get it, and wash up after it yourself."

In New York last fall, my neighbors—named Jones—had a couple named Smith over for dinner. Mr. Smith kept telling his wife to get up and help Mrs. Jones. Click! Click! The two women radicalized at once.

A woman I know in St. Louis, who had begun to enjoy a little success writing a grain company's newsletter came home to tell her husband about lunch in the executive dining room. She had planned a funny little story about the deeply humorous pomposity of executives, when she noticed her husband rocking with laughter. "Ho ho, my little wife in an executive dining room." Click!

Last August, I was on a boat leaving an island in Maine. Two families were there with me, and the mothers were discussing the troubles of cleaning up after a rental summer. "Bob cleaned up the bathroom for me, didn't you, honey?" she confided, gratefully patting her husband's knee. "Well, what the hell, it's vacation," he said fondly. The two women looked at each other, and the queerest change came over their faces. "I got up at six this morning to make sandwiches for the trip home from this 'vacation,' " this first one said. "So I wonder why I've thanked him at least six times for cleaning the bathroom?" Click! Click!

In suburban Chicago, the party consisted of three couples. The women were a writer, a doctor, and a teacher. The men were all lawyers. As the last couple arrived, the host said, heartily, "With a roomful of lawyers, we ought to have a good evening." Silence. Click! "What are we?" asked the teacher. "Invisible?"

In an office, a political columnist, male, was waiting to see the editor-in-chief. Leaning against a doorway, the columnist turned to the first woman he saw and said, "Listen, call Barry Brown and tell him I'll be late." Click! It wasn't because she happened to be an editor herself that she refused to make the call.

In the end, we are all housewives, the natural people to turn to when there is something unpleasant, inconvenient, or inconclusive to be done. It will not do for women who have jobs to pretend that society's ills will be cured if all women are gainfully employed. In Russia, 70 percent of the doctors and 20 percent of construction workers are women, but women still do *all* the housework. Some revolution. As the Russian women's saying goes, it simply freed us to do twice the work.

They tell us we are being petty. The future improvement of civilization could not depend on who washes the dishes. Could it? Yes. The liberated society—with men, women and children living as whole human beings, not halves divided by sex roles—depends on the steadfast search for new solutions to just such apparently unimportant problems, on new answers to tired old questions. Such questions as:

Denise works as a waitress from 6 A.M. to 3 P.M. Her husband is a cabdriver, who moonlights on weekends as a doorman. They have four children. When her husband comes home at night, he asks: *"What's for dinner?"*

Jonathan and Joanne are both doctors. They have identical office hours. They come home in the evening to a dinner cooked by the housekeeper. When they go to bed, he drops his clothes on the floor and she picks them up. In the morning he asks: *"Where is my pink and orange striped shirt?"*

In moments of suburban strife, Fred often asks his wife, Alice, "Why haven't you mended my shirt and lubricated the car? *What else have you got to do but sit around the house all day?"*

According to insurance companies, it would cost Fred $8000 to $9000 a year to replace Alice's services if she died. Alice, being an average ideal suburban housewife, works 99.6 hours a week—always feeling there is too much to be done and always guilty because it is never quite finished. Besides, her work doesn't seem important. After all, Fred is paid for doing whatever it is he does. Abstract statistics make no impact on Alice. "My situation is different," she says. Of course it is. All situations are different. But sooner or later she will experience—in a blinding click—a moment of truth. She will remember that she once had other interests, vague hopes, great plans. She will decide that the work in the house is less important than reordering that work so she can consider her own life.

The problem is, what does she do then?*

TOTAL READING TIME _____

Immediately answer the following questions without referring to the selection.

1. Choose the statement that best expresses the thesis.
  (a) Men must arm themselves against a female revolution.
  (b) Women are beginning to realize the unfairness of their being totally responsible for housework.
  (c) Women are beginning to prefer careers to housework.
  (d) A woman's place is in the kitchen.

2. According to the author, one can expect women in the future to demand a live-in maid.　　　　　　　　　　　　　　　　T　　F

3. Why were the "two women radicalized at once" over Mr. Smith telling

his wife to help Mrs. Jones with dinner? _____

_____

4. The men in the examples take a woman's role as homemaker for granted.　　　　　　　　　　　　　　　　　　　　　T　　F

5. The problem of sex discrimination in Russia has been solved.　　T　　F

6. Insurance companies estimate that it would cost approximately $9000 annually to replace a housewife's services.　　　　　　　　T　　F

7. The author seems to be saying that despite the fact that women are often frustrated and unfulfilled, they still believe the natural order of things to be in their best interest.　　　　　　　　　　　　T　　F

8. As in Russia, working women in America are still almost totally responsible for the care of home and families.　　　　　　　　T　　F

9. Why is the cabdriver's question, "What's for dinner?" unfair since he

has two jobs and his wife has only one? _____

_____

10. What does "click!" mean?
  (a) the turning on of a light bulb **(b)** the realization of a chore to be done **(c)** the shock of recognition that something is unfair

Turn to the Rate Chart in the Appendix to get your words per minute for this selection. Then record your scores below and on the progress chart in the Appendix.

WORDS PER MINUTE _____

% COMPREHENSION _____

---

*From "The Housewife's Moment of Truth" by Jane O'Reilly. Reprinted by permission of the author.

1. Write a paragraph describing a time in your life when you were expected to act or think a certain way simply because of your sex. (Examples: you were expected to fight someone because you were a boy even though you weren't angry, or you were expected to play dolls quietly when you really wanted to play baseball.) Explain why you think this situation was unfair.

2. Discuss whether or not you agree with the point of view expressed in any of the selections in this Lesson. Write a paragraph with a topic sentence that sums up your opinion. Expand on your topic sentence with supporting details.

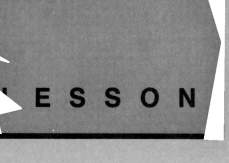

LESSON

11

Reading Deeper for Inferences

IN THIS LESSON, YOU WILL

1. continue perception and comprehension;

2. learn three common literary devices (tone, irony, and satire) used in fiction;

3. learn to draw even *deeper inferences* in more imaginative paragraphs and articles.

► *Exercise 11A—Phrase Perception (Variation)*

Each column of twenty items has only one key phrase. Mark each repeated phrase. Work through both columns vertically before checking your time.

Key Phrase	**Key Phrase**
bear in mind	*the right station*
bear in window	the eighth station
bears in mind	the bright station
bears in the wind	the richest station
bear in winter	the right stanchion
bare in mind	the right state
beer in mind	the right station
bear in mind	the mighty station
bearing minds	the right station
mindless bear	the rigged station
barring minds	the right states
bear in mind	the station's right
bear in mid-winter	the right stallion
bear in mind	tight little station
bear on your mind	the right station
hear in mind	the straight station
hear in the wind	the fight station
read your mind	the right station
bear in mind	the fighting station
read and mind	the night station
bearing in mind	the right station

TIME _____

ERRORS _____

► *Exercise 11B—Phrase Perception (Variation)*

Each column of twenty items has only one key phrase. Mark each repeated phrase. Work through both columns vertically before checking your time.

Key Phrase	**Key Phrase**
cope with life	*a slow drawl*
copout from life	a low trawler
cope with strife	a low shawl
cope with life	a low drawling
copper has life	as low a drawl
coping with life	a lower drawl
cape with knife	a slight frawl
cop wins life	a slow down
cope with light	a slow drawl
cops with lifer	a slow crawl
cope with life	as slowly crawl
come with life	a southern drawl
run from life	a slow draw
cope within	as slow a draw
coping with line	a slow drowning
cope with line	a slow howl
coping wins life	a low drawl
cold without life	a slow drawl
cope with life	a loud drawl
cope with knife	our slow drawl
poke with knife	a slow drawl

TIME _____

ERRORS _____

► *Exercise 11C—Word Comprehension (Variation)*

Choose the **antonym** (opposite word) of the key word in **boldface** print.

Key Word

1.	a **cryptic** note	clear	affectionate	secret
2.	to **curtail** parties	hide	stop	increase
3.	**boisterous** talk	noisy	quiet	interesting
4.	**frugal** with gifts	lavish	tasteless	economical
5.	to hold in **esteem**	respect	dishonor	safekeeping
6.	to **elongate** his arm	cut off	lengthen	shorten
7.	**futile** advice	significant	necessary	useless
8.	becoming **listless**	enthusiastic	attentive	inactive
9.	a **slothful** worker	lazy	sorry	energetic
10.	to **bolster** his ego	tear down	save	support
11.	a **plausible** story	harmful	incredible	believable
12.	an **eloquent** sermon	well-expressed	awkward	long
13.	a **chagrined** smile	poised	leering	embarrassed
14.	to offend the **clientele**	customers	relatives	owners
15.	to **disintegrate** slowly	decay	improve	move
16.	a **grotesque** body	well-shaped	distorted	huge
17.	to reach the **apex**	side	peak	bottom
18.	to **revoke** privileges	examine	issue	cancel
19.	a **turbulent** marriage	calm	terrible	agitated
20.	to act with **intensity**	force	weakness	friendship

TIME _____

ERRORS _____

► *Exercise 11D—Word Comprehension (Variation)*

Choose the **antonym** (opposite word) of the key word in **boldface** print.

Key Word

1.	to **dispel** our fears	drive away	ridicule	encourage
2.	**fallacious** thinking	sound	indirect	false
3.	**spontaneous** laughter	unplanned	forced	silly
4.	a **glib** compliment	awkward	unbelievable	too-smooth
5.	**exuberant** applause	sincere	lavish	lukewarm
6.	a **dynamic** company	new	listless	energetic
7.	to **glean** rumors	spread	falsify	gather
8.	to **enthrall** an audience	irritate	captivate	bore
9.	an **imperative** request	interesting	unneeded	urgent
10.	a **phenomenal** singer	ordinary	shrill	extraordinary
11.	a **deficient** performance	defective	efficient	flawless
12.	an **invigorating** day	stimulating	calming	insufferable
13.	to **dilate** an opening	fill up	expand	narrow
14.	an **illegitimate** business	legal	illegal	bankrupt
15.	**torrid** weather	hot	cold	dry
16.	an **alluring** face	repulsive	friendly	fascinating
17.	**havoc** in the crowd	leader	commotion	order
18.	a **portly** gentleman	stout	thin	mannerly
19.	a **pessimistic** personality	positive	gloomy	changeable
20.	a **prelude** to the play	introduction	ticket	conclusion

TIME _____

ERRORS _____

► *Exercise 11E—Phrase Comprehension (Variation)*

Mark every *verb* in the phrases and clauses below. (A verb expresses action or state of being.) Some items have none. Try to follow the action described in the phrases.

1. 32° temperature
2. good butchering weather
3. neighbors come early
4. catch razorback hog
5. shoot in head
6. right between eyes
7. stab in heart
8. 6-inch knife blade
9. bleed until drained
10. drop in huge vat
11. of scalding water
12. hair comes off
13. scrape off remaining hair
14. wash hog well
15. hog now white
16. tie up back legs
17. swing hog off ground
18. take the knife
19. rip downwards
20. through the breastbone
21. stop at neck
22. saw off head
23. remove liver and heart
24. remove intestines
25. wash out intestines
26. soak for 2 or 3 days
27. fry intestine walls
28. southern delicacy—chitlings
29. saw down backbone
30. lay 2 halves on table
31. cut hind quarter off
32. for the ham
33. take out ribs
34. cut between
35. front and back quarter
36. for bacon
37. front quarter
38. is for roasts
39. pork chops are
40. from backbone
41. take the trimmings
42. of lean meat
43. grind up together
44. 1/4 fat and 3/4 lean
45. add seasoning
46. makes sausage
47. give to neighbors
48. their fair share
49. everybody has
50. meat for winter

TIME _____

ERRORS _____

NOTE: You are using both your skimming and scanning skills in these phrase exercises.

► *Exercise 11F—Phrase Comprehension (Variation)*

Mark every *verb* in the phrases and clauses below. Some items have none. Again, follow the action. (Who repairs the flat tire?)

1. the long drive home
2. is a rainy night
3. the thunder thunders
4. the lightning lights
5. family in car
6. the children fight
7. hillbilly singer whines
8. on the radio
9. cigar smoke in air
10. air too warm
11. wife studies map
12. small explosion is heard
13. a blown-out tire
14. low curses inside
15. drives over to side
16. coveralls over dress
17. husband with umbrella
18. puts block under wheel
19. prevents rolling
20. flashlight on
21. puts flares around car
22. opens trunk
23. gets out tools
24. jack and tire irons
25. jacks up car

26. only a little
27. removes hub cap
28. loosens lug nuts
29. jacks it up higher
30. removes lug nuts
31. flat tire off
32. replaces with new tire
33. lug nuts on
34. lowers the jack
35. tightens lug nuts
36. hub cap back on
37. tools into trunk
38. flat tire into trunk
39. wife washes hands
40. husband lowers umbrella
41. back in the car
42. children asleep on seat
43. engine starts quickly
44. headlights on
45. windshield wipers on
46. cigar lights up
47. nasal voice sings
48. on the radio
49. the open road
50. the long drive home

TIME _____

ERRORS _____

Can you recognize subtle inferences?

How good are you at determining the *tone* of someone's voice? Do you listen to what is behind someone's words? Do you recognize sarcasm when you hear it? Do you ever hear someone say one thing and know he or she means the opposite?

Because you have probably honed your listening skills to a fine edge, you may have answered these questions positively and confidently. However, could you answer with the same confidence if these questions were applied to your reading skills? Are you aware when an author uses these same subtle, complex expressions?

In earlier Lessons in this book, most of the reading selections have been nonfiction. The inferences you have been asked to draw have been fairly simple and direct. In more imaginative writing (such as the reading selections in this Lesson and in Lesson 12), you will be asked to look deeper, interpret more carefully what you read. For this more complex, evaluative reading, you need to be familiar with some subtler techniques used by many writers. You need to be able to draw deeper inferences about *tone, irony,* and *satire.*

How does a listener determine *tone?*

Here is an example involving *tone.* An aspiring actor appeared before a director who was casting a new play. "All right," said the director, "give me this line seven different ways." He handed the actor a slip of paper on which he had written one word—"thunder." What did the director want? No doubt he wanted to see whether this fellow was indeed an actor, for any good actor should be able to say "thunder" and express several different moods or ideas. Imagine yourself saying "thunder" seven times to express simple irritation or joy or fear or anger or discovery or relief or worry. What is different in your voice as you say the word? Mainly, the *tone* of your voice expresses those different emotions, although you might add facial expression and perhaps some gestures to aid the sound of your voice.

How does a writer express tone?

What happens, though, when we are *reading* the play that the director is casting? The playwright will simply have written the word "thunder" on the page. The page has no voice or facial expression. How will we know how to hear it in our mind's ear as we silently read it in the book? To read it properly and intelligently, we must know the story up to that point. We must also know the character who is to speak that word. What situation caused him to say it? Did he just break a shoelace? Was he surprised to hear thunder in the distance? Is he a farmer upset because of the long drought that threatens his crops? Is he a weirdo who becomes unhinged when nature turns violent? When we know some of these things, as we should if we have read the play carefully up to that point, we can read that word silently with our eyes and at the same time "hear" it in the tone that fits the character and the situation.

Tone is the writer's attitude toward his subject.

In all your reading you need to be aware of *tone.* It is used in this sense to mean the writer's attitude toward subject, characters, perhaps even toward himself or herself. We can't speak to others without revealing a bit of ourselves, no matter what we say. Writers also reveal themselves, sometimes unconsciously, sometimes on purpose, in the way they put their words down on the paper. From the *way* they put their ideas down, we can often infer meanings beyond or even different from what is actually stated.

Irony—to say one thing and mean the opposite

One inference device writers use to express tone is *irony* (saying one thing and meaning exactly the opposite). We all do this every day; it would be a dull world if we didn't. For example, suppose that your friend is fifteen minutes late for an appointment with you. When he or she finally comes in, you say, "Well, I'm glad you're on time as usual." Are you glad, really? Is your friend on time, really? The answer is no to both questions, but look at what you actually said. Did you deliberately lie? No, you made use of irony, a type of tone. (You may have called this device "sarcasm.") And, unless your friend is totally stupid, he or she will realize that you are unhappy at being kept waiting.

Examples of *irony*

Watch for this in some of the material that you read. A humorist like Art Buch-wald may write, "I'm sure glad this country doesn't have a foreign policy because if it did I'd have to explain it to my relatives." He's not really glad, and in spite of his playful touch, there's a sharp poke at the government in his remark. A critic like Dorothy Parker could chop an actress like Katherine Hepburn into small pieces with a savage ironic twist: "She runs the gamut of emotions from A to B."

Satire—to ridicule something or someone

Irony, of course, is a basic tool for the writing of *satire*, which is the act of holding something or somebody up to ridicule. Writers often say just the opposite of what they mean, thus hoping to jolt readers into understanding the main ideas. Perhaps the most famous satirist in our language was Jonathan Swift, who lived more than two hundred years ago. In the imaginary country of Lilliput in *Gulliver's Travels*, he shows us these little humanlike creatures only six inches tall who have their political parties—the Big-enders and the Little-enders. They battle fiercely over whether an egg should be cracked at the big end or the little end. Why such a petty argument? What is he really saying? As we read carefully Swift's description of the two parties and their silly antics, we come to realize that these fictional parties are very much like the Whigs and the Tories in the England of his day. We realize that the Lillputians' big political fights are no more ridiculous, time wasting, and pointless than those of the real politicians, whether in England two hundred years ago or in America today. We can laugh as we read the story, but if our inference antennae are properly extended, we soon sober a bit when we realize that these pompous little Lilliputians are very much like us—or at least those around us.

Satire—sometimes too subtle to see

Although Swift wrote thousands of words of blasting satire attacking the human cruelties and stupidities of his day, he was very much aware that many readers could not or would not make the inferences that he hoped they would. "Satire," he said, "is a sort of glass (mirror) in which beholders do discover everybody's face but their own. And that is why so very few are offended by it."

Theme: Imaginative Prose

In the reading selections that follow, you will need to consciously look for tone, irony, and satire in order to understand the deeper inferences. The readings so far in this book have been mostly non-fiction, taken from newspapers, magazines, and text-books. The selections in this Lesson are drawn from more imaginative forms of writing like novels and classic essays.

Practice Paragraphs

These paragraphs are character sketches by well-known authors. By paying careful attention to the details, you will be able to "infer" the dominant impression the author wants to create.

A. Miss Abbott had a pink nose and came from a small town in South Mississippi. She pronounced words like "night," "bright," and "sight" with the *i's* prolonged and nasal, a sure sign of hillcountry origins. The only book she read through and through, she told us, was the Bible, and you lived to believe her, and to rue the day she got hold of that book. . . . Miss Abbott's religion was Christianity by fear and by rote—so tenacious it got you by the extremities and never let go; . . . she wanted you to believe she herself was in radio contact with the Deity, and had hung the moon for Him on day number six. When she talked about the time she had been saved, a moist glint began creeping into her eyes, which invariably meant the sermon was on its way. She learned to play a little plastic flute, the kind you could get in Woolworth's for a quarter, and she would play us rousing hymns and Christian marches, heedless of the saliva trickling down that instrument onto the floor. After the music she would preach to us on sin and redemption, there being more of the former than the latter, or what the Old Testament said about niggers or Japs, or why we would all end up in hell if God caught us in a backfire. She would not drink Coca-Colas, she said, because of their alcoholic content. Sometimes she would lapse into a sweet, unexpected silence and gaze out the nearest window for endless minutes. Her features would be bathed in gentle peace. Then I knew Miss Abbott was praying to herself.*

1. The author's tone, or attitude, toward Miss Abbott, is one of

   (a) respect. **(b)** ridicule. **(c)** affection. **(d)** hatred.

2. List the details that suggest Miss Abbott was a hypocrite. (What traits contradict her claim of being a good Christian?)

   _____

   _____

   _____

   _____

*Willie Morris, *North Toward Home*. Oxford, MS: Yoknapatawpha Press.

B. (1) He was a rich man: banker, merchant, manufacturer, and what not. (2) A big, loud man, with a stare, and a metallic laugh. (3) A man made out of a coarse material, which seemed to have been stretched to make so much of him. (4) A man with a great puffed head and forehead, swelled veins in his temples, and such a strained skin to his face that it seemed to hold his eyes open and lift his eyebrows up. (5) A man with a pervading appearance on him of being inflated like a balloon, and ready to start. (6) A man who could never sufficiently vaunt himself a self-made man (7) A man who was always proclaiming, through that brassy speaking-trumpet of a voice of his, his old ignorance and his old poverty. (8) A man who was the Bully of humility.*

1. Most of the sentences (or fragments) in this paragraph describe the man's physical appearance. Which three sentences make implications about his *internal* makeup? _____

2. The words "Bully" and "humility" in the last sentence seem contradictory. Explain how they fit in this characterization.

_____

_____

_____

C. Miss Baez sat very still in the front row. She was wearing a long-sleeved navy-blue dress with an Irish lace collar and cuffs, and she kept her hands folded in her lap. She is extraordinary looking, far more so than her photographs suggest, since the camera seems to emphasize an Indian cast to her features and fails to record either the startling fineness and clarity of her bones and eyes or, her most striking characteristic, her absolute directness, her absence of guile. She has a great natural style, and she is what used to be called a lady. . . . Joan Baez was a personality before she was entirely a person, and like anyone to whom that happens, she is in a sense the hapless victim of what others have seen in her, written about her, wanted her to be and not to be. The roles assigned to her are various, but variations on a single theme. She is the Madonna of the disaffected. She is the pawn of the protest movement. She is the unhappy analysand. She is the singer who would not train her voice, the rebel who drives the Jaguar too fast, the Rima who hides with the birds and the deer. Above all, she is the girl who "feels" things, who has hung on to the freshness and pain of adolescence, the girl ever wounded, ever young.**

1. The author's description of Joan Baez is full of

(a) sarcasm. (b) respect and sympathy. (c) complete admiration.
(d) criticism.

---

*From Charles Dickens, *Hard Times.*

**Excerpt adapted from "Where the Kissing Never Stops" from *Slouching Towards Bethlehem* by Joan Didion. Copyright © 1966 by Joan Didion. Reprinted by permission of Farrar, Straus and Giroux, Inc.

2. What is meant by the statement that Miss Baez is "the hapless victim of what others have seen in her"? _____

_____

_____

_____

Words in Context

For each *italicized* word, choose the best meaning below.

► *Long Reading 11G*

1. It is a *melancholy* time to those who walk through this great town, or travel in the country. **(a)** fearful **(b)** sad **(c)** cheerful **(d)** meditative

2. Therefore, let no man talk to me of these and the like *expedients,* till he has at least some glimpse of hope that there will be ever some hearty and sincere attempt to put them in practice. **(a)** necessary evil **(b)** means to an end **(c)** outdated device **(d)** fantasies

3. They would have avoided the lack of common sustenance, with neither house nor clothes to cover them from the *inclemencies* of the weather. **(a)** unpredictability **(b)** natural beauty **(c)** harshness **(d)** rainy season

This article was written by Jonathan Swift, an eighteenth-century writer known for his biting satire. Its purpose was to attract the attention of England to the hardships the mother country imposed on Ireland. Though he wrote the essay over 200 years ago, he proposes his unusual solution to a problem that is current in the United States— what to do with our poor people.

Preview: *In 40 seconds or less, read the title (longer than usual) and the first and last paragraphs, looking for the thesis. Then write what you think the thesis is.*

_____

_____

Wait for a signal from your instructor before you begin reading. (Reread the parts you just previewed.) Read carefully and be suspicious of what Swift says on a literal level.

A MODEST PROPOSAL
For Preventing the Children of Poor People in Ireland from Being a Burden to their Parents or Country, and for Making them Beneficial to the Public

Jonathan Swift

It is a melancholy time to those who walk through this great town, or travel in the country. They see the streets, the roads, and cabin doors crowded with beggars of the female sex, followed by three, four, or six children all in rags and begging every passenger for an alms. These mothers, instead of being able to work for their honest livelihood, are forced to employ all their time in strolling to beg sustenance for their helpless infants. These children grow up and either turn thieves, for lack of work, or leave their dear native country. . . .

I think it is agreed by all parties that this enormous number of children in the arms, or on the backs, or at the heels of their mothers, and frequently of their fathers is, in the present deplorable state of the kingdom, a very great additional grievance. Therefore, whoever could find out a fair, cheap and easy method of making these children sound, useful members of the commonwealth would deserve . . . to have his statue set up for a preserver of the nation.

But my intention is very far from being confined to provide only for the children of professed beggars. It is of a much greater extent and shall take in the whole number of infants at a certain age, who are born of parents . . . as little able to support them as those who demand our charity in the streets.

As to my own part, I have turned my thoughts for many years upon this important subject. I have maturely weighed the several schemes of our [advisors] and have always found them grossly mistaken in their computation. It is true, a child just dropped from its mother may be supported by her milk for a year with little other nourishment. The child may not cost more than two shillings, which the mother may certainly get, or the value in scraps, by her lawful occupation of begging. It is exactly at one year old that I propose to provide for them so that, instead of being a burden on their parents or the parish, or lacking food and clothing for the rest of their lives, they shall, on the contrary, contribute to the feeding and partly to the clothing of many thousands.

There is likewise another great advantage in my scheme. It will prevent the voluntary abortions and that horrid practice of women murdering their bastard children, alas! too frequent among us, sacrificing the poor innocent babes. I doubt their actions are to avoid the expense than the shame, which would move tears and pity in the most savage and inhuman breast.

The number of souls in this kingdom is usually reckoned one million and a half. Of these I calculate there may be about two hundred thousand couples, whose wives are breeders. From this number I subtract thirty thousand couples who are able to maintain their own children (although I apprehend there cannot be so many, under the present distresses of the kingdom). But that being granted, there will remain a hundred and seventy thousand breeders. I again subtract fifty thousand for those women who miscarry, or whose children die by accident or disease within the year. There only remains one hundred and twenty thousand children of poor parents annually born. The question therefore is how this number shall be reared and provided for.

The answer, as I have already said, under the present situation of affairs, is utterly impossible by all the methods hitherto proposed. For we can neither employ them in handicraft or agriculture. We neither build houses (I mean in the country) nor cultivate land. They can very seldom pick up a livelihood by stealing till they arrive at six years old, except where they are quick to learn. . . .

I am assured by our merchants that a boy or girl before twelve years old is no salable commodity. Even when they come to this age they will not yield above three pounds and a half a crown at most, on the exchange. This sale cannot [reimburse] the parents or kingdom, the charge of nutriment and rags having been at least four times that value.

I shall now therefore humbly propose my own thoughts, which I hope will not be liable to the least objection.

I have been assured by a very knowing American of my acquaintance in London that a young healthy child well nursed is at a year old a most delicious, nourishing, and wholesome food, whether stewed, roasted, baked or boiled. I make no doubt that it will equally serve in a fricassee or a ragout.

I do therefore humbly offer it to public consideration that of the hundred and twenty thousand children already computed, twenty thousand may be reserved for breed, whereof only one-fourth part to be males. This number is more than we allow to sheep, black cattle, or swine. My reason is that these children are seldom the fruits of marriage, a circumstance not much regarded by our savages. Therefore one male will be sufficient to serve four females. The remaining hundred thousand may, at a year old, be offered in sale to the persons of quality and fortune through the kingdom. The mother should be advised to let them suck plentifully in the last month, so as to render them plump and fat for a good table. A child will make two dishes at an entertainment for friends. When the family dines alone, the fore or hind quarter will make a reasonable dish. Seasoned with a little pepper or salt, it will be very good boiled on the fourth day, especially in winter.

I have reckoned upon a medium that a child just born will weigh twelve pounds. In a year, if tolerably nursed, it will increase to twenty-eight pounds.

I grant this food will be somewhat dear and therefore very proper for landlords. As they have already devoured most of the parents, they seem to have the best title to the children. . . .

Those who are more thrifty (as I must confess the times require) may flay the carcass of the children. The skin, artifically dressed, will make admirable gloves for ladies and summer boots for fine gentlemen. . . . I rather recommend buying the children alive and dressing them hot from the knife as we do roasting pigs. . . .

I think the advantages, by the proposal which I have made are obvious and many, as well as of the highest importance.

First, . . . this plan would greatly lessen the number of papists, with whom we are yearly overrun. They are the principal breeders of the nation. . . .

Secondly, the poorer tenants will have something valuable of their own, to help pay their landlord's rent. Their corn and cattle have already been seized, and money is a thing unknown to them.

Thirdly, whereas the maintenance of a hundred thousand children, from two years old and upwards, cannot be computed at less than ten shillings a piece per year, the nation's stock will be thereby increased fifty thousand pounds per year. Plus, the profit of a new dish will be introduced to the tables of all gentlemen of fortune in the kingdom, who have any refinement in taste. And the money will circulate among ourselves, the goods being entirely of our own growth and manufacture.

Fourthly, the constant breeders not only will gain eight shillings sterling per year by the sale of their children. They will also be rid of the charge of maintaining them after the first year.

Fifthly, this food would likewise bring great custom to taverns. The merchants will certainly be so prudent as to procure the best receipts for dressing it to perfection. Consequently, they will have their houses frequented by all the fine gentlemen, who justly value themselves upon their knowledge in good eating. A skillful cook, who understands how to oblige his guests, will contrive to make it as expensive as they [can].

Sixthly, this would be a great inducement to marriage, which all wise nations have either encouraged by rewards or enforced by laws and penalties. It would increase the care and tenderness of mothers toward their children. After all, they will be sure of a settlement for life because of the poor babes, provided in some sort by the public, to their annual profit instead of expense. We should see an honest competition among the married women, which of them could bring the fattest child to the market. Men would become as fond of their wives during the time of their pregnancy as they are now of their mares in foal, their cows in calf, or sows when they are ready to give birth. Men will be less likely to beat or kick their wives (as is too frequent a practice) for fear of a miscarriage. . . .

I can think of no one objection that will possibly be raised against this proposal, unless it should be urged that the number of people will be thereby much lessened in the kingdom. This I freely own, and it was indeed one principal design in offering it to the world. I desire the reader will observe that I calculate my remedy for this one individual kingdom of Ireland, and for no other than ever was, is, or, I think, ever can be upon earth.

Therefore, let no man talk to me of other expedients [like using] clothes nor household furniture, except what is of our own growth and manufacture. Do not talk to me of introducing thrift, prudence, and temperance. Do not talk to me of learning to love our country. Do not talk to me of quitting our animosities and petty fighting. Lastly, do not talk to me of putting a spirit of honesty, industry, and skill into our shopkeepers, who, if a resolution could now be taken to buy only our native goods, would immediately unite to cheat us.

Therefore, I repeat, let no man talk to me of these and the like expedients, till he has at least some glimpse of hope that there will be ever some hearty and sincere attempt to put them in practice.

But as to myself, having been wearied out for many years with offering vain, idle, visionary thoughts, and at length utterly despairing of success, I fortunately fell upon this proposal. As it is wholly new, it has something solid and real, of no expense and little trouble, full in our own power, and whereby we can incur no danger in displeasing ENGLAND. For this kind of commodity will not bear exportation, the flesh being of too tender a consistence to [last] a long [time] in salt. Perhaps, however, I could name a country which would be glad to eat up our whole nation without it.

After all, I am not so violently bent upon my own opinion as to reject any offer proposed by wise men, which shall be found equally innocent, cheap, easy, and effective. But before something of that kind shall be advanced in contradiction to my scheme, I desire the author or authors will be pleased to consider two points. First, as things now stand, how will they be able to find food and clothing for a hundred thousand useless mouths and backs? . . . And, secondly, I desire those politicians, who dislike my overture, that they will first ask the parents of these mortals this question. Would they not at this day think it a great happiness to have been sold for food at a year old in the manner I prescribe? They thereby would have avoided such a perpetual scene of misfortunes as they have since gone through by the oppression of landlords and the impossibility of paying rent without money or trade. They would have avoided the lack of common sustenance, with neither house nor clothes to cover them from the inclemencies of the weather. Most of all, they would have avoided the inevitable prospect of [bringing] the same or greater miseries upon their breed forever.

I profess, in the sincerity of my heart, that I have not the least personal interest in endeavoring to promote this necessary work. I have no other motive than the public good of my country, by advancing our trade, providing for infants, relieving the poor, and giving some pleasure to the rich. I have no children by which I can propose to get a single penny, the youngest being nine years old, and my wife past childbearing.*

TOTAL READING TIME _____

Answer the following questions without looking back at the article.

1. Write a sentence that gives the thesis for the article.

_____

_____

2. Swift is completely serious about his proposal to sell babies for food.　　**T**　　**F**

3. A result of his proposal, Swift suggests, is that women will treat their children better because of their value.　　**T**　　**F**

4. In his statement that landlords are entitled to the children because they have already devoured the parents, the author is literally accusing these landlords of cannibalism.　　**T**　　**F**

5. At what age does Swift recommend that a child be sold for food?

(a) one year **(b)** six years **(c)** twelve years **(d)** fifteen years

6. He recommends that an equal number of males and females be reserved for breeding.　　**T**　　**F**

7. Why does the author go into such lengthy detail about the preparation

of the children for food? _____

_____

8. The author seems to direct his sharpest criticism at which of the following groups? **(a)** children **(b)** parents **(c)** landlords **(d)** papists

9. Give any one of the author's six stated advantages to his proposal. ____

_____

10. When the author says "let no man talk to me of other expedients" like

thrift or honesty or patriotism, what does he really mean? _____

_____

Turn to the Rate Chart in the Appendix to get your words per minute for this selection. Then record your scores below and on the progress chart in the Appendix.

WORDS PER MINUTE _____

% COMPREHENSION _____

WRITING AND DISCUSSION ACTIVITIES

1. Rewrite either Practice Paragraph A (on Miss Abbott) or any long paragraph from "A Modest Proposal" *without* using irony or satire. Say simply and directly what you think the author really means.

2. Write a paragraph describing a major personality trait (greed, hypocrisy, arrogance) of someone you know. If you can, use irony or satire.

12

Interpreting Literature

IN THIS LESSON, YOU WILL

1. continue perception and comprehension exercises;

2. pick out other common literary elements (character, conflict, and theme) used in imaginative writing;

3. practice *interpreting literature* in poems and short stories.

► *Exercise 12A—Phrase Perception (Variation)*

Each column of twenty items has only one key phrase. Mark each repeated phrase. Work through both columns vertically before checking your time.

Key Phrase	Key Phrase
immune to colds	*internal stress*
immune to chills	eternal stress
immersed in colds	international stress
immune to colds	internal stress
immune to cold	interminable stress
immune to cold	interior stress
imagine colds	internal stress
among these clods	eternal rest
inured to colds	entirely stress
immunity to colds	intrinsic stress
immune to colds	internal stress
impugn my colds	enter the stress
immune to the cold	eternal trees
immense cold	internal stars
immune to colds	eternal stares
an immense cold	internal satire
immunize against colds	internal stress
immunity to cold	internal stress
immune to clods	interminable stars
immune to colds	interesting stress
immense coffin	interred dress

TIME _____

ERRORS _____

► *Exercise 12B—Phrase Perception (Variation)*

Each column of twenty items has only one key phrase. Mark each repeated phrase. Work through both columns vertically before checking your time.

Key Phrase	**Key Phrase**
varsity baseball	*uncanny look*
university baseball	uncanny book
version of baseball	uncanny brook
varsity basketball	unkind look
various baseballs	uncanny look
varnished baseballs	granny look
varsity baseball	uncanny hook
various basketballs	uncanned cook
university base walls	a nanny look
university baseball	uncanny look
inner city baseball	unplanned book
varsity baseball	unplanned look
varsity baseball	unmanned boat
verse about baseball	banned book
varsity team	unfanned food
varsity racketball	uncared-for look
variation baseball	unkind cook
varsity baseball	uncalled-for look
vanished baseball	uncanny look
varsity baseball	uncanny look
next year, the pros!	must be a witch

TIME _____

ERRORS _____

► *Exercise 12C—Word Comprehension (Variation)*

Look for whole-part relationships and mark the part(s). To illustrate this relationship: a *toe* is a part of the whole *foot;* a *fender* is a part of the whole *car.* (Words expressing this relationship are common transitions between ideas in writing.) There may be more than one answer.

EXAMPLE:

orange	basket	p~~e~~el	lamp	s~~e~~ed	glue

Key Word (whole)

1.	bottle	bat	mother	neck	cells	steak
2.	lamp	base	chair	arm	shade	ankle
3.	kangaroo	scales	ear	sorrow	lipstick	pouch
4.	skirt	trousers	shoes	zipper	dress	rascal
5.	stocking	heel	nails	collar	hammer	toe
6.	wagon	horse	wheel	road	cloud	thunder
7.	desert	traffic	whistle	sand	oak	red
8.	ocean	water	dream	briefcase	salt	paper
9.	book	rug	binding	branch	words	page
10.	bank	golf	basketball	money	vault	nightclub
11.	apple	core	cider	seed	foot	peel
12.	saw	grass	blade	check	handle	magazine
13.	bathroom	tub	stove	soap	refrigerator	towel
14.	egg	skillet	shell	yolk	boil	white
15.	classroom	desk	logs	mink	blackboard	cat
16.	pen	file	ink	sweater	ring	tissue
17.	fish	hair	wings	scales	legs	pencil
18.	street	plane	notes	box	fire	pavement
19.	telephone	elephant	cord	lips	receiver	teeth
20.	watch	belt	cushion	stem	chain	crystal

TIME _____

ERRORS _____

► *Exercise 12D—Word Comprehension (Variation)*

Look for whole-part relationships and mark the part(s). There may be more than one answer.

Key Word (whole)

1.	body	stocking	arm	hat	pill	leg
2.	house	home	family	roof	steps	rake
3.	shoe	track	sole	sock	shadow	heel
4.	car	engine	trip	selfish	wheel	accident
5.	lawn	lost	grass	virtue	knife	bird
6.	cigarette	cigar	teeth	tobacco	board	picture
7.	flower	vase	petal	cut	stem	plant
8.	face	veil	neck	nose	nail	lips
9.	kitchen	stove	bed	sink	car	bathroom
10.	tree	forest	leaf	meadow	trunk	branch
11.	hand	finger	toenail	shoe	wrist	palm
12.	forest	wagon	trees	street	dream	firm
13.	office	clouds	rabbit	desk	tennis	typewriter
14.	cow	horse	hoof	plow	farm	pouch
15.	eye	brow	kneecap	iris	honor	pupil
16.	pencil	park	lead	paper	eraser	powerful
17.	bird	wing	sky	snake	scales	bathroom
18.	coat	hat	stockings	sleeve	hanger	collar
19.	window	scene	pane	door	frame	factor
20.	hammer	tongs	blade	handle	tongue	hatchet

TIME _____

ERRORS _____

► Exercise 12E—Phrase Comprehension (Variation)

Mark each noun in these phrases that represents an animate object (containing human or animal life). Example: the fat finger. Some phrases have none; some have more than one. Try to follow the plot.

1. the overcast sky
2. high on a hill
3. towering stone mansion
4. howl of a coyote
5. a door creaking
6. the monkey's paw
7. the whistling wind
8. the chain clanking
9. sudden glimpse of mummy
10. candles snuffed out
11. a starving black rat
12. the mad doctor
13. in a dank, dark basement
14. blood on the coat
15. a twisted arm hanging
16. glaring bloodshot eyes
17. one foot sliding behind
18. sharpening of a blade
19. eyes on last victim
20. hoarse croaking laugh
21. footsteps up the stairs
22. whining cries of a child
23. lightning outside a window
24. vultures hovering above
25. bat wings rustling in attic

26. bedroom on West Wing
27. pale sleeping girl
28. under a red velvet spread
29. the slim trembling hand
30. an eyelid fluttering
31. stirred by unknown fears
32. bird caught in a trap
33. steps coming closer
34. clawlike hand reaching
35. doorknob slowly turning
36. heavy door creaking open
37. frightened eyes piercing the dark
38. blade illuminated by lightning
39. shrill scream shattering quiet
40. desperate struggle beginning
41. knife near throat
42. lips looming near
43. yellow teeth bared
44. fangs piercing throat
45. not a drop wasted
46. body falling to floor
47. mad doctor dead
48. pink flush returning
49. to girl's pale cheeks
50. return of Vampira

TIME _____

ERRORS _____

► *Exercise 12F—Phrase Comprehension (Variation)*

Mark each noun in these phrases that represents an animate object (has human or animal life). Some phrases have none; some have more than one. Notice the descriptive details establish a setting.

1. small southern town
2. five hundred people
3. the courthouse square
4. magnolia trees on lawn
5. old men on benches
6. whittling and spitting
7. old pick-up trucks
8. bird splattered windshield
9. farmer walking into courthouse
10. to pay his taxes
11. farmer's wife shopping
12. six dry-goods stores
13. horse and wagon
14. causing traffic jam
15. coon dog scratching fleas
16. noon-day sun shining
17. long, hot summer
18. spilled ice cream cone
19. on the pavement
20. flies buzzing around
21. teenagers lined up
22. outside the movie house
23. *Son of Swamp Monster*
24. store clerk rushing
25. back to work

26. shirtsleeves rolled up
27. perspiration on arms
28. college kids hanging around
29. the local dairy treat
30. waitress chewing gum
31. boy on motorcycle
32. roars up
33. waitress giggling
34. manager in front
35. shakes his fist
36. only bank in town
37. customers lined up
38. cashiers handling money
39. children in cowboy boots
40. scuffling on floor
41. mothers grabbing hands
42. holding on tight
43. sound of music
44. and marching feet
45. trumpets off-key
46. the high school band
47. around the courthouse square
48. hands waving
49. hearts beating
50. too much excitement

TIME _____

ERRORS _____

Interpreting literature is really a matter of using all the reading skills you have learned thus far. You find the main idea (or theme). You connect the details, and see a pattern emerge. You read between the lines (or draw inferences).

What is literature?

The word "literature" comes from the Latin *littera*, which means "letter." In the most general sense, then, literature means anything written. But in the way you most often hear the word used, literature refers to poetry, novels, short stories and plays.

Why interpret literature?

Interpreting literature means *appreciating* literature. To appreciate it, you must first understand it. In this Lesson, we will study three of the most common aspects of literature: *character, conflict* and *theme*. Understanding these three basic elements of literature will help you appreciate and enjoy it more.

► *Character*

Observe personality traits

The character who usually interests us the most in a story is the main character. The most entertaining main characters are often the most real, even though they are fictional. They have a mixture of personality traits, some good, some not so admirable, just as real people do. Characters who are realistic in this way we call *rounded*. Characters who are all one-sided and unrealistic we often call *flat* or *stereotyped*. As an aware reader, train yourself to notice (1) characters' personality traits and (2) whether these traits make the characters rounded or flat.

► *Conflict*

Without conflict, there is no story, no play, and often no poem. What is conflict? It is the central problem or group of problems the main character has. Conflict is often what keeps us fascinated when we read a story or watch a play or film. We want to see how the main character handles or *resolves* the conflict he or she is struggling with.

Identify the conflict

Conflict can take many forms. The main character's conflict or problem can be a *physical* one. For example, the main character may actually have to fight another person or a deadly snake or even a serious disease. But just as often, the conflict is on a *psychological* level. This kind of conflict can come in two types: external or internal (or both). In an external psychological conflict, the main character struggles to get his or her way with another character, or struggles to be understood. Stories about conflicts between friends, lovers, or parents and children usually fall into this category of conflict. But in some stories, the psychological conflict is an internal one, meaning inside the main character. For example, the main character may struggle against his or her own bad habits or vices or real desires. Very often, though, a character faces all types of conflict—physical and psychological—in the same story. A twenty-one-year-old son may find himself struggling so hard to prove himself to his father (an external psychological conflict with another character) that he and the father may actually come to blows (a physical conflict). And one of the reasons the son may find it so hard to gain his father's respect is that he is constantly struggling to conquer his own hot temper (an internal psychological conflict).

As you read, look for the main character's conflict or problem. Notice whether it is physical, external psychological or within herself, or a mixture. Then notice the way the main character resolves or handles the conflict. How the main character resolves the conflict can lead you to the theme.

► *Theme*

Infer the theme

The theme is similar to an implied main idea. It is the generalization or statement that we can make about life based on what happens in a particular story, poem, or work of art. For example, Shakespeare's play *Othello* is about a man who strangles his wife because he believes—wrongly—that she has been unfaithful to him. He learns that he has killed what he most loved. We might say, then, that the theme is that unproven jealousy can lead to tragic results.

Seldom in literature do authors state their themes for us. Instead, they imply the theme by the kind of characters and conflict they create and by the way the characters resolve those conflicts and by whether the characters learn from their experiences. We readers must infer the author's dominating idea or theme, but our inference is always a guess. And we should be ready to change our idea of the theme as we understand the work of literature better. Even so, an effort to state the theme can make the reading more rewarding because it forces us to put ourselves in the writer's mind. Just as with other kinds of reading, seeing the whole—whether it's the theme or the thesis—helps us understand the parts better.

► *Summary*

1. Notice the personality traits of the main character. Do these traits make the character rounded or flat?

2. Identify the conflict of the main character. Is the conflict physical or psychological? If psychological, is the conflict external or internal? Or is the conflict a combination?

3. Look at how the character resolves his or her conflict. Has the character learned anything from how the conflict turned out? Have you, the reader, learned anything? Your general statement of the work's main idea is the theme.

Theme: Conflicts in Literature

The selections from imaginative prose in the last Lesson offered you a taste of nonfiction. The readings in this Lesson, all by well-known writers, will broaden your sampling of literature and give you a chance to practice your interpretive skills.

Practice Passages

Read the following passages from a short story, a play, and a poem carefully. Examine the techniques the authors use to express their themes.

A. Francis Macomber was very tall, very well built if you did not mind that length of bone, dark, his hair cropped like an oarsman, rather thin-lipped, and was considered handsome. He was dressed in the same sort of safari clothes that Wilson wore except that his were new. He was thirty-five years old, kept himself very fit, was good at court games, had a number of big-game fishing records and had just shown himself, very publicly to be a coward.*

1. A careless reading might result in a view of Macomber as the typical handsome hero. List the descriptive words that contradict that view, show a conflict between his appearance and his character.

   _____

   _____

   _____

2. What is the significance of Macomber's safari clothes being new?

   _____

3. How are these words—"and had just shown himself, very publicly to be a coward"—*ironic* (or creating a reversal of expectations)?

   _____

B. Like flies are we to the wanton gods;
they kill us for their sport.**

1. What is the author's tone in these two lines?

   (a) religious   **(b)** cynical   **(c)** light and playful

2. List the images (word pictures) used to show the relationship between "us" and "the gods."

What is being described	Images used for comparison
us	_____
the gods	_____

---

*From Ernest Hemingway, "The Short Happy Life of Francis Macomber."
**From William Shakespeare, *King Lear,* IV, i, 1.27

3. What is the theme or point of the two lines?

_____

_____

C. The following poem is written by John Donne, a seventeenth-century British poet. (You may need to use your dictionary.) Read the poem at least twice before you answer the questions below.

> Go and catch a falling star,
>   Get with child a mandrake root,
> Tell me where all past years are,
>   Or who cleft the devil's foot:
> Teach me to hear mermaids singing,
>   To keep off envy's stinging,
>   And find
>   What wind
> Serves to advance an honest mind.
>
> If thou be'st born to strange sights,
>   Things invisible go see,
> Ride ten thousand days and nights
>   Till Age snow white hairs on thee;
> Thou, when thou return'st, wilt tell me
> All strange wonders that befell thee,
>   And swear
>   No where
> Lives a woman true and fair.
>
> If thou find'st one, let me know;
>   Such a pilgrimage were sweet.
> Yet do not; I would not go,
>   Though at next door we might meet.
> Though she were true when you met her,
> And last till you write your letter,
>   Yet she
>   Will be
> False, ere I come, to two or three.*

1. In the first stanza, the poet assigns someone seven tasks to perform.

What do all these tasks have in common? _____

_____

2. In stanza two, what is the final and most difficult task assigned? ___

_____

3. Explain the sudden dramatic shift in the third stanza. Or why does the poet change his mind about going on the _pilgrimage_, or journey, himself? What is his internal conflict?

_____

_____

_____

---

*From John Donne, "Song."

Words in Context

For each *italicized* word, choose the best meaning below.

► *Short Reading 12G*

1. She was a dear little creature, so *guileless* and good-natured. [Extra Clue: *Guile* means *trickiness; less* means *without.*]

    (a) smiling **(b)** simple **(c)** foolish **(d)** passionate

2. Even Miss Pinkerton, that *austere* and god-like woman, ceased scolding her after the first time. [Extra Clue: From Greek *austeros,* meaning *dry* or *harsh.*]

    (a) stern **(b)** violent **(c)** religious **(d)** pompous

► *Short Reading 12H*

3. She looked like a child, but she had the dismal *precocity* of poverty. [Extra Clue: A child who speaks with an adult vocabulary is said to be precocious.]

    (a) misery **(b)** symptoms **(c)** horrors **(d)** maturity

4. Her father, *reprobate* as he was, was a man of talent. [Extra Clue: Opposite of an honorable person.]

    (a) artist **(b)** loving father **(c)** morally unprincipled person **(d)** gambler

► *Long Reading 12I*

5. You must go away from here and from the *impertinences* of these men. [Extra Clue: The antonym for *impertinent* is *respectful.*]

    (a) impudences **(b)** hostile behavior **(c)** conversation **(d)** importance

The following selections are from a nineteenth-century British novel, Vanity Fair, *by William Makepeace Thackeray. The first Short Reading introduces one of the two major characters, who are a study in contrasts.*

Preview: *In 15 seconds or less, read the title and first sentence of each paragraph. Then write at least one personality trait you discovered about Amelia.* _____

_____

Wait for a signal from your instructor before you begin. Circle your WPM after one minute. Continue to look for Amelia's character traits as you read.

Amelia
from *Vanity Fair*

William Makepeace Thackeray

	WPM
Now Miss Amelia Sedley was a young lady who deserved all	11
that Miss Pinkerton (the schoolmistress at Chiswick Hall) said in her	22
praise. Amelia could sing like a lark, dance gracefully, embroider	32
beautifully, and spell as well as the dictionary itself. She also had	44
such a kindly, smiling, tender, gentle, generous heart of her own. She	56
won the love of everybody who came near her, from Miss Pinkerton	68
herself down to the poor girl in the scullery, and the one-eyed tart-	80
woman's daughter. She had twelve intimate and bosom friends out	90
of the twenty-four young ladies.	94
Even envious Miss Briggs never spoke ill of her. High and	105
mighty Miss Saltire (Lord Dexter's grand-daughter) allowed that	113
Amelia's figure was genteel. And as for Miss Swartz, the rich girl	125
from St. Kitt's, on the day Amelia went away, she was in a passion of	140
tears. They were obliged to send for Dr. Floss and make her tipsy.	153
Amelia was a dear little creature, so guileless and good-	162
natured. I am afraid, however, that her nose was rather short than	174
otherwise, and her cheeks a great deal too round and red for a	187
heroine. But her face blushed with rosy health, and her lips with the	199
freshest of smiles. She had a pair of eyes, which sparkled with the	212
brightest and honestest good humor, except indeed when they filled	222
with tears, and that was a great deal too often. For that silly thing	236
would cry over a dead canary bird; or over a mouse, that the cat had	251
seized upon; or over the end of a novel, were it ever so stupid.	265
And as for saying an unkind word to her, were any persons	277
hardhearted enough to do so—why, so much the worse for them.	289
Even Miss Pinkerton, that austere and god-like woman, ceased scold-	299
ing her after the first time. Although she no more comprehended	309
sensibility than she did algebra, she gave all masters and teachers	320
particular orders to treat Miss Sedley with the utmost gentleness, and	331
harsh treatment was injurious to her.	337

Immediately answer the following questions without referring to the selection.

1. Amelia's most admired qualities were
   (a) her singing and dancing.
   (b) her sparkling eyes and fresh smile.
   (c) her embroidery and spelling.
   (d) her sensitivity and kindness.

2. What is the author's tone in the line "for that silly thing would cry over a dead canary bird." (a) completely admiring (b) gently satiric (c) critical

3. The author is making fun of Miss Swartz, who went into a passion of tears at Amelia's departure.   T   F

4. Because Miss Pinkerton was a sensitive, though strict, schoolmistress, she was kind to Amelia.   T   F

5. What seems to be Amelia's character flaw?

_____

Record your scores below and on the progress chart in the Appendix.

WORDS PER MINUTE _____

% COMPREHENSION _____

The second selection introduces Amelia's friend Rebecca.

Preview: *In 15 seconds or less, read the title and the first sentence of each paragraph. Then write at least two character traits you discovered about Rebecca.* _____

Wait for a signal from your instructor before you begin. Circle your WPM after one minute. As you read, look for character traits for Rebecca that are different from those of Amelia.

Rebecca
from *Vanity Fair*

William Makepeace Thackeray

	WPM
Rebecca was seventeen when she came to Chiswick, and was	10
bound over as an articled pupil. Her duties were to talk French. Her	23
privileges were to live cost free, with a few guineas a year and gather	37
scraps of knowledge from the professors who attended the school.	47
She was small and slight in person, pale, sandy-haired, and with eyes	59
habitually cast down. When they looked up they were very large,	70
odd, and attractive.	73
By the side of many tall and bouncing young ladies in the	85
establishment, Rebecca Sharp looked like a child, but she had the	96
dismal precocity of poverty. Many a dun had she talked to and	108
turned away from her father's door. Many a tradesman had she	119
coaxed and wheedled into good-humor, and into the granting of one	130
meal more. She sat commonly with her father, who was very proud of	143
her wit, and heard the talk of many of his wild companions—often	156
but ill-suited for a girl to hear. But she had never been a girl, she said;	172
she had been a woman since she was eight years old.	183
The rigid formality of Chiswick Hall suffocated her. The	192
prayers and the meals, the lessons and the walks, which were	203
arranged with a monotonous regularity, oppressed her almost be-	211
yond endurance. She looked back to the freedom and the beggary of	223
her old home with so much regret that everybody, herself included,	234
fancied she was consumed with grief for her father. She had a little	247
room in the garret, where the maids heard her walking and sobbing	259
at night. But it was with rage, not grief. She had not been much of a	275
dissembler, until now her loneliness taught her to pretend. She had	287
never mingled in the society of women. Her father, reprobate as he	299
was, was a man of talent. His conversation was a thousand times	311
more agreeable to her than the talk of such of her own sex as she now	326
encountered.	327
The pompous vanity of the old schoolmistress, the foolish	336
good humor of her sister, the silly chat and scandal of the elder girls,	350
and the frigid correctness of the governesses equally annoyed her.	360
She had no soft maternal heart, this unlucky girl; otherwise the	371
prattle and talk of the younger children, with whose care she was	383
chiefly entrusted, might have soothed and interested her. She lived	393
among them for two years, and not one was sorry that she went away.	407

The gentle, tenderhearted Amelia Sedley was the only person to   417
whom she could attach herself in the least. And who could help at-   429
taching herself to Amelia?   433

The happiness, the superior advantages of the young women   442
round about her, gave Rebecca inexpressible pangs of envy. She   452
determined at any rate to get free from the prison in which she   465
found herself, and now began to act for herself. For the first time she   479
began to make connected plans for the future.   487

Immediately answer the following questions without referring to
the selection.

1. State the thesis (or theme) of the selection in a complete sentence.

_____

_____

2. Her being at Chiswick Hall caused her to change.   T   F

3. She didn't make friends with any of the other girls—not even Amelia.   T   F

4. The author presents Rebecca as a totally unsympathetic character.   T   F

5. What are some of Rebecca's positive traits? _____

_____

Record your scores below and on the progress chart in the Appendix.

WORDS PER MINUTE _____

% COMPREHENSION _____

This reading reunites Amelia and Rebecca for a final conflict almost two decades after their schoolgirl days.

Preview: *In 30 seconds or less, read the title and the first sentence of each paragraph. Then write what you think their conflict is about.* _____

_____

Wait for a signal from your instructor before you begin. Look for evidence that both women are round, rather than flat, characters.

The Sacrifice
from *Vanity Fair*

William Makepeace Thackeray

[Many years pass; both Amelia and Rebecca marry and have a son each. Amelia becomes a widow and is courted for years to no avail by a Major Dobbin, a gentle, dependable man. She refuses to marry him in memory of her late husband, the more exciting George Osborne.

Rebecca, in the meantime, has been deserted by her husband because she had been taking presents from another man and probably had been unfaithful. Her son is also taken away from her, an act which does not upset her unduly. She has been living a life of not-too-genteel poverty when she is rescued by Amelia and taken into her home—against Dobbin's wishes. He knows Rebecca's reputation and character.

Rebecca takes advantage of her improved situation and lives a little more discreetly. She soon becomes aware that Amelia is pining for Major Dobbin, who has gone away. He finally gave up on his courtship of Amelia because of her stubborn clinging to her husband's memory. The two women go to Bath, where Amelia is being courted by two unsuitable men—old friends of Rebecca's.]

"She mustn't stay here," Rebecca reasoned with herself. "She must go away, the silly little fool. She is still whimpering after that gaby of a husband—dead (and served right!) these fifteen years. She shan't marry either of these men. No, she shall marry the bamboo-cane (Major Dobbin). I'll settle it this very night."

So Rebecca took a cup of tea to Amelia in her private apartment. She found that lady in the company of her miniatures, and in a most melancholy and nervous condition. She laid down the cup of tea.

"Thank you," said Amelia.

"Listen to me, Amelia," said Rebecca, marching up and down the room before the other, and surveying her with a sort of contemptuous kindness. "I want to talk to you. You must go away from here and from the impertinences of these men. I won't have you harassed by them; and they will insult you if you stay. I tell you they are rascals. Never mind how I know them. I know everybody. You are no more fit to live in the world than a baby in arms. You must marry, or you and your precious boy will go to ruin. You must have a husband, you fool. One of the best gentlemen I ever saw has offered you a hundred times, and you have rejected him, you silly, heartless, ungrateful little creature!"

"I tried—I tried my best, indeed I did, Rebecca," said Amelia, "but I couldn't forget—." She finished the sentence by looking up at her husband's portrait.

"Couldn't forget *him!*" cried out Rebecca, "that selfish humbug, that low-bred cockney-dandy, that padded booby, who had neither wit, nor manners, nor heart. He was no more to be compared to your friend with the bamboo-cane that you are to Queen Elizabeth! Why, the man was weary of you, and would have jilted you, but that Dobbin forced him to keep his word. He owned it to me. He never cared for you. He used to sneer about you to me, time after time. He made love to me the week after he married you."

"It's false! It's false, Rebecca!" cried out Amelia, starting up.

"Look there, you fool," Rebecca said, still with provoking good humor. She took a little paper out of her belt, opened it, and flung it into Amelia's lap. "You know his handwriting. He wrote that to me—wanted me to run away with him. He gave it to me under your nose, the day before he was shot—and served him right!" Rebecca repeated.

Amelia did not hear her; she was looking at the letter. It was that which George had put into the bouquet and given to Rebecca on the night of the Duke of Richmond's ball. It was as she said: the foolish young man had asked her to go away with him.

Amelia's head sank down, and she commenced to weep. Her head fell to her bosom, and her hands went up to her eyes. And there for awhile, she gave way to her emotions, as Rebecca stood on and regarded her. Who shall analyze those tears, and say whether they were sweet or bitter? Was she most grieved because the idol of her life was tumbled down at her feet? Or was she indignant that her love had been so despised? Or was she glad because the barrier was removed which modesty had placed between her and a new, a real affection? "There is nothing to forbid me now," she thought. "I may love him with all my heart now. Oh, I will, I will, if he will but let me, and forgive me." I believe it was this feeling which rushed over all the others which agitated that gentle little bosom.

Indeed, she did not cry so much as Rebecca expected—the other soothed and kissed her—a rare mark of sympathy with Rebecca. She treated Amelia like a child, and patted her head. "And now let us get pen and ink, and write to him to come this minute," she said.

"I—I wrote to him this morning," Amelia said, blushing exceedingly.

Rebecca screamed with laughter, and the whole house echoed with her shrill laughter.

TOTAL READING TIME _____

Immediately answer the following questions without referring to the selection.

1. Choose the statement that best expresses the thesis (or theme).
   (a) Amelia was a good woman and Rebecca a bad one.
   (b) Both Rebecca and Amelia had human frailties and virtues.

(c) Amelia was foolish for sacrificing her life for a worthless man.

(d) Rebecca's sacrifice, telling Amelia the truth about her husband, was for nothing.

2. For all her faults, Rebecca was a loving mother.   T   F

3. Rebecca seemed to have selfish motives for telling Amelia about her husband.   T   F

4. Amelia wouldn't marry Major Dobbin because of loyalty to her late husband.   T   F

5. According to Rebecca, Amelia's husband respected his wife even though he was unfaithful to her.   T   F

6. Amelia had no way of knowing whether Rebecca was telling her the truth about her husband.   T   F

7. The author believed Amelia's tears were because

(a) her husband had been unfaithful.

(b) he hadn't loved her.

(c) she was finally free to love Major Dobbin.

(d) her idol had fallen.

8. Rebecca's shrill laughter at the end indicates that she recognizes the irony of her confession.   T   F

9. What keeps Amelia from being a stereotypical "good" character? _____

_____

10. What keeps Rebecca from being a stereotypical "bad" character? _____

_____

Turn to the Rate Chart in the Appendix to get your words per minute for this section. Then record your scores below and on the progress chart in the Appendix.

WORDS PER MINUTE _____

% COMPREHENSION _____

WRITING AND DISCUSSION ACTIVITIES

1. Write a paragraph describing a person you know who has both negative and positive traits.

2. Write a paragraph describing a conflict between two people you know. Try to account for the reasons the people are in conflict.

3. Discuss the use of irony in the reading selections in this Lesson.

HOMEWORK

HOW TO USE THE DICTIONARY

You are probably thinking now that you already know how to use the dictionary. You know the alphabet; so you know how to look up a word. You can find the correct spelling if you have an idea of how the word starts. You know how to find the meaning of a word.

But you have only just *begun* to learn how to use the dictionary. When you look up the definition of a word, do you know why that word might have up to fourteen different definitions listed? Which one do you pick?

There are around twenty other kinds of information (besides spelling and definition) that can be given about a word. How many can you think of? Do you know how to use the aids in the front or back of your dictionary? Perhaps you have never looked at these aids before or after the alphabetized list of words. Also, how do you learn to pronounce words you do not know? Can you pronounce an unfamiliar word after you look it up in your dictionary?

You will find the answers to these questions and to many, many more while working through the following exercise.

► *Exercise 1*

For this exercise you need a large unabridged (uncut) dictionary, an abridged hardcover dictionary, and a paperback dictionary. The exercise might be done as a class project, small group work, or individual work. When you finish, you will know the differences between the three types of dictionaries and which dictionary to choose for a particular problem. (Remember, you can find all three types of dictionaries in your library if they are not available at home or in the classroom.)

1. How many entries (the alphabetized words plus information such as spelling, definition, etc.) are in each dictionary?

   Tip: You do not have to count the words or the pages.

   In the unabridged dictionary _____

   In the abridged hardcover dictionary _____

   In the paperback dictionary _____

2. What special sections or charts do you find in the abridged hardcover dictionary that are not in the paperback?*

   _____

   _____

   _____

   _____

   What special sections or charts do you find in the unabridged dictionary that are not in the abridged hardcover?

   _____

   _____

   _____

   _____

---

*Do not spend too much time on this question. Use abbreviations as much as possible.

3. Most paperback dictionaries do not have a special biography section. Therefore where can you find Albert Einstein's birthdate in your paperback dictionary?

_____

4. Look in all three dictionaries and find the page numbers for the chart of abbreviations and symbols used in the entries of each dictionary.

In the unabridged dictionary _____

In the abridged hardcover dictionary _____

In the paperback dictionary _____

5. On what page do you find information about usage labels? (Example: archiac)

Tip: These labels may be listed as status or subject labels.

In the unabridged dictionary _____

In the abridged hardcover dictionary _____

In the paperback dictionary _____

6. Find the guide words (two words above the line of each page of entries) in any of the dictionaries. Explain how these guide words help you find a word more quickly. _____

_____

7. Find the main pronunciation key in all three dictionaries. Then find the pronunciation key at the bottom of every other page throughout any of the dictionaries. Explain how the sample words in the pronunciation key help you pronounce words. _____

_____

8. How is the pronunciation of a word set apart from the rest of the entry?

_____

How is the etymology (origin) of a word set apart from the rest of the entry?

_____

9. Draw the symbol for "derived from" in the etymology for an entry. _____

10. Look up a couple of words that have long entries and list at least ten different kinds of information given about the words. (Remember, give the *type* of information, not the information itself. Two answers are given.)

_____spelling_____	_____
_____	_____
_____definitions_____	
_____	_____
_____	_____
_____	_____

Check the answers with your instructor.

► *Exercise 2*

Do this exercise individually using a paperback dictionary recommended by your instructor.

1. Give the date and complete title of your dictionary. _____

   _____

2. When was Richard M. Nixon born? _____

3. What is the capital of Rhode Island? _____

4. **(a)** What verb forms are given for the regular verb *reward?*

   _____

   (b) What verb forms are given for the irregular, intransitive verb *lie?*

   _____

5. List all the parts of speech for *cool.* (Give the whole word, not the abbreviation for the part of speech.) _____

   _____

6. Rewrite the following words, showing their syllable division the same way your dictionary does. (You do not need to give the pronunciation.)

   (a) examination _____

   (b) commodious _____

   (c) valedictorian _____

   (d) euthanasia _____

7. Give the plural spelling of the following words.

   (a) belief _____   **(e)** tomato _____

   (b) elf _____   **(f)** sash _____

   (c) sister-in-law _____   **(g)** thesis _____

   (d) phenomenon _____   **(h)** fox _____

8. How many definitions are listed for *order?* _____

9. Give the complete etymology for the following words. (Do not use abbreviations.)

   (a) bane _____

   (b) lollipop _____

   (c) obloquy _____

   (d) quarry _____

10. What is a slang definition for *squeal?* _____

11. **(a)** What is the preferred or central definition for *regular?* _____

   _____

   (b) What is the definition for *sharp* used in music? _____

   _____

12. What is the definition for *relief* used in baseball? _____

   _____

13. What do the following abbreviations stand for?

   (a) M.A. _____

   (b) R.I. _____

   (c) ck. _____

   (d) Bart. _____

14. (a) Give the definition of the suffix (word part at the end of a word) -*ic*. _____

   _____

   (b) Give two words ending in -*ic*. _____

15. (a) Give the definition of the prefix word (word part at the beginning of a word) *intra-*. _____

   (b) Give two words beginning with the prefix *intra-*. _____

16. When you add suffixes to many words, you must double a final consonant, drop an *e*, or add an *i*. Your dictionary gives these inflectional changes. Look up the correct spelling for the following words, and write the complete word (root plus suffix) in the blank.

   (a) courage + ous _____

   (b) convey + ing _____

   (c) patrol + ed _____

   (d) acknowledge + ment _____

17. Look up the definitions for these commonly confused pair of words. Then write a sentence using each word. Make sure your sentences clearly show the difference between the words in each pair.

   (a) continuous _____

   continual _____

   (b) principle _____

   principal _____

   (c) allusion _____

   illusion _____

   (d) implication _____

   inference _____

18. How do you find the number *4* or *8* in your dictionary? _____

   _____

19. (a) Does your dictionary have word combinations like *radio frequency*? _____

   (b) Would *radio frequency* come before or after *radiology*? _____

   (c) Would the entry *William McKinley* come before the entry *Machiavellian* in your dictionary? _____

   (d) Would the word *ma* come before or after McKinley and Machiavellian?

   _____

20. Write all the pronunciation symbols and marks for the following words. Using the pronunciation key at the bottom of every other page, prepare to pronounce the words in class.

    (a) ungulate _____

    (b) desuetude _____

    (c) satyriasis _____

    (d) farinaceous _____

    (e) demesne _____

    (f) dementia _____

    (g) Zeitgeist _____

    (h) deleterious _____

Check the answers with your instructor.

TWENTY WAYS TO COMPLIMENT YOUR FRIENDS

Read the following carefully to determine how the descriptive adjectives in **bold-faced print** are used. Let the context help you determine each word's meaning.

It was the twenty-year reunion for class of 1968, Puddle Creek High School. As Mark drove down the winding old Puddle Creek Road, he thought of some of his old classmates that he hoped to see. He was especially curious to see the ¹**agile** Sally Faye. He loved to watch her ²**lithe** young body moving on the basketball court. She could weave and bob and dribble her way across the court and sink a basket in a flash of the eye. Sally Faye was well coordinated off the court too. He remembered her ³**nimble** fingers flying across the typewriter and piano keys with equal skill.

Another person he hoped to see was Randall, the senior class president. How Mark envied his speaking ability! Randall was ⁴**articulate** on every subject, always able to talk convincingly about anything. He was so ⁵**fluent** that he made even the speech teachers seem like stammering, stuttering idiots in contrast. Mark would never forget how ⁶**eloquent** Randall was in defending senior class privileges—every reason ⁷**plausible.**

The person Mark was sure would attend was the ⁸**affable** Artie Joe. This good-natured class clown would probably be the first to arrive and the last to leave. He would keep the alumni amused with his ⁹**droll** remarks. Though he poked fun at everyone, his jokes were ¹⁰**benign;** they had no bite.

Mark knew the most outstandingly dressed couple there would be the favorite class sweethearts, Ginger Lee and Freddy. She would be looking ¹¹**exotic** in some rich-colored, gypsy-style, swirling dress to match her striking dark features and flashing eyes. He would look ¹²**immaculate** as usual, dressed in ¹³**impeccable** taste. He would probably be wearing an expensively tailored three-piece suit, perhaps beige and brown, with a handmade tie. This inseparable couple would know all the latest dance steps.

And surely Phyllis would be there—¹⁴**vivacious** as ever. Her ¹⁵**effervescent** personality would sparkle and shine, brightening up the party. She would dazzle them all with her ¹⁶**scintillating** wit.

Mark was curious if Alphonse, the class brain, would honor them with his presence. He used to be jealous that Alphonse seemed ¹⁷**proficient** in all subjects, seeming to have no weak areas. He was equally ¹⁸**diligent** in every course, spending as much time in English as in Math or P.E. His study habits were ¹⁹**exemplary.** He studied four hours a day, every day, at the same time and same place. He always studied at a desk, sitting in a straight-back chair, with good lighting over his left shoulder. His answers in class were ²⁰**astute,** right on the mark.

As Mark drove through the night, he worried that he might still be in awe of these shining lights of the Puddle Creek class of 1968.

► *Exercise*

Pick the best definition for the words to the left as they were used in the preceding passage.

1. *agile* (a) aggravating (b) active (c) clumsy

2. *lithe* (a) limber (b) brittle (c) muscular

3. *nimble* (a) slow (b) strong (c) quick

4. *articulate* (a) speaking well (b) artistic (c) talking a lot

5. *fluent* (a) boastful (b) smooth talking (c) intelligent

6. *eloquent* (a) emotional (b) persuasive (c) loud

7. *plausible* (a) believable (b) possible (c) doubtful

8. *affable* (a) rich (b) funny (c) agreeable

9. *droll* (a) slapstick (b) complimentary (c) dryly comical

10. *benign* (a) poisonous (b) mild (c) healthy

11. *exotic* (a) unusual and striking (b) classy (c) beautiful but dumb

12. *immaculate* (a) slovenly (b) neat (c) spotless

13. *impeccable* (a) expensive (b) faultless (c) gaudy

14. *vivacious* (a) amusing (b) weird (c) lively

15. *effervescent* (a) bubbling (b) devious (c) kind

16. *scintillating* (a) sarcastic (b) sparkling (c) sweet

17. *proficient* (a) average (b) competent (c) recognized

18. *diligent* (a) hardworking (b) smart (c) busy

19. *exemplary* (a) well organized (b) to be criticized (c) praiseworthy

20. *astute* (a) correct (b) shrewd (c) pompous

Check the answers with your instructor and record your score below.

% CORRECT _____

TWENTY WAYS TO INSULT YOUR ENEMIES

Read the following carefully to determine how the descriptive adjectives in **bold-faced print** are used. Let the context help you determine each word's meaning.

Mark drove up to the old gymnasium, where the Puddle Creek High School reunion, class of 1968, was being held. He entered the brightly lit room, decorated with balloons and streamers. The first person he saw was former star athlete Sally Faye. What a shock! Her lithe young body had become fat. No longer agile, she had become [1]**slothful**—her movements slow and [2]**listless;** her once nimble fingers were now swollen and arthritic.

Mark ducked into another direction and bumped into Randall, Big Man on Campus, who immediately began boasting about his important executive position with an international banking firm. How could he ever have thought Randall fluent, Mark wondered to himself. The former class president was merely [3]**loquacious.** Randall's fluency with words now seemed [4]**glib.** His tone was [5]**condescending,** his whole manner [6]**supercilious.**

Fortunately they were interrupted by Artie Joe, formerly beloved class clown, loudly trying to get everyone's attention. People were shying away from his [7]**boisterous** behavior. His antics were too [8]**juvenile** and his jokes too [9]**asinine** for people pushing forty to laugh at. As the evening progressed and Artie Joe dipped into the spiked punch more and more, he became [10]**surly** and threatening. His remarks were especially [11]**snide** to those who had laughed most at his jokes in high school.

At one point Mark saw Ginger Lee swirl by—but not with her class sweetheart Freddy. He was dancing with Phyllis on the other side of the gym, carefully avoiding contact with Ginger Lee. Ginger Lee no longer looked exotic to Mark. She now appeared too [12]**flamboyant.** Her dress was [13]**gaudy** with its loud clashing colors, beads, bows, ribbons, and ruffles. Her once distinctive dance style now seemed to Mark only [14]**eccentric.**

The years had been equally unkind to Freddy. Mark realized that Freddy's cool poise hid a [15]**humdrum** personality. His careful attire seemed conservative and unimaginative. Mark quickly became bored with Freddy's [16]**bland** conversation and drifted away to find the class genius, Alphonse. Alphonse told Mark that he was still in graduate school, working on his fourth degree. He seemed so pale and [17]**cadaverous** that he looked as if he had been in prison for ten years. He had dark circles under his eyes, and his frame appeared [18]**gaunt** from improper diet and lack of exercise. His conversation was [19]**tedious;** it was like talking with an encyclopedia. Alphonse's mind was so full of trivia that he wandered from one subject to another and back again in an [20]**incoherent** fashion.

Mark silently slipped out of the gym thinking that perhaps he had not turned out so badly after all.

► *Exercise*

Pick the best definition for the words to the left as they were used in the preceding passage.

1. *slothful* (a) lazy (b) mean (c) sick

2. *listless* (a) without warmth (b) without ambition (c) without energy

3. *loquacious* (a) phony (b) very talkative (c) too friendly

4. *glib* (a) surface; too easy (b) using big words (c) bilingual

5. *condescending* (a) lowering oneself (b) insulting (c) hypocritical

6. *supercilious* (a) superficial (b) arrogant (c) easy to anger

7. *boisterous* (a) smelly (b) obnoxious (c) noisy

8. *juvenile* (a) immature (b) criminal (c) ignorant

9. *asinine* (a) retarded (b) silly (c) too serious

10. *surly* (a) rude (b) strong (c) cursing

11. *snide* (a) funny (b) stupid (c) sarcastic

12. *flamboyant* (a) showy (b) vulgar (c) greasy

13. *gaudy* (a) dull colored (b) cheaply colorful (c) too thin

14. *eccentric* (a) odd (b) clumsy (c) sexy

15. *humdrum* (a) singsong (b) boring (c) snappy

16. *bland* (a) low-voiced (b) colorless (c) loud

17. *cadaverous* (a) sickly (b) corpselike (c) evil

18. *gaunt* (a) ill (b) out of shape (c) thin and bony

19. *tedious* (a) tiresome (b) tender (c) depressing

20. *incoherent* (a) coarse (b) disordered (c) uninformed

Check the answers with your instructor and record your score below.

% CORRECT _____

WORD ANALYSIS

Word analysis is one more way that a reader can unlock the meanings of words. You may learn a word through its use, in context, you may use a dictionary, or you may consciously analyze the word. If English is your native language, you already practice word analysis unconsciously. For example, you know that the last word, "unconsciously," in the previous sentence is the "way you practice." Why do you know this? Because of the little two-letter ending *-ly*. You probably also know that the two-letter beginning *-un* means *not*. The whole word then means "without being conscious of doing it."

In this way, one English word can stand for several words or for a whole phrase. If you can consciously learn how these word parts work and memorize some uncommon parts as well as common ones, you can unlock even more words, especially in more difficult and technical reading. (What word beginnings and endings do you see in this sentence and the previous sentence?)

The three major parts of an English word are called the *root, prefix,* and *suffix.* In the remaining Homework sections you will learn how important these word parts are in unlocking the meaning of unfamiliar words. The root is discussed first, because it is the only essential part of the word. A word consists of *at least* a root. *We will* italicize *the* words *in this sentence that are root* words only. Do you see any beginnings or endings on those italicized words that can be removed and still leave a basic word? (Your answer should be no.)

But if you can remove a part, one that you have seen attached to many other words, and still have a basic word remaining, then that letter or part is probably a *prefix* or *suffix.* Can you do this to the words "removed," "attached," and "words"? If you took off a part from the beginning of the word, the part is called a *prefix.* If you took off a part from the end, it is called a *suffix.*

To remember the order of these three possible word parts in a word, read the word from left to right as usual → and think Prefix-Root-Suffix, or PRS. If you still forget your word parts, think of this Word Animal, made of the letters P, R, and S. (The eye is not a word part, only an eye!)

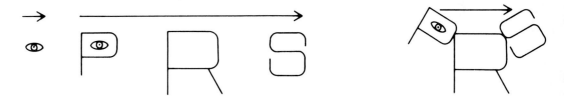

Now look at these words: *removed, incapable, rewording.* We have written the basic word below within the R or root. Add the detachable parts to the root, in the right place on the Animal. (The first one has been done for you.)

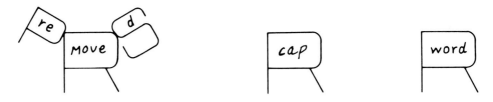

If you did this correctly, you are already a good word analyst!

Look at the table of contents again and notice how many Homework sections are devoted to roots, prefixes and suffixes.

While eighty roots, forty prefixes, and forty-seven suffixes may sound like a lot of word parts to memorize, you probably know many of them already. If you do not, your vocabulary is gravely hampered because these 167 parts are basic to the English language and therefore extremely important. As you advance through your studies, you will learn dozens more, formally through learning lists like these, and informally through your reading and general vocabulary growth.

TWENTY COMMON GREEK AND LATIN ROOTS

We begin our word analysis with a list of twenty common root words that English has borrowed from two ancient languages, Latin and Greek. You will see these roots in many English words, often combined with prefixes and suffixes. Note that a borrowed root does not always make a familiar English word by itself. "Cent" and "cult" are whole words, but "cogni" and "cor" are not. (Also note that the root is usually a stressed syllable in a word.)

Directions: First memorize the root with its original meaning. Then study the example of the root at work in the English language. If you cannot determine the meaning of any example, look up the word in your dictionary. Then jot down any other examples you can think of.

	Root	Original Meaning	English Example	Your Examples
1.	(a)equus	equal, even	equivalent	_____
			equinox	_____
2.	anima	breath, spirit	animate	_____
		mind	magnanimous	_____
3.	*ann, enn	year	annuity	_____
			biennial	_____
4.	anthropo	man	anthropology	_____
			philanthropy	_____
5.	*astro	star	astronomy	_____
			astral	_____
6.	*aud, audit	to hear	auditory	_____
			audio-frequency	_____
7.	*auto	self	automation	_____
			autobiography	_____
8.	bellum	war	rebel	_____
			belligerent	_____
9.	*bene	good, well	benefactor	_____
			benign	_____

10.	*bio	life	autobiography	_____
			biopsy	_____
11.	cap, cept	to take	capture	_____
			accept	_____
12.	*capit	head	capitol	_____
			caption	_____
13.	cede, ceed	to yield, to go	recede	_____
			accessory	_____
14.	cent	hundred	centennial	_____
			centimeter	_____
15.	*chron	time	chronological	_____
			chronic	_____
16.	*civ	citizen	civility	_____
			civilization	_____
17.	cogni	to know	connoisseur	_____
			incognito	_____
18.	cor	heart	core	_____
			courage	_____
19.	*crat, cracy	rule	plutocrat	_____
			democracy	_____
20.	*cred, credit	to believe	credible	_____
			creditor	_____

———
*Also presented in *Reading Faster and Understanding More, Book 1,* and included here for review.

► *Exercise*

Use your knowledge of the original meaning of the root to choose the answer most closely related to the *italicized word*. Write the letter of the answer in the blanks. Do not look back at the list until finished.

_____ 1. In his weakened condition, he was barely *audible*.

(a) able to stand (b) visible (c) able to be heard

_____ 2. He crossed the Alps safely because he was *cognizant* of the dangers.

(a) concerned about (b) aware (c) unaware

_____ 3. As the word itself suggests, *biology* is the study of

(a) living things (b) chemical compounds (c) physical systems

_____ 4. After taking a long draw from her cigarette, she slowly rose to her feet and toasted her new status of *centenarian*.

(a) winner of a marathon (b) someone who is a hundred years old (c) a type of veterinarian

_____ 5. An *asterisk* gets its name from its shape.

(a) starlike (b) circular (c) flowerlike

_____ 6. Atilla and his Huns were noted for their *bellicose* tendencies.

(a) artistic (b) warlike (c) agricultural

_____ 7. The beautiful streets, public buildings, and parks of the city of Santa Barbara are the source of much *civic* pride.

(a) architectural (b) of the citizens (c) financial

_____ 8. No matter how hectic the workload in our office, my boss always responds with *equanimity*.

(a) enthusiasm (b) an even temperament (c) lots of laughs

_____ 9. According to this *chronology*, you entered high school in 1968.

(a) high school yearbook (b) newspaper clipping (c) a list given in order of time

_____ 10. Even though she was dripping with sweat, it was hard for me to give any *credence* to her story about winning the cross-country race.

(a) belief (b) attention (c) sympathy

_____ 11. World power in the future may be controlled by the *technocrats*.

(a) space-age computers (b) those who rule technology (c) technical details

_____ 12. The man gave his best friend's wife a *cordial* welcome.

(a) indifferent (b) frosty (c) friendly

_____ 13. *Perennial* flowers are not only beautiful but practical since you need plant them only once.

(a) appearing in the spring (b) prize winning (c) reappearing yearly

_____ 14. Rocks, though they may make nice pets, are still *inanimate*.

(a) not lasting in popularity (b) not alive (c) not warm and clever

_____ 15. If I were a dictator, I know I would be a *beneficent* one.

(a) kind **(b)** scared **(c)** powerful

_____ 16. "We have no evidence *anthropoids* inhabited this earth until relatively recently in the earth's history," intoned the professor.

(a) large horses **(b)** creatures resembling man **(c)** dinosaurs

_____ 17. Through *autohypnosis* many people successfully change their lives.

(a) the power of positive thinking **(b)** deep hypnosis **(c)** self-hypnosis

_____ 18. The task of the Tactical Air Command is to *intercept* enemy planes.

(a) assist **(b)** prevent progress of **(c)** shoot down

_____ 19. After hotly debating his point for several hours, he suddenly *conceded.*

(a) won **(b)** grew tired **(c)** gave in

_____ 20. *Per capita,* New Yorkers pay more in property taxes than residents of most other states.

(a) for each household **(b)** for each individual **(c)** for each family of four

Check the answers with your instructor and record your score below.

% CORRECT _____

TWENTY MORE GREEK AND LATIN ROOTS

As in the previous assignment, first memorize the root with its original meaning. Study the example of the root at work in the English language. If you cannot determine the meaning of any example, look up the word in your dictionary. Then jot down any other examples you can think of.

	Root	Original Meaning	English Example	Your Examples
1.	cult	to care for	cult	_____
			agriculture	_____
2.	cycle	wheel, circle	cycle	_____
			cyclone	_____
3.	dem	people	democracy	_____
			demographic	_____
4.	dent	tooth	denture	_____
			indent	_____
5.	derma	skin	hypodermic	_____
			pachyderm	_____
6.	*dic, dict	to say, to speak	indicative	_____
			valedictorian	_____
7.	duc, duct	to lead	educate	_____
			conductor	_____
8.	*fac, fact	to make	facile	_____
			factory	_____
9.	*fin	end, to complete	finale	_____
			infinite	_____
10.	*gen, gene	birth, origin	genealogy	_____
			eugenics	_____
11.	geo	earth	geology	_____
			geophysics	_____
12.	*gram	to write	diagram	_____
			gramophone	_____

*Also presented in *Reading Faster and Understanding More, Book 1,* and included here for review.

13.	*graph	to write	graffiti	_____
			graphology	_____
14.	hetero	other	heterosexual	_____
			heterodox	_____
15.	*homo	same	homopathy	_____
			homogeneous	_____
16.	hydra	water	hydraulic	_____
			hydrogen	_____
17.	*jac, ject	to throw	eject	_____
			interject	_____
18.	*log, logo	word, study	apology	_____
			mineralogy	_____
19.	loqui, locut	talk	loquacious	_____
			elocution	_____
20.	luc, lus	light	translucent	_____
			illustrate	_____

► *Exercise*

Using your knowledge of the original meaning of the root, choose the answer most closely related to the *italicized word.* Write the letter of the answer in the blank. Do not look back at the list until you have finished.

_____ 1. He is always *engendering* new designs.

(a) overlooking (b) creating (c) distrusting

_____ 2. She was able to *induce* her friends to follow her.

(a) flatter (b) threaten (c) lead

_____ 3. My childhood sweetheart has rushed me a *cryptogram.* [*Crypt* means "secret."]

(a) message written in secret code (b) secret box of chocolates (c) secret music box

_____ 4. *Dermabrasion* is a rubbing technique often used by beauty parlors.

(a) fingernail shaping (b) hair removal (c) skin scraping

_____ 5. According to the popular *dictum,* he is a man-on-the-go.

(a) philosophy (b) saying (c) advertisement

_____ 6. The fiery words of the *demagogue* swayed the crowd.

(a) one who agitates people with words (b) one who likes to hear himself talk (c) one who has a cause he is willing to die for

---

*Also presented in *Reading Faster and Understanding More, Book 1,* and included here for review.

_____ 7. Neal spends much of his time *cultivating* the friendship of his co-workers.

(a) wishing for (b) ignoring (c) tending to

_____ 8. A daily use of *dentifrice* can save you hours of pain and agony later.

(a) common sense (b) household safety (c) preparation for cleaning the teeth

_____ 9. The *calligraphy* on the invitation was very delicate and full of detail.

(a) handwriting (b) painting (c) scroll

_____ 10. "Apparently, my dear, her interest in her marriage was merely *cyclical*," purred the lady from behind her fan.

(a) superficial (b) based on money (c) came and went

_____ 11. The police pointed out that, oddly enough, the check for $1,000,000 bore a *facsimile* of my signature.

(a) sample (b) old version (c) reproduction

_____ 12. He has a reputation for writing in a *colloquial* style.

(a) sincere (b) elegant and carefully structured (c) informal, like talking

_____ 13. There was a tone of *finality* in his voice as he sang to the judge.

(a) completeness (b) sorrow (c) freshness

_____ 14. His explanation helped to *elucidate* the difficult lesson in trigonometry.

(a) prepare (b) cast light on (c) tear apart

_____ 15. *Homonyms* are words that have

(a) similar sounds (b) opposite meanings (c) abbreviated forms

_____ 16. A future source of world energy may lie in *geothermal* resources. [*Thermal* means "heat."]

(a) heat from the sun (b) heat from the sea (c) heat from the earth

_____ 17. The *projectile* was found on my lawn.

(a) lizardlike creature (b) object that is thrown (c) carton of film

_____ 18. The *hydroplane* made good time between Spain and Morocco.

(a) jet airplane (b) high-speed water craft (c) commuter plane

_____ 19. A *eulogy* involves _____ of praise.

(a) words (b) music (c) study habits

_____ 20. I like a large college because the students are more likely to be *heterogeneous*.

(a) of the same sex (b) doing upper-division study (c) from varied backgrounds

Check the answers with your instructor and record your score below.

% CORRECT _____

EVEN MORE GREEK AND LATIN ROOTS

Again, memorize the common root with its original meaning. Notice how the original meaning helps explain the English word. Look up any word you do not know in your dictionary. Then jot down any other examples you can think of.

	Root	Original Meaning	English Example	Your Example
1.	mania	madness, derangement	maniacal nymphomania	_____ _____
2.	manus	hand	manuscript manacle	_____ _____
3.	*metr	measure	seismometer metrology	_____ _____
4.	micro	small	microbe microelectronics	_____ _____
5.	*mit, miss	to send	intermittent missive	_____ _____
6.	mono	one	monogamy monochrome	_____ _____
7.	mor	dead	mortal morgue	_____ _____
8.	ocul	eye	binocular monocle	_____ _____
9.	*path	feeling, suffering	pathos pathologist	_____ _____
10.	ped	foot	pedestal impediment	_____ _____
11.	pel, puls	drive	propel impulse	_____ _____
12.	*phil, philo	to love	philander philharmonic	_____ _____

_____
*Also presented in *Reading Faster and Understanding More, Book 1,* and included here for review.

13. *phobia	fear	hydrophobia	_____
		acrophobia	_____
14. *phon	sound	phoneme	_____
		phonology	_____
15. *photo	light	photosynthesis	_____
		photophobia	_____
16. pod	foot	podium	_____
		tripod	_____
17. *poly	many	polysyllable	_____
		polytechnic	_____
18. pon, pos	to place	component	_____
		transpose	_____
19. *popul	people	populace	_____
		populous	_____
20. *port	to carry	portfolio	_____
		rapport	_____

▶ *Exercise*

Using your knowledge of the original meaning of the root, choose the answer most closely related to the *italicized word*. Write the letter of the answer in the blank. Do not look at the list until you have finished.

_____ 1. My blind date was a bore; she carried on a constant *monologue* throughout the evening.

(a) conversation with strangers (b) pleasing chat (c) long, uninterrupted speech

_____ 2. *Vox populi* is a term that means voice of the

(a) people. (b) government. (c) pope.

_____ 3. Her strong sense of ambition *compels* me to rest a lot.

(a) forbids (b) pays (c) drives

_____ 4. Certain skin diseases respond well to *phototherapy*, which is a treatment using

(a) chemicals. (b) light. (c) sound.

_____ 5. The king was recently *deposed* from his throne.

(a) removed (b) suffering from an illness (c) praised

_____ 6. A *bibliophile* is a person who _____ books.

(a) mends (b) writes (c) loves

---

*Also presented in *Reading Faster and Understanding More, Book 1,* and included here for review.

_____ 7. The ideas in that book are dull and *pedestrian*.

   (a) plodding (b) quoted often (c) sharply defined

_____ 8. The *emissary* of the king is here and will not stop talking.

   (a) messenger sent by another (b) foreign affairs officer (c) official historian

_____ 9. She *manipulated* the cards so well everyone thought she was a gambler.

   (a) bet (b) read (c) handled

_____ 10. His thoughts have become *morbid* ever since he lost his job and family.

   (a) about revenge (b) about death (c) about vacation

_____ 11. The word *geometry* literally means of the earth.

   (a) division (b) measurement (c) worship

_____ 12. She would have had a better time on their date if he weren't such an *egomaniac*. [*Ego* means "I."]

   (a) independent and self-sufficient (b) suffering from poor eyesight (c) overly concerned with himself

_____ 13. The psychiatrist helped him to overcome his many *phobias*.

   (a) experiences (b) fears (c) problems

_____ 14. He thought an *oculist* might discover the cause of his headaches.

   (a) ear-nose-and-throat doctor (b) eye doctor (c) specialist in brain disorders

_____ 15. My mother has a lot of *empathy* for other people.

   (a) helpful advice (b) identification with feelings (c) secret anger

_____ 16. Even though he often puts his foot in his mouth, he has never had to visit a *podiatrist*.

   (a) nutritionist (b) speech therapist (c) foot doctor

_____ 17. A *polygon* is a figure with _____ sides.

   (a) seven (b) many (c) three

_____ 18. Instead of keeping stacks of old newspapers, libraries usually put the information on *microfilm*.

   (a) tiny filmstrips (b) recording tape (c) large-screen television

_____ 19. If our language had a *phonetic* spelling system, few people would make spelling errors.

   (a) based on sound (b) based on historical developments (c) based on visual aspects

_____ 20. Although her *deportment* is conventional, her ideas are sensational.

   (a) way of carrying or conducting oneself (b) section or subdivision of an office (c) educational background.

Check the answers with your instructor and record your score below.

% CORRECT _____

STILL MORE GREEK AND LATIN ROOTS

By this time you have begun to understand just how much our English language owes to the influence of Greek and Latin. Here are twenty more roots to add to your growing foundation. Again, memorize the root with its original meaning. Look up any word you do not know in your dictionary. Then jot down any other examples you can think of.

	Root	Original Meaning	English Example	Your Examples
1.	*psych	mind	psychoanalysis	_____
			psychopath	_____
2.	rupt	to break	bankrupt	_____
			disrupt	_____
3.	*scrib, script	to write	scribe	_____
			nondescript	_____
4.	sect	to cut	insect	_____
			vivisect	_____
5.	*sens, sent	to feel	sensation	_____
			sentient	_____
6.	*spec, spect	to look at	spectrum	_____
			perspective	_____
7.	spir	to breathe	inspire	_____
			conspire	_____
8.	tain, ten	to hold	container	_____
			tenet	_____
9.	*tele	distant	telecast	_____
			telekinesis	_____
10.	*tempor	time	extemporaneous	_____
			temporal	_____
11.	tend, tens	to stretch	extend	_____
			attention	_____
12.	terra	earth	terrestrial	_____
			inter	_____

*Also presented in *Reading Faster and Understanding More, Book 1,* and included here for review.

13.	the	god	theology	_____
			atheist	_____
14.	*therm	heat	thermal	_____
			thermodynamics	_____
15.	vene, vent	to come	revenue	_____
			adventure	_____
16.	vers, vert	to turn	anniversary	_____
			convert	_____
17.	*vid, vis	to see	providence	_____
			visionary	_____
18.	*viv, vit	to live, life	vivacious	_____
			vital	_____
19.	*voc, vocat	to call	evoke	_____
			avocation	_____
20.	volens	wishing,	volunteer	_____
		willing	benevolence	_____

► *Exercise*

Using your knowledge of the original meaning of the root, choose the answer most closely related to the *italicized word*. Write the letter of the answer in the blank. Do not look back at the list until you have finished.

_____ 1. At the end of the church service, the minister gave an *invocation*.

  (a) call for help **(b)** prayer of thanksgiving **(c)** dismissal

_____ 2. He longs to be on *terra firma* once again.

  (a) the lake **(b)** the earth **(c)** the farm

_____ 3. To climb Mt. Whitney requires enormous *vitality*.

  (a) liveliness and energy **(b)** muscular development **(c)** experience and courage

_____ 4. Be careful or you'll *rupture* that line!

  (a) twist **(b)** drop **(c)** break

_____ 5. The *vista* before us had the beauty of a painting by Joseph Turner.

  (a) lakeshore **(b)** view **(c)** attractive woman

_____ 6. Despite the difficulty of getting into medical school, she is *tenacious* in her desire to be a doctor.

  (a) confident **(b)** uncertain **(c)** holding stong to

---

*Also presented in *Reading Faster and Understanding More, Book 1,* and included here for review.

_____ 7. *Thermopane* glass is not a good conductor of _____.

        (a) light **(b)** moisture **(c)** heat

_____ 8. Members of the delegation will *convene* at 3:00 P.M. in the bar.

        (a) vote **(b)** meet **(c)** depart

_____ 9. Much to his pleasure he was named president *pro tem* of the service club.

        (a) honorary **(b)** elect **(c)** for the time being

_____ 10. Whenever he winked at her, she would *avert* her eyes and groan.

        (a) blink **(b)** turn away **(c)** widen

_____ 11. A *teletypewriter* is for material _____.

        (a) to be used on television **(b)** that is transmitted from or sent afar **(c)** typed at extremely high speeds

_____ 12. With great zest he began to *dissect* the frog.

        (a) cut up **(b)** eat **(c)** catch

_____ 13. Because of the hero's constant *introspection,* the play did not have much action in the first act. [*Intro* means "within."]

        (a) love duets with the heroine **(b)** serious illness **(c)** soul searching

_____ 14. Most paper is unsuitable for making clothing because it lacks *tensile* strength.

        (a) waterproof **(b)** fire-resistant **(c)** stretching

_____ 15. He was *insensible* to the fact he was standing on my hand.

        (a) aware **(b)** unaware **(c)** unconcerned about

_____ 16. Except for a few *respiratory* problems, he is in excellent health.

        (a) stomach **(b)** breathing **(c)** back

_____ 17. He asked for the *typescript* of thc trial.

        (a) tape-recording **(b)** news photos **(c)** typed copy

_____ 18. "Should you marry me," said the aging duke to the young woman, "I insist it be of your own *volition.*"

        (a) love **(b)** free will **(c)** need

_____ 19. *Psychosis* is a serious illness of the _____.

        (a) liver **(b)** heart **(c)** mind

_____ 20. Maria is a *polytheist.*

        (a) member of the union **(b)** believer in many gods **(c)** many-talented student

Check your answers with your instructor and record your score below.

% CORRECT _____

PREFIXES

In Lessons 4, 5, 6, and 7, you discovered the idea of word parts. You also learned some common root words that English has borrowed from Greek and Latin. Our Word Animal so far has only a body ⊢. Now we will add a head! The word "prefix" is itself an example of a word made up of a root plus a prefix, or a P—R combination:

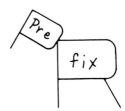

The head of an animal precedes, or goes before, the body. So what does "pre-" mean? _____ A prefix adds to, modifies, or reverses the meaning of the root.

TWENTY COMMON PREFIXES

Memorize this list of common prefixes, with their original meanings. Just as in root words, the original meaning of each prefix helps you understand the English word. Jot down any other examples you can think of. (Note: Prefixes seldom are usable English words by themselves. That is why they are listed here with hyphens.)

	Prefix	Original Meaning	English Example	Your Examples
1.	ab-	away from, down	abnormal, abate	_____ _____
2.	ad-	to, toward	addict, adhere	_____ _____
3.	ambi-, amphi-	on both sides, around	ambiguous amphitheater	_____ _____
4.	arch-	chief, principal	archangel, archbishop	_____ _____
5.	bi-	two	biannual, bifocals	_____ _____
6.	circum-	around	circumnavigate, circumspect	_____ _____
7.	con-, com-	with, together	congregate, commence	_____ _____
8.	extra-	outside, beyond	extraneous, extradite	_____

9.	inter-	among, between	interject, intermingle	_____
				_____
10.	mal-	bad, wrong	malice, maladjusted	_____
				_____
11.	*in- (im-, il-, ir-)	not, opposite of	ineligible	_____
	[in- may also		impeccable	_____
	mean inside]		illegitimate	_____
			irreligious	_____
12.	*a-	not, without	amoral, atypical	_____
13.	*dis-	not	dissimilar, disinterested	_____
	[dis- may also			_____
	mean apart]			_____
14.	*un-	not	unreal, unlikely	_____
15.	*non-	not	nonproductive, nonaddictive	_____
16.	*in-	inside, within	ingest, indebted	_____
	[in- may also			_____
	mean not]			_____
17.	*intra-	inside, within	intramuscular, intramural	_____
18.	*e-, ex-	out, away from	egress	_____
			exhale	_____
19.	*de-	away, down	depart, depress	_____
20.	*dis-	apart	dismember, disperse	_____

► *Exercise*

Using your knowledge of the original meaning of the prefix, choose the answer most closely related to the *italicized word*. Write the letter of the answer in the blank. Do not look back at the list until you have finished.

_____ 1. The teacher said there were many *extraneous* ideas in my paper.

(a) deeply pondered (b) unusual (c) off the subject

_____ 2. For a speech teacher, he is almost *inarticulate*.

(a) not well spoken (b) overly talkative (c) having an accent

_____ 3. If you ask her for help, you will hear a great deal of sweet *circumlocution*.

(a) swearing (b) beating about the point (c) well-expressed eagerness

_____

*Also presented in *Reading Faster and Understanding More, Book 1,* and included here for review.

4. In the past, governments would *decapitate* lawbreakers.

   (a) burn at the stake (b) cut off the head (c) put in the stocks

5. If I say that I can *commiserate* with your misfortune, I mean that I

   (a) can comment on it objectively. (b) sympathize with you. (c) am glad it did not happen to me.

6. He would like to have that blemish *excised.*

   (a) cut away (b) hidden (c) beautified

7. A *binary* star is composed of _____ parts.

   (a) two (b) ten (c) one hundred

8. An *intracardiac* problem would be located _____ the heart.

   (a) next to (b) under (c) inside

9. My *archenemy* gives me reason to live.

   (a) friend (b) former enemy (c) chief enemy

10. After her *incarceration* was over, she began to live a successful life.

    (a) being jailed in (b) graduation (c) medical operation

11. My feelings about snakes are *ambivalent.*

    (a) firmly decided (b) both for and against (c) negative

12. Because of an allergy, she must wear things that are *nonmetallic.*

    (a) manmade (b) not metal (c) plastic or metal

13. "If you wish to be successful," said the famous musician, "you must not blindly *adhere* to the rules."

    (a) stick to (b) ignore (c) revise in your favor

14. He persists in believing that he is *unaccountable* for his bad luck.

    (a) not responsible (b) deserving (c) about to change

15. His brother always *interceded* for him when he got in trouble.

    (a) was glad (b) pleaded his case (c) was sorry

16. She is *disinclined* to change her opinion.

    (a) not ready to (b) about to (c) known

17. If I wish a *malady* upon you, I am hoping you have

    (a) wealth. (b) an illness. (c) a good journey.

18. That movie was totally *asexual.*

    (a) sexually suggestive (b) nonsexual (c) against sex

19. The king *abdicated* his throne.

    (a) secured the safety of (b) stepped up to (c) stepped down from

20. He floats around as if he were *disembodied.*

    (a) in a trance (b) removed from his body (c) on a natural high

Check the answers with your instructor and record your score below.

% CORRECT _____

TWENTY MORE PREFIXES

Memorize this list of common prefixes and their original meanings. Jot down any examples you can think of.

Prefix	Original Meaning	English Example	Your Examples
1. mis-	wrong, ill	mispronounce, misgiving	_____
			_____
2. multi-	many	multicolored,	_____
		multimillionaire	_____
3. poly-	many	polygamy, polytheism	_____
			_____
4. pro-	before, forward	procession, proficient	_____
			_____
5. re-	again, back	reassure, recede	_____
			_____
6. retro-	back	retrogress, retrospect	_____
			_____
7. semi-	half	semifinal, semiannually	_____
			_____
8. syn-, sym-	together	synonym,	_____
		sympathy	_____
9. trans-	across	transpire, transition	_____
			_____
10. tri-	three	triangle, tripod	_____
			_____
11. *pro-	for, in favor of	pro-abortion, propaganda	_____
12. *anti-	against	anti-abortion, antithesis	_____
13. *contra-	against	contravene	_____
counter-		counterpoint	_____
14. *post-	after	postwar, posthumous	_____

*Also presented in *Reading Faster and Understanding More, Book 1,* and included here for review.

15.	*pre-	before	prewar, precedence	_____
16.	*ante-	before	antedate, antecedent	_____
17.	*sub-	under	subordinate, subsist	_____
18.	*hypo-	under	hypoglycemia, hypothetical	_____
19.	*hyper-	above	hypertension, hyperventilate	_____
20.	*super-	above	superimposed, supernatural	_____

► Exercise

Choose the meaning most closely related to the *italicized word* and write the letter in the blank at left.

_____ 1. The warring nations finally reached a *trilateral* agreement

(a) final (b) three-sided (c) temporary

_____ 2. His public statements indicate that he is *prorevolutionary.*

(a) in favor of revolution (b) against revolution (c) indifferent to revolution

_____ 3. Moss that grows on trees is an example of *symbiosis.*

(a) the nature of the southern landscape (b) a dangerous parasite (c) different organisms living together

_____ 4. He has a *superfluity* of money.

(a) excess (b) lack (c) large amount

_____ 5. To call this establishment first-class is a *misnomer.*

(a) wrong term (b) compliment (c) insult

_____ 6. He is saving to buy an *antebellum* home in the South.

(a) housing tract (b) pre-Civil War (c) with acreage

_____ 7. Alfredo is a world traveler and *polyglot.* (*Glot* means "tongue.")

(a) one who presents travel lectures (b) international business-man (c) one who speaks many languages

_____ 8. We take an *antibiotic* to

(a) promote growth. (b) kill bacteria. (c) help us sleep.

_____ 9. "There certainly were a dreadful *multitude* of ugly women in Bath." (Jane Austen)

(a) small group (b) large number (c) organization

_____ 10. Most of his tales are full of *hyperbole.*

(a) exaggeration (b) violence (c) romance

_____ 11. In *retrospect* I realize I made the right decision.

(a) full honesty (b) looking back on it (c) looking objectively

_____ 12. She had talked to him before his anger *subsided.*

(a) went down (b) built up (c) exploded

---

*Also presented in *Reading Faster and Understanding More, Book 1,* and included here for review.

_____ **13.** Much to my surprise, I found a *semiconscious* man on my doorstep.

   (a) mentally developed **(b)** almost passed out **(c)** drunken

_____ **14.** She had carefully *predetermined* the amount of money needed.

   (a) arranged in advance **(b)** saved over a long period of time
   (c) removed from the bank

_____ **15.** The quickest way to *revitalize* yourself after a day in class is to exercise.

   (a) improve your memory **(b)** organize your notes **(c)** feel energetic again

_____ **16.** As a child, I was so *hypo-active*, I was given a tonic.

   (a) overly active **(b)** too sloppy **(c)** underactive

_____ **17.** Amanda's devotion to her career has helped her to *transcend* her problems at home.

   (a) rise above **(b)** worsen **(c)** clear up

_____ **18.** She is planning to do *postdoctoral* study next year.

   (a) after she receives the Ph.D. **(b)** before she receives the Ph.D.
   (c) study for a master's degree

_____ **19.** Skip the *prologue* and get to the heart of this romance!

   (a) music **(b)** introductory words **(c)** first half

_____ **20.** *Contraband* is items _____.

   (a) used in law enforcement **(b)** that are against the law **(c)** sold in music stores

Check the answers with your instructor and record your score below.

% CORRECT _____

SUFFIXES

Lesson 8 explained the P or Prefix part of a word. You now know that a word may be only a root (for example, the eleven words preceding the parenthesis). Or the root word may have a *prefix* at the beginning, as in the words "*pre*fix," "*re*read," and "*pre*ceding." Or it may have a *suffix* at the end, as in the words "end*s*" and "end*ing.*"

More complicated words may have both a prefix and a suffix, and sometimes more than one of each. Can you analyze the word "preceding" by finishing the animal?

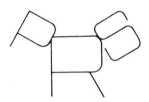

Our English language has many more suffixes than prefixes. Also, many have the same meaning. In some cases it takes years of listening, reading, and writing to know which one of several suffixes, all meaning the same thing, is the correct suffix for your word. Do we call a talkative person "word*y,*" "word*ish,*" "word*ic,*" "wor-d*ive,*" or "word*al*"? Those suffixes all mean "having the quality of."

However, some classification of English suffixes by meaning is possible, and often helpful. If nothing else, you will begin to notice suffixes and their effect on words they are attached to. The most important reason for learning suffixes is that they give you flexibility in using words you already know. And, since adding a suffix will often change the part of speech of a word, their study will give you some insights into the structure of our language.

We'll start with suffixes that generally indicate that a word is a noun.

TWENTY-FIVE NOUN SUFFIXES

By "noun" we mean a thing—a person, a place, an idea, a quality, an object of some sort. If you are not sure whether a word is being used as a noun, you can apply five tests:

1. Put *a, an,* or *the* before it (a *bone,* an *hour,* the *thought*).
2. Put an *-s* on it for a plural (more than one) (*bones, hours, thoughts*).
3. Precede it with a descriptive word (dry *bones,* wee *hours,* deep *thoughts*).
4. Make it the subject of a sentence (His *bones* are buried in the yard).
5. Make it the object of a preposition (There's dust around those *bones*).

If the word sounds right and makes sense in most of these uses, then it is a noun. For example, try the five tests out on the word "if". 1. an *if* 2. the *ifs* 3. a bright *if* 4. Her *if* is plain to see. 5. with *if,* beside *if.* Does *if* pass these tests for a noun? _____

Now try the five tests with the word "love." Can love be used as a noun? _____
Love, of course, is a root word; it does not have a suffix—yet. But if we were to add a suffix to *love* to make it a noun, what would we use? Try the preceding five tests with the words "love-ly," "lov-ing," "love-liness." Which ending is a noun suffix? Does that word fit most of the five conditions? Can love also be used as a verb—as in "He *loves* her"?

Because there are so many suffixes, we have grouped those with similar meanings together. (**Note:** some noun suffixes, unfortunately, are also used as adjective suffixes. An example is *-ent:* He is my *dependent*—noun. He is a very *dependent* person—adjective.)

For more practice in spotting nouns, see Phrase Comprehension exercises 9E and 9F.

Directions: Memorize this list of common noun suffixes, with their meanings. Notice how the meaning helps explain the examples. Add any other examples you can think of.

	Suffix	Original Meaning	Examples	Your Examples
1.	*-s, -es	simple plural	rhythms	_____
			reflexes	_____
2.	-ette		novelette, sermonette	_____
	-ie, -y		Annie, lassie, piggy	_____
	-let	little	booklet, streamlet	_____
	-ling		nestling, princeling	_____
	-ule		globule	_____
3.	*-ism	state of,	despotism	_____
		doctrine	capitalism	_____
4.	-ese		Japanese, Burmese	_____
	-er	inhabitant of	southerner	_____
	-ian		Bostonian	_____
5.	-cide	killing	matricide	_____
			homocide	_____
6.	-dom	place, condition,	Christendom,	_____
		rank	boredom, dukedom	_____
7.	-itis	inflammation,	tonsillitis	_____
		disease	bronchitis	_____
8.	*-ee	one who receives	examinee	_____
		an action	addressee	_____

---

*Also presented in *Reading Faster and Understanding More, Book 1,* and included here for review.

9.	*-er		examiner	_____
	-ar	one who,	beggar	_____
	-or	a thing that	protector, generator	_____
10.	*-an, -ian	one who	artisan, pediatrician	_____
11.	*-ist, -tist	one who	conformist, egotist	_____
12.	*-ant, -ent	one who	defendant, resident	_____
13.	-eer, -ier	one who	auctioneer, bombardier	_____
14.	-ster	one who	prankster, youngster	_____
15.	-ess	one who, female	authoress, tigress	_____
16.	-acy	state of	privacy, accuracy	_____
17.	*-ance, -ence	state of,	governance	_____
		quality of	competence	_____
18.	*-tude, -lude	state of	altitude	_____
		quality of	interlude	_____
19.	*-ion, -tion	state of,	fusion, relaxation	_____
	-sion	quality of	revulsion	_____
20.	*-ity, -ty	state of	publicity	_____
		quality of	certainty	_____
21.	*-ment	state of	enlargement	_____
		quality of	enlightenment	_____
22.	*-ness	state of,	courteousness	_____
		quality of	hardiness	_____
23.	*-ship, -hood	state of	courtship	_____
		quality of	childhood	_____
24.	*-ary, -ery	a place for	aviary, monastery	_____
	-ory		armory	_____
25.	-arium, -orium	a place for	solarium	_____
			auditorium	_____

*Also presented in *Reading Faster and Understanding More, Book 1,* and included here for review.

► *Exercise*

Decide from the context what *noun suffix* must be added to the word in parentheses. Then write the entire word in the blank, changing the spelling if necessary.

(Use suffixes meaning "little")

1. In the "chase scene" of this (novel) _____, (Susan) _____, our little heroine, holds her (handkerchief) _____ tightly and daintily steps over the (brook) _____, taking care not to frighten the (duck) _____, or get a (glob) _____ of water upon her tiny velvet slippers.

(Use suffixes indicating "inhabitants of")

2. The (New York) _____ calmly took a bite out of the big apple as his (Peking) _____ dog gave his regards to Broadway and the astonished (Boston) _____ looked the other way.

(Use a suffix indicating the female gender)

3. The famous (actor) _____ on the plane little suspected that the (steward) _____ was not only an (heir) _____ but a (prince) _____ too.

(Use suffixes meaning "one who")

4. She was not (climb) _____ enough to venture higher without the help of a (mountain) _____.

5. "Oh, my (protect) _____ and (defend) _____," the (drama) _____ wrote, "I would have surely been a (gone) _____ without your help."

6. Against my expressed wishes, that (prank) _____, (gang) _____ and (rough) _____, my brother-in-law Freddy, turned my new Cadillac into a dune buggy.

7. The letter indicated I would receive, as the (pay) _____, the yearly sum of a thousand dollars from my (guard) _____ as long as I remained a (ten) _____ of the old house.

(Use suffixes meaning "state" or "quality of")

8. In (recognize) _____ of your (encourage) _____ and (assist) _____ during my times of (solitary) _____ and (depend) _____, I offer my (grateful) _____, (loyal) _____, and (friend) _____.

9. It may seem like (lunatic) _____, but the crime of (pirate) _____ is still committed on the high seas.

10. Having just turned twenty-one, the youth celebrated his new (man) _____ with a little (relax) _____ at the local bar.

Check the answers with your instructor and record your score below.

% CORRECT _____

SEVEN VERB SUFFIXES

The list of *noun suffixes* in Lesson 10 was long. To balance it, this list of *verb suffixes* will be short.

First, what do we mean by *verb*? A verb is a word or words that show action or just existence. (*Is* and *show* in that sentence are verbs.) Along with the noun subject, the verb makes the skeleton, the basic part of a sentence. For example, in these basic sentences, the subject is underlined once and the verb twice.

God is. The people were. Jody waited. He had been waiting.

In Lesson 10, you learned five tests for a noun. To test a word to see if it's a verb, you can apply these tests:

1. Put he, she, or it before the word and add an -s to it. (He *guarantees.*)
2. Change the time (tense) to past, continuing present, or future. (He *guaranteed.* He is *guaranteeing.* He will *guarantee.*)

Try the tests out on the word "college." She *colleged.* She is *colleging.* She will *college.* Do you think that the word "college" is usually a verb?

Now try the tests on the word "act." Can *act* be used as a verb?

Like the test word (*love*) in Lesson 10, *act* is a root word. But also like *love*, we can add suffixes to *act* and still have a verb. (Extra credit: What *noun* suffixes can you add to *act*? Check Lesson 10 if you have forgotten.) Try the tests for a verb on the word "activate." Is it a verb form?

Most verb endings indicate *tense* or time. English has few verb suffixes other than the regular -s, -ed, and -ing (works, worked, working) and occasionally -en, -t (written, burnt). These endings are so much a part of the word that many people don't think of them as suffixes at all. We start our list with them because, to communicate clearly, you need them when you speak or write.

For more practice in spotting verbs, see Phrase Comprehension exercises 11E and 11F.

Directions: Memorize this list of common verb suffixes, with their meanings. Notice how the meaning helps clarify the examples. Add any other examples you can think of.

	Suffix	Meaning	Examples	Your Examples
1.	*-s	third person singular, present tense (he, she, it)	declares, expels	_____ _____ _____
2.	*-ing	present participle	declaring, expelling	_____
3.	*-ed, -t	past participle	declared, dwelt	_____

---

*Also presented in *Reading Faster and Understanding More, Book 1*, and included here for review.

4.	*-ate	to make, to cause	marinate, salivate	_____
		to be		_____
5.	*-en	to make, to cause	enlighten	_____
		to be	strengthen	_____
6.	*-fy, -ify	to make, to cause	intensify	_____
		to be	fortify	_____
7.	*-ize	to make, to cause	synthesize	_____
		to be	jeopardize	_____

▶ *Exercise*

Decide from the context what verb suffix must be added to the word in parentheses. Then write the entire word in the blank, changing the spelling where necessary. (**Note:** Keep verb tense consistent within each sentence. Many verbs can be either present or past tense.)

1. The wife (sympathy) _____ with her husband's desire for a vacation but (insist) _____ the Superbowl was not her idea of a resort.

2. When he was a child, she (pacific) _____ him by stroking his hair.

3. In the past the hero (kneel) _____ in adoration and (sanctify) _____ the heroine's hand with a chaste kiss.

4. He (mad) _____ his mother as he (fast) _____ the corsage to her skin by mistake.

5. Now the computer is (reply) _____ slowly to letters that inquire about possible errors.

6. That couple could (deep) _____ and (strength) _____ their friendship by making fewer cutting comments.

7. As he (notary) _____ the document, his feelings of joy (intensify) _____ about the good fortune that would soon be his.

8. He (expel) _____ his breath in sudden anger and (declare) _____ that he had (deal) _____ with her thoughtlessness long enough.

9. The book he was (peruse) _____ (fertile) _____ his imagination.

10. In one terrifying moment the car (swerve) _____ across three lanes of traffic and (maneuver) _____ to safety.

Check the answers with your instructor and record your score below.

% CORRECT _____

---

*Also presented in *Reading Faster and Understanding More, Book 1,* and included here for review.

NINETEEN ADJECTIVE SUFFIXES
AND ONE ADVERB SUFFIX

In Lesson 10, you learned some (but not all!) of the suffixes that show a word is being used as a noun—electrici*an*, fix*er*, fix*ation*, national*ism*, and so on. In Lesson 11, you learned most of the verb suffixes that show a word is being used as an action word or a verb—electri*fy*, fix*ate*, national*ize*, and so on. This last group of suffixes is used to show that a word is being used as either an adjective or adverb.

Again, we should review what is meant by an adjective and an adverb. They are words that modify (describe) other words. An adjective describes a noun or pronoun; an adverb describes a verb, adjective, or another adverb. An adverb indicates how, when, where, why, or to what degree.

As in the last lesson, we can take a skeleton sentence and add an adjective and an adverb like this:

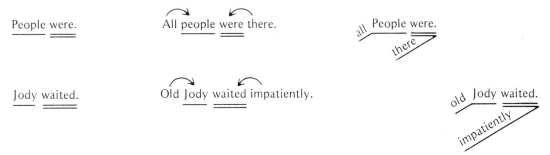

Is the adjective "old" in that sentence a root word, or does it also have a prefix and suffix? What about the adverb "impatiently"? If you say that *im* is a prefix and *ly* is a suffix, you have kept on top of the vocabulary building exercises so far.

Do you remember, from Lesson 10, the problem some students face when they want to describe a person as "wordy," "wordish," "wordal," "wordic," or "wordive"? These are all possible adjective endings, describing a noun, and English has so many that it is easy to be confused. Sometimes the only way to make the choice is to read and listen until "the *ear* knows." As in the noun suffixes in Lesson 10, as many as possible are grouped together by similar meaning.

Luckily, the adverb ending in English is usually *-ly;* so you can learn that one easily and quickly. (Stop and underline carefully the adverb endings that have evidently been carefully and pointedly added in this paragraph!)

Nineteen Adjective Suffixes

Memorize this list of adjective suffixes, with their meanings. Study the samples and jot down any additional examples you can think of.

Adjective Suffix	Meaning	Examples	Your Examples
1. *-er	comparative (of two)	naughtier, tenser	_____ _____
2. *-est	superlative (of more than two)	naughtiest, tensest	_____ _____

*Also presented in *Reading Faster and Understanding More, Book 1,* and included here for review.

3.	*-able, -ible	able to be	durable, incorrigible	_____
4.	-oid	in the form of	anthropoid, ovoid	_____
5.	-esque	having the nature of	picturesque, romanesque	_____
6.	*-ic	having the nature of	phonic, manic	_____
7.	*-ish	having the nature of	feverish, reddish	_____
8.	-ose, -ous	having the nature of	morose, glamorous	_____
9.	*-tious, -cious	having the nature of	nutritious, suspicious	_____
10.	*-ive, -ative	having the nature of	restive, curative	_____
11.	*-ant, -ent	having the nature of	redundant, effervescent	_____
12.	-ac, *-an, -al	having the nature of	cardiac, partisan, abdominal	_____
13.	*-ar	having the nature of	solar, familiar	_____
14.	-some	having the nature of	winsome, loathsome	_____
15.	-fic	having the nature of	specific, soporific	_____
16.	*-y, -ly	having the nature of	earthy, scholarly	_____
17.	*-ful	full of	fanciful, artful	_____
18.	*-less	without, free of	restless, artless	_____
19.	-ward	direction	homeward, leeward	_____

One Adverb Suffix

20.	*-ly	in a certain manner	humanely	
			incorrigibly	_____
			fancifully	
			winsomely	_____
			picturesquely	_____

Note: While most -ly endings are adverbs, a small group of words ending in -ly are adjectives: homely, brotherly, friendly, lively, leisurely, and so on.

─────────────

► *Exercise 1—Adjective Suffixes*

Choose the best adjective suffix for the word in parentheses and write the entire word in the blank, changing the spelling if necessary. Example: that (moment) *momentous* day

1. her (girl) _____ charms
2. a (cellulose) _____ film
3. a (democracy) _____ organization
4. the (fruit) _____ endeavor
5. his (continue) _____ resistance

────────
*Also presented in *Reading Faster and Understanding More, Book 1,* and included here for review.

6. an (unforget) _____ character

7. a (destruct) _____ kit

8. a (mourn) _____ sound

9. an (impression) _____ young man

10. the (smart) _____ brother [comparing two]

11. a (fever) _____ pace

12. a (fire) _____ temper

13. a (back) _____ glance

14. the (weary) _____ task

15. a (without *fear*) _____ attitude

16. a (scholar) _____ essay

17. an (amateur) _____ performance

18. a (love) _____ lass

19. a (specify) _____ song

20. a (burden) _____ undertaking

21. (commune) _____ living

22. the (able to *restore*) _____ powers

23. a (nutrition) _____ repast

24. a (seduce) _____ look

25. an (admire) _____ act

26. an (elude) _____ quality

27. the (witty) _____ sister [comparing three]

28. a (care) _____ remark

29. a (knight) _____ quest

30. a (quarter) _____ report

► *Exercise 2—Adverb Suffixes*

Attach the adverb suffix to the word in parentheses and write the entire word in the blank.* In some cases the word in the blank is a noun and must first be given an adjective suffix before the adverb suffix can be added.

Example: to write (fancy) *fancifully*

1. is (athletic) _____ fit

2. inquires (full of *purpose*) _____

3. kisses (loving) _____

4. is (hypnotic) _____ charming

5. to be (instant) _____ regretful

6. to admit (public) _____

7. to be rude (period) _____

---

*Spelling tip: If you add *ly* to words ending in *y*, usually you change the *y* to *i*. Example: *busy* + *ly* = *busily.*

8. was (impossible) _____ true
9. will (like) _____ rain
10. to address (similar) _____
11. a (nutrition) _____ prepared meal
12. an (incredible) _____ easy problem
13. to speak (hurry) _____
14. please (kind) _____ forward
15. a (time) _____ topic
16. he talks (matter-of-fact) _____
17. he (witty) _____ comments
18. (without *fear*) _____ charges ahead
19. to sweat (continue) _____
20. she is (happy) _____ married

Check the answers with your instructor and record your score below.

% CORRECT _____

POSTTESTS

1. Comprehension and Rate Posttest
2. Vocabulary Posttest

Read the following selection as rapidly as you can but with good comprehension. Wait for a signal from your instructor before you begin reading.

I Was a Speed-Reading Dropout

J. M. Flagler

If, since beginning this article, you have already finished it, you are a speed reader.

In the past few fast-paced years, courses in rapid reading have spread throughout the land, both on campus and off. Human word-devouring machines have been churned out by the hundred thousand. As I see it, all this bodes no good for writers. When I do an article, I prefer the reader to hang around it for a while. Stay. Sift your fingers through the rare coin of my syntax. Gambol—barefoot, if you will—in the rich meadows of metaphor. Let's not race over my brilliantly (not to say painfully) wrought points.

The fact is, though, I am probably fighting the tide of history. Never has the eye been washed with a greater outpouring of printed matter, from new books (more than thirty thousand a year in the United States alone) to thick reports by corporate subcommittees on *The Feasibility of Installing Plasticine Soap Dishes in Executive Washrooms.* At the same time, never has the eye been more loath to read. If television doesn't make words obsolete, the speed-reading movement may.

Most speed-reading systems seem to regard words as but pesky obstacles to reading. They advocate wolfing them down in clumps. "Why savor words?" said one speed-reading school executive. . . . Why savor words? Well, for one thing, some of them give a good deal of pleasure. The word "savor," for instance. Roll it around on the tongue. Savory, isn't it? Still, it must be conceded that the vast majority of printed pages are as indigestible as cold French fries. It is also undoubtedly true that the method by which we are taught to read in grade school serves many of us poorly in our attempt to keep up with the flood of required reading, let alone reading for enjoyment and personal enlightenment.

There are almost as many reading theories as there are reading experts. However, most seem to agree that the traditional reading-aloud system so long and so securely established in schools leaves many of us with the bad habit of subvocalization. In other words, later in life, we continue to "read aloud," but under our breath. Insecurely, we also tend to read back over words; ten to fourteen "regressions" a page is typical. Emotional hang-ups caused by early reading anxieties may help slow us even more. The national reading-rate average is 250 words a minute; the average for college graduates only 350.

We are for the time being stuck with the printed word as the chief instrument for transmitting knowledge. It therefore stands to reason that we could do well to read faster (except when reading articles about speed reading). Some college-based reading-improvement experts believe 600 to 800 words is a realistic national average goal. On the face of it then, a speed-reading course is as logical a response to a felt need as a hat factory. With this wisdom in mind, I recently signed up for a course myself. As a writer, I can sulk all I want about words getting short shrift, but the fact is that I am also a reader, and not a consistently fast reader. . . .

I decided to sign on with one of the (Evelyn Wood's Reading Dynamics) institutes, partly because of the name, with its suggestions of Charles Atlas and "Dynamic Tension." No longer would 98-pound weaklings kick literary sand in my face at cocktail parties, simply because I was lagging behind in reading. . . .

. . . I have always been puzzled, not to say chagrined, by the curious flaw in my reading ability that made me take an age to get through any book read for pleasure and nonprofit. Since I started *War and Peace,* there have been three wars and even a few periods of peace, and I'm still slogging through the book. Speed-reading success stories served to inflame my interest. I knew of one graduate who tossed off a novel every morning on his bus ride to work from uptown to Midtown Manhattan. Riffling through pages like a gambler through a deck of cards, he had the satisfaction of astounding his fellow passengers, as they barely groped past page one of their newspapers . . .

. . . (Reading Dynamic's) guarantee—to triple reading rate or money back—seems like a fairly safe bet, as far as I am concerned. By the end of my first class, I had jumped my achievable word-per-minute rate from a measly 345 to 1300!

Actually, classwork plays a minor part in the speed-reading time-work schedule. You pay largely for the privilege of doing homework—an hour a day minimum, six days a week, for the two and one-half hour weekly class. The Evelyn Wood course takes eight weeks to complete, and is conducted in a typical bare classroom. . . . A shirt-sleeved young male instructor with an antiseptically modern, brightly lit teaching style presided over a class of twenty, largely salesmen and students. From the first moment, he plunged us into our subject at a cheerlessly relentless pace. "It hurts, but it works," he said of the course.

In short order, I could see what he meant by the first part of the statement. For one thing, the basic tool of speed reading is the hand. (A slew of paperback books, a pencil and/or pen, a good deal of self-discipline and free time, and anywhere from $150 to $275 are among the other prerequisites for the usual triple-your-speed course.). . .

"Use the hand as a pacer," we were urged—seemingly at every turn of a page—either to underline or to make sweeps, loops, "lazy L's," or "G whorls." All these gestures are designed to hasten the sluggard eye down a page or column. After the first class, my hand began to develop reader's cramp.

The two and one-half hours flew by, but not the demanded hour of homework for each of the next six days. Homework involves more than simply practicing with a different paperback book each night. I found also that a considerable amount of time was required to digest the mess of directions that I had bolted down in class. Then, too, homework required written comments on each segment we read from the paperback books. Conceivably, if normal academic contemplation were employed, the course would have taken a college semester. As it was, an hour's homework invariably came closer to two for this long-time refugee from scholastic discipline. The curdling of my disposition was correspondingly doubled by the end of the week.

Not that the technique didn't begin to pay off. In fact, I had gone through only three class sessions when laboring over home studies one evening I found myself racing through *Moby Dick* at 5000 words a minute. Since my previous practice high had been something like 2700 words and faltering, I assumed that I had misread my watch. A careful recheck proved that I *was* reading at 5000 words.

At that point, the realization crept up on me that for the first time in my scattered academic life, I would not make the grade. I was heading hell-bent to becoming a speed-reading dropout. For, as my reading rate escalated, comprehension seemed to fall rapidly. (Classroom tests indicated that it was no worse than standing still, but I was having more trouble recalling details for my written homework reports than a witness at a five-car accident.) I even became alarmed that, as the rate approached the rapid-reading equivalent of the speed of light, perhaps knowledge already accrued would be drained out of my system. On top of that, I was reading more but enjoying it less. Both nerves and muscles tensed as I whizzed a frozen clawlike hand through the pages. It was a matter—in humorist Gordon Cotler's phrase—of coiling up with a good book.

Finally, my conscience as a writer began to creep into play. It was all well and good to race through J. Edgar Hoover's *Masters of Deceit* at a four-minute-mile pace. Hoover has a job other than writing to fall back on. But when I found myself completing John Steinbeck's *The Pearl* in eleven minutes, I felt like a traitor to the cause. If a fellow professional puts in months, years, on a book, who am I to dishonor the effort by tossing it off with dessert and coffee, so to speak. I never could face up to my fourth class.

Shame at being a dropout has since been lessened somewhat by the knowledge that I am not alone. A spokesman for one prominent commercial speed-reading organization conceded that only 70 percent of its enrollees go the full route. It also gives me a warm feeling to know that Evelyn Wood keeps a lamp lighted for me. I have been assured that, if I ever come to my senses, they owe me five more class sessions.

Most academic reading experts, while conceding that too many people read slowly, assert that the physical limitations of the eye determine an outer limit for reading speed—anywhere from 800 to 1200 words, even assuming a fast pair of eyes and an exceptional intelligence. They claim that anything beyond is scanning or skimming—terms forbidden by the Reading Dynamics lexicon—and thus of dubious value to comprehension. To somebody laboring along at our national average of 250 wpm, of course, whether a step-up in their prose consumption is reading or scanning may seem academic indeed. However, another argument raised by the middle-speed theorists is that force-fed rates work only for a short while. Unless speed-reading practices artificially maintained during courses are continued afterward, the tendency is to slump back into old habits. Recognizing this, Reading Dynamics conducts lifetime refresher courses free for their graduates, who now number more than four hundred thousand. Maybe someday I'll make it too. It's the age of the dropout, after all.*

TOTAL READING TIME _____

*J. M. Flagler, "I Was A Speed-Reading Dropout." From *Look* Magazine, October 21, 1969. Copyright © Cowles Communications, Inc. 1969. Reprinted by permission.

Immediately answer the following questions without referring to the selection.

1. Choose the statement that best expresses the thesis.
  (a) The author believes it is better to read slowly and savor every word.
  (b) Although the author generally agrees with the need for most people to increase their reading speed, he is poking fun at commercial speed-reading courses.
  (c) The author believes that learning to read faster can improve one's social life.
  (d) Although the author dropped out of the Reading Dynamics course, he still recommends it to slow readers.

2. Because of the tremendous amount of printed matter, the author seems to think few people will agree with his tendency to read slowly and savor words.   T   F

3. The author does not agree that the traditional reading aloud in schools causes subvocalization.   T   F

4. According to some college reading experts, a realistic national average goal for reading is
  (a) 300 to 500 (b) 600 to 800 (c) 900 to 1200 (d) 1200 or above

5. The author found the homework much easier than the classwork in the reading course.   T   F

6. The hand is the most important tool of speed reading in the Reading Dynamics course.   T   F

7. The author suggests that speed reading offends his writer's instincts.   T   F

8. The author dropped out of Reading Dynamics after his third class.   T   F

9. The major pattern of organization in this article is
  (a) classification. (b) time sequence. (c) addition.

10. The author's *primary* purpose is to
  (a) inform, (b) persuade, (c) entertain,
  and his *secondary* purpose is to
  (a) inform. (b) persuade. (c) entertain.

Check your answers with your instructor. Then turn to the Rate Chart in the Appendix to get your words per minute for this selection. Finally, record your scores below and on the progress chart in the Appendix on page 368.

WORDS PER MINUTE _____

% COMPREHENSION _____

This test, like the Pretest, is made up mostly of words taken from the Homework sections. "Word Comprehension," and "Words in Context" exercises. If you have done the exercises and read the Short and Long Readings in this book, you will know most of the words. A few words from the Pretest are repeated in this test.

A. Matching, 1–5

In the blank before each vocabulary word on the left, write the letter of the best definition on the right.

_____	1. salvage	(a)	pretend
_____	2. enhance	(b)	dry
_____	3. curtail	(c)	reduce
_____	4. arid	(d)	save
_____	5. feign	(e)	heighten

B. Short Definitions, 6–15

In the blank at the left, write the letter of the word that is being defined.

_____ 6. odd

(a) dormant (b) exotic (c) eccentric (d) senile

_____ 7. beat

(a) flail (b) segregate (c) dissect (d) mediate

_____ 8. levels

(a) silhouettes (b) strata (c) panoramas (d) caper

_____ 9. honor

(a) sham (b) abolition (c) homage (d) incision

_____ 10. lengthen

(a) elongate (b) forgo (c) smite (d) compile

_____ 11. calm

(a) intent (b) rustic (c) sultry (d) tranquil

_____ 12. stoop

(a) relent (b) smudge (c) condescend (d) endorse

_____ 13. scornful

(a) treacherous (b) disdainful (c) immune (d) mammoth

_____ 14. system

(a) regimen (b) velocity (c) cluster (d) provision

_____ 15. change

(a) pretense (b) turbulence (c) mutation (d) apex

In the blank at the left, write the letter of the best definition for the *italicized word*.

_____ 16. no strong *sentiment* or tenderness

(a) wrong-doing (b) feeling (c) power (d) gloom

_____ 17. suffering from *vascular* disease

(a) spots on the lungs (b) excessive coughing (c) system of blood or lymph vessels (d) condition caused by white blood cells destroying red

_____ 18. *cropping* the roses in the garden

(a) smelling (b) planting (c) cutting off (d) trampling

_____ 19. in a *solicitous* tone

(a) expressing concern (b) hypocritical (c) sarcastic (d) harshly critical

_____ 20. high degree of *sociability*

(a) friendliness (b) intelligence (c) vulgarity (d) energy

_____ 21. to *gloat* over her success

(a) give it up (b) act modestly (c) act too satisfied (d) help others

_____ 22. Inside that *hovel*

(a) elegant mansion (b) wretched shack (c) haunted house (d) apartment building

_____ 23. to *capitulate* without a groan

(a) give in (b) go into business (c) feel happiness (d) feel hopeful

_____ 24. of blood, *sinews*, and flesh

(a) intelligence (b) passion (c) tendons (d) corruption

_____ 25. *exhorting* people on the street

(a) fighting with (b) singing to (c) giving warnings to (d) greeting warmly

_____ 26. *eliciting* no assurance

(a) forcing (b) drawing forth (c) begging for (d) winning

_____ 27. *derogatory* comments

(a) truthful (b) insulting (c) angry (d) complimentary

_____ 28. an *innate* sense of respect

(a) learned (b) inborn (c) artistic (d) reluctant

_____ 29. erupting *convulsively*

(a) cleanly (b) blowing gently (c) shaking violently (d) suddenly

_____ 30. *comparable* to children

(a) different from (b) similar (c) bigger than (d) leading up to

D. Context—Sentences, 31–40

In the blank at the left, write a *T* if the statement is true; write an *F* if the statement is false. (Emphasis is on the correct use of the *italicized word* rather than on facts.)

_____ **31.** His closet held shirts of *myriad* colors.

_____ **32.** The happy couple treated each other with respect and *antipathy.*

_____ **33.** Flowers picked from *random* fields are often just alike.

_____ **34.** People with the gift of gab are seldom *articulate.*

_____ **35.** I am *complacent* in my job and am not looking for another.

_____ **36.** Michael, an enthusiastic party-goer, loves to *fraternize.*

_____ **37.** When she is motionless, she *gesticulates* frequently.

_____ **38.** Filled with *remorse,* she promised not to break the law again.

_____ **39.** He certainly is an *adept* surgeon; eight out of ten patients he operates on die.

_____ **40.** The dress was too *gaudy* with its loud colors and rhinestone trim.

E. Roots, Prefixes, and Suffixes—Matching, 41–50

In the blank at the left, write the letter of the best definition for the root, prefix, or suffix.

Roots

_____ **41.** cult

_____ **42.** bellum

_____ **43.** mono

_____ **44.** tend, tens

_____ **45.** duc, duct

(a) war

(b) to lead

(c) to stretch

(d) to care for

(e) one

Prefixes and Suffixes

_____ **46.** -arium, -orium

_____ **47.** mal-

_____ **48.** ambi-

_____ **49.** -ize

_____ **50.** -ward

(a) to make or cause to be (verb)

(b) on both sides, around

(c) direction (adj.)

(d) a place for (noun)

(e) bad, wrong

Check your answers with your instructor and record your score below and on the progress chart in the Appendix on page 368.

% CORRECT _____

Finally, contrast the results of the Pretest and the Posttest.

APPENDIX

1. Additional Perceptual Drills
2. Scanning Instruction and Exercises
3. Personal Vocabulary List
4. Alphabetical List of Prefixes, Roots, and Suffixes
5. Rate Chart for Long Readings
6. Progress Chart for Short and Long Readings
7. Progress Chart for Pretest and Posttest
8. Answer Keys for Lessons 1–12 and Scanning Exercises

Perceptual Drill 1

1. Circle the *cl* combination each time you see it. Example: (cl̲aw.) Write your time and number of errors at the end of each drill.
   (a) climb call click casual callow cold calf collar
   (b) casual clench chorus clack cull climber lick
   (c) lull clam calorie calcium calendar clear cling
   (d) calm clearly walk clan close curl closet clef
   (e) club aisle acclaim clone acrid claim clothes clue
   (f) chick claw clasp clean crass class calk clumsy
   (g) chink clink cancel clap clamp clunker chorus acclimate

   TIME _____

   ERRORS _____

2. Circle the *st* combination each time you see it. (Example: po̲st̲.)
   (a) sting sat string past tryst mask astir sty strap
   (b) stud haste sister satrap straight Steve inset
   (c) astra fast finest misstep visit hasty studying
   (d) stone staple rest restaple restive hose strange
   (e) worst slit instant insert resist step story just
   (f) restaple retain ask must story stain unspoiled
   (g) listen stampede asked trust often strength star

   TIME _____

   ERRORS _____

3. Have someone read out loud to you one word from line (a). Point to it as quickly as you can. Continue through each line in both drills.

Perceptual Drill 2

To expand your peripheral vision horizontally (left and right), fix your eyes on the dot in the middle of each line in each pyramid. Try to see the figures or words on each side of the dot. As your eyes move vertically down each pyramid, *stretch* your eye span until the outside corners of your eyes tingle.

1.
```
        4
       341
      82453
     9264516
    827141623
   91452438996
```

2.
```
        b
       s  s
     pr  b  l
      y  b  ro
     lk  b e  t
   e  y b  n  no s
```

3.
```
          A
         bi-
         ped
        is an
        animal
       that goes
      on two legs
     such as a man
  or a woman or birds
  or some trick horses.
```

4.
```
          i
         + 1
         = 2
       and two
       rabbits
      can make
     more rabbits
  than you ever wanted.
```

5.
```
          A
         gnu
        is an
       antelope
      that is also
   called a wildebeest.
```

6.
```
          A
         gnu
         gets
       its name
      from the
     Kaffir word
    "nqu." or would
   you rather call it
  by its proper Latin name
which is a Connochaetes taurinus?
```

Perceptual Drill 3

To expand your peripheral vision vertically (above and below):

1. Fixate on the black dot and try to read the items above and below it.

				faster
		9	form	latter
	7	1	for	madder
4	2	0	if	harder
•	•	•	•	•
8	6	5	I	banner
	3	7	in	dinner
		8	mine	shiner
				winter

2. Fixate on each dot and try to read the items above and below it.

Yeung D S
Yewell Frank
   •
Yglesias Terry
Yhookas Pancho
   •
Yi Chung Loo
Yick James
Yim Archibald
   •
Yinger Maryanne
Yip Kate
Ylanan Agonistes
   •
Ynson Yolanda
Yodo Restrt
Yoga Kundalini
   •
Yogurt International
Yoh H. I. Co.

Perceptual Drill 4

1. Take an index card (or a folded piece of paper) and cover up the bottom half of the first line in the following paragraph. Try to read the line even though you see only the top half of the letters. Repeat the process on the other lines, still trying to follow the idea presented.

    "Comprehension" simply means understanding what you read. You not only have to understand each sentence, but you have to see relationships between sentences in a paragraph, between paragraphs in a short reading, between sections in an article or chapter, between chapters in a book. You must know what topic is being discussed. You must know the main idea(s) the writer is presenting about the topic. You must follow the organization of details as the writer enlarges upon the main idea. You must keep sight of the structural scheme, the differences between the large, general ideas and the small, specific ideas. And you must retain or remember all or most of this, or why bother to read at all?

2. Now take the card and cover up the top half of the first line and read it again. You will notice that you get fewer clues from the shape of the bottom half of the letters. There are more differences in the configurations of the top half. Conclusion: Faster readers tend to focus on the top or above the line.

1. In the following paragraph, note how the words are arranged into natural phrase clusters. Try to fix your eyes only once per phrase (on the dot in the middle) and still follow the meaning of the paragraphs.

A person with a rate of less than
250 words per minute almost always reads
word by word. This method is so slow
and inefficient that it actually hinders
comprehension. In learning to read
by meaningful word groups, a person
enables his brain to function much closer to
its capacity and almost invariably
improves his comprehension. No matter how hard
some people try to ignore the fact, reading is
a learned process, in which certain techniques
operate more successfully than others. No one
is born knowing how to read; he must
be taught. He can be taught well or poorly.
What most often happens, however —and this
seems to be what the "slower, slower" people
are fighting for —is that he is not taught at all.
Left to his own devices, he typically develops
a surprising number of bad reading habits,
among which is the habit of reading too slowly
for maximum comprehension or enjoyment.*

2. In the next paragraph, many of the functional and repetitive words are missing. Only the key words remain. Try to follow the meaning of the paragraph through reading these key words.

We should not forget obvious aids
physical process reading. One, good lighting spread
evenly room, not concentrated
desk or book. Two, good posture breathing permit
oxygen reach eyes brain, area of
body uses high proportion of
total energy. Three, get plenty rest; fatigue affects
eyesight. Four, have eyes checked for defects
near-point (reading) distance year two.

---

*Adapted from George Guomo, "How Fast Should a Person Read?" Adapted from *The Saturday Review,* April 21, 1962. Copyright © 1962 by the Saturday Review/World, Inc.

Look at the key unit of shapes on the left and try to find the identical unit among the units on the right. Mark the repeated unit, and work your way through the drill as rapidly as you can.

Key Unit

1. GDP	PDG	GDP	PGD	BGD	ODP
2. wmuv	wumv	vumw	mwuv	wmuv	wnuv
3. $\frac{1}{2}\ \frac{2}{4}$	$\frac{1}{4}\ \frac{1}{2}$	$\frac{1}{3}\ \frac{1}{2}$	$\frac{1}{2}\ \frac{2}{3}$	$\frac{2}{1}\ \frac{4}{2}$	$\frac{1}{2}\ \frac{2}{4}$
4. $hb\frac{1}{3}$	$hb\frac{1}{3}$	$hb\frac{1}{2}$	$bh\frac{1}{3}$	$hb\frac{2}{3}$	$hp\frac{1}{3}$
5. + %;	= + %	% +;	+ %;	+ %,	+ % ÷
6. 8968	9868	6898	8968	8986	8936
7. 27530	27538	27530	25730	27503	03572
8. il2x4	li2x4	il4x2	ilx42	il2x5	il2x4
9. xxxxxx	xxxxx	xxxxxx	xxxxx	xxxxxxx	xxx
10. XXVII	XVII	XXXVII	XXVII	XXVIII	XXVI

Note which type of symbol you found most difficult to perceive.

2. SCANNING INSTRUCTION AND EXERCISES

Definition of *scanning*

The reading skill called "scanning" takes skimming a step further. It might be defined as selective skipping. **When you scan print, you are looking for one thing in particular.** You have a specific question or word or number in mind, and you run through the material at high speed until you find the answer. Then you stop, fixate, and read only what you need.

Scanning can be the simple task of finding the exact word or number—as in our perception drills. Or it can be more difficult, as when the wording of your information is different from the wording of your question. The different kinds of scanning often overlap. The important points is that *you recognize what you are looking for.*

How fast?

The scanning rates many experts suggest may be frightening. They speak of 2000 wpm and up. Actually, you have already practiced scanning many times, at 2000 wpm and much more. In fact, a words-per-minute rate is rather meaningless in scanning because you are selecting so little and ignoring so much. Keep in mind, however, that you are rapidly processing even the material you choose not really to *read.*

Simple scanning

When you scan, you begin, as in all reading, with a purpose. Here are some of the simplest reasons to use your scanning ability.

1. Finding a name in the phone book, a word in the dictionary, "Cleaners" in the yellow pages, or page 00 in this book;

2. Locating a certain street or town on a map;

3. Looking for news of a specific athlete, meeting, or auto accident in the news-paper;

4. Finding the subject, author, or title you want in the library's card catalog or on the shelf;

5. Using office skills such as filing, billing, and checking for errors;

6. Locating information in a book index or table of contents;

7. Looking for a specific item as you do in the number, letter, word, or phrase perception drills in this book.

Complex scanning

The following scanning tasks require some translation of your ideas, some flexibility of where to look. But they still assume that you have a specific question and will know when you find the answer:

1. Looking in the movie ads or TV guides for "any good show" (you may, in the process, rule out all westerns, porno films, etc.);

2. Looking in the classified newspaper ads for rentals, furniture, etc., that are available in your area or in your price range;

3. Finding how many buses or planes travel between two cities and when;

4. Using a reference guide or a book index for information, say, on "Women's Lib"—it may be listed under "Sex Discrimination," "Employment," or "Equal Rights";

5. Looking for answers to multiple-choice questions;

6. Looking for similar words, phrases, and sentences in the comprehension exercises in this book.

Sharp focus

When you scan, you zero in on specific answers like a hawk swooping down on a mouse. The image is not extreme if you have ever done a research paper or worked in a busy office. You do need good perception, a clear idea of what you're looking for, and the discipline to ignore everything else.

Follow these guidelines when you scan:

How to scan

1. Clearly fix in your mind the information for which you are scanning.

2. Use any headings or subheadings to find quickly the part of the page (or chapter or book) that probably contains your information.

3. Look for synonyms, alternate ways your information might be worded. For example, information about "whales" might be listed under "marine life" or "oceanography," or even "mammals."

The following exercises should help you become faster and more accurate in your scanning ability.

► ***Exercise 1—Scanning***

Scan the opposite page for answers to the following questions.

You have decided to enroll in a community college. So you scan the college catalog to familiarize yourself with the requirements.

STARTING TIME _____

1. Under what circumstance could you get a "W" grade? _____

_____

2. If you withdraw from a regular course during the twelfth week because you are

not passing, might you get a "U" grade? _____

_____

3. The last day to change your class program is found in the semester schedule of

classes and where else? _____

_____

4. Where do you file to withdraw from one or all of your classes? _____

_____

5. If a class has a number beginning with 90–99, what kind of class is it? _____

_____

FINISHING TIME _____

Check your answers with the key at the back of the book and record your scores below.

TOTAL SCANNING TIME _____

NUMBER OF ERRORS _____

► *Exercise 1—Scanning*

College Regulations

It is important that every student give careful attention to his educational objectives and the program of studies before he registers. Deadline date for change of program, refund of A.S. Membership, etc., are indicated in each semester's schedule of classes and in the Student Handbook.*

Attendance and Student Request to Withdraw from a Class

Since attendance is considered necessary for normal progress in a class, the student is expected to be in class regularly and on time.

First Ten Weeks: A student may withdraw from a single class or from all classes during the first ten weeks without penalty. Proper forms for withdrawal are available in the Counseling Office.

After Ten Weeks: A student may withdraw from a single class or from all classes by filing proper forms available in the Counseling Office. A grade check will be made with the instructor. If the student was passing the course at the time of his last attendance, he will receive a "W" grade. If he was failing, he may be given a "U" (unsatisfactory withdrawal) grade.

Exception: This policy does not apply to "classes for adults" numbered 90–99. All students who withdraw will be given "W" grades in these classes.

Attendance and Instructor Request to Drop a Student

A student may be dropped from a class when, in the instructor's judgment, the number of absences has become excessive. Such judgment should be based exclusively on the student's prospect for successfully completing the course. When a student is dropped from class, he will receive a "W" grade, except under the following conditions: If the last attendance occurs after the 10th week and if the student was doing failing work, the instructor may assign a "U" grade. *Exception:* This policy does not apply to classes numbered 9000–9999. All students who withdraw will be given "W" grades in these classes. Failure to follow these procedures by discontinuing attendance in class may result in "U" (unsatisfactory withdrawal) grades and possible disqualification from college.

*From Santa Monica College General Catalog, 1974–76.

► *Exercise 2—Scanning*

Scan the opposite page for answers to the following questions.

You consider drafting as a possible career. Again, scan the college catalog for requirements.

1. If you are not interested in the Associate in Arts Degree, what are the other three general academic goals that you might pursue in preparation for employment? _____

    _____

2. How many units would you need for an Occupational Certificate? _____

    _____

3. For an A.A. degree in Drafting Technology, how many units must you take in the major? _____

    _____

4. How many courses are available for "selection" in the major? _____

    _____

5. Where do you find a page listing the General Education courses? _____

    _____

Check your answers with the key at the back of the book and record your scores below.

► *Exercise 2—Scanning*

Major in Drafting Technology

Employment in the field and an Associate in Arts Degree in Drafting Technology are the primary purposes of this major.*

A. Associate in Arts Degree—60 Units

1. The major consists of 20 units including:
    Drafting Technology 3, Advanced Drafting, and other courses selected from:
    Drafting Technology 2, Fundamentals
    Drafting Technology 35AB, Advanced Drafting and Layout
    Electronic Engineering Technology 5, Computer Fundamentals
    Manufacturing Engineering Technology 1, Machine Processes
    Manufacturing Engineering Technology 2, Metal Joining
    Manufacturing Engineering Technology 3, Metal Casting
    Manufacturing Engineering Technology 7, Welding Processes
    Manufacturing Engineering Technology 10, Numerical Controls
    Manufacturing Engineering Technology 11AB, Tool Design
    Manufacturing Engineering Technology 14, Numerical Controls
2. The required General Education courses are included in the Santa Monica College graduation requirements listed on a page following this section on majors.

B. Occupational Certificate

A Certificate in Drafting Technology or Tool Design may be earned by completing 20 units with a C or better grade point average. Courses are to be selected from those listed above for the major.

C. Vocational Diploma

A Vocational Diploma is awarded to students who complete 40 units or more in Drafting Technology with a C grade point average. Courses are those listed in the major and other courses in the Metal Trades. Units may be counted toward the Associate in Arts Degree as well as this diploma.

D. Transfer

1. *Drafting and Design, California State University at Fresno*
    Art 11, 12; Construction Technology 5, 6, 7, 8, 9
    Drafting, California Polytechnic State University at San Luis Obispo
    Chemistry 1; General Engineering 7; Electricity 40 or 40X; Electronic Engineering Technology 12, 13, or 13X; Mathematics 2, 7, 8; Manufacturing Engineering Technology 1, 10; Physics 6, 7
    California State University at San Jose
    The Technical and Architectural option in the Industrial Studies major is also a study area related to the Santa Monica Drafting major.
2. General Education
    The California State University and Colleges General Education pattern is listed on a page following this section on majors.

---

*From Santa Monica College General Catalog, 1974–76.

► *Exercise 3—Scanning*

Scan the opposite page for answers to the following questions.

Try to decide which English course to take by scanning the schedule of classes.

STARTING TIME _____

1. You can't take World Literature or English Literature I and II without first taking what course? _____

2. If you want to take Harrell's Monday class, English 48, will it conflict with Chodos' English 4? _____

3. If you are given a grade of C in English I, can you then enroll in Dodge's Advanced Composition class? _____

4. Is English 98 a college-level course? _____

5. Is there a class in Creative Writing on Monday evenings? _____

FINISHING TIME _____

Check your answers with the key at the back of the book and record your scores below.

TOTAL SCANNING TIME _____

NUMBER OF ERRORS _____

► *Exercise 3—Scanning*

Section Number	Time	Room	Instructor	
ENGL 30 BEGINNING CREATIVE WRITING				**3 UNITS**
1318	9:30–11 TT	LA 124	CastyA H	
1319	11 MWF	LA 136	CastyA H	
5354	**7–10 WED**	**SMHSH213**	**Bilson B T**	
1320	9–12 SAT	LA 231	Ellman D M	
ENGL 31 ADVANCED COMPOSITION				**3 UNITS**
Prereq—Engl I With Grade B				
1321	8–9:30 TT	SA 10	Dodge R H	
ENGL 46 POWER READING				**3 UNITS**
Prereq—Group C—Engl Placement Test				
Offered Only On A Credit-No Credit Basis.				
One Hour Per Week Required in the Learning Center				
1322	8 MWF	SA 12	Dye A G	
1323	9 MWF	SA 12	Dye A G	
1324	12–1:30 TT	SA 12	Saintleon S K	
1325	1:30–3 TT	SA 12	Saintleon S K	
1326	3–4:30 TT	SA 12	George P C	
5355	**7–10 TUES**	**SA 12**	**Hearn W G**	
5356	**7–10 WED**	**SA 12**	**George P C**	
5357	**7–10 THURS**	**SA 12**	**Hearn W G**	
ENGL 47 ADVANCED POWER READING				**3 UNITS**
Prereq—Group B—Engl Placement Test				
One Hour Per Week Required in the Learning Center				
1327	9:30–11 TT	SA 12	Dye A G	
ENGL 48 POWER AND SPEED READING				**3 UNITS**
Prereq—Engl 1 or B in Engl 21 or 47				
One Hour Per Week Required in the Learning Center				
1328	11 MWF	SA 12	Dye A G	
1329	12 MWF	SA 12	Dye A G	
5358	**7–10 MON**	**SA 12**	**Harrell W M**	
1330	9–12 SAT	SA 12	Harrell W M	
ENGL 98 CORRECT USAGE				**0 UNITS**
For Completion of High School Requirements				
9808	**7–10 MON**	**SMHST215**	**Harris J K**	
9809	**7–10 WED**	**SMHST215**	**Harris J K**	
	ENGLISH LITERATURE			
ENGL 4 WORLD LITERATURE II				**3 UNITS**
Prereq—Engl 1				
1331	12 MWF	LA 236	Marsh J E	
5359	**7–10 MON**	**SC 274**	**Chodos J W**	
ENGL 5 ENGLISH LITERATURE I				**3 UNITS**
Prereq—Engl 1				
1332	9 MWF	LA 231	Doten D G	
1333	9:30–11 TT	LA 231	Marrant D E	
5360	**7–10 WED**	**LA 231**	**Doten D G**	
ENGL 6 ENGLISH LITERATURE II				**3 UNITS**
Prereq—Engl 1				
1334	12 MWF	LA 231	Theiss N L	
5361	**7–10 TUES**	**LA 220**	**Dodge R H**	
	Master Numbers over 5000 in Bold Type indicate Evening Sessions			

*From Santa Monica College Schedule of Classes, Spring 1975.

► *Exercise 4—Scanning*

Scan the opposite page for answers to the following questions.

You learn to use the dictionary in your English class—by scanning for answers.

STARTING TIME _____

1. What is the population of Gibraltar? _____

2. From what language did we borrow the word **gigolo**? (Look in the brackets [ ].)

   _____

3. What are the two ways of spelling the noun plural of **GI**? _____

   _____

4. What part of speech is **ghoulish**? _____

   _____

5. How many meanings are listed for the simple word **gift**? _____

   _____

FINISHING TIME _____

Check your answers with the key at the back of the book and record your scores below.

TOTAL SCANNING TIME _____

NUMBER OF ERRORS _____

► *Exercise 4—Scanning*

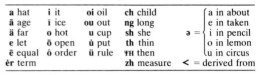

a hat	i it	oi oil	ch child		a in about
ā age	ī ice	ou out	ng long		e in taken
ä far	o hot	u cup	sh she	ə =	i in pencil
e let	ō open	u̇ put	th thin		o in lemon
ē equal	ô order	ü rule	ᴛʜ then		u in circus
ėr term			zh measure	< = derived from

ghost writ er (gōst′rĭ′tər), *n.* person who writes something for another person who pretends to be the author.

ghoul (gül), *n.* **1** (in Oriental stories) a horrible demon that robs graves and feeds on corpses. **2** person who robs graves or corpses. **3** person who enjoys what is revolting, brutal, and horrible. [< Arabic *ghūl*]

ghoul ish (gü′lish), *adj.* like a ghoul; revolting, brutal, and horrible. —**ghoul′ish ly,** *adv.* —**ghoul′ish ness,** *n.*

GHQ or **G.H.Q.,** General Headquarters.

GHz, gigahertz.

GI or **G.I.** (jē′ī′), *adj., n., pl.* **GI's** or **G.I.'s** (jē′īz′). —*adj.* **1** government issue: *GI shoes, GI socks.* **2** INFORMAL. conforming to regulations; standard: *GI uniforms.* **3** of, having to do with, or for a member of the armed forces: *a GI loan.* —*n.* INFORMAL. **1** an enlisted soldier in the United States Army; serviceman. **2** member or former member of any of the armed forces of the United States. [< the initial letters of the phrase "Government Issue"]

GI or **G.I.,** **1** gastrointestinal. **2** general issue. **3** government issue.

Gia co met ti (jä′kō met′ē), *n.* **Alberto,** 1901-1966, Swiss sculptor and painter.

gi ant (jī′ənt), *n.* **1** an imaginary being having human form, but larger and more powerful than a person. **2** person or thing of great size, strength, or importance. —*adj.* like a giant; huge: *a giant potato.* [< Old French *geant* < Latin *gigantem* < Greek *gigas*]

gi ant ess (jī′ən tis), *n.* woman of great size, strength, or importance.

gi ant ism (jī′ən tiz′əm), *n.* **1** condition of being a giant. **2** gigantism.

giant panda, panda (def. 1).

giant sequoia, a very large evergreen tree of California, belonging to the same family as the redwood, often growing to a height of over 300 feet (92 meters); sequoia; big tree.

giant star, a very bright star of vast size and low density, such as Arcturus.

giaour (jour), *n.* a Moslem term for a person who does not believe in the Moslem religion. [< Turkish *giaur*]

gib ber (jib′ər, gib′ər), *v.i.* chatter senselessly; talk in a confused, meaningless way: *The monkeys gibbered angrily at each other.* —*n.* senseless chattering. [imitative]

gib be rel lic acid (jib′ə rel′ik), a plant hormone, first discovered in a fungus, that increases size and the rate of growth. *Formula:* $C_{19}H_{22}O_6$ [< New Latin *Gibberella,* name of the fungus]

gib be rel lin (jib′ə rel′ən), *n.* any of a group of hormones that are synthesized in the protoplasm of plants and that increase the rate and amount of growth. Gibberellic acid is a gibberellin.

gib ber ish (jib′ər ish, gib′ər ish), *n.* senseless chatter; confused, meaningless talk or writing.

gib bet (jib′it), *n.* **1** an upright post with a projecting arm at the top, from which the bodies of criminals were hung after execution. **2** gallows. —*v.t.* **1** hang on a gibbet. **2** hold up to public scorn or ridicule. **3** put to death by hanging. [< Old French *gibet,* diminutive of *gibe* club]

gib bon (gib′ən), *n.* any of various small apes of southeastern Asia and the East Indies that live in trees and have very long arms and no tail. [< French]

Gib bon (gib′ən), *n.* **Edward,** 1737-1794, English historian.

gib bos i ty (gi bos′ə tē), *n., pl.* **-ties.** **1** gibbous condition. **2** protuberance; swelling.

gib bous (gib′əs), *adj.* **1** curved out; humped. **2** (of a heavenly body) so illuminated as to be convex on both margins. A gibbous moon is more than half full but less than full. See **phase** for diagram. **3** humpbacked. [< Latin *gibbosus* < *gibbus* hump] —**gib′bous ly,** *adv.* —**gib′bous ness,** *n.*

gibbon about 3 ft. (91 cm.) tall

Gibbs (gibz), *n.* **Josiah Willard,** 1839-1903, American mathematician and physicist, whose theories form the basis of modern physical chemistry.

gibe (jīb), *v.,* **gibed, gib ing,** *n.* —*v.i.* speak in a sneering way; jeer; scoff; sneer. —*n.* a jeer; taunt; sneer. Also, **jibe.** [perhaps < Old French *giber* handle roughly < *gibe* staff] —**gib′er,** *n.* —**gib′ing ly,** *adv.*

gib let (jib′lit), *n.* Usually, **giblets,** *pl.* the heart, liver, or gizzard

of a fowl. [< Old French *gibelet* stew of game]

Gi bral tar (jə brôl′tər), *n.* **1** seaport and fortress on a high rock on the Mediterranean Sea, near the S tip of Spain. It is a British colony. 30,000 pop. ; 2 sq. mi. (5 sq. km.) **2 Rock of,** the large rock on which this fortress stands. **3** a strongly fortified place; impregnable fortress or stronghold. **4 Strait of,** strait between Africa and Europe, connecting the Mediterranean Sea with the Atlantic. 8½ to 23 mi. (14 to 37 km.) wide.

gid dy (gid′ē), *adj.,* **-di er, -di est.** **1** having a whirling feeling in one's head; dizzy. **2** likely to make dizzy; causing dizziness: *a giddy dance.* **3** never or rarely serious; frivolous; fickle: *a giddy person.* [Old English *gydig* mad, possessed (by an evil spirit) < *god* a god] —**gid′di ly,** *adv.* —**gid′di ness,** *n.*

Gide (zhēd), *n.* **André,** 1869-1951, French novelist and critic.

Gid e on (gid′ē ən), *n.* (in the Bible) a hero of Israel who defeated the Midianites and was a judge of Israel for forty years.

gie (gē), *v.t., v.i.* SCOTTISH AND DIALECT. give.

gift (gift), *n.* **1** something given freely; present: *a birthday gift.* See synonym study below. **2** act of giving freely: *The land came to her by gift from an aunt.* **3** power or right of giving: *The job is within his gift.* **4** natural ability; special talent: *a gift for painting.* —*v.t.* **1** present or make a gift to. **2 gift with,** present as a gift to: *to gift a person with several new books.* **3** give as a gift: *to gift copies of a best seller to one's friends.* [Middle English *gifte* < Scandinavian. Related to GIVE.]

Syn. 1 Gift, present mean something given to express friendship, admiration, interest, etc. **Gift** usually applies to what is given to a person, organization, or institution to benefit it: *The university received a gift of a million dollars.* **Present** always suggests a personal connection and applies to what is given a friend, relative, or other close person: *We bought a wedding present for our cousin.*

gift ed (gif′tid), *adj.* having natural ability or special talent; unusually able: *Beethoven was a gifted composer.*

gift of gab, ability to talk persuasively or glibly.

gift-wrap (gift′rap′), *v.t.,* **-wrapped, -wrap ping.** wrap (a parcel, gift, etc.) in fancy paper and with decorative trimmings.

gig¹ (gig), *n.* **1** a light, open, two-wheeled carriage drawn by one horse. **2** a long, light ship's boat moved by oars or sails. [origin uncertain]

gig² (gig), *n., v.,* **gigged, gig ging.** —*n.* a fish spear. —*v.t.* spear (fish) with a gig. [origin uncertain]

gig¹ (def. 1)

gig³ (gig), *n.* SLANG. **1** a gathering or meeting of jazz or rock musicians. **2** a single engagement or playing time of a jazz or rock group, or solo entertainer. **3** any work or interest that is habitual.

giga-, *combining form.* one billion: *Gigavolt = one billion volts.* [< Greek *gigas* giant]

gig a hertz (jig′ə hèrts), *n., pl.* **-hertz.** unit of frequency equal to one billion hertz.

gi gan tic (jī gan′tik), *adj.* **1** of, having to do with, or like a giant: *In folklore, Paul Bunyan was a gigantic lumberjack.* **2** huge; enormous. [< Greek *gigantos*] —**gi gan′ti cal ly,** *adv.*

gi gan tism (jī gan′tiz′əm), *n.* **1** abnormal growth or size of the body or part of the body, usually caused by malfunction of the pituitary gland. **2** condition of being a giant.

gig a volt (jig′ə vōlt′), *n.* one billion volts.

gig gle (gig′əl), *v.,* **-gled, -gling,** *n.* —*v.i.* laugh in a silly or undignified way. —*n.* a silly or undignified laugh. [imitative] —**gig′gler,** *n.* —**gig′gling ly,** *adv.*

gig gly (gig′lē), *adj.* having the habit of giggling: *a giggly pupil.*

gig o lo (jig′ə lō), *n., pl.* **-los.** man who is paid for being a woman's dancing partner, escort, or lover. [< French]

gig ot (jig′ət), *n.* **1** a leg-of-mutton sleeve. **2** leg of mutton, veal, etc. [< French]

Gi la (hē′lə), *n.* river flowing from SW New Mexico across S Arizona into the Colorado River. 630 mi. (1014 km.)

Gila monster, a large, poisonous lizard of the southwestern

3. PERSONAL VOCABULARY LIST

Record any words and their definitions here that you missed in the Word Comprehension or Phrase Comprehension exercises. Use this page as an ongoing review chart.

4. ALPHABETICAL LIST OF PREFIXES, ROOTS, AND SUFFIXES

Alphabetical list of word parts studied in the Homework sections, Lessons 4 through 12.

Roots

root word	meaning
1. (a)equus	equal, even
2. anima	breath, spirit, mind
3. *ann, enn	year
4. anthropo	man
5. *astro	star
6. *aud, audit	to hear
7. *auto	self
8. bellum	war
9. *bene	good, well
10. *bio	life
11. cap, cept	to take
12. *capit	head
13. cede, ceed	to yield, to go
14. cent	hundred
15. *chron	time
16. *civ	citizen
17. cogni	to know
18. cor	heart
19. *crat, cracy	rule
20. *cred, credit	to believe
21. cult	to care for
22. cycle	wheel, circle
23. dem	people
24. dent	tooth
25. derma	skin
26. *dic, dict	to say, to speak
27. duc, duct	to lead
28. *fac, fact	to make
29. *fin	end, to complete
30. *gen, gene	birth, origin
31. *geo	earth
32. *gram	to write

---

*Also presented in *Reading Faster and Understanding More, Book 1,* and included here for review.

33.	*graph	to write
34.	hetero	other
35.	*homo	same
36.	hydra	water
37.	*jac, ject	to throw
38.	*log, logo	word, study
39.	loqui, locut	talk
40.	luc, lus	light
41.	mania	madness, derangement
42.	manus	hand
43.	*metr	measure
44.	micro	small
45.	*mit, miss	to send
46.	mono	one
47.	mor	dead
48.	ocul	eye
49.	*path	feeling, suffering
50.	ped	foot
51.	pel, puls	drive
52.	*phil, philo	to love
53.	*phobia	fear
54.	*phon	sound
55.	*photo	light
56.	pod	foot
57.	*poly	many
58.	pon, pos	to place
59.	*popul	people
60.	*port	to carry
61.	*psych	mind
62.	rupt	to break
63.	*scrib, script	to write
64.	sect	to cut
65.	*sens, sent	to feel
66.	*spec, spect	to look at
67.	spir	to breathe
68.	tain, ten	to hold
69.	*tele	distant
70.	*tempor	time
71.	tend, tens	to stretch

---

*Also presented in *Reading Faster and Understanding More, Book 1,* and included here for review.

72.	terra	earth
73.	the	god
74.	*therm	heat
75.	vene, vent	to come
76.	vers, vert	to turn
77.	*vid, vis	to see
78.	*viv, vit	to live, life
79.	*voc, vocat	to call
80.	volens	wishing, willing

Prefixes

	prefix	**meaning**
1.	*a-	not, without
2.	ab-	away from, down
3.	ad-	to, toward
4.	ambi-, amphi-	on both sides, around
5.	*ante-	before
6.	*anti-	against
7.	arch-	chief, principal
8.	bi-	two
9.	circum-	around
10.	con-, com-	with, together
11.	*contra-, counter-	against
12.	*de-	away, down
13.	*dis-	not, without
14.	*dis-	apart
15.	*e-, ex-	out, away from
16.	extra-	outside, beyond
17.	*in- (im-, il-, ir-)	not
18.	*in- (im-)	inside, into
19.	inter-	among, between
20.	*intra-	inside, within
21.	*hyper-	above
22.	*hypo-	under
23.	mal-	bad, wrong
24.	mis-	wrong, ill
25.	multi-	many
26.	*non-	not

---

*Also presented in *Reading Faster and Understanding More, Book 1,* and included here for review.

27.	poly-		many
28.	*post-		after
29.	*pre-		before
30.	*pro-		for, in favor of
31.	pro-		before, forward
32.	re-		again, back
33.	retro-		back
34.	semi		half
35.	*sub-		under
36.	*super-		above
37.	syn-, sym-		together
38.	trans-		across
39.	tri-		three
40.	*un-		not

Suffixes

	suffix	part of speech	meaning
1.	-ac, -an	adj.	having the nature of
2.	*-able, -ible	adj.	able to be
3.	-acy	n.	state of
4.	*-an, -ian	n.	one who
5.	*-ance, -ence	n.	state of, quality of
6.	*-ant, -ent	n.	one who
7.	*-ant, -ent	adj.	having the nature of
8.	*-al, -ar	adj.	having the nature of
9.	-arium, -orium	n.	a place for
10.	*-ary, -ory	n.	a place for
11.	*-ate	v.	to make, cause to be
12.	-cide	n.	killing
13.	-dom	n.	place, condition
14.	*-ed, -t	v.	past participle
15.	-ed	adj.	having the nature of
16.	*-ee	n.	one who receives an action
17.	*-en	v.	to make, cause to be
18.	-eer, -ier	n.	one who
19.	*-er, -ar, -or	n.	one who, a thing which
20.	*-er	adj.	comparative (of two)
21.	-ese, -er, -ian	n.	inhabitant of

---

*Also presented in *Reading Faster and Understanding More, Book 1,* and included here for review.

22.	-esque	adj.	having the nature of
23.	-ess	n.	one who, feminine
24.	*-est	adj.	superlative (of more than two)
25.	-ette (-ie, -y, -let -ling, -ule)	n.	little noun
26.	-fic	adj.	having the nature of
27.	*-fy, -ify	v.	to make, cause to be
28.	*-ful	adj.	full of
29.	*-ic, *-ish	adj.	having the nature of
30.	*-ing	v.	present participle
31.	-ing	adj.	having the nature of
32.	*-ion, -tion, -sion	n.	state of, quality of
33.	*-ism	n.	state of, doctrine
34.	*-ist, -tist	n.	one who
35.	-itis	n.	inflammation, disease
36.	*-ive, -ative	adj.	having the nature of
37.	*-ize	v.	to make, cause to be
38.	*-less	adj.	without, free of
39.	*-ly	adv.	in a certain manner
40.	*-ment	n.	state of, quality of
41.	*-ness	n.	state of, quality of
42.	-oid	adj.	in the form of
43.	-ose, -ous	adj.	having the nature of
44.	*-s	v.	third person singular, present tense
45.	*-s, -es	n.	plural of noun
46.	-some	adj.	having the quality of
47.	*-ship, -hood,	n.	state of, quality of
48.	-ster	n.	one who
49.	*-tious, -cious	adj.	having the nature of
50.	*-tude, -lude	n.	state of, quality of
51.	*-ty, -ity	n.	state of, quality of
52.	-ward	adj.	in the direction of
53.	*-y, -ly	adj.	having the nature of

*Also presented in *Reading Faster and Understanding More, Book 1,* and included here for review.

5. RATE (WPM) CHART FOR LONG READINGS

Match the Long Reading (left column) with the time (top line) taken for reading it. The number at the point these two meet is your WPM (or how fast you read).

READINGS ↓	TIME → 1:00	1:10	1:20	1:30	1:40	1:50	2:00	2:10	2:20
Pretest	1571	1347	1178	1047	943	857	786	725	673
LR 1I	935	801	701	623	560	510	467	431	400
LR 2I	1332	1141	999	888	799	726	666	614	570
LR 3I	1728	1481	1296	1152	1037	943	864	798	741
LR 4I	1282	1098	961	854	769	699	641	591	549
LR 5I	1265	1084	948	843	758	690	632	583	542
LR 6G	1288	1104	966	859	773	703	644	594	552
LR 6H	1332	1142	999	888	799	727	666	615	571
LR 7G	1642	1407	1232	1095	985	896	821	758	704
LR 7H	1572	1347	1179	1048	943	857	786	726	674
LR 8I	1542	1321	1156	1028	925	841	771	711	661
LR 9G	873	748	655	582	524	476	437	403	374
LR 9H	1647	1412	1235	1098	988	898	824	760	706
LR 10I	1008	864	756	672	604	549	504	465	432
LR 11G	2075	1779	1556	1383	1245	1132	1038	958	889
LR 12I	916	785	687	610	549	499	458	422	392
Posttest	1628	1395	1221	1085	997	880	814	751	698

READINGS ↓	TIME → 2:30	2:40	2:50	3:00	3:10	3:20	3:30	3:40	3:50
Pretest	628	589	554	524	496	471	449	428	410
LR 1I	374	350	330	311	295	280	267	254	243
LR 2I	532	499	470	444	420	399	380	363	347
LR 3I	691	648	610	576	546	518	494	471	451
LR 4I	512	480	452	427	404	384	366	349	334
LR 5I	506	474	446	421	399	379	361	344	330
LR 6G	515	483	455	429	407	382	368	351	336
LR 6H	533	500	470	444	421	400	381	363	347
LR 7G	657	616	580	547	519	493	469	448	428
LR 7H	629	590	555	524	496	472	449	429	410
LR 8I	617	578	544	514	487	463	441	421	402
LR 9G	349	327	308	291	276	262	249	238	228
LR 9H	659	618	581	549	520	494	471	449	430
LR 10I	403	377	355	336	318	302	288	274	262
LR 11G	830	778	732	692	655	623	593	566	541
LR 12I	366	343	323	305	289	274	261	249	238
Posttest	650	611	574	542	513	488	465	444	425

READINGS ↓	TIME → 4:00	4:10	4:20	4:30	4:40	4:50	5:00	5:10	5:20
Pretest	393	377	363	349	337	325	314	304	295
LR 1I	233	224	215	207	200	193	187	180	175
LR 2I	333	319	307	296	285	275	266	257	249
LR 3I	432	415	399	384	370	358	346	334	324
LR 4I	320	307	295	284	274	265	256	248	240
LR 5I	316	303	291	281	271	261	253	244	237
LR 6G	332	309	297	286	276	266	258	249	242
LR 6H	333	320	307	296	285	276	266	258	250
LR 7G	411	394	379	365	352	340	328	318	308
LR 7H	393	377	363	349	337	325	314	304	295
LR 8I	386	370	356	343	330	319	308	298	289
LR 9G	218	210	201	194	187	181	175	169	164
LR 9H	412	395	380	366	353	341	329	319	309
LR 10I	252	241	232	224	215	208	201	195	189
LR 11G	519	498	479	461	445	429	415	402	390
LR 12I	229	219	211	203	196	189	183	177	171
Posttest	407	391	376	362	349	337	326	315	305

READINGS ↓	TIME → 5:30	5:40	5:50	6:00	6:10	6:20	6:30	6:40	6:50
Pretest	286	277	269	262	255	248	242	236	230
LR 1I	170	164	160	155	151	147	143	140	136
LR 2I	242	235	228	222	215	210	204	199	194
LR 3I	314	305	296	288	280	273	266	259	253
LR 4I	233	226	219	213	207	202	197	192	187
LR 5I	230	223	216	210	205	199	194	189	185
LR 6G	234	227	221	215	209	203	198	193	188
LR 6H	242	235	228	222	216	210	205	200	195
LR 7G	299	290	281	274	266	259	253	246	240
LR 7H	286	277	269	262	255	248	242	236	230
LR 8I	280	272	264	257	250	243	237	231	226
LR 9G	159	154	150	146	142	138	134	131	128
LR 9H	299	291	282	275	267	260	253	247	241
LR 10I	183	177	172	168	163	159	155	151	147
LR 11G	377	366	356	346	336	328	319	311	304
LR 12I	166	161	157	152	148	144	140	137	134
Posttest	296	287	279	271	264	257	250	244	238

READINGS ↓	TIME → 7:00	7:10	7:20	7:30	7:40	7:50	8:00	8:10	8:20
Pretest	224	219	214	209	205	201	196	192	189
LR 1I	133	130	127	124	121	119	116	114	112
LR 2I	190	185	181	177	173	170	166	163	159
LR 3I	247	241	236	230	225	221	216	212	207
LR 4I	183	178	174	170	167	163	160	156	153
LR 5I	180	176	172	168	164	161	158	154	151
LR 6G	184	180	176	172	168	164	161	158	155
LR 6H	190	186	182	178	174	170	167	163	160
LR 7G	235	229	224	219	214	210	205	201	197
LR 7H	225	219	214	210	205	201	197	192	189
LR 8I	220	215	210	206	201	197	193	189	185
LR 9G	125	122	119	116	114	111	109	107	105
LR 9H	235	230	225	220	214	210	206	202	198
LR 10I	144	140	137	134	131	128	126	123	120
LR 11G	296	290	283	277	271	265	259	254	249
LR 12I	130	127	124	122	119	116	114	112	109
Posttest	232	227	222	217	212	208	204	199	195

READINGS ↓	TIME → 8:30	8:40	8:50	9:00	9:10	9:20	9:30	9:40	9:50	10:00
Pretest	185	181	178	175	171	168	165	163	160	157
LR 1I	110	107	105	103	101	100	98	96	95	94
LR 2I	156	153	150	148	145	142	140	137	135	133
LR 3I	203	199	196	192	189	185	182	179	176	173
LR 4I	150	147	145	142	139	137	134	132	130	128
LR 5I	148	145	143	140	137	135	133	130	128	126
LR 6G	152	149	146	143	141	138	136	133	131	129
LR 6H	157	154	151	148	145	143	140	138	135	133
LR 7G	193	189	186	182	179	176	173	170	167	164
LR 7H	185	181	178	175	171	168	165	163	160	157
LR 8I	181	178	175	171	168	165	162	160	157	154
LR 9G	103	100	99	97	95	94	92	90	89	87
LR 9H	194	190	186	183	180	176	173	170	167	165
LR 10I	118	116	114	112	109	108	106	104	102	101
LR 11G	244	239	235	231	226	222	218	215	211	208
LR 12I	107	105	103	101	99	98	96	94	93	92
Posttest	192	188	184	181	178	174	171	168	166	163

6. PROGRESS CHART FOR SHORT AND LONG READINGS

Short Readings			Long Readings		
	WPM	% Comprehension		WPM	% Comprehension
SR 1G					
SR 1H			LR 1I		
SR 2G					
SR 2H			LR 2I		
SR 3G					
SR 3H			LR 3I		
SR 4G					
SR 4H			LR 4I		
SR 5G					
SR 5H			LR 5I		
			*LR 6G		
			*LR 6H		
			**LR 7G		
			**LR 7H		
***SR 8G					
***SR 8H			***LR 8I		
			LR 9G		
			LR 9H		
SR 10G					
SR 10H			LR 10I		
			LR 11G		
SR 12G					
SR 12H			LR 12I		

---

*Readings for outlining have no comprehension score.
**Study-reading speed should be slower than other speeds.
***Skimming speed should be double the other speeds.

7. PROGRESS CHART FOR PRETEST AND POSTTEST

Contrast your scores on the Pretest (taken when beginning this book) and the Posttest (taken after finishing this book).

I. Comprehension and Rate

	How Fast Should a Person Read?	% Comprehension	WPM
Pretest:			
Posttest:	I Was a Speed-Reading Dropout	% Comprehension	WPM
Difference:			

II. Vocabulary

	% Correct
Pretest:	
Posttest:	% Correct
Difference:	

ANSWER KEYS—LESSON 1

Exercise 1C: **1.** elaborate **2.** ponder **3.** bad-tempered **4.** outermost part **5.** reject **6.** odor **7.** spiteful **8.** extra **9.** forced **10.** desire **11.** worship **12.** subside **13.** ability **14.** smother **15.** omit **16.** agile **17.** impressive **18.** mourn **19.** nap **20.** prank

Exercise 1D: **1.** destroy **2.** steal **3.** disapprove **4.** scold **5.** conquered **6.** recover **7.** boring **8.** story **9.** agree **10.** famous **11.** disturb **12.** sleeplessness **13.** unreadable **14.** copy **15.** take apart **16.** receding **17.** point **18.** cut off **19.** permanent **20.** joy

Practice Paragraphs:

A. **1.** **(b)** [This is the only possible answer in this paragraph. The person who reads "more than one word at a glance" can read two or three times as fast as the person who reads (c) "one whole word at a time." Note the transition word *similarly,* which points out the similarity between the driver who sees more than one car and the reader who sees more than one word. Answers (a) and (d) are irrelevant.]

    2. "Use your Peripheral Vision" or "Read out of the Corners of your Eyes"

    3. [Check with your instructor.]

B. **1.** **(c)** ["Instead of" are the key words in the correct answer.]

    2. "Stop Margin-Reading and Read Faster"

    3. [Check with your instructor.]

C. [Check with your instructor. The answers are in the Instructor's Manual.]

Words in Context: **1.** (a) **2.** (b) **3.** (c) **4.** (b) **5.** (a) **6.** (d) **7.** (b) **8.** (d)

Short Reading 1G: **1.** (c) **2.** F **3.** her diary **4.** T **5.** (c)

Short Reading 1H: **1.** The author's mother is suspicious of him. **2.** F **3.** sugar bowl **4.** F **5.** (b)

Long Reading 1I: **1.** (c) **2.** T **3.** almost seven **4.** F **5.** T **6.** F **7.** T **8.** T **9.** (a) **10.** (b)

Exercise 2C: 1. fluent 2. stubborn 3. dry 4. detest 5. cautious 6. excessive 7. termination 8. hide 9. fake 10. brave 11. surprising 12. corpse 13. suggest 14. poor 15. decline 16. silent 17. starved 18. petty 19. vague 20. noble

Exercise 2D: 1. repeat 2. emblem 3. fit 4. wander 5. wonderful 6. capture 7. give up 8. give in 9. split 10. turn aside 11. dead 12. opponent 13. charm 14. strike 15. cut off 16. learner 17. plan 18. masterful 19. concrete 20. honor

(Your answers for 2E and 2F may be a little different. Check with your instructor.)

Exercise 2E: 1. ape; can be 2. executive; went 3. bobwhite; has 4. they; constructed 5. people; flavor 6. ambassador; received 7. book; has been made 8. candidates; are chosen 9. Gulf Stream; flows 10. leaves and berries; are used

Exercise 2F: 1. Lyndon Johnson; took 2. simile; is 3. politician; gave 4. terra cotta; is used 5. terrorists; have made 6. woman; wore 7. God; dwells 8. Martin Van Buren; was 9. people; suffer 10. he; won

Practice Paragraphs:

A. 1. Biofeedback Training for Migraines 2. Biofeedback has been effective in treating migraine headaches. 3. Yes (1) [Sentence (2) explains how migraine headaches work. Sentences (3) through (8) explain how biofeedback works. And sentence (9) gives statistics about the method's success.]

B. 1. Breathing and Relaxation. 2. Your breathing affects how relaxed or tense you are. 3. Yes (2) [Note that all the details in the paragraph have to do with your manner of breathing. Sentence (1) presents the topic, *breathing;* but (2) is better as a topic sentence because it makes a statement about breathing—*that breathing can tell you how relaxed you are.*]

C. [Check with your instructor. The answers are in the Instructor's Manual.]

Words in Context: 1. (c) 2. (a) 3. (d) 4. (c) 5. (c) 6. (b)

Short Reading 2G: 1. (d) 2. T 3. T 4. depression 5. (c) (*Bonus: T*)

Short Reading 2H: 1. Tension can be controlled through learning to find and then relax the tense muscles. 2. T 3. T 4. (c) 5. (b) (*Bonus: last*)

Long Reading 2I: 1. (b) 2. (a) 3. increased sexual performance 4. T 5. F 6. F 7. F 8. T 9. F 10. (a) (*Bonus: first or last*)

Exercise 3C: 1. disgusting   2. willful   3. deep hole   4. confirm   5. helper   6. disturbance   7. adjust   8. custom   9. stick   10. huge   11. manage   12. stop   13. misfortunes   14. rhythm   15. forceful   16. dark   17. accumulate   18. exceed   19. examination   20. hold back

Exercise 3D: 1. praise   2. complicated   3. clever   4. tastefully   5. calculate   6. understanding   7. shrinking   8. necessary   9. helping   10. hard work   11. search   12. unplanned   13. commotion   14. introduction   15. warning   16. destroyed   17. follower   18. defect   19. overcome   20. strong

Exercise 3E: 1. traveling about   2. big picture   3. bitter lemon   4. carved letters   5. ordinary error   6. ripped paper   7. short doze   8. silent spot   9. fat volume   10. serious attempt   11. to fall   12. backward position   13. careful reexamination   14. pleasant praise   15. additional income   16. to disagree forcefully   17. engaging in merriment   18. find a solution   19. complete price   20. fits in most cases.

Exercise 3F: 1. complete tale   2. weird blunder   3. very worried   4. plainly opposite   5. as arranged   6. bad nightmare   7. short meeting   8. clean carpet   9. close haircut   10. lonely area   11. comic actor   12. being brave   13. caught crook   14. appearing serene   15. sad look   16. expecting problems   17. being content   18. endless emptiness   19. completed job   20. easy to handle

Practice Paragraphs:

A.   1. Popularity of Historical Romances with Women   2. A lot of women are reading historical romances for escape and adventure.   3. Yes (5) [Sentences (1) through (3) catch your attention but do not introduce the topic. Sentence (4) presents the topic but does not sum it up. Sentence (5) defines the topic and prepares for the examples that follow.]

B.   1. Need for Literacy among Blue-Collar Workers   2. Blue-collar workers today need to be educated to be able to perform their jobs.   3. Yes (7) is the closest to a topic sentence.

C.   [Check with your Instructor. The answers are in the Instructor's Manual.]

Words in Context: 1. (c)   2. (a)   3. (a)   4. (a)   5. (b)   6. (c)   7. (b)   8. (c)   9. (a)   10. (c)

Short Reading 3G: 1. (d)   2. F   3. T   4. his hand   5. (b) (*Bonus:* first)

Short Reading 3H: 1. Key believes many advertisements are sending subliminal messages to people.   2. skulls   3. F   4. F   5. (c) (*Bonus:* the last two)

Long Reading 3I: 1. (b)   2. F   3. F   4. F   5. F   6. T   7. F   8. T   9. wait for the repairmen   10. frighten or charm the repairmen (*Bonus:* first sentence of the third to last paragraph)

Exercise 4C: 1. unaware 2. fight 3. acceptable 4. separate 5. odd 6. horrifying 7. final 8. anger 9. gather 10. sleeping 11. view 12. outline 13. levels 14. group 15. curious 16. appoint 17. beat 18. assess 19. lacking 20. cut

Exercise 4D: 1. different 2. destroy 3. sneaky 4. relieve 5. improve 6. ordinary 7. important 8. innocent 9. well-bred 10. available 11. mud 12. constant 13. hard-working 14. undeveloped 15. depressed 16. confusion 17. shy 18. amusing 19. judgment 20. recuperate

Exercise 4E: 2, 5, 6, 9 (perhaps 1)

Exercise 4F: 4, 9 (perhaps 7)

Practice Paragraphs:

A. 1. The cockroach has several traits that have caused it to survive for a long time. 2. Yes (2) [Sentence (1) is an introductory statement, and sentences (3) through (8) discuss its traits as a survivor.] 3. The major pattern is *cause and effect;* a minor pattern is *contrast.* 4. adapts easily; eats anything; has few enemies; is inedible.

B. 1. The author's joy on receiving the dog was so great she couldn't speak. 2. Yes (2) expresses her overall feeling. [Sentence (1) gives the reason for her joy.] 3. *Time sequence* and *description* are the major patterns; *contrast* is a minor pattern. 4. She couldn't speak, turned away, and had to be alone.

C. [Check with your instructor. The answers are in the Instructor's Manual.]

Words in Context: 1. (a) 2. (b) 3. (c) 4. (b) 5. (c) 6. (d) 7. (a) 8. (c) 9. (a) 10. (c)

Short Reading 4G: 1. (b) 2. T 3. T 4. They were killed and eaten. 5. (b) (*Bonus:* time sequence, cause and effect)

Short Reading 4H: 1. A person with a little wit may be able to turn what seems like a bad situation into a good one. 2. gold horn 3. F 4. T 5. (d) (*Bonus:* description, cause and effect, time sequence)

Long Reading 4I: 1. (c) 2. T 3. F 4. (a) 5. T 6. F 7. T 8. T 9. He learned that the Yahoos, whom he resembled, were disgusting beasts. 10. (b) (*Bonus:* Refer to paragraph 4)

Exercise 5C: 1. stop 2. isolated 3. illness 4. skilled 5. economical 6. lengthen 7. burn 8. inactive 9. hungry 10. ask 11. support 12. lazy 13. useless 14. respect 15. soaked 16. sideways 17. break 18. noisy 19. pretend 20. secret

Exercise 5D: 1. believable 2. destroy 3. crush 4. embarrassed 5. decay 6. unknown 7. peak 8. agitated 9. ill 10. force 11. alteration 12. select 13. passion 14. rotten 15. cancel 16. distorted 17. god 18. customers 19. well-expressed 20. part

Exercise 5E: 1. go faster 2. perceive a unit 3. at the start 4. gone seven days 5. seems incredible 6. can be counted on 7. trip to seashore 8. often argue 9. dull, empty scenery 10. hide information 11. talk about people 12. period of stress 13. make experts wonder 14. accomplishment in air 15. courageous reply 16. huge mistake 17. inspire wonder 18. usual living quarters 19. being sad 20. perhaps enough

Exercise 5F: 1. runner without clothes 2. pleasant sight 3. artificial praise 4. punctual every time 5. smart choice 6. look over 7. extremely glad 8. in slow motion 9. careful handling 10. arrogant behavior 11. descend rapidly 12. high-priced cloth 13. crying man 14. stalled car 15. panicky gesture 16. serpent on lawn 17. hurt leg 18. worried giggle 19. tight fist 20. take away all

Practice Paragraphs:

A. 1. The author, when very young, learned about widespread prejudice. 2. No, but (7) is close. 3. until then, but in those days, and, sometimes, unfortunately 4. examples, cause and effect 5. being called "dago" and "wop" trying to hide being Italian; "took a lot of abuse for being different"; getting into fights; teachers calling him "little wop." Second level.

B. 1. The author is proud to be a Greek immigrant who is running for President. 2. Yes, (7) 3. now, then, and 4. description, contrast, time sequence 5. wide toothy smile; thick black hair; swarthy forehead; position of hands on hips. Second level.

C. [Check with your instructor. The answers are in the Instructor's Manual.]

Words in Context: 1. (b) 2. (c) 3. (c) 4. (b) 5. (d) 6. (a) 7. (a) 8. (d) 9. (b) 10. (c) 11. (b)

Short Reading 5G: 1. (c) 2. (a) 3. to twist the truth 4. F 5. (b) (*Bonus:* second; so that, for instance, and, soon)

Short Reading 5H: 1. The narrator started acting deaf because some white people acted as if he were too dumb to hear or speak. 2. (c) 3. F 4. F 5. He may have pretended he couldn't hear or speak. (*Bonus:* cause and effect; because)

Long Reading 5I: 1. (c) 2. T 3. (c) 4. She was a majorette. 5. T 6. F 7. T 8. T 9. She agreed to take *odori* lessons. 10. F

Bonus:

when	time sequence, description, effect	(4th sentence)
like	comparison	(5th sentence)

Exercise 6C: 1. false 2. foam 3. too-smooth 4. anger 5. energetic 6. gather 7. urgent 8. defective 9. stimulating 10. supreme 11. watchful 12. apex 13. extraordinary 14. unbeatable 15. captivate 16. skilled 17. lavish 18. search 19. unplanned 20. disperse

Exercise 6D: 1. persistent 2. catchable 3. illegal 4. fascinating 5. pay back 6. festive 7. filled 8. instinct 9. stout 10. gloomy 11. watch 12. introduction 13. irritate 14. sponsor 15. commotion 16. hot 17. destruction 18. center 19. expand 20. engaged

Exercise 6E: 1, 5, 8

Exercise 6F: 2, 6, 10

Practice Paragraphs:

A. 1. *time sequence, example, description, contrast, addition* (transitions: three years ago, now, last year, finally—all reinforce time sequence)

   2. My Friend's Pursuit of Total Beauty

   My friend will try anything to become beautiful.
   I. First project—nose job
      A. Before—distinctive Roman nose suited to long, thin face
      B. Now—cute little pixie nose—out of place
   II. Second project—search for inner peace
      A. Transcendental Meditation, Yoga, EST, Bio-Energetics, Biofeedback
      B. Result—lost her high pressure sales job because of being so peaceful.
   III. Third project—hair permanent, bleaching, and streaking
      A. Wanted to look like Madonna
      B. Has frizzled blond hair
      Conclusion. Final result: tranquil snub-nosed gypsy with yellow Brillo-pad hair

B. 1. *classification, description, comparison, contrast, addition*

   2. Three Types of Headaches

   3. There are three types of headaches—tension, migraine, and cluster.
   I. Tension headache
      A. Most common and least painful
      B. Muscular—dull ache in scalp, jaw, neck, and shoulders
   II. Migraine headache
      A. Affects twice as many women as men
      B. Muscular and vascular contractions—throbbing pressure
      C. Flashing lights, dots, or lines seen by some before migraine strikes
      D. Nausea and vomiting experienced by others
   III. Cluster headache
      A. Most severe and least common
         1. Only 1.5 percent of population affected
         2. Victim unable to function
      B. Focus on eyes, neck, and temples
      C. Like a hot branding poker rammed into head
      D. Tendency to hit quickly, one after another

C. [Check with your instructor. The answers are in the Instructor's Manual.]

Words in Context: **1.** (c) **2.** (a) **3.** (d)

Long Reading 6G: **1.** (c)

2. Model Outline:

Preparing for Tests

Thesis: Students can improve their performance on tests if they improve their attitude toward tests and understand the reasons for tests.

Introduction.

A.   The average student learns in order to pass tests.

B.   Students need to master test-taking skills because of future aptitude, achievement, placement, adaptability, and promotion tests.

I.   Students need to examine their attitudes toward tests.

A.   Many students see tests as a personal battle.
1.   They see themselves in a contest with the teacher.
2.   They react unwisely when the test is returned.
a.   They throw the test away without looking at mistakes.
b.   They ask the teacher why points were taken off instead of asking what they should have included.

B.   Many students are afraid of taking tests.
1.   Fear causes tension and inability to think clearly or creatively.
2.   Fear conditions the mind for failure.
3.   Students afraid of tests have the following traits:
a.   Their test grades are lower than their daily recitation grades.
b.   They complain about the teacher.
c.   They criticize the test.
d.   They prepare for tests at the last minute.
e.   They study with another unprepared student.

C.   Students need to develop a positive attitude toward tests.
1.   They need to adopt an attitude of challenge, self-confidence, and content-reliability.
2.   They need to adopt a cooperative relationship with the teacher and the test itself.

II.   Students need to understand the reasons for tests.

A.   Tests motivate students to learn.

B.   Tests give students a chance to show their knowledge.

C.   One test will predict what future tests will be like.

D.   Tests point out students' weaknesses and progress.

E.   Tests give students experience in making decisions.

Conclusion.   If you approach tests with an honest and determined effort for self-improvement, your grade will take care of itself.

Long Reading 6H: **1.** (d)

2. Model Outline:

Taking Tests

Thesis: You can improve your performance on tests if you familiarize yourself with the two types of tests and their requirements.

I.   Familiarize yourself with the following points about objective tests.

A.   There are two types of objective, or short answer, tests.
1.   Recall of detail is required for filling in blanks.
2.   Recognition of correct answers is required for multiple choice, true and false, and matching.

B. Consider these six suggestions for taking objective tests.
   1. Pay attention to "where and how" instructions.
   2. When questions are numerous, first answer the ones you know.
   3. Notice qualifying words (usually, always, most, never, some), especially in true-false questions.
   4. Don't let your own opinions cause you to misread a question.
   5. Don't change answers too quickly; trust your response.
   6. Be neat and orderly.
II. Familiarize yourself with the following points about subjective tests.
   A. The subjective, or essay, test demands more of the student.
      1. The test may consist of short-answer (paragraph) or discussion (lengthy essay) questions.
      2. Subjective tests are more personal than objective tests.
      3. Subjective tests measure your ability to recall what you have learned and to organize it intelligently.
      4. Subjective tests require good writing with *no generalities.*
   B. Consider these six requirements for writing good subjective tests.
      1. Read through all the essay questions before writing for better use of time.
         a. Write a sketchy outline.
         b. Write key words in the margin.
      2. Write in the margin the time allotted for answering the first question and answer exactly what is asked of you.
      3. Reread the question to determine steps to be taken.
         a. Decide how much detail to include.
         b. Mentally organize the topics and accompanying details.
         c. Plan an effective opening statement.
      4. Try to write what the teacher would consider a model answer—clear and easy to grade.
      5. Concentrate on one question at a time and mentally use a numbering system to prevent overwriting or getting off the subject.
      6. Check over the test paper before turning it in and after it has been graded.
         a. Reserve ten minutes of the test hour to check for errors.
         b. Rely on your first impression before changing an answer.
Conclusion. Examine errors marked by your teacher to avoid repeating them.

Exercise 7C: 1. many 2. irregular 3. adjusted 4. agree 5. scrutinize 6. inborn 7. goal 8. system 9. conditional 10. friendly 11. intense 12. trick 13. resupply 14. masculine 15. front 16. high point 17. troubled 18. grotesque 19. trusting 20. prevent

Exercise 7D: 1. disperse 2. difficult 3. many-sided 4. change 5. small hill 6. bold 7. system 8. commit 9. deadly 10. grim 11. patronizing 12. unbelieving 13. digress 14. adviser 15. approach 16. neglectful 17. foolish 18. obscure 19. frank 20. suitability

Exercise 7E: 1. giving approval to 2. earning income 3. a stack of wastes 4. barred opportunity 5. an affectionate hug 6. his biggest mistake 7. glutted with presents 8. a variety of edibles 9. measles shot 10. a noble person 11. be confused 12. awful conduct 13. a searching intelligence 14. unsettling experience 15. a gay journey 16. a serious conflict 17. the offender 18. foreseen marriage 19. wild get-together 20. vanished dinosaur

Exercise 7F: 1. feelings of remorse 2. to reply yes 3. satisfy need for drink 4. twice-a-year event 5. additional statement 6. becoming rich 7. might blow up 8. abundance of flora 9. a light stroke 10. book about someone else 11. endurance of the best 12. snobbish behavior 13. questioning look 14. surprise treachery 15. extraordinary ability 16. behaving properly 17. a noisy disturbance 18. uplift mental condition 19. a good appetite 20. disgusting illness

Words in Context: 1. (b) 2. (d) 3. (b) 4. (a) (**Note:** Model outlines for 7G and 7H are in the Instructor's Manual.)

Long Reading 7G: 1. (b) 2. (c) 3. F 4. T 5. F 6. F 7 & 8. See p. 170 9. Wait a few days to see if it continues; then tell them that the barking dog bothers you. Point out that you could have called the pound but that you want to find a solution good for both of you. 10. T

Long Reading 7H: 1. (a) 2. T 3. When one person insists on trying to defeat you or to harm others, defeating him is the only way to stop the behavior (or any example of your own that illustrates this point). 4. (a) 5. T 6. F 7. no-lose 8. F 9. T 10. finding a tailor-made solution that fits everyone's needs.

Exercise 8C: 1. calm 2. distinguished 3. risky 4. hatred 5. scornful 6. peaceful 7. wrong 8. joyful 9. restore 10. doubtful 11. inflammatory 12. widespread 13. forewarning 14. question 15. curt 16. blasphemous 17. restrain 18. mournful 19. disgust 20. determined

Exercise 8D: 1. survey 2. ancient 3. burden 4. emotionless 5. enthusiasm 6. prayer 7. accidental 8. revenge 9. aversion 10. elated 11. theory 12. sensual 13. compete 14. uncontrollable 15. disturbed 16. timely 17. abolish 18. credit 19. later 20. better

Exercise 8E: 1, 7 (perhaps 6 and 8)

Exercise 8F: 1, 2, 6

Words in Context: 1. (b) 2. (a) 3. (c) 4. (a) 5. (d) 6. (b) 7. (c) 8. (a) 9. (b) 10. (c)

Short Reading 8G: 1. (c) 2. (a) 3. *The Sea Around Us* 4. Pesticides poisoned the fish and animals that would be eaten by people. 5. F

Short Reading 8H: 1. As a young girl, Golda had an extraordinary speaking ability and a dedication to a homeland for Jews. 2. F 3. Since married women were not allowed to teach in local schools, she was afraid Golda would be an old maid. 4. T 5. (c)

Long Reading 8I: 1. (a) 2. T 3. He cut off his son's hair 4. F 5. F 6. (b) 7. T 8. F 9. T 10. T

Exercise 9C: 1. plain 2. pleasant 3. accept 4. necessary 5. degrade 6. increase 7. inability 8. let out 9. add 10. stiff 11. give 12. approve 13. compliment 14. ruin 15. interesting 16. defy 17. unknown 18. readable 19. bind 20. depressing

Exercise 9D: 1. agreeable 2. approve 3. cheap 4. uncover 5. genuine 6. cowardly 7. infer 8. rich 9. increase 10. talkative 11. satisfied 12. important 13. clear 14. ordinary 15. common 16. take 17. win 18. living 19. sew on 20. abstract

Exercise 9E: 1. airport 2. car, flies 3. streets 4. structures 5. voice 6. words 7. *parking 8. *loading, unloading 9. passengers 10. taxi 11. passenger, coat 12. baggage 13. porter, tip 14. doors 15. counter 16. check 17. concourse 18. heels 19. escalator 20. arrival, gate 21. scramble, ticket 22. assignment, window 23. flight 24. tension, voices 25. police 26. rumors, bomb 27. waiting, lobby 28. eyes, mink 29. cushions 30. butts 31. smell, smoke 32. drinks 33. hamburgers 34. grease, chins 35. children 36. soldier, wife 37. chatter, languages 38. announcement 39. passengers, plane 40. stewardess 41. class 42. window 43. champagne 44. belt 45. smoking 46. demonstration, stewardess 47. voice, speaker 48. apology, delay 49. take-off 50. explosion, air
*Note: Parking, loading, and unloading are gerunds, which function as nouns.

Exercise 9F: 1. scene 2. road 3. shack 4. outhouse, back 5. door 6. trees 7. tires, yard 8. patches, grass 9. chickens 10. roof 11. porch 12. cracks, walls 13. smell, urine 14. wallpaper 15. chairs 16. bottoms 17. stove 18. bedstead 19. paint 20. mattress 21. seams 22. table 23. bench 24. peas, stove 25. onions 26. pork, pan 27. biscuits, oven 28. sunset, trees 29. time 30. daughter 31. milkbucket 32. gate 33. cowpen 34. ground 35. boots, mud 36. pigs 37. mules 38. barn 39. cow, stall, cud 40. flies 41. head, belly 42. hands, machines 43. dog 44. squirt, head 45. dog 46. milkbucket 47. kitchen 48. milk, strainer 49. biscuits 50. supper, table

Practice Paragraphs:

A. 1. Dr. Belsky thinks that infants who are not cared for most of the time by their parents may suffer from psychological problems. 2. to inform 3. to persuade against day care for infants 4. opinion. Note the qualifying words like "seem" and "likely." 5. There are not enough facts to support the opinions, although psychological problems are difficult to prove.

B. 1. Employers are being encouraged to help employees make child support payments easier through voluntary payroll deductions. 2. to inform, perhaps to persuade people to improve compliance with child-support payments. 3. Sentence (8) is the most factual—perhaps (2) and (3); all other sentences are opinion. 4. Yes. The source is a reputable newspaper. 5. Sentence 8 is an effective argument for the author's opinion, perhaps the only one needed.

C. [Check with your instructor. The answers are in the Instructor's Manual.]

Words in Context: 1. (c) 2. (a) 3. (b) 4. (b) 5. (b)

Long Reading 9G: 1.   The author believes that the right to possess arms is important to America's freedom and equality. 2. (b) 3.   to equate these restrictive societies with what he considers the restrictive practice of gun control. 4.   to make a connection between a hero who defended his country and American citizens who bear arms 5. (a) 6. (b) 7. F 8.   It makes him appear more objective, for being against gun control is considered conservative. 9. (b) 10. (b)

Long Reading 9H: 1.   Handguns should be restricted because they are concealable and dangerous. 2. F 3. yes 4. (b) 5. target-shooting 6.   Most hunters consider handguns less humane for hunting because they tend to wound instead of kill. 7. (a) 8. (b) 9.   no (His arguments are logical and well-supported.) 10. (d)

Exercise 10C: 1. let out 2. light 3. shy 4. aid 5. tiny 6. dispute 7. obedient 8. delightful 9. weak 10. leader 11. thriving 12. conclusion 13. peace 14. planned 15. useless 16. growing 17. stupid 18. simple 19. condemn 20. lose

Exercise 10D: 1. conscious 2. plentiful 3. unbearable 4. active 5. integrate 6. minor 7. typical 8. insignificant 9. similar 10. relapse 11. forthright 12. sad 13. aggravate 14. bold 15. worsen 16. order 17. exceptional 18. happy 19. sophisticated 20. closed

Exercise 10E: 2, 5, 7

Exercise 10F: 1, 5, 10

Practice Paragraphs:

A. 1. The author believes that men are entitled to the same choice women often have about whether to work or be supported.

2. Examples: The author thinks of his income as "our money" and of her income as "my money." Her friend, after letting her husband support her for seven years, doesn't like the idea of supporting him for a while.

3. One may infer that the author is trying to accept liberation from both women's and men's traditional sex roles. However, she is having trouble adjusting. Part of her wants to be supported whenever she is in trouble. Part of her is upset at the idea of a man being supported by a woman. She sees herself, her women friends, and men all as struggling to get out of a prison of expectations.

B. 1. A perfect appearance is not considered an asset for a man.

2. Women are judged, much more than men are, for their appearance—and judged feature by feature.

3. The wording of the last sentence—"merely a 'pretty face' "—is a put-down of women. What is considered a woman's best asset is being devalued. The author goes on to say in the next line: "Think of the depreciation of women—as well as of beauty—that is implied in that judgment."

C. [Check with your instructor. The answers are in the Instructor's Manual.]

Words in Context: 1. (c) 2. (b) 3. (d)

Short Reading 10G: 1. (b) 2. T 3. (a) 4. T 5. (a) Men, like dessert, are extra, unnecessary, and possibly bad for you. (b) Men are *justice*, what you deserve, if you depend on them.

Short Reading 10H: 1. In most matters of etiquette, the author relies on his own judgment. 2. (c) 3. F 4. T 5. (b)

Long Reading 10I: 1. (b) 2. F 3. They realize *Mr.* Smith himself could help Mrs. Jones. 4. T 5. F 6. T 7. F 8. T 9. Since they have four children, his wife really has two jobs also. 10. (c)

Exercise 11A: "bear in mind" repeated four times   "the right station" repeated five times

Exercise 11B: "cope with life" repeated three times   "a slow drawl" repeated three times

Exercise 11C: 1. clear 2. increase 3. quiet 4. lavish 5. dishonor 6. shorten 7. necessary 8. enthusiastic 9. energetic 10. tear down 11. incredible 12. awkward 13. poised 14. owners 15. improve 16. well-shaped 17. bottom 18. issue 19. calm 20. weakness

Exercise 11D: 1. encourage 2. sound 3. forced 4. awkward 5. lukewarm 6. listless 7. spread 8. bore 9. unneeded 10. ordinary 11. flawless 12. calming 13. narrow 14. legal 15. cold 16. repulsive 17. order 18. thin 19. positive 20. conclusion

Exercise 11E: 3. come 4. catch 5. shoot 7. stab 9. bleed 10. drop 12. comes 13. scrape 14. wash 16. tie 17. swing 18. take 19. rip 21. stop 22. saw 23. remove 24. remove 25. wash 26. soak 27. fry 29. saw 30. lay 31. cut 33. take 34. cut 38. is 39. are 41. take 43. grind 45. add 46. makes 47. give 49. has

Exercise 11F: 2. is 3. thunders 4. lights 6. fight 7. whines 11. studies 12. is heard 15. drives 18. puts 19. prevents 21. puts 22. opens 23. gets 25. jacks 27. removes 28. loosens 29. jacks 30. removes 32. replaces 34. lowers 35. tightens 39. washes 40. lowers 43. starts 46. lights 47. sings

Practice Paragraphs:

A. 1. (b). [All the descriptive details are negative, but not to the point of (d) hatred.]

2. Christianity by fear and rote; belief that she had a special connection to God; emphasis on sin; refusal to drink Coca-Colas, racist attitudes

B. 1. 6, 7, 8, [These sentences are the only ones giving personality traits.] 2. His loud, aggressive boasting of his modest beginnings explain the contradiction in terms.

C. [Check with your instructor. The answers are in the Instructor's Manual.]

Words in Context:

1. (b) 2. (b) 3. (c)

Long Reading 11G:

1. The author proposes the sale of infants for food to dramatize the terrible conditions in Ireland caused by English landlords. 2. F 3. T 4. F 5. (a) 6. F 7. to make the horror of his proposal real and to make readers aware of the horrors of the poverty in which the children live. 8. (c) 9. Refer to pages 000 through 000. 10. He has heard these empty promises too often to believe they will be kept.

Exercise 12A: "immune to colds" repeated four times   "internal stress" repeated five times

Exercise 12B: "varsity baseball" repeated five times   "uncanny look" repeated four times

Exercise 12C: 1. neck 2. base, shade 3. ear, pouch 4. zipper 5. heel, toe 6. wheel 7. sand 8. water, salt 9. binding, words, page 10. money, vault 11. core, seed, peel 12. blade, handle 13. tub, soap, towel 14. shell, yolk, white 15. desk, blackboard 16. ink 17. scales 18. pavement 19. cord, receiver 20. stem, chain, crystal

Exercise 12D: 1. arm, leg 2. roof, steps 3. sole, heel 4. engine, wheel 5. grass 6. tobacco 7. petal, stem 8. nose, lips 9. stove, sink 10. leaf, trunk, branch 11. finger, palm 12. trees 13. desk, typewriter 14. hoof 15. iris, pupil 16. lead, eraser 17. wing 18. sleeve, collar 19. pane, frame 20. handle

Exercise 12E: 4. coyote 6. paw 11. rat 12. doctor 15. arm 16. eyes 17. foot 19. eyes, victim 22. child 24. vultures 25. wings 27. girl 29. hand 30. eyelid 32. bird 34. hand 37. eyes 41. throat 42. lips 43. teeth 44. fangs, throat 46. body 47. doctor 49. cheeks 50. Vampira

Exercise 12F: 2. people 5. men 8. bird 9. farmer 11. wife 13. horse 15. dog, fleas 20. flies 21. teenagers 23. Son, Monster 24. clerk 27. arms 28. kids 30. waitress 31. boy 33. waitress 34. manager 35. fist 37. customers 38. cashiers 39. children 41. mothers, hands 44. feet 46. band 48. hands 49. hearts

Practice Passages:

A. 1. that length of bone; hair cropped like an oarsman; rather thin-lipped [These images suggest sharpness.]

2. The new clothes suggest either inexperience or the strong desire to *look* the part of the hunter.

3. Macomber's being shown up as a coward contradicts both his expectations of himself and probably the readers' expectations of him—again, not the *hero* image.

B. 1. (b)

2. us = helpless, insignificant flies
the gods = wanton (or reckless and playful) children

3. We are as helpless as flies in the hands of the gods (or fate). They toy with us and would just as soon destroy us as not.

C. [Check with your instructor. The answers are in the Instructor's Manual.]

Words in Context: 1. (b) 2. (a) 3. (d) 4. (c) 5. (a)

Short Reading 12G: 1. (d) 2. (b) 3. T 4. F 5. She seemed too good to be true, too sensitive because of her background.

Short Reading 12H: **1.** Rebecca was not as good as the other girls, but she learned to be a survivor. **2.** T **3.** F **4.** F **5.** She was witty, strong, ambitious, and loving with her father.

Long Reading 12I: **1.** (b) **2.** F **3.** F **4.** T **5.** F **6.** F **7.** (c) **8.** T **9.** Amelia is a little foolish and hypocritical when she professes her undying love for her late husband even though she has already written to Major Dobbin. **10.** Rebecca generously sacrifices her reputation and endangers her friendship and well-being when she confesses the affair.

Exercise 1: **1.** If you withdraw from a class after ten weeks and are passing at the time of your last attendance **2.** yes **3.** Student Handbook **4.** Counseling Office **5.** "classes for adults"

Exercise 2: **1.** Occupational Certificate, Vocational Diploma, or Transfer **2.** 20 **3.** 20 **4.** 10 **5.** following this section on majors

Exercise 3: **1.** Engl 1 **2.** Yes **3.** No **4.** No **5.** No

Exercise 4: **1.** 30,000 **2.** French **3.** GI's or G.I.'s **4.** adj. (adjective) **5.** 7